Liberalism and Its Discontents

Also by Alan Brinkley

Voices of Protest:
Huey Long, Father Coughlin, and the Great Depression

The Unfinished Nation:
A Concise History of the American People

The End of Reform:
New Deal Liberalism in Recession and War

LIBERALISM AND ITS DISCONTENTS

ALAN BRINKLEY

HARVARD UNIVERSITY PRESS
Cambridge, Massachusetts, and London, England

Printed in the United States of America
Second printing, 2000

First Harvard University Press paperback edition, 2000

Library of Congress Cataloging-in-Publication Data

Brinkley, Alan.
Liberalism and its discontents / Alan Brinkley.
p. cm.
Includes index.
ISBN 0-674-53017-9 (cloth)
ISBN 0-674-00185-0 (pbk.)
1. United States—Politics and government—1933–1945. 2. United States—Politics and government—1945–1989. 3. Liberalism—United States—History—20th century. 4. Right and left (Political science)—History—20th century. I. Title.
E743.B755 1998
320.51'3'0973—dc21 97-40654

For Elly

Contents

Preface

What is liberalism? What has happened to it? There are probably no satisfactory answers to those questions—and certainly no answers that would satisfy the many contenders in today's battles over liberalism's past and future. But these are, nevertheless, the questions that have shaped the essays that are gathered in this book—just as they have shaped much of my life as a historian.

When I was growing up in the 1950s and 1960s, surrounded by adults who considered themselves liberals and in a political world that appeared dominated by their beliefs, the answers to these questions seemed obvious. Liberalism was the set of political ideas that had descended from the New Deal and that had shaped the steady postwar expansion of federal social and economic responsibilities. The achievements of liberalism were everywhere visible: the robust growth of the American economy, stabilized (at times at least) by the active use of Keynesian policies; the gradual expansion of the New Deal welfare and social insurance system, which had lifted millions of elderly people (and many others) out of poverty; and beginning in the early 1960s, the alliance between the federal government and the civil rights movement, an alliance that most white liberals believed gave liberalism a powerful moral claim to accompany its many practical achievements. There were, of course, conservative and reactionary forces in American life, and liberals often spoke ominously about them. But the right, they generally believed, was a force at the margins of American life, without the resources to shake the great edifice of liberal achievement.

Faith in both the value and the durability of liberalism shaped not only the politics, but also much of the scholarship of the postwar era. When I began studying history in high school and college in the 1960s, much of what I read was the product of the "consensus" scholars, who—while their work was hardly as celebratory as their many critics have claimed—had few doubts about the centrality of liberalism both to their own time, and to the whole of the American experience. Liberalism was, many of them argued, the only important political tradition in our national history. Some regretted that (for how, they asked, could such a pragmatic and materialistic creed sustain a vigorous and productive culture?). For others, it was a source of satisfaction. But in a society still fearful of totalitarian threats from the left and the right, the apparent dominance and stability of the liberal order was almost always a source of at least modest comfort. Whatever its flaws, most liberals believed, the alternatives were clearly worse.

By the end of the 1960s, of course, this secure liberal universe was already beginning to crumble. It soon collapsed, and it has never recovered. Today liberalism stands in apparent disarray—the word itself has become a term of widespread opprobrium. Even many of its erstwhile defenders scramble to disassociate themselves both from the label and from the policies it has come to symbolize.

The attacks on liberalism in these postliberal years have focused generally on two supposed failings, failings that are in some ways mutually exclusive but that many critics cite interchangeably. One complaint, popular among leaders of the traditional right, is the claim that liberalism is a paternalistic, statist creed that has concentrated authority in the hands of government and a few elites at the expense of individual liberty. Liberalism is, in short, a threat to freedom and prosperity. Another complaint, which has found a substantial following among conservative intellectuals and has even generated significant support among some liberals (or erstwhile liberals), is the argument that liberalism is too wedded to liberty; that its excessive, indeed nearly exclusive, emphasis on rights and freedoms makes no room for a definition of the public good; that liberalism leaves society without a moral core and hence vulnerable to the destabilizing whims of fractious minorities and transitory passions. Liberalism is, in other words, a threat to community.

Whether or not these claims are accurate is, in a way, beside the point. So many people have come to perceive in liberalism a danger of too much (or too little) freedom, too much (or too little) order that it is impossible to dismiss such criticisms as simply ill-informed or illogical. It is therefore necessary to ask what there is about modern liberalism that has made so many people consider it, in effect, an empty vessel into which to pour these widely varying discontents.

One purpose of these essays, then, is to help illuminate the ways in which liberalism has changed in the years since the beginning of the

New Deal, how different it has become from the set of ideas that sustained Franklin Roosevelt and his followers in the early and mid-1930s. Answering that question has occupied much of my recent scholarly life and was the basis of my book *The End of Reform: New Deal Liberalism in Recession and War* (1992). Some of the essays here are extensions of arguments suggested in that study; others are efforts to examine some of liberalism's later incarnations—and the successes and failures they experienced in the years after the war. Liberalism has been a victim of profound changes in the economic, social, and cultural life of the nation and the world—changes for which it was not primarily responsible but for which, as the dominant political creed of its time, it received much of the blame. But liberalism has also suffered from some of its own internal weaknesses and incongruities, and from the unwillingness or inability of many liberals to look skeptically or critically at their own values and assumptions. Understanding where postwar liberalism came from, therefore, is part of understanding where it has gone, and why.

But the problems liberalism has experienced are not simply a result of its own internal weaknesses, or of the broad forces it has failed to control. For despite the claims of the "consensus" scholars that liberalism is the only important political tradition in America, nothing has become clearer over the past thirty years—both in historical scholarship and in our experience as a society—than that the consensus argument, on that point at least, was wrong. Just as liberalism has never been a uniform or stable creed, so it has never been uncontested. There have been powerful alternative political traditions at work throughout the twentieth century—and indeed throughout American history. I explored some of those traditions in my first book, *Voices of Protest: Huey Long, Father Coughlin, and the Great Depression* (1982), in which I argued for the presence of a broad, if somewhat inchoate, populist impulse in the 1930s. Since that time, I have become interested in other non- or antiliberal impulses, on both the right and the left. Several of the essays here are products of my imperfect efforts to understand them.

Finally, this book includes several commentaries on the way historians themselves have explained (or failed to explain) both liberalism and its alternatives in the last half-century or so. Perhaps unsurprisingly, I have been particularly interested in the scholarly generation that shaped my own education and training, the generation that interpreted the past through the prism of its own turbulent youth and produced the idea of the "consensus." The great scholarly achievements of these historians are, I believe, notable for their breadth, richness, and complexity, but also for the way they reflect the assumptions of the liberal world of the postwar era—a world that collapsed more quickly and more completely than almost any of them could have imagined. I have commented at some length here on the work of several of the historians and writers of that time. I have also commented on some of the problems my own generation of historians has encountered as we have tried to create our own frameworks for understanding the past. Historians have made dramatic and mostly welcome changes in the scope and character of scholarship over the last quarter century and more; and it is both natural and appropriate that we have often congratulated ourselves on our achievements and defended ourselves against the frequent attacks—many of them ill-informed and dishonest—on the directions in which we have moved. But for all the diversity and openness of the new scholarship of recent decades, there remain important aspects of the American past to which we have been insufficiently attentive. And there has been, as well, an increasing isolation of our profession from much of the public that historians once addressed. In creating an increasingly rich, diverse, and disaggregated scholarly world, we ourselves have become part of the story of what the collapse of the liberal order has produced.

Most of these essays have been published previously in various scholarly and non-scholarly journals. Some of them I prepared originally as lectures. Several I wrote specifically for this book. Because their origins are diverse, their formats are as well. Some have elaborate scholarly documentation. Others have relatively sparse notes or no notes at all, but brief bibliographical essays instead. I have revised all of them—some extensively, some only modestly. But they remain to some degree products of the moments in which I wrote them.

It would be futile to try to thank all the many people who have contributed to these essays. But I have benefited from the perceptiveness and generosity of countless friends, colleagues, students, and editors in the course of the years during which I wrote the material that appears in this book. I do want to offer special thanks to Aida Donald, for suggesting that I create this book; to Anna Safran, for her careful, intelligent editing of the manuscript; to the Russell Sage Foundation, which provided me with a stimulating and supportive place in which to work on it; and to my wife, Evangeline Morphos, who read and commented on most of these essays and improved them enormously—although not nearly as enormously as she has improved the life of their author.

1

The Rise of Franklin Roosevelt

In 1945, shortly after Franklin Roosevelt died, Woodie Guthrie wrote a song he called "Dear Mrs. Roosevelt"—a song intended to serve as both a condolence and a tribute. In it Guthrie described several important events and accomplishments of Roosevelt's life (not all of them accurately) and punctuated his account with the refrain "The world was lucky that he walked."

Through much of his life, of course, Franklin Roosevelt could not walk, as Guthrie probably knew. But to Guthrie, as to many other Americans of his generation, he seemed for a time to bestride the earth; and the literal truth of his life seemed less important than the powerful image he had—half purposefully, half inadvertently—created in the popular imagination.[1] Even a half-century later, Roosevelt's reputation seems unusually malleable. Public figures across the ideological spectrum try to seize a piece of his legacy—at times to justify their efforts to dismantle it—without much concern about who Roosevelt himself actually was or what he actually did. In the popular mind, Roosevelt the icon has transcended Roosevelt the president, Roosevelt the politician, Roosevelt the New Dealer, and Roosevelt the man. He has become a figure of myth: a man for all seasons, all parties, and all ideologies.

But Roosevelt the man was not an icon. He was, rather, a complicated, elusive, at times even devious figure. He was both a friend of the common people, as Woody Guthrie believed, and a creature of the American aristocracy. He was both a great statesman and a consummate defender of his own political self interest. He was generous as well as vindictive. He was capable of broad vision and petty deceit. He had millions of friends and no intimates. Even those who felt closest to him knew only a small part of his carefully concealed inner self. The New Deal he constructed, and which changed the landscape of American public life for the rest of the century and beyond, reflected the urgency of the crisis he inherited in 1933 and the accumulated legacy of nearly half a century of rising reform sentiment. But it also reflected his own curious personality and the strangely rarefied world that had shaped it.

Roosevelt was born on January 30, 1882, on his family's estate in Dutchess County, New York. His father, James, came from (and largely modeled himself after) a long line of wealthy, landed gentlemen who dabbled in business but usually devoted no great effort to it. James himself worked at times as a railroad executive, invested in coal mines, and once took part in an unsuccessful effort to build a canal across Nicaragua. But by the time his son Franklin was born, he was 53 years old and relatively inactive in business—a widower with a grown son, two years into a second marriage to a woman half his age. Sara Delano, Franklin's mother, was a wealthy, attractive woman acutely aware of both her own and her husband's distinguished lineages. As a couple, they strove to live their lives and raise their child in a manner reminiscent of the English aristocracy—a goal symbolized, perhaps, by the elaborate remodeling Sara supervised of the house on her husband's estate in Hyde Park. Once a rambling and relatively modest Victorian home named "Springwood," it gradually became an imposing, formal country manor with a neo-classical granite facade.

Franklin grew up, therefore, in a remarkably cosseted environment—insulated from the normal experiences of most American boys both by his family's wealth and by their intense and at times almost suffocating love. Until he was fourteen years old, he lived in a world almost entirely dominated by adults: his Swiss tutors, who supervised his lessons at home or during the family's annual travels through Europe; his father, who sought to train his son in the life of a landowner and gentleman; and above all his mother, who devoted virtually all her energies to the raising of her only child—bathing and dressing him herself until he was eight years old and giving him only slightly more independence after that. It was a world of extraordinary comfort, security, and serenity. But it was also a world of reticence and reserve, particularly after 1891, when James Roosevelt suffered the first of a series of heart attacks that left him a semi-invalid. Franklin responded to James's condition protectively. He tried to spare his father anxiety by masking his own emotions and projecting a calm, cheerful demeanor. He would continue hiding his feelings behind a bright, charming surface for the rest of his life.

In the fall of 1896 Franklin left his parents for the first time to attend Groton, a rigorous boarding school in a small Massachusetts town whose mission, according to its imperious headmaster, Endicott Peabody, was the training of the American elite. Groton was something of a shock to Roosevelt. He had never before attended school with other children. He had never had any close friends of his own age and had some difficulty making them now. Physically slight, he attained little distinction in athletics, which dominated the life of the school. He did reasonably well academically, but he went through his four years at Groton something of an outsider—denied the principal honors of the school, disliked by many of his classmates for what seemed to them a cocky demeanor and an irritating gregariousness.

Entering Harvard College in 1904, he set out to make up for what he considered his social failures at Groton. He worked hard at making friends, ran for class office, and became president of the student newspaper, the *Crimson*, at a time when the position carried more social than journalistic distinction. (Roosevelt's own contributions to the newspaper consisted largely of such obvious things as editorials calling for greater school spirit.) And although he and his family were Democrats, he became conspicuous in his enthusiasm for his distant cousin Theodore Roosevelt, even affecting some of the president's famous mannerisms (the wearing of a pince-nez, the frequent and hearty use of such well-known Roosevelt exclamations as "De-lighted" and "Bully"). But Roosevelt failed to achieve what he craved most: election to the most exclusive of the Harvard "final clubs," the Porcellian—the club to which his own father and his celebrated cousin Theodore had belonged. He joined another, less prestigious, club instead. It was, he reportedly said later, "the greatest disappointment of my life"—a disappointment that continued to gnaw at him even several years afterward. In 1906, when he attended Alice Roosevelt's wedding at the White House, he watched Theodore Roosevelt jovially summon his fellow Porcellians (among them Alice's new husband, Nicholas Longworth) to a closed-door meeting from which Franklin was, of course, excluded.

During Franklin's first year at Harvard his ailing father finally died, and Sara Roosevelt took a house in Boston to be near her son. Franklin was devoted to his mother and always attentive and loving towards her. But he was beginning to chafe at her efforts to control him—efforts buttressed by her iron grip on the family finances and her unwillingness (up to her death in 1941) to allow her son any real financial independence. Even as president, Franklin continued to receive an "allowance" from his mother. His years at Harvard were the beginning of his lifelong effort to balance her expectations against his determination to create a life of his own. Unwilling to challenge her openly, he did so covertly, intensifying his already well-developed secretiveness. Indeed, he concealed from his mother the most important experience of his Harvard years: his courtship of his distant cousin, Eleanor Roosevelt, the president's niece.

Franklin and Eleanor had known each other slightly as children, and they began to spend time together during the 1902 social season in New York when Eleanor made her debut. Few suspected at the time that he was becoming attracted to her. The handsome, charming, and somewhat glib Franklin seemed to have little in common with Eleanor, a quiet, reserved, and intensely serious young woman who struggled all her life to mask the insecurities she had acquired in a lonely childhood during which both her parents had died. But Franklin perhaps saw in her qualities of commitment, compassion, and intellect that he feared he himself lacked. By the end of his senior year at Harvard they were secretly engaged. When he finally told Sara of his plans, she tried to dissuade him, convinced that Eleanor lacked the poise and self-assurance to be a proper wife to her son. But Franklin stood firm. He and Eleanor were married in New York on March 17, 1905, in a ceremony at which Theodore Roosevelt, who gave his niece away, was the real center of attention.

By the time of his marriage Roosevelt was a student at Columbia Law School. He never completed the requirements for his degree, but he passed the bar exams and spent several years desultorily practicing law in New York City. Already, however, he was principally interested in politics; and in 1910 he accepted an invitation from Democratic party leaders in Dutchess County to run for the state Senate—an invitation based, like many other political opportunities he would encounter in his early career, both on his position as a leading county aristocrat and as a man whose name (and marriage) linked him to the most magnetic political figure of the age. Profiting from a split among the Republicans (long the dominant power in Dutchess County politics) and from his own energetic denunciation of party bosses, he won what had originally seemed a hopeless race.

Roosevelt made few friends at first among his fellow legislators, most of whom considered him naive and arrogant. Surrounded by tough, pragmatic politicians who had fought their way up from obscurity, Roosevelt stood out as a fey aristocrat—with his self-consciously upper-class accent and language, his conspicuously expensive clothes, and his disconcerting tendency to speak with his chin jutting out and his nose in the air. Many of his colleagues considered him a lightweight, even a fraud; they took to calling him (playing on his initials) "Feather Duster" Roosevelt. But in fact he compiled a creditable, if modest, record protecting the interests of upstate farmers (his own constituents among them) and opposing the New York City Democratic machine, Tammany Hall.

In 1912 he won reelection easily—in part because he had by then enlisted the aid of Louis M. Howe. A former journalist turned political operative, Howe seemed Roosevelt's opposite in almost every way. He was short, disheveled, withered, and in many ways coarse. He was bluntly outspoken and self-consciously gruff. He was also a brilliant political strategist, who would be indispensable to Roosevelt's career for the next twenty years. Sara Roosevelt loathed him, and even Eleanor (who later came to depend on him almost as much as her husband did) felt uneasy around Howe at first. But Franklin seemed instinctively to understand that Howe could help him overcome the political limitations of his background, and he paid no attention to the complaints of his family. Howe managed Roosevelt's 1912 campaign, taught him to drop many of his aristocratic mannerisms, and helped him make alliances with politicians of backgrounds very different from his own. He taught him that in politics an upper-class lineage was something to overcome and not to flaunt. He also helped fan what was already Roosevelt's own strong inclination: to envision an important national political career, even to dream of the presidency.

Roosevelt did not serve out his second term in the legislature. Early in 1913 Woodrow Wilson, the new Democratic president whom Roosevelt had energetically supported, offered him an appointment as assistant secretary of the navy. Roosevelt eagerly accepted, not least because it was from that same position that Theodore Roosevelt had launched his own national political career fifteen years earlier. Franklin enjoyed the new job and the Washington social life that came with it, and he plunged into both with a sometimes reckless enthusiasm.

In the Navy Department he was brashly assertive and often almost openly insubordinate to his remarkably tolerant superior, Secretary of the Navy Josephus Daniels. But with the help of Louis Howe, he ran the day-to-day affairs of the fast-growing department with reasonable efficiency. He also kept his hand in New York politics and tried unsuccessfully in 1914 to seize the Democratic nomination for the United States Senate away from the Tammany candidate. From that experience he concluded that, while hostility to Tammany was good politics in Dutchess County, it was a serious, perhaps insurmountable, obstacle to statewide (and hence national) success. From 1914 on he worked to develop cordial, even if always slightly distant, relations with Tammany leaders.

Roosevelt remained in the Navy Department throughout World War I. He lobbied strenuously for preparedness during the nearly three years between the outbreak of the conflict in Europe in 1914 and the American entry into it in 1917. Later, he successfully promoted the laying of a large barrage of antisubmarine mines in the North Sea, supervised the production of small vessels to defend the American coasts, and intruded himself into deliberations of naval strategy and tactics that were not normally the province of the assistant secretary. He also became involved, perhaps inadvertently, in a controversy that would haunt him for years. In 1918 the navy began an attempt to "clean up" the area around the large naval base at Newport, Rhode Island, after receiving complaints about prostitution and homosexuality there. In the process, enlisted men were dispatched to entrap sailors and others (including a prominent Protestant clergymen) in homosexual acts. How much Roosevelt himself knew of these controversial tactics was long a matter of dispute, but he signed at least one authorization for the investigation. A scandal erupted when the operation became public, and it simmered for years. In 1921 a Senate investigation (dominated by Republicans) openly chastised him for his part in the operation.

In the meantime, Roosevelt was experiencing a personal crisis that was even more threatening to his future. Almost from the moment he arrived in Washington in 1913, he was a fixture in the city's active social life—a lively, handsome, gregarious presence at innumerable dinners, dances, and receptions. In the process he often found himself at odds with his wife, to whom such social events were seldom less than an ordeal. Eleanor often stayed home with the children when Franklin went out. At times, she even left parties early, alone. Perhaps in part as a result of his wife's painful reserve, Franklin found himself drawn to the poised, attractive, gregarious young woman whom Eleanor had hired as her social secretary in 1913: Lucy Mercer. Eventually they formed a romantic relationship, which blossomed during the summer months when Eleanor and the children were at the family's summer home on Campobello Island and Franklin remained behind in Washington. The relationship continued until Eleanor discovered it late in 1918, when she found some letters between her husband and her secretary. It was a decisive moment in their marriage. Aware that a divorce would end his political career (and, his mother threatened, her financial support), Franklin refused Eleanor's offer to terminate their marriage and promised to end all relations with Lucy Mercer (a promise he kept until many years later when, during World War II, he began to see her occasionally again). But Eleanor was deeply wounded, withdrew from any real intimacy with her husband, and began slowly to build her own, independent public career. Their marriage survived on the basis of shared public commitments and residual respect and affection. But from 1918 on, they lived increasingly separate lives. Roosevelt's relationship with his wife, like his relationship with many others, became characterized by surface charm, emotional distance, and elaborate patterns of deception.

Despite the occasional travails of his first experience in Washington, Roosevelt emerged from his eight years in the Navy Department with a significantly enhanced reputation. That, combined with his famous name, made him immediately attractive to national Democratic leaders. And in 1920 they secured for him the party's nomination for vice president on the ill-fated ticket headed by Ohio governor James M. Cox. Roosevelt campaigned energetically and at times rashly (as when, in defending the League of Nations, he falsely claimed that he had written the constitution of Haiti and thus had that nation's vote "in his pocket"). But he emerged from the experience with little of the blame for the Democrats' crushing defeat and with many new friends among party leaders.

In 1921 Roosevelt returned to private life for the first time since his election to the New York State Senate eleven years earlier—a thirty-six-year-old man with a national reputation and an apparently limitless future. His public image was of an attractive and articulate young politician, but he had no broad reputation for strong commitments to anything in particular. Nor did he deserve such a reputation. Unlike his cousin Theodore, who had always been distinguished by the passion with which he held and promoted his convictions, Roosevelt had a real aversion to deep ideological commitments; throughout his life he sought politically pragmatic routes through the thickets of dogma surrounding him.

But he was not without beliefs. From Theodore Roosevelt, his first political idol, he had derived a lasting commitment to a highly nationalistic view of government, a belief that Washington had an important role to play in the life of the nation, and that America had a large destiny in the world. From Woodrow Wilson, the president he had served, he drew a belief in internationalism and, perhaps equally important, an acute sense of the political dangers in moving too quickly, as he believed Wilson had tried to do, towards thrusting the United States into cooperative relationships with other nations. From the progressive political battles he had observed but rarely joined in his youth, he acquired a general sense that in the modern industrial world there were dangerous sources of instability and great imbalances of power, and that concerted public action was necessary to address the problems they caused. But he identified himself clearly with no one faction within the highly eclectic array of progressive reformers. In later years he would draw with equal facility from many different, often incompatible, advisers and clusters of belief.

Back in New York, he became a vice president of a bonding company and formed a legal partnership, intending all the while to focus primarily on politics. But in August 1921 a personal disaster seemed to shatter all his hopes. Tired and distracted by the embarrassing investigations into the Newport affair, he joined his family at their summer home on Campobello Island (several weeks after visiting a Boy Scout outing outside New York, where he may have been exposed to the poliomyelitis virus). A few days later, he fell ill.

The disease appeared first as a fever after a strenuous morning of outdoor activity with his children. Within days, he had lost the use of both his legs and was in excruciating pain. Months later, his doctors, after a belated diagnosis of the disease as polio, told him that he would never walk again. But Roosevelt refused to believe them, and he spent most of the next seven years in a futile search for a cure. He tried innumerable forms of therapy, some medically respectable and others indistinguishable from quackery. At times he seemed determined simply to will himself to walk—as in his repeated and always unsuccessful efforts to carry himself on crutches to the end of the long driveway of his family home in Hyde Park. He spent winters on a houseboat in Florida, hoping the sun and the fresh air would help revive his legs. He became particularly attached to the spa-like baths he discovered in Warm Springs, Georgia, and he spent much of his personal fortune buying an old resort hotel there, converting it into a center for polio patients, and becoming the ebullient leader of dispirited groups of men and women—exhorting them to work toward recovery, as he had done, and providing (if unintentionally) an example of how the power of denial and bravado could help someone who could not regain the use of his legs regain some control of his life.

Although Eleanor Roosevelt had nursed her husband devotedly through the first traumatic months of his illness, the polio ultimately increased their estrangement. She sided with her husband and Louis Howe against Sara to support Franklin's determination to return to politics, a course his mother bitterly opposed. But even this alliance damaged their relationship, for Eleanor became as a result a party to a bitter intra-family struggle from which her husband wanted nothing so much as to escape. His struggle for recovery made Franklin more self-centered than ever. Confined for the first time to his home, he engaged in elaborate strategies to protect himself from the demands of his family, even to pit them against one another, and finally to distance himself from them.

For years he spent months at a time away from home and became accustomed, as he would remain for the rest of his life, to building around himself a protective (and constantly changing) circle of friends, aides, and flatterers who helped him sustain the atmosphere of superficial gaiety and and lighthearted banter in which he had always felt most comfortable. Marguerite "Missy" LeHand, his personal secretary beginning in 1920, remained the one constant, daily presence in his life—serving as aide, companion, and (when Franklin and Eleanor were apart, as they often were) hostess. In some senses, she was almost a surrogate wife. She was almost certainly in love with him. He was heavily dependent on her, but probably not romantically involved. (Indeed, it seems likely that after contracting polio, Roosevelt never again had sexual relations.) Roosevelt and LeHand remained together for two decades, until she became incapacitated after a stroke in 1941. Eleanor

Roosevelt may have felt some jeaolousy toward Missy's increasingly public role in her husband's life, but she never revealed it if so. Instead, she cultivated a close relationship of her own with LeHand, whose devotion to Franklin made it easier for Eleanor to continue building a life of her own.

Eventually, Roosevelt became at least partially reconciled to his continuing paralysis and learned to disguise it for public purposes by wearing heavy leg braces, supporting himself—first with crutches and later with a cane and the arm of a companion—and using his hips to swing his inert legs forward. He tried to compensate for the discomfort he feared his disability might create in those around him with an aggressively cheerful countenance. As he labored to move in and out of rooms, and while aides lifted him in and out of cars and trains, he smiled broadly, waved, chattered, told jokes—anything to distract others from his physical limitations. He carefully staged most of his public appearances so that the public would often see him standing, but rarely walking. When he traveled by train, he almost always spoke from the rear platform. When he moved about by automobile, he spoke to crowds from the back seat of an open car or used specially constructed ramps to have himself driven as close to the podium as possible. He painted his steel braces black and had his trousers cut long to obscure them from the public. Later, when he was president, White House aides ensured that no one ever photographed the president in any way that would reveal his disability. Of all the thousands of photographs of him in the Roosevelt Library in New York, only two—taken by relatives—show him sitting in a wheelchair.

So effective was the deception (and so cooperative was the press in preserving it) that few Americans knew during his lifetime that Roosevelt could not walk. On the contrary, most believed that he had suffered, struggled, and recovered from his affliction—much as Theodore Roosevelt had rebuilt himself from a frail, asthmatic child into a husky, energetic adult. Prior to contracting polio, Roosevelt had been a slight and slender man—charming, attractive, but in appearance at least not entirely "manly" in the way Theodore had seemed and in the way many Americans wished their leaders to be. His strenuous efforts to strengthen his upper body so that he could move himself about without his legs gave him a new appearance of physical power—broad shoulders, a heavily muscled chest, and a ramrod-straight posture. In drawings and political cartoons, he was almost always portrayed as a strong, muscular man, and almost always shown standing, running, leaping, even boxing—a testament to his success in conveying an image of energy and mobility despite his physical limitations.

Roosevelt rarely talked about his own feelings, and he talked least of all about the impact of paralysis on him. But contracting polio was clearly one of the most important events of his life. His determination to hide his condition from those around him strengthened what was already his natural inclination to dissemble, to hide behind an aggressive public geniality, and to reveal as little about himself as possible. Eleanor Roosevelt later claimed that polio also gave him patience and increased his understanding of "what suffering meant." Whatever else it did, the ordeal made him more serious and determined. Gradually, he transferred his steely new resolve away from his efforts to walk and toward an attempt to resume a public career.

After the polio attack, Eleanor and Louis Howe—having supported Franklin against Sara in his desire to resume a public life—worked together to keep his name alive in New York politics during the long years of his attempted rehabilitation. Through much of the 1920s Roosevelt maintained his ties to politics largely through correspondence (much of it orchestrated by Howe) and through the increasing public activities of his wife. He developed a close political (although never personal) relationship with Al Smith, the Tammany-supported governor of New York. But he also forged ties to other groups in the Democratic party and presented himself as a bridge between its two bitterly divided wings: one (represented by Smith) largely eastern, urban, Catholic, and ethnic; the other (represented by William Jennings Bryan and William McAdoo) largely southern, western, rural, and Protestant. Only by uniting those warring factions, he believed, could the Democrats hope to challenge the dominance of national politics Republicans had sustained since 1896—a dominance broken only by Woodrow Wilson's triumphs over a divided GOP in 1912 and 1916.

In 1924 Roosevelt attended the disastrous Democratic National Convention, in which the party's two great factions did battle for 103 ballots before spurning both Smith and McAdoo and nominating the pallid and uncontroversial John W. Davis of South Carolina instead. Before that dreary battle, a grim-faced Roosevelt had dragged himself laboriously to the podium on crutches and placed Smith's name in nomination. He made no further public appearances until 1928, when he again nominated Smith for president at the national convention—this time "walking" to the podium without crutches, one hand holding a cane and the other clutching his son's arm. He smiled broadly throughout. It was an important personal triumph and helped lay to rest public doubts about his health. It also signaled his readiness to resume an active political career. He did so more quickly than even he had expected. After months of resisting pressure from Smith and other party leaders to run for governor of New York in 1928, he finally agreed—fearful that if he did not, no comparable opportunity would emerge again. He campaigned energetically and buoyantly, partly to dispel the persistent rumors of weakness and poor health. And in a year in which Al Smith lost his home state to Herbert Hoover in the presidential contest by 100,000 votes, Roosevelt won his own race by a narrow margin.

His four years as governor coincided with the first three and a half years of the Great Depression. More quickly than President Hoover, and more quickly than most Democratic leaders, he concluded that the economy would not recover on its own, "that there is a duty on the part of government to do something about this." There was relatively little a state government could do to fight a national Depression; but Roosevelt pushed for a series of modest reforms that, if nothing else, reinforced his image as an energetic progressive. He promoted the development of public electric power, struggled to lower utilities rates, and reduced the tax burden on New York farmers. Later, he created a state agency to provide relief to the unemployed and began calling for national unemployment insurance and other government programs to assist the jobless. But he was careful not to seem reckless or radical. He criticized Hoover for failing to balance the budget and even denounced the Republican administration at times for intruding the government too far into the life of the economy.

From the moment of his landslide reelection to a second two-year term as governor of New York in 1930, he was an obvious front-runner for the 1932 Democratic presidential nomination. And with the help of Louis Howe and James A. Farley, a talented New York political organizer who had helped orchestrate Roosevelt's two gubernatorial campaigns, he accumulated pledges from delegates throughout the country—particularly in the South and the West, where antipathy to Al Smith (Roosevelt's chief rival for the nomination) was strong. Even so, he approached the Democratic National Convention far from certain of victory. Smith had defeated him in the Massachusetts primary. House Speaker John Nance Garner of Texas had won the California primary.

Their delegate strength, combined with that of other candidates and favorite sons, denied Roosevelt through three ballots the two-thirds vote the Democratic party then required for nomination. But on the fourth ballot Garner released his delegates (after being offered the vice-presidential nomination), and the votes from Texas gave Roosevelt the margin he needed. The following day, he broke with tradition by flying to Chicago—the first major-party presidential candidate ever to travel in an airplane and the first ever to appear personally before a convention to accept its nomination. In his speech to the delegates he pledged "a new deal for the American people." Within weeks, the phrase had become a widely accepted label for his as yet undefined program.

His task in the fall campaign was a relatively simple one: avoid doing anything to alarm the electorate while allowing Herbert Hoover's enormous unpopularity to drive voters to the Democrats. Roosevelt traveled extensively and gave speeches filled with sunny generalities. He was unfailingly ebullient. He continued to criticize Hoover for failing to balance the budget and for expanding the bureaucracy, but he also occasionally gave indications of his own vaguely progressive agenda. In the most important speech of the campaign, at the Commonwealth Club in San Francisco, he outlined in broad terms a new set of government responsibilities: providing "enlightened administration" to help the economy revive and distribute "wealth and products more equitably," and giving "everyone an avenue to possess himself of a portion of that plenty sufficient for his needs through his own work."

The presidential campaign brought together the people who had guided Roosevelt's career in the past and some of those who would shape his presidency thereafter. Louis Howe and James Farley remained his principal political strategists. Eleanor Roosevelt continued to serve as a surrogate for her husband even while she was developing an important reputation of her own. But 1932 also brought Roosevelt into contact with new aides and advisers. Perhaps most notable was a group of academic advisers (dubbed the "brains trust" by reporters), chief among them three Columbia University professors: Raymond Moley, Adolf A. Berle, Jr., and Rexford G. Tugwell. They helped write his campaign speeches (including the Commonwealth Club address) and, more important, began developing ideas for his presidency based on their own growing belief in the need for a rational plan for American economic life.

Roosevelt found himself particularly attracted at first to the "brains trust" vision of of a harmonious economy, a vision inspired in large part by the American experience of mobilization for World War I. Like many members of his generation, he viewed the experiments in industrial organization of the war years as possible models for a peacetime economic order; and he was interested both in the ideas of Berle, Moley, and others in creating a new "cooperative commonwealth" in which business, labor, and government would work together to stabilize the economy, and in the more statist ideas of those who, like Tugwell, believed in a more direct form of government economic planning. But proponents of "harmony" and planning were not the only people who had his ear. Roosevelt listened to a broad and eclectic group of advisors and exhorters from throughout the Democratic party: the inveterate antimonopolists of the South and the West, who urged him to look skeptically at the power of great corporations; the public-power advocates, who had struggled throughout the 1920s to bring the federal government into the development of hydroelectric projects so as to challenge the utilities monopolies; other advocates of public works and state investment in infrastructure, who sought to use government to spur the economic development of underdeveloped regions of the country; agrarian reformers, who had spent a decade promoting a plan for stabilizing farm prices (embodied in the McNary-Haugen bills that Congress had twice passed and Calvin Coolidge had twice vetoed); the social workers and welfare strategists of his own state, of whom his wife was one, who argued strenuously for an expanded federal role in relief and social insurance.

Even before the 1932 election, the Roosevelt circle was a large and diverse one. Among the significant figures who moved into his orbit as he prepared for the White House were Felix Frankfurter, the brilliant Harvard Law School professor and frequent critic of monopoly, whose network of talented students ultimately populated many New Deal agencies; Henry A. Wallace, the visionary Iowa reformer who became Roosevelt's secretary of agriculture; Harry Hopkins, the impassioned social worker and (at least at first) close friend of Eleanor Roosevelt, who became the New Deal's "minister of relief" and eventually the president's closest adviser; even Jesse Jones, the conservative Texas banker and champion of state investment in infrastructure projects, whom Roosevelt retained as director of the Reconstruction Finance Corporation and later named secretary of commerce. Roosevelt never lacked for talented aides and advisers. His challenge was to mediate among their diverse and often conflicting views.

Roosevelt won the presidency handily, with 57 percent of the popular vote to Hoover's 40, and with 472 electoral votes to Hoover's 59. Democrats won solid control of both houses of Congress. But most observers interpreted the results less as a mandate for Roosevelt (whose plans remained largely unknown to the public and perhaps even to himself) than a repudiation of Hoover. There were still many skeptics who shared Walter Lippmann's dismissive view of Roosevelt before the election as "a pleasant man who, without any important qualifications for the office, would very much like to be president."

In the four months between his victory and his inauguration, Roosevelt did little to dispel those doubts. The Depression worsened considerably that winter and reached its nadir in the first months of 1933. More than 25 percent of the workforce was now unemployed, while many others struggled with part-time work or dramatically reduced wages. Early in 1933 a series of bank failures deepened the crisis. President Hoover, conservative Democrats, and leading business figures all urged the president-elect to restore the confidence of business and financial elites by pledging himself to fiscal and monetary orthodoxy. Roosevelt ignored their advice, but he offered few clues to his own plans. The most dramatic event of his "inter-regnum" was an attempted assassination in Miami in February, in which Roosevelt was not injured but in which Anton Cermak, the mayor of Chicago, was killed. The president-elect responded to the incident with the same unruffled calm he had displayed since the election.

Several weeks before the 1933 presidential inauguration, the cartoonist Peter Arno prepared a cover illustration for the *New Yorker* magazine. It portrayed Franklin Roosevelt and Herbert Hoover riding together in an open car, wearing top hats, following the traditional route from the White House to the Capitol for the swearing-in ceremony. Gaping crowds lined the route. Hoover was slumped in his seat, glum, unsmiling, looking sideways—somewhat suspiciously—at his successor. Roosevelt was smiling broadly, head raised, staring ebulliently at the crowds. In the aftermath of the assassination attempt, the *New Yorker* decided not to run that cover. But on March 4, 1933, photographers captured the actual scene of the ride to the Capitol, a scene uncannily similar to the one Arno had imagined weeks before: Hoover, the repudiated president, sour and silent, as if aware that after years at the center of public life he faced thirty years of marginalization and near-oblivion; and Franklin Roosevelt, beaming, insouciant, and inscrutable, his head thrust high, his arm outstretched, riding toward his rendezvous with destiny.

2

The New Deal Experiments

Historians have expressed impatience with Franklin Roosevelt at times. He was, they have complained, a man without an ideological core and thus unable to exercise genuine leadership. He was a compromiser, a trimmer. He "was content in large measure to follow public opinion," Richard Hofstadter once wrote, and thus charted no clear path. He allowed the existing political landscape to dictate his course, James MacGregor Burns lamented, instead of reshaping the Democratic party to serve his own purposes. Such complaints were common among Roosevelt's contemporaries as well, most of all among those who had invested the greatest hopes in him. There seemed to be something almost slippery about the man—with his eagerness to please everyone with whom he talked, with his ability to persuade people expressing two opposing views that he agreed with them both, with his tendency to allow seemingly contradictory initiatives to proceed simultaneously. "When I talk to him, he says 'Fine! Fine! Fine!,'" Huey Long once complained. "But Joe Robinson [one of Long's ideological nemeses] goes to see him the next day and again he says 'Fine! Fine! Fine!' Maybe he says 'Fine' to everybody." Henry Stimson, Roosevelt's Secretary of War from 1940 on, was constantly frustrated by this enigmatic man—so much so that not long after Roosevelt died, Stimson privately expressed relief that in Harry Truman, the new president, he finally had someone willing to make a clearcut and unequivocal decision. Roosevelt's fundamentally political nature—his rejection of all but a few fixed principles and his inclination to measure each decision against its likely popular reaction—may have been a significant weakness, as some of his critics have claimed, or his greatest strength, as others insist. But it was the essence of the man.[1]

So too was the New Deal a confusing amalgam of ideas and impulses—a program that seemed to have something in it to please everyone except those who sought a discernible ideological foundation for it. "Take a method and try it," Roosevelt liked to say. "If it fails, admit it frankly and try another. But above all, try something." Such statements have sometimes led critics and admirers alike to conclude that the New Deal reflected nothing but pragmatic responses to immediate problems, that it was, as Hofstadter described it, little more than a "chaos of experimentation." "To look upon these programs as the result of a unified plan," Roosevelt's erstwhile adviser Raymond Moley wrote in a sour memoir published after his falling out with the president, "was to believe that the accumulation of stuffed snakes, baseball pictures, school flags, old tennis shoes, carpenter's tools, geometry books, and chemistry sets in a boy's bedroom could have been put there by an interior decorator." But the New Deal also reflected Roosevelt's instinct for action—his belief in, if nothing else, the obligation of the leaders of government to work aggressively and affirmatively to deal with the nation's problems.[2]

Roosevelt was no ideologue, but neither he himself nor the New Deal he created existed in an ideological vacuum. The blizzard of experiments that coexisted, and sometimes clashed, within the Roosevelt administration was the product not just of short-term, pragmatic efforts to solve immediate problems. It was the product too of the well of ideologies that he and other New Dealers had inherited from the reform battles of the first third of the century and from which they felt at liberty to pick and choose as they saw fit. The New Deal may have had no coherence, but it did have foundations—many of them.

Roosevelt entered office convinced that he faced three urgent tasks. He needed to devise policies to end the Great Depression. He needed to create programs to help the millions in distress weather hard times until prosperity returned. And he needed, most New Dealers believed, to frame lasting reforms that would prevent a similar crisis from occurring again. He made strenuous efforts to fulfill all of these tasks. And while he succeeded fully at none of them, he achieved a great deal in the trying.

Roosevelt's first and most compelling task was to restore prosperity. But in truth the New Dealers had no idea how to end the Depression because they had only the vaguest idea of what had caused it. Some believed the Depression was a result of overproduction, which had driven down prices and launched the spiraling deflation. Others sensed that it was a result of underconsumption, of the inadequate incomes of working people and hence the inadequate markets for industrial goods. Some believed the problem was the composition of the currency, others that it was a lack of "business confidence." Few people in any of these groups (and in many others, with different diagnoses still) had any persuasive prescriptions for how to solve the problems they cited. Virtually no one yet understood the Keynesian economic ideas that would in later years inspire concerted, and at times effective, government efforts to fight recessions.

Just as the Federal Reserve Board in the first years of the Depression had raised interest rates at a time of massive deflation when rates should have gone down, Roosevelt entered office convinced that one of his most pressing tasks was to reduce federal spending to protect the government's solvency, at a time when the most effective response to the crisis would have been substantial deficits. In his first week in office, he won passage of the Economy Act, which slashed the federal payroll and reduced veterans benefits. And while he never succeeded in actually balancing the budget, for more than five years he never stopped trying. In time-honored fashion, Roosevelt also tinkered with the currency. First he sabotaged an international economic conference that was meeting in London to stabilize world currencies. (He sent his adviser, Raymond Moley, to represent him there. Then he repudiated the agreements Moley was attempting to craft by releasing what became known as the "bombshell" message, in which Roosevelt informed the conference that the United States would not abide by its results whatever they might be. The meeting quickly dissolved in failure.) Then he loosened the dollar's attachment to the gold standard. Later, he engaged in a fanciful program of buying gold on the international market in an effort to lower the value of the dollar and make American goods more attractive in world markets—an arcane strategy that may have done little harm but certainly did no good. Roosevelt did act effectively to stem the dangerous banking crisis that was his most immediate challenge on taking office. He declared a "bank holiday," passed emergency bank legislation to give the government authority to review the financial health of banks before allowing them to reopen, and later won passage of more substantial banking reforms that created federal insurance of banking deposits and strengthened the Federal Reserve System.

That stopped the financial panic and saved the banks. But to the larger crisis in the nation's economy he had no effective solution.

Many historians and economists now agree that the best, perhaps the only, way to end the Great Depression quickly in 1933 would have been to increase total spending rapidly and substantially. And since the private sector was trapped in a deflationary spiral that made such increases virtually impossible for businesses and individuals, the only agent for doing so was the government. But during their first five years, most New Dealers recognized the need for public spending only dimly—and constantly sought to balance that recognition against their lingering commitment to fiscal orthodoxy. Not until 1938, after a premature effort to balance the budget had helped trigger a severe recession, did Roosevelt openly endorse the idea of public spending as a stimulus to economic growth—validating the core of what would soon be known as Keynesian economics in the process. Even then, the fiscal stimulus was much smaller than what the economic conditions required.[3] In the meantime, the New Deal had to content itself with a largely inadvertent contribution to purchasing power and total spending: its public works projects and its increasingly elaborate programs of relief to the distressed and the unemployed. Only during World War II did government spending increase dramatically enough to bring the Depression wholly to an end.

Perhaps Roosevelt's most important contribution to the nation's short-term economic fortunes was to dispel the broad sense of panic that was threatening to destroy not just the banking system but the entire financial and industrial structure of the nation. He did so in part through the flurry of legislation he steered through a compliant Congress in his famous first "hundred days." But he did so as well by thrusting his own personality into the center of public life. His firm and confident inaugural address—with its ringing promise that "the only thing we have to fear is fear itself" and its stern warnings of quasi-military responses to the crisis if more conventional means did not work—established him as a leader determined to do whatever it took to avert disaster. His warm, comforting "fireside chats" over the radio, in which he patiently explained what the government was doing and what it meant to ordinary people, made him the first president whose voice and image became an ordinary part of everyday life.

Soon portraits of Roosevelt were appearing in the living rooms and kitchens of farmers, working people, and others all over the country.

Roosevelt did not end the Depression. But he challenged the despair that had gripped so many Americans in the last, lugubrious year of the Hoover presidency and helped them to believe that the government could do something about their problems.

In the absence of an effective program for ending the Depression, the New Deal's efforts to provide relief became all the more important. State, local, and private relief efforts were collapsing under the unprecedented demands placed on them, and Roosevelt stepped into the void with a series of new programs. In his first months in office, he created the Civilian Conservation Corps (CCC), which took young, unemployed, urban men and gave them jobs working in national parks and forests. This was a plan the president (who retained a preference for the countryside despite his many years in New York City and who voiced his cousin Theodore's faith in the value of the "strenuous life"—a life, of course, now barred to him) particularly liked. He created the Federal Emergency Relief Administration (FERA), which offered financial assistance to state relief agencies, and some months later the Civil Works Administration (CWA), a federally managed jobs program administered by the former social worker Harry Hopkins. The New Deal launched other programs as well, offering financial assistance to imperiled homeowners, farmers, and small businesses. Even taken together, these early relief programs were modest when measured against the gravity of the problems they were trying to address. For the people they helped, they were a godsend. For millions of others, they were simply an alluring but unattainable promise.

These early experiments in providing relief revealed both the extent and the limits of the New Deal commitment to social welfare. Roosevelt and those around him clearly rejected the rigid conservative views of those who considered any aid to the poor dangerous and improper. In 1931, as governor of New York, Roosevelt had challenged that orthodoxy. Government had a clear responsibility, he told the state legislature, "when widespread economic conditions render large numbers of men and women incapable of supporting either themselves or their families because of circumstances beyond their control which make it impossible for them to find remunerative labor. To these unfortunate citizens aid must be extended by government—not as a matter of charity but as a matter of social duty."[4] As president, he continued to reject the conservative arguments against social assistance.

But Roosevelt, Hopkins, and most of the other critical figures who shaped the New Deal welfare state also feared the debilitating effects of what was still widely known as "the dole." Harry Hopkins, looking at the effects of the FERA in 1933, said, "I don't think anybody can go on year after year, month after month accepting relief without affecting his character in some way unfavorably. It is probably going to undermine the independence of hundreds of thousands of families. . . . I look upon this as a great national disaster." The president himself proclaimed in 1934, "I do not want to think that it is the destiny of any American to remain permanently on the relief rolls."[5] Instead, the New Deal turned to an approach with which it felt much more comfortable: work relief, providing the unemployed with jobs. "Give a man a dole, and you save his body and destroy his spirit," Hopkins said. "Give him a job . . . and you save both the body and the spirit. It saves his skill. It gives him a chance to do something socially useful."[6] Both the CCC and the CWA had been experiments in work relief. In 1935, with unemployment still a serious problem, the New Deal created a much larger experiment: the Works Progress Administration (WPA).

The mission of the WPA was to fund public works programs across the nation. Hopkins became its administrator; and while he hoped to provide useful and necessary work, his first priority was to provide immediate assistance to the unemployed. Hopkins spent the money allotted to him lavishly, rapidly, and with remarkable creativity. The WPA built hospitals, schools, airports, theaters, roads, hotels in national parks, monuments, post offices, and federal buildings all over the country. It created some of the most imaginative government projects in American history: the Federal Theater Project, which hired actors, directors, playwrights, and other unemployed theater people to write and produce plays, skits, and revues; the Federal Arts Project, which recruited unemployed artists, paid them a wage, and put them to work creating public art; the Federal Writers' Project, which hired writers to produce state and city guidebooks and to collect oral histories from ordinary men and women (including former slaves). Most of all, the WPA pumped desperately needed money into the economy. In the process, it raised popular expectations of government and helped legitimize the idea of public assistance to the poor. But it did not become the model for a lasting federal role in social welfare. Congress abolished it in 1943, and federally funded jobs programs have been rare and generally modest in the years since.

What did become important and lasting parts of the American welfare state were two forms of government aid created by the Social Security Act of 1935, the single most important piece of social legislation in American history. The first was public assistance, which the framers of the Act considered to be the less important of the two—a relatively small, limited commitment, they believed, to help certain specified categories of people who clearly were unable to help themselves. It institutionalized, in effect, the longstanding distinction in American attitudes toward poverty between the deserving and undeserving poor, or (as the New Dealers themselves described them) between employables and unemployables.

New Dealers had opposed generalized relief because they feared giving a dole to people who could and should work. But the Social Security Act identified groups of people who, its framers believed, could not and should not work. Specifically, it provided direct assistance to the disabled (primarily the blind), to the elderly poor (people presumably too old to work), and most important (although no one realized at the time how important it would be) to dependent children. The Aid to Dependent Children (ADC) program (later Aid to Families with Dependent Children) eventually achieved dimensions far beyond even the wildest imaginings of those who created it and struggled constantly for legitimacy for over sixty years until finally succumbing to conservative opposition in 1996.

The Social Security Act also set up two important programs of social insurance: unemployment compensation and the old age pensions that we now associate most clearly with the name Social Security. Unlike ADC, these insurance programs had little difficulty achieving political legitimacy. Indeed, they remained through the end of the twentieth century among the most popular, even sacrosanct, of all the functions of the federal government. Unemployment insurance and old-age pensions were able to entrench themselves so successfully in part because they were nearly universal—because virtually everyone who worked stood to benefit from them. But they were also popular because they represented such a safe and conservative approach to welfare that many people (including many New Dealers) did not consider them welfare at all. They were, Americans came to believe, "insurance," much like private-sector insurance and pension plans. They were funded not out of general revenues, but out of special, separate taxes on employers and workers, whose revenues went into presumably inviolable trust funds.

(Social Security was not even included in the official federal budget until the late 1960s.) Recipients would, in theory, receive benefits they had earned and paid for (although in fact the program was more redistributive than its popular image suggested, and many people received either much more or much less in benefits than they had paid into it in contributions).

The Social Security Act, in other words, set up two forms of welfare—separate and highly unequal. Public assistance (most notably ADC) was the product of assumptions about the difference between the deserving and the undeserving, and it was both stingier in its benefits and much more vulnerable to public hostility than its social-insurance partner in birth. Social insurance, which rested on no such distinction, was more generous from the beginning and enjoyed much greater public support. It is no coincidence that one of these programs—public assistance—was a program whose benefits went disproportionately to women and that the other—social insurance—was a program whose benefits went, at least at first, principally to white men. That was not because the Social Security program was devised by men; many women were centrally involved in shaping these programs as well. It was because both the men and the women who created these programs agreed that women should be treated differently; that public policy should assume that married women would be supported by their husbands and that only when a man was absent from the home should a woman be eligible for assistance. Women, unlike men, would need public assistance when left alone, particularly when left alone with children.

This was, then, a system (in both its public assistance and social insurance elements) that was designed to preserve the traditional family wage system. Unemployment insurance and old-age pensions provided a safety net for the wage earner or retiree (although not at first to all earners, since until the 1940s the program excluded large categories of working people—including agricultural workers, domestics, and other groups that were largely black or female or both). ADC provided assistance, somewhat grudgingly, primarily to those unfortunate women and children who found themselves outside the family wage system.[7]

The most ambitious effort of the first hundred days was a series of measures to reshape the American economy in more basic and lasting ways. The reform effort took several different forms. Some reflected the belief in government regulation of concentrated power that New

Dealers had derived from the progressive reform crusades of the early twentieth century and from their suspicion of what Louis Brandeis had once called the "curse of bigness." Their inspiration was Woodrow Wilson's New Freedom, or at least those elements of it (mostly rhetorical) that warned of the power of large corporate institutions and envisioned a more decentralized and competitive economy. At the instigation of such self-proclaimed Brandeisians as Felix Frankfurter, Thomas Corcoran, and Benjamin Cohen, and with the enthusiastic support of the inveterate antimonopolist Sam Rayburn in the House of Representatives, the New Deal created a new agency to regulate the stock and bond markets—the Securities and Exchange Commission, which set out to prevent the kind of reckless speculation and occasional fraud that had helped create instability in the financial markets in 1929. It produced the Federal Communications Commission, the Civil Aeronautics Board, and other agencies to supervise sensitive areas of the economy. Later, the same forces helped inspire a controversial (and only partially successful) effort in 1935 to break the power of utilities monopolies: the Utilities Holding Company Act. Later still, they won passage of the Fair Labor Standards Act of 1938, which created a minimum wage, a forty-hour work week, and a ban on child labor; and they pressed for the creation of the Temporary National Economic Committee—a highly publicized inquiry into monopoly power run jointly by the White House and Congress from 1938 to 1943, which produced mountains of data but failed to inspire any concrete reforms.

Other New Dealers envisioned a much more forceful kind of national planning, rooted in the progressive era's faith in system, process, and expertise. Implicit in their efforts were acceptance of large-scale organization as the basic feature of the modern economy and belief in the need for some kind of centralized coordination and control. "The essential conditions of efficiency," Herbert Croly had written early in the century, "is always concentration of responsibility." Among the New Dealers who shared that belief was Rexford Tugwell. He was certain that new administrative structures could be created, new techniques of management and control devised, that would allow a modern society to achieve what Walter Lippmann had once called "mastery" over the forces that threatened to overwhelm it. Among his heroes was Theodore Roosevelt, who had begun in 1910 to articulate the ambitious vision of state supervision of the economy he called the "New Nationalism." "We should," the earlier Roosevelt had declared, "enter upon a course of supervision, control, and regulation of these great corporations—a regulation which we should not fear, if necessary, to bring to the point of control of monopoly prices."[8]

No effective centralized planning mechanisms ever emerged out of the New Deal, to Tugwell's lasting chagrin—despite the efforts of a series of committed but politically ineffective agencies charged with "planning" that survived within the government from 1933 to 1943. But the Roosevelt administration did launch some important, if limited, federal planning efforts. The most prominent of them was the Tennessee Valley Authority (TVA), a dramatic experiment in flood control and public power that was also for a time an ambitious effort to plan the future of an entire region.

The TVA's most extravagant planning efforts ultimately came to naught. Its more lasting significance may have been as a spur to another New Deal approach to political economy: a wide-ranging experiment in what the historian Jordan Schwarz has called "state capitalism" and what in today's political discourse is more often known as "public investment."[9] The commitment to public investment was not new to the Roosevelt administration, as New Dealers were quick to point out in response to their critics. The federal government had invested in roads, waterways, railroads, universities, and other public projects throughout its history. It had built the Panama Canal. Herbert Hoover, whom New Dealers spent a generation demonizing as a reactionary, had created the Reconstruction Finance Corporation (RFC) in 1932, which included among its many missions government investment in public works, and which remained under Franklin Roosevelt one of the government's most important economic instruments. But the New Deal went much further than any previous administration in making the state an instrument of capitalist development. It spent billions of dollars constructing highways and bridges, building dams and other hydroelectric projects, creating irrigation systems and other water projects in California and the Southwest. Its Rural Electrification Administration carried electrical power to millions of rural Americans.

Federally financed infrastructure projects provided short-term stimuli to the economy by creating jobs and markets for industrial goods. But they had an even more important long-term legacy. The New Deal's public works projects were concentrated disproportionately in the Southwest and the West, in part because men committed to the development of those regions played critical roles in allocating resources—among them Jesse Jones of Texas, chairman of the RFC. As a result (and by design), they laid the groundwork for the postwar transformation of the American Southwest from an arid, sparsely populated region with limited economic growth into a booming "Sunbelt."

Most New Dealers considered their most important initiatives to be their efforts to reform the two major segments of the modern economy: industry and agriculture. In that effort, the most powerful traditions were not the great progressive battles between Theodore Roosevelt and Woodrow Wilson, between the New Nationalism and the New Freedom, but the more immediate and more resonant legacy of World War I.

The historian William Leuchtenburg was among the first to note the critical role the war played in shaping the New Deal's approach to the Depression. The war, he argued, became the Roosevelt administration's principal metaphor. In his inaugural address, the new president promised to treat the task of fighting the Depression "as we would treat the emergency of war"; and he called on the "great army of the people" to embrace the effort "with a unity of duty hitherto invoked only in time of armed strife."[10] But the war was not just a metaphor; it was a model. For the wartime experiments in economic mobilization had inspired bright dreams among many reformers of an "ordered economic world" that might be recreated in peacetime. The War Industries Board of 1918, many liberals fervently (and not entirely accurately) believed, had successfully rationalized and coordinated industrial activity under the supervision of the "super-manager" Bernard Baruch. Surely, influential New Dealers argued (just as many aspiring reformers had argued through the 1920s), something similar could work comparable miracles now. The most important result of such beliefs was the National Industrial Recovery Act (NIRA) of June 1933.[11]

The origins of the NIRA were inauspicious. It was drafted hastily and pushed through Congress suddenly—a response not just to longstanding visions of reform, although it was that, but also to several alternative industrial-recovery measures moving through Congress that the president did not like: a wages and hours bill, sponsored by Senator Hugo Black of Alabama, which proposed imposing a 30-hour work week on industry as a way to spread work around and reduce unemployment;

and a number of proposals for "vast public works programs," programs much vaster than Roosevelt was willing to consider. The NIRA was, in part, an effort by Roosevelt to forestall these measures.

Even so, many New Dealers believed it was the most important piece of legislation in American history. And it was packed with provisions designed to placate the many warring factions who had a stake in reform. It created the Public Works Administration, to satisfy the many demands for new job-creation measures—a large and important program that built dams and other major infrastructure projects, but that proceeded so carefully and punctiliously under the directorship of Secretary of the Interior Harold Ickes that it failed to provide much in the way of short-term economic stimulus. The NIRA also tried to protect small businesses from monopoly power, but with regulations too weak to have any real impact. And it provided a legal guarantee of organized labor's right to organize and bargain collectively with employers (Section 7a, the first such guarantee the government had ever provided in peacetime, albeit one with no effective enforcement mechanisms). At its heart, however, was the effort to impose on the Depression economy the same kind of enlightened coordination that New Dealers liked to believe Baruch and his War Industries Board had imposed on the wartime economy. As such, it was a victory for an industry-led trade-association movement, orchestrated by Gerard Swope of General Electric, which had been arguing for two years that if businesses could be released from antitrust pressures and allowed to cooperate in setting production levels, prices, and wages, they could break the deflationary spiral and restore prosperity.[12]

The act created a new federal agency, the National Recovery Administration (NRA), with authority to work with representatives of business and labor to produce wage and price codes to stabilize various industries. Within each major industry, a new code authority would set floors below which no one could lower prices or wages; it would also set quotas for production and would have the power to enforce compliance. Government administrators would play a role in the process, but the real authority would lie with the business leaders themselves. The NRA would, in effect, allow industries to operate as cartels. It has often been described, with considerable justification, as an effort to create an American form of corporatism. "Many good men voted this new charter with misgivings," Roosevelt said in signing the bill. "I do not share their doubts. I had a part in the great cooperation of 1917 and 1918 and it is my faith that we can count on our industry once more to join in our general purpose to lift this new threat."[13]

The NRA swung into action quickly and impressively. Within weeks almost every major industry had drawn up a code and had agreed to abide by its provisions; and the agency's energetic director—General Hugh Johnson, former director of the World War I draft—succeeded in whipping up broad popular excitement about the experiment and its iconography. The famous NRA Blue Eagle seemed to be everywhere—in shop windows, and on posters, emblazoned on banners carried in "Blue Eagle" parades (one of which, in New York, was the largest parade in the city's history—larger than the great celebration that had greeted Charles Lindbergh on his return from Paris nearly a decade before). Thousands of school children in San Francisco celebrated the NRA by assembling on a playing field in the shape of an eagle for photographers. The owner of the Philadelphia professional football team renamed it the "Eagles" in honor of the agency.

But the initial enthusiasm could not disguise the fundamental problems at the heart of the experiment. And within a year, the entire effort was a shambles. There were many reasons for this. The codes served the needs of large economic organizations reasonably well. They allowed big industrial firms to keep their prices up without having to fear being undercut by competitors. But small businesses often could not compete with larger firms *unless* they undercut them in price; forcing small businesses to charge the same as large ones, which the codes tried to do, often meant robbing them of their only access to the market. Despite Section 7a, the code authorities permitted labor virtually no role at all in setting their guidelines. Workers organized, but companies continued to refuse to bargain with them. And the codes, therefore, became vehicles not just for keeping prices up but for keeping wages down. Perhaps most damningly, the NRA catered to industry fears of overproduction; and it became a vehicle that helped manufacturers move in the direction of lower production, lower wages, and higher prices at a time when the economy needed just the opposite. Criticism mounted, and the NRA attempted to correct the problems; but its efforts to intervene more forcefully in the process produced opposition from business leaders, who resented this government interference in their internal affairs and who were, in any case, becoming disillusioned with the codes, which were not working as well as they had hoped. By the end of 1934 the NRA was in chaos. And in the spring of 1935 it was ruled unconstitutional by the Supreme Court and abolished. The administration made no attempt to replace it.

The NRA was a failure, but it was not without legacies. It had emerged out of the efforts of businessmen to achieve one of their most cherished goals (cartelization), and it did help create some longstanding cartels in a few particularly troubled sectors of the economy, including oil, lumber, and aviation. On the whole, however, the NRA ended up contributing to the development that many of its supporters from the corporate world had most feared: the creation of an organized movement of independent labor unions sanctioned and protected by the government. The one aspect of the NRA that Congress did move to revive after the 1935 Supreme Court decision was Section 7a—the provision guaranteeing collective bargaining rights to workers. In 1935 it passed the National Labor Relations Act (the Wagner Act)—along with Social Security one of the two most important pieces of New Deal legislation—which not only restored but greatly strengthened 7a. It created the National Labor Relations Board, which had authority to police labor-management relations and to use federal power to stop unfair labor practics. The framers of the NIRA had accepted the provisions that led to the mobilization of trade unions, assuming that within the harmonious economy they believed the NRA would create, unions would work cooperatively with management. But once the NRA was gone, the unions remained—not as partners in an effort to coordinate the industrial economy, but as adversarial organizations challenging the prerogatives of business. The effort to create a cooperative economy had, inadvertently, contributed to creating a more competitive one: an economy increasingly characterized by the clash of powerful interest groups.

In May 1933, a month before Congress passed the NIRA, the administration won passage of legislation creating the Agricultural Adjustment Administration (AAA). The agricultural economy had been in something like a Depression since the mid-1920s. And in an age when agriculture played a much larger role in the nation's economy than it later would, and when farmers were a much more important political force than they would later become, the crisis of the agrarian economy seemed as urgent to New Dealers as the crisis of the industrial one. The principal problems facing farmers were excess production and falling prices. The AAA, therefore, was an effort to end the chronic agricultural overproduction and lift inadequate prices by limiting production and subsidizing farmers. It embodied the demands of the so-called McNary-Haugenites—representatives of agricultural interests who had battled throughout the 1920s to create federal protection for farm prices. But it went in some ways much further than these earlier proposals had done.

The AAA paid farmers to take acreage out of production. In the meantime, the government would guarantee them an equitable price for the goods they did produce. Like the NRA, the AAA included provisions for protecting small producers (in this case family farmers, tenants, and sharecroppers); and it contained provisions for guarding against excessive concentration or monopoly. But also like the NRA, the AAA in practice largely ignored those provisions. Roosevelt had insisted that farmers themselves take the lead in designing and administering reforms. And the AAA soon came to be dominated by the American Farm Bureau Federation, which represented larger farmers and whose leaders had, in fact, helped draft the bill. The Farm Bureau played a major role in administering the AAA (much as trade associations had inspired and later dominated the NRA). The National Farmers Union, a rival organization representing primarily small producers, was largely shut out. Most landowners simply ignored the provisions requiring them to keep tenants on the land and to share AAA benefits with them. The program was particularly hard on African Americans, who formed a large proportion of the landless farmers in the South and who had even less political leverage than their white counterparts. The workings of the AAA became part of the process that drove many black farmers off the land and into towns and cities.

But in other respects the AAA was a striking success. It stabilized farm prices; it limited production; it won and retained the support of most commercial farmers. By 1936 farm prices had risen significantly for most major commodities, and American farmers had become a much better organized and more powerful interest group than ever before. The American Farm Bureau Federation, in particular, had expanded dramatically and was able to put great pressure on Congress on behalf of its demands. When the Supreme Court struck down the AAA as unconstitutional in 1935 (at about the same time it struck down the NIRA), farmers were able to get is major provisions re-enacted in slightly different form to meet the Court's objections. The essential AAA programs thus survived and became the basis for the system of federal subsidization of farming that continued into the 1990s.

The NRA and the AAA were efforts—very similar efforts in many ways—to introduce order, harmony, and coordination into the two major sectors of the American economy. Both tried to stabilize unstable economies through restrictions on production and floors under prices. Both relied heavily on representatives of the private sector (the NRA on trade associations, the AAA on the Farm Bureau) to design and administer the programs. Both gave the government authority to enforce cooperation and punish violations. Both contained provisions to protect weaker members of the economy: workers and small businessmen in industry; tenant farmers and sharecroppers in agriculture. And both largely ignored those provisions.

And yet the results of these two experiments were dramatically different. The NRA utterly failed to stabilize industrial prices and production; its administrative structure dissolved in chaos; its legal authority was struck down by the Supreme Court and never revived. The most important remnant of the experiment was the one element that businessmen had most opposed: the elevation of organized labor. The AAA, on the other hand, succeeded impressively in stabilizing farm prices and production; its administrative bodies worked reasonably effectively and attracted wide support; when the Court struck them down, they were quickly replaced. The one area where the AAA did not live up to its original goals was the only area where the NRA inadvertently did: the protection of the working class of the agricultural world, the sharecroppers and tenant farmers.

There are several reasons for this difference in results. Perhaps the most basic was that the agricultural and industrial economies were not at all alike. American industry was highly diverse, deeply fragmented, with large and perhaps irreconcilable divisions between the interests of large organizations and small ones, and between management and labor. No one element within the industrial economy was capable of dominating and bringing order to it; big business, small business, labor were all too powerful to be subordinated entirely to the others and too diverse and internally divided to be entirely dominant on their own. The agricultural economy was considerably more homogeneous. There were important competing factions within it, to be sure—large and small farmers, landlords and tenants—but the large interests were relatively more powerful, and the smaller interests relatively weaker, than their counterparts in industry. The agricultural economy could work reasonably harmoniously on the basis of cooperation among its most powerful members; the industrial economy could not.

Another difference, as Theda Skocpol, Kenneth Finegold, and other scholars have argued, was in the administrative capacities of the two agencies. Both the NRA and the AAA required elaborate bureaucracies to supervise the complex economic arrangements they envisioned. The NRA was established more or less from scratch, outside any existing department. There were no existing institutions, no experts, no reliable information on which those running the agency could rely. It really had no choice but to turn to the industries and their trade associations to run the program. But the industries were themselves so fragmented that they couldn't bring order to the economy either. Given the absence of administrative capacity within the government, it is difficult to imagine how the NRA could possibly have worked. The AAA, by contrast, was part of Agriculture Department and benefited from that department's elaborate institutional network of statisticians and administrators. Agriculture was the only sector of the American economy that had already developed a public policy elite of government experts schooled in agricultural economics, experts with long experience in various federal farm programs, some of which had been in existence for twenty or thirty years. There was a tradition of government involvement with agriculture, even if a limited one; and the AAA built on and profited from that tradition.[14]

In retrospect, the New Deal has often seemed as significant for its failures and omissions as for the things it achieved. It did not end the Great Depression and the massive unemployment that accompanied it; only the enormous public and private spending for World War II finally did that. It did not, the complaints of conservative critics notwithstanding, transform American capitalism in any genuinely profound way; except for relatively limited reforms in labor relations and the securities markets, corporate power remained nearly as free from government regulation or control in 1945 as it had been in 1933. The New Deal did not end poverty or produce any significant redistribution of wealth. There was a significant downward distribution of wealth and income between 1929 and 1945—the first in more than a century and, as of the 1990s at least, also the last. But virtually all of that shift occurred during (and as a result of) World War II. Many of the New Deal's most prominent and innovative efforts—its work relief programs, its community and national planning initiatives, its community-building efforts, its public works agencies—did not survive the war.

Nor did the New Deal do very much to address some of the principal domestic challenges of the postwar era. Roosevelt was not unsympathetic to the problems of African Americans, and he made sure that his relief programs offered benefits (even if not always equal ones) to blacks as well as whites. But he was never willing to challenge the central institutions of racial oppression in American life, fearful that to do so would damage the Democratic party in the South and lose him the critical support of powerful southerners in Congress. Nor did the New Deal make much more than a symbolic effort to address problems of gender inequality. Roosevelt appointed the first woman cabinet member, Secretary of Labor Frances Perkins, and he named more women to secondary positions in government than any president had ever done. Eleanor Roosevelt, through the prominent role she played in her husband's administration, helped serve as a symbol to many women of the possibilities of active public service. But New Deal programs (even those designed by New Deal women) continued mostly to reflect traditional assumptions about women's roles and made few gestures toward the aspirations of women who sought economic independence and professional opportunities. The interest in individual and group rights that became so central to postwar liberalism—the source of both its greatest achievements and its greatest frustrations—was faint, and at times almost invisible, within the New Deal itself.

For all its limitations, however, the Roosevelt administration ranks among the most important in American history. The New Deal created a series of new state institutions that greatly, and permanently, expanded the role of the federal government in American life. The government was now committed to providing at least minimal assistance to the poor, the unemployed, and the elderly; to protecting the rights of workers and unions; to stabilizing the banking system; to regulating the financial markets; to subsidizing agricultural production; and to doing many other things that had not previously been federal responsibilities. As a result of the New Deal, American political and economic life became much more competitive than ever before, with workers, farmers, consumers, and others now able to press their demands upon the government in ways that in the past had been available only to the corporate world. (Hence the frequent description of the government the New Deal created as a "broker state," a state brokering the competing claims of numerous groups.) The New Deal literally transformed much of the American landscape through its vast public works and infrastructure projects. It revolutionized economic policy (although not until near its end) with its commitment to massive public spending as an antidote to recession. And it created broad new expectations of government among the American people, expectations that would survive—and indeed grow—in the decades that followed.

The New Deal also produced a new political coalition that sustained the Democrats as the majority party in national politics for more than a generation after its own end. After the election of 1936, the Democratic party could claim the support of its traditional constituencies in the white South and the urban immigrant cities of the East and Midwest. It could also claim a much larger share than in the past of the working-class and farm votes, the vast majority of the African-American vote in the North, and the overwhelming support of liberals and progressives of all stripes—many of whom had once found a home in the Republican party.

And the Roosevelt administration generated or gave new life to a broad set of political ideas. Some of them faded from the New Deal even before Roosevelt's death and have played a relatively small role in American political life in the years since—but they resonate, if perhaps only faintly, with the impulses of many Americans in the late twentieth century as they search for answers to the seemingly intractable economic and social dilemmas of their own time. There were experiments in fostering new forms of community—through the Tennessee Valley Authority, the Farm Security Administration, the Resettlement Administration, and other agencies—that sought to provide alternatives to the harsh, competitive individualism of the staggering capitalist economy of their day. There were innovative forms of social assistance, most notably the work relief programs of the Works Progress Administration, which rested on a notion of the government as employer of last resort. And there was the continuing and at times impassioned effort to control the effects of monopoly—to keep the issue of concentrated economic power where it had been, at least intermittently, since the late nineteenth century and where it would not be again in the half century after Roosevelt's death: at the center of American political life. Roosevelt was the last president to talk openly about the power of the "moneychangers in the temple," the "economic royalists," and the "new industrial dictatorship." No leading political figure since has spoken so directly about the forces of "organized money." They were—he said in his extraordinary speech accepting the Democratic nomination in 1936—"unanimous in their hatred for me, and I welcome their hatred." "I should like to have it said of my first Administration," he continued, "that in it the forces of selfishness and lust for power met their match. . . . I should like to have it said of my second Administration that in it these forces met their master."[15] That language—a language only rarely dominant, and more rarely decisive even within the New Deal itself—has since become almost entirely lost to American politics, even though the problems it attempted to address—the problems associated with highly concentrated economic power and widening disparities of wealth and income—have survived.

But the Roosevelt administration also produced other ideas that have endured more hardily—ideas known to later generations as New Deal liberalism, ideas that sketched a vision of a government that would compensate for rather than challenge the limitations of capitalism, ideas that embraced Keynesian economics and a vision of a sturdy welfare state, ideas that remained a source of inspiration and controversy for decades and that helped shape the next great experiments in liberal reform in the 1960s. Roosevelt may have had no coherent philosophy of his own. The New Deal may have been an amalgam of inconsistent and even contradictory measures. Its experiments may have seemed no more than what Rexford Tugwell once dismissively described as "pitiful patches" on an inadequate government, an exercise in "planting protective shrubbery on the slopes of a volcano." But the cumulative effect of Roosevelt's leadership and the New Deal's achievements was a dramatically changed political world that continues, more than half a century later, to define our own.

3

The Late New Deal and the Idea of the State

Alvin Hansen had been one of the principal economic advisers to the New Deal for nearly three years when he traveled to Cincinnati in March 1940 to speak to a group of businessmen. After his address, someone asked him what must have seemed to most people in the audience a perfectly reasonable question: "In your opinion is the basic principle of the New Deal economically sound?" Hansen could not answer it. "I really do not know what the basic principle of the New Deal is," he replied. "I know from my experience in the government that there are as many conflicting opinions among the people in Washington under this administration as we have in the country at large."[1]

Hansen's confusion was not uncommon in the frantic, at times incoherent, political atmosphere of the late New Deal. The Roosevelt administration had moved in so many directions at once that no one could make sense of it all. Everyone was aware, of course, of what the New Deal had done—of the laws it had helped pass, of the programs it had created, of the institutions it had launched or reshaped. But as Hansen suggested, few could discern in all this any "basic principle," any clear prescription for the future.

Only a few years later, however, most American liberals had come to view the New Deal as something more than an eclectic group of policies and programs. By the end of World War II, it had emerged as an idea: a reasonably coherent creed around which liberals could coalesce, a concept of the state that would dominate their thought and action for at least a generation. To some extent, battered and reviled as it has become, it remains at the center of American political life still.

What follows is an attempt to explain how and why liberal ideas of what the federal government should do evolved in response first to the recession of the late 1930s and then to the experience of World War II. The liberal concept of the state was not, of course, the only or even the most important factor in determining the form American government would assume. Nor was liberal ideology ever a uniform or static creed. But the broad outlines of what came to be known as "New Deal liberalism" remained fairly consistent for several decades after World War II; and those ideas played a major role at times in shaping the significant expansions of federal responsibility that have transformed American government and, in more recent years, American politics.

The United States was one of the slowest of the advanced industrial nations to define an important social and economic role for its national government. The American state did not remain static, certainly, in the last decades of the nineteenth century and the first decades of the twentieth; but it grew slowly, haltingly, incompletely.[2] The Great Depression, which would have been a difficult challenge for any state, was thus doubly intimidating in the United States because Americans had as yet made few decisions about what their government should do and how it should do it. As a result, the New Deal was not only an effort to deal with the particular problems of the 1930s; it was also a process of building government institutions where none existed, of choosing among various prescriptions for an expanded American state.

Through the first four years of the Roosevelt administration, however, making choices seemed to be nearly the last thing New Dealers were interested in doing. Instead, they moved unashamedly, even boastfully, in innumerable directions, proud of their experimentalism, generally unconcerned about the eclecticism of their efforts. Richard Hofstadter may have exaggerated when he described it as a program bereft of ideologies, "a chaos of experimentation." The New Deal was, in fact, awash in ideologies. What it lacked, however, was any single principle to bind its many diverse initiatives together.[3] There were occasional pleas, both in and out of the administration, for greater ideological coherence; predictions that without it the New Deal would ultimately collapse in terminal confusion. But as long as the administration seemed politically unassailable, and as long as the economy seemed on the road to recovery, it was easy to ignore such warnings.

In 1937, however, both the political and the economic landscape changed. The president's ill-advised plan for "packing" the Supreme Court, first proposed a few weeks after his second inauguration, sparked a long-festering revolt among conservatives within his own party and caused an erosion of both his congressional and popular strength from which he was never fully to recover. An even greater blow to the administration's fortunes, and to its confidence, was the dismaying and almost wholly unanticipated recession that began in October 1937—an economic collapse more rapid and in some ways more severe than the one following the crash of 1929. The new recession quickly destroyed the illusion that the Great Depression was over. And it forced a serious reevaluation among American liberals of the policies and philosophy of the New Deal. Out of the tangle of ideas and achievements of the early New Deal, many came now to believe, had to come a coherent vision that could guide future efforts. It was necessary, in short, to define the concept of New Deal liberalism.

In the late 1930s a number of potential definitions were available to those engaged in this effort, and there seemed little reason at the time to assume that any one of them would soon prevail. Two broad patterns of governance, in particular, competed for favor. Each had roots in the first years of the New Deal and in earlier periods of reform; each had important defenders.

For a time, at least, it seemed that the principal impact of the 1937 recession on American liberalism would be an enhanced belief in the value of an "administrative" or "regulatory" state, a government that would exercise some level of authority over the structure and behavior of private capitalist institutions. Efforts to reshape or "tame" capitalism had been central to American reform ideology since the late nineteenth century and had been particularly prominent in the first years of the New Deal. Indeed, believing that something was wrong with capitalism and that it was the responsibility of government to fix it was one of the most important ways in which progressives and, later, liberals had defined themselves through the first decades of the twentieth century.

In the immediate aftermath of the 1937 collapse, a powerful group of younger New Dealers embraced this tradition again and, without fully realizing it, began to transform it. They were something of a fresh force within the New Deal, a new generation of liberals moving into the places vacated by the original "brain trusters," most of whom had by then departed from public life. Some occupied important positions of influence in the administration itself: Thomas Corcoran (often considered their unofficial leader), Benjamin Cohen, Thurman Arnold, Leon Henderson, James Landis, and Robert Jackson, among others. Some made their influence felt as writers for the *New Republic*, the *Nation*, and other magazines and journals. Felix Frankfurter (who had once taught some of them at Harvard Law School and who served as a one-man employment agency for New Deal agencies) maintained his links from Cambridge. Henry Wallace and Harold Ickes served at times as their allies in the cabinet. They were known as the "New Dealers," a term that had once referred to the administration and its supporters as a whole but that now usually described a particular group within that larger orbit.

Several things distinguished them from other members of the administration and other advocates of reform. One was their hostility to an idea that had entranced progressives for decades and had played a major role in the early years of the New Deal—the idea of an associational economy, in which government would promote and regulate the cartelization of private industries so as to reduce destructive competition and maintain prices. The associational vision had shaped the first and most celebrated of the New Deal's reform experiments, the National Recovery Administration of 1933–1935.[4] And the concept continued to evoke a vague, romantic affection in some corners of the administration. Donald Richberg and others continued to lobby in the late 1930s for a revival of NRA-like policies, and the president showed an occasional inclination to agree with them.[5] But to the younger liberals of the late 1930s the failure of the NRA was proof of the bankruptcy of the associational vision. They referred repeatedly to the "NRA of unhappy memory," the "NRA disaster," the "ill-conceived NRA experiment." The attempt to create a cartelistic "business commonwealth" capable of ordering its own affairs had, they claimed, produced only increased concentrations of power and artificially inflated prices. "The NRA idea is merely the trust sugar-coated," the *Nation* argued, "and the sugar coating soon wears off."[6]

A second, related characteristic of these younger liberals was their rhetoric. Most rejected the conciliatory tone of the early New Deal, which had sought to draw the corporate world into a productive partnership with government. They favored, instead, the combative language of Franklin Roosevelt's 1936 campaign, with its sharp denunciation of "economic royalists." To much of the press and the public, what typified the "New Dealers" was a strong antipathy toward the corporate world and a fervent commitment to using government to punish and tame it.[7]

In fact attitudes toward businessmen varied greatly among the "New Dealers," and few were as hostile to corporate capitalism as their rhetoric at times suggested. Some did indeed believe that the new recession was a result of a corporate conspiracy: a deliberate "strike" by capital designed to frustrate and weaken the administration.[8] But even many of those who articulated this theory were careful to draw distinctions between "tyrannical" capitalists and those more "enlightened" business leaders who were already embracing some elements of the New Deal.

Whatever their opinions of corporate capitalism, however, virtually all the New Dealers agreed that a solution of the nation's greatest problems required the federal government to step into the marketplace to protect the interests of the public. The events of 1937 and 1938 had proved, they believed, that the corporate world, when left to its own devices, naturally frustrated the spontaneous workings of the market; that business leaders often conspired with one another to impose high "administered prices" on their customers; that the result was an artificial constriction of purchasing power and hence an unnecessarily low level of production. Only through a vigorous campaign against monopoly, therefore, could the economy be made to operate at full capacity.

Thus, on the surface at least, the most powerful impulse within the New Deal, beginning early in 1938, was the revival of the old crusade against "monopoly." Rhetorical assaults on economic concentration echoed throughout the administration as New Dealers tried to forge an explanation for the setbacks of the year before. The president made the issue the centerpiece of an important 1938 message to Congress, in which he called for the creation of what became the Temporary National Economic Committee (TNEC) to examine "the concentration of economic power in American industry and the effect of that concentration upon the decline of competition." At about the same time, Roosevelt appointed Thurman Arnold, a professor at Yale Law School and a prolific political theorist, to succeed Robert Jackson as head of the Antitrust Division of the Justice Department. Arnold quickly made his office one of the most active and conspicuous in the federal government.[9]

In fact, however, it was not the "atomizers," the believers in the Brandeisian concept of a decentralized, small-scale economy, who were moving to the fore. For while the antitrust activists of the late New Deal used familiar antimonopoly rhetoric, their efforts had very little to do with actually decentralizing the economy. They were not much concerned about the sizes of economic units as such; not much interested in punishing "bigness" or expanding opportunities for small producers. They were committed, instead, to defending the consumer and to promoting full production by expanding the regulatory functions of the state.

The record of Thurman Arnold was one indication of the form the "antimonopoly" impulse was now assuming. Arnold well deserved his reputation as the most active and effective director in the history of the Antitrust Division. By the time he left the Justice Department in 1943, he had radically expanded both the budget and the staff of his division; and he had filed (and won) more antitrust cases than the Justice Department had initiated in its entire previous history.[10]

But Arnold was not using the antitrust laws to promote anything remotely resembling the Brandeisian concept of decentralization. On the contrary, he had been arguing for years, in his books, articles, and speeches, that the idea of "atomizing" the economy was nostalgic folly; that large-scale institutions were an inevitable, perhaps even desirable, consequence of industrialism; and that any effort to dismantle them would be not only futile but dangerous.[11] In *The Folklore of Capitalism*, his celebrated 1937 book chronicling the meaningless ideological "rituals" Americans used to disguise political and economic realities, he gave special attention to what he considered one of the most vacuous of such rituals—the antitrust laws. They were, he wrote, "the answer of a society which unconsciously felt the need of great organizations, and at the same time had to deny them a place in the moral and logical ideology of the social structure. They were part of the struggle of a creed of rugged individualism to adapt itself to what was becoming a highly organized society."[12]

The role of the Antitrust Division, Arnold believed, was not to defend "smallness" or to break up combinations, but to supervise the behavior of corporations. Size by itself was irrelevant. "I recognize the necessity of large organizations in order to attain efficient mass production," he wrote in 1939, shortly after assuming office. "I recognize that trust-busting for the mere sake of breaking up large units is futile." Three years later, as he neared the end of his tenure, he was saying the same thing, even more emphatically: "Big Business is not an economic danger so long as it devotes itself to efficiency in production and distribution. . . . There can be no greater nonsense than the idea that a mechanized age can get along without big business."

How was government to measure "efficiency in production and distribution"? Arnold's answer was simple: by the price to the consumer. Whatever artificially inflated consumer prices (and thus reduced economic activity)—whether it was the anticompetitive practices of a giant monopoly, the collusive activities of smaller producers acting to stabilize their markets, or (and here he raised the ire of some of his fellow liberals) the excessive demands of such powerful labor organizations as the building trades unions—was a proper target of antitrust prosecution. Any organization that did not harm the consumer, regardless of its size, had nothing to fear. Hence the antitrust laws became in Arnold's hands vehicles for expanding the regulatory scope of the state, not tools for altering the scale of economic organizations. Enforcement, he claimed, "is the problem of continuous direction of economic traffic. . . . The competitive struggle without effective antitrust enforcement is like a fight without a referee."[13]

Arnold was saying little that was inconsistent with the actual history of antitrust law enforcement, and certainly nothing that was inconsistent with the previous record of the New Deal in confronting economic concentration. It was, however, a statement sharply at odds with the long-standing ideology of antimonopoly. Arnold's views were more reminiscent of Theodore Roosevelt's nationalistic view of the economy (or Thorstein Veblen's concern with efficiency) than of the more truly antimonopolist views of the populists or Brandeis or the Wilson of 1912.[14] No one recognized that more clearly than the old midwestern progressives to whom antitrust still meant (as William Borah put it in a hostile exchange during Arnold's confirmation hearings) "breaking up monopolies." Suspicious of Arnold from the start, they viewed his tenure in the Justice Department as a disaster—which, by their standards, it turned out to be. His success in using the antitrust laws to police rather than forestall "bigness" was a serious, perhaps final, blow to the old concept of those laws as the route to genuine decentralization. That was precisely Arnold's intention.[15]

The TNEC, similarly, was an antimonopoly inquiry more in name than in substance. It included among its members such inveterate congressional antimonopolists as Borah, Rep. Hatton Sumners of Texas, and Sen. Joseph O'Mahoney of Wyoming (the chairman). But most of the congressional members soon lost both interest and faith in the committee as the real work of the investigation fell increasingly under the control of the young New Dealers appointed to represent the administration: Arnold, Jerome Frank, William O. Douglas, Isador Lubin, and (directing the investigative staff) Leon Henderson, men far less concerned about the size of the institutions of the economy than about their effects on consumers and their accountability to the state. At times subtly, at times explicitly, the TNEC inquiry debunked old antimonopolist assumptions that small enterprises were inherently preferable to large ones; it cited time and again the value of efficiencies of scale; and it sought to find new devices with which government could intervene in the economy to protect the public from the adverse effects of a concentration of power that it seemed to concede was now inevitable.[16]

The work of the TNEC dragged on for nearly three years. The committee examined 655 witnesses, generated 80 volumes and over 20,000 pages of testimony, published 44 monographs, and, as time passed and the inconclusiveness of the enterprise became clear, gradually lost the attention of both the public and the president. Its final report, issued in April 1941, attracted virtually no serious attention in a nation already preoccupied with war; and the entire episode was soon largely dismissed as a "colossal dud" or, more charitably, a "magnificent failure." "With all the ammunition the committee had stored up," *Time* Magazine commented at the end, "a terrific broadside might have been expected. Instead, the committee rolled a rusty BB gun into place [and] pinged at the nation's economic problems."[17]

The feeble conclusion of the TNEC inquiry illustrated the degree to which the antimonopoly enthusiasms of 1938 had faded by 1941. But the character of the inquiry during its three years of striving illustrated how the rhetoric of antimonopoly, even at its most intense, had ceased to reflect any substantive commitment to decentralization. If economic concentration was a problem, and most liberals continued to believe it was, the solution was not to destroy it but to submit it to increased control by the state.

The New Dealers of the late 1930s used many different labels to describe their political ideas: "antimonopoly," "regulation," "planning." But while once those words had seemed to describe quite distinct visions of reform, they were coming now to describe a common vision of government—a vision of capable, committed administrators who would seize control of state institutions, invigorate them, expand their powers

when necessary, and make them permanent actors in the workings of the marketplace. The task of liberals, William Douglas wrote in 1938, was "to battle for control of the present government so its various parts may be kept alive as vital forces of democracy." What Americans needed above all, Thurman Arnold argued, was a "religion of government which permits us to face frankly the psychological factors inherent in the development of organizations with public responsibility."[18]

James Landis, chairman of the Securities and Exchange Commission from 1935 to 1937 and later dean of Harvard Law School, published in 1938 a meditation on his own experiences in government in which he expressed something of this new faith. "It is not without reason," he wrote in *The Administrative Process*, "that a nation which believes profoundly in the efficacy of the profit motive is at the same time doubtful as to the eugenic possibilities of breeding supermen to direct the inordinately complex affairs of the larger branches of private industry." But the impossibility of finding "supermen" to manage the economy (as some progressives had once dreamed) was, Landis believed, not a reason to retreat from state activism. It was a reason to enlarge the federal bureaucracy, to substitute for the unattainable "super manager" the massed expertise of hundreds of individual administrators. "A consequence of an expanding interest of government in various phases of the industrial scene," he insisted, "must be the creation of more administrative agencies. . . . Efficiency in the processes of governmental regulation is best served by the creation of more rather than less agencies."[19]

Increasing the regulatory functions of the federal government was not, of course, an idea new to the 1930s. Curbing corporate power, attacking monopoly, imposing order on a disordered economic world—those had been the dreams of generations of reformers since the advent of large-scale industrialization. But the concept of an administrative state that was gaining favor in the late New Deal, while rhetorically familiar, was substantively different from the visions that had attracted reformers even five years earlier. Younger liberals continued to use the language of earlier reform impulses; but without ever quite saying so, they were rejecting one of the central features of those impulses.

For decades, American reformers had dreamed of creating a harmonious industrial economy, a system that could flourish without extensive state interference and produce enough wealth to solve the nation's most serious social problems. There had been widely varying ideas about how to create such an economy, from the associational visions of creating a smoothly functioning, organic whole out of the clashing parts of modern capitalism to the antimonopolist yearning for a small-scale decentralized economy freed of the nefarious influence of large combinations. But the larger dream—the dream of somehow actually "solving" the problems of modern capitalism—had been one of the most evocative of all reform hopes and the goal of most progressives and liberals who advocated an expanded state role in the economy.

By the end of the 1930s, faith in such broad solutions was in retreat. Liberal prescriptions for federal economic policy were becoming detached from the vision of a harmonious capitalist world. The state could not, liberals were coming to believe, in any fundamental way "solve" the problems of the economy. The industrial economy was too large, too complex, too diverse; no single economic plan could encompass it all. Americans would have to accept the inevitability of conflict and instability in their economic lives. And they would have to learn to rely on the state to regulate that conflict and instability.

This new vision of the state was in some ways more aggressive and assertive than the prescriptions it replaced. And it was the very limits of its ultimate ambitions that made it so. The new breed of administrators would operate from no "master plan." Nor would they ever reach a point where economic reforms obviated the need for their own services. Rather, they would be constantly active, ever vigilant referees (or, as Arnold liked to put it, "traffic managers"), always ready to step into the market to remove "bottlenecks," to protect efficiency and competition, and to defend the interests of consumers, who were replacing producers as the ultimate focus of liberal concern.[20] The regulators would not, could not, create lasting harmony and order. They would simply commit the state to the difficult task of making the best of an imperfect economic world.

The aggressively statist ideas of the new liberals aroused intense and constant controversy—controversy that revealed how untenable their position really was. The idea of perpetual, intrusive government involvement in the workings of the economy, with no hope of ever setting things right in a way that would permit the government to withdraw, was a rebuke both to the antistatist impulses deeply embedded in American political culture and to the natural yearning for simple, complete solutions to important problems. Even most liberals were never fully comfortable with the idea that there was no real "answer" to the economic question. So it is perhaps unsurprising that when an alternative "solution" of an appealing, almost dazzling simplicity began to emerge, it found a ready, even eager, following.

While some New Dealers were expressing enthusiasm for an expanded regulatory state, others within the administration were promoting a different course of action that would ultimately become more important in shaping the future of liberalism. They proposed that the government make more energetic use of its fiscal powers—its capacity to tax and spend—to stimulate economic growth and solve social problems. Advocates of the fiscal approach, like advocates of regulation, were principally interested in aiding consumers and increasing mass purchasing power. But they seized on different tools. Theirs was a vision of an essentially compensatory government, which would redress weaknesses and imbalances in the private economy without directly confronting the internal workings of capitalism. Such a state could manage the economy without managing the institutions of the economy.

There were few signs early in 1937 that new, more ambitious fiscal policies were on the horizon. Instead, the administration began the year in a confident mood and seemed prepared to return to the still appealing orthodoxies of balanced budgets and reduced spending. The Depression, it appeared, was finally over. Unemployment remained disturbingly high, to be sure, but other signs—factory production, capital investment, stock prices—were encouraging. Inspired by these apparent successes, fiscal conservatives pressed their case with an almost gleeful vigor.

Leading the campaign for "fiscal responsibility" was Secretary of the Treasury Henry Morgenthau, Jr., whose relentless private efforts to win Roosevelt's support for a balanced budget belied his public image as a passive sycophant with no strong ideas of his own. Morgenthau and his allies admitted that deficit spending had been necessary during the economic emergency, but they had never credited the concept with any real legitimacy. And now that the New Deal had "licked the Great Depression," as a treasury official wrote in 1937, it was time to put the nation's finances back in order. The president, who had never been fully reconciled to the budget deficits he had so consistently accumulated, was receptive to such arguments. In the spring of 1937 he agreed to a series of substantial cuts in federal spending that would, he believed, balance the budget in 1938.[21]

The idea of a balanced budget was appealing for reasons beyond inherited dogma. Morgenthau managed to persuade the president that only by eliminating deficits could the New Deal truly prove its success; federal spending, he argued, had become a crutch, propping up an economy that—because of the administration's achievements—could now stand on its own. Roosevelt, moreover, recalled the charges of fiscal irresponsibility he had leveled against Hoover in 1932 and saw a balanced budget as a way to vindicate his earlier attacks. Economists in the Treasury Department argued further that there was a danger now of inflation and that trimming the federal deficit would contribute to price stability.[22]

There were dissenters. Chief among them was Marriner Eccles, chairman of the Federal Reserve Board, who called efforts to balance the budget "dangerously premature" and defended deficits as "a necessary, compensatory form of investment which gave life to an economy operating below capacity."[23] But nothing could prevail in the spring of 1937 against the sunny optimism and strenuous bureaucratic infighting of Morgenthau and his allies. "The President gave me . . . everything that I asked for," Morgenthau gloated in the spring of 1937. "It was a long hard trying fight but certainly at some time during the weeks that I argued with him he must have come to the conclusion that if he wants his Administration to go forward with his reform program he must have a sound financial foundation."[24]

The economic collapse of the fall of 1937 destroyed hopes for a balanced budget in 1938. More significantly, it discredited many of the arguments supporting those hopes. "No one can doubt," the *New Republic* wrote, "that the sudden withdrawal of hundreds of millions of dollars of federal relief funds, the smashing of thousands of projects all over the country, did contribute materially to the creation of our present misery."[25] Within a few months, even many erstwhile defenders of fiscal orthodoxy had come to believe that the spending cuts of the previous spring had been an important, perhaps even a decisive, cause of the recession. The center of power in the debate over fiscal policy suddenly shifted.

Morgenthau and his allies in the Treasury Department continued to argue strenuously for fiscal conservatism even in the face of the new disasters. But they were now arguing almost alone. Throughout the early months of 1938, Eccles arranged meetings with sympathetic administration officials to press the case for spending and quickly mobilized influential supporters—Henry Wallace, Harold Ickes, Harry

Hopkins, Aubrey Williams, Leon Henderson, Lauchlin Currie, Mordecai Ezekiel, Beardsley Ruml, Isador Lubin—committed to a vigorous new antirecession program. In March a group of spending advocates assembled in Warm Springs, where the president was vacationing. And while Williams, Ruml, and Henderson huddled at a nearby inn preparing ammunition, Hopkins sat with the president in the "Little White House," spread the evidence out on the rickety card table Roosevelt liked to use as a desk, and persuaded him to shift his course.[26] A few weeks later, the president sent a message to Congress proposing a substantial new spending program: an additional $1.5 billion for work relief, another $1.5 billion for public works, and an expansion of credit of approximately $2 billion. It was not enough, some critics maintained. But at a time when the nation's peacetime budget had never exceeded $10 billion, most considered $5 billion substantial indeed.[27]

What was particularly significant was the way Roosevelt explained the new proposals. In his first term, he had generally justified spending programs as ways to deal with specific targeted problems: helping the unemployed, subsidizing farmers or homeowners or troubled industries, redeveloping the Tennessee Valley. Now he justified spending as a way to bring the economy as a whole back to health.[28] "We suffer primarily from a lack of buying power," he explained in a fireside chat early in 1938 (its text drawn in part from a Beardsley Ruml memo). It was time for the government "to make definite additions to the purchasing power of the nation." He accompanied his announcement (as he was fond of doing) with references to the historical precedents for his decision:

> In the first century of our republic we were short of capital, short of workers and short of industrial production; but we were rich in free land, free timber and free mineral wealth. The Federal Government rightly assumed the duty of promoting business and relieving depression by giving subsidies of land and other resources.
>
> Thus, from our earliest days we have had a tradition of substantial government help to our system of private enterprise. But today the government no longer has vast tracts of rich land to give away. . . . [N]ow we have plenty of capital, banks and insurance companies loaded with idle money; plenty of industrial productive capacity and several millions of workers looking for jobs. It is following tradition as well as necessity, if Government strives to put idle money and idle men to work, to increase our public wealth and to build up the health

and strength of the people—to help our system of private enterprise to function.[29]

Roosevelt's comfortable references to the past failed to mask the unprecedented nature of his statement. Government spending, the president now implied, was no longer a necessary evil, to be used sparingly to solve specific problems. It was a positive good, to be used lavishly at times to stimulate economic growth and social progress. Without fully realizing it, he was embracing the essence of what would soon be known as Keynesian economics. He was ushering in a new era of government fiscal policy.

In some respects fiscal activism was no newer to the 1930s than the regulatory innovations with which it coexisted. Federal subsidization of private interests was as old as the federal government itself. But the kind of spending New Dealers supported throughout the 1930s, and the rationale they were gradually developing to justify it, suggested an important departure. In the past, government subsidies had almost always promoted the productive capacities of the nation. They had been designed to assist the builders of roads, bridges, dams, railroads, and other essential elements of the economic infrastructure. They had encouraged settlement of the West and the development of new agricultural frontiers. More recently, they had assisted banks and other financial institutions to weather the storms of the Depression.

But ideas about government spending changed significantly in the late New Deal. Instead of advocating federal fiscal policies that would contribute directly to production and economic development, liberals pressed for policies that would promote mass consumption. Alvin Hansen, one of the first important American economists to grasp and promote the teachings of Keynes, took note of this important shift in outlook. The best way to ensure a prosperous future, he was arguing in the late 1930s, was "to work toward a higher consumption economy," to make consumer demand the force driving production and investment instead of the other way around. And the most efficient way to create such demand was for the government to pump more spending power into the economy—through public works, social security, federal credit mechanisms, and other methods. "Consumption," he argued, "is the frontier of the future."[30]

These two broad approaches to the problems of the economy—increased state regulation and increased use of fiscal policy—coexisted relatively easily in the late 1930s. Indeed, many New Dealers considered them two halves of a single strategy and seldom thought very much about the differences between them. Both were efforts to deal with what most liberals believed was the principal cause of the Great Depression: inadequate purchasing power. Both aimed to promote full production through stimulating consumption.[31]

What bound these two strategies together most closely was an assumption about the American economy that suffused liberal thought in the late 1930s and helped drive efforts to discover a new role for the state. Even before the 1937 recession, doubts had been growing within the New Deal about the nation's capacity ever again to enjoy the kind of economic growth it had experienced in the half-century before the Great Depression. The setbacks of 1937 only reinforced those concerns. The economy had been dragging for nearly a decade; sluggish growth and high unemployment were beginning to seem part of the natural order of things. Out of those fears emerged the concept of the "mature economy."[32]

The idea that economic expansion was not (and could not become) limitless drew from a long tradition of such predictions in America, stretching back at least to the nineteenth century. (It also, of course, anticipated some of the no-growth ideologies of the 1970s.) It had particularly close ties to Frederick Jackson Turner's "frontier thesis," which remained in the 1930s a staple of American historical interpretation. Sen. Lewis Schwellenbach of Washington, an ardent New Dealer (and later secretary of labor under Truman) suggested the connection in a 1938 speech: "So long as we had an undeveloped West—new lands—new resources—new opportunities—we had no cause to worry. We could permit concentration of wealth. We could permit speculation of our heritage. We could permit waste and erosion by wind and water, but we caught up with ourselves. We reached our Last Frontier."[33]

It was not simply the exhaustion of land and other natural resources that presented problems. Nor was it the slackening population growth of the 1930s, which had led many analysts to predict very slow future increases and a leveling off at 175 million around the year 2000.[34] The most important source of "economic maturity," defenders of the concept claimed, was the end of "capital accumulation." The great age of industrial growth was finally over. The basic industries were now built. No new sectors capable of matching railroads, steel, and automobiles as engines of expansion were likely to emerge. And since economic growth alone would no longer be sufficient to meet the needs of society, new forms of management were now essential if the nation's limited resources were to be sensibly and fairly allocated. "Hereafter," wrote the popular economist Stuart Chase, "unless I have completely misjudged the trend of the times and the temper of the people, economic systems are going to be run deliberately and directly for those ends which everybody knows they should be run for. . . . The welfare of the community will be paramount."[35]

The mature-economy idea provided powerful support to arguments for increasing the regulatory functions of the state. An economy in which dynamic growth was no longer possible placed nearly unbearable pressures on players in the marketplace to avoid risks and thus to collude to raise (or "administer") prices. Only a strong administrative state could combat this dangerous trend. But the same concept also added strength to arguments for greater government spending. In the absence of large-scale private investment, only the government had the resources (and the broad "national" view of the economic problem) necessary to keep even modest economic growth alive.

The writings of Alvin Hansen illustrate how the belief in economic maturity was helping to fuse regulatory and spending ideas. Hansen agreed that "the age of capital investment is past." The result, he argued, was "secular stagnation"—a concept that became one of his principal contributions to Keynesian theory (and one that Keynes himself never entirely accepted). Private institutions, Hansen argued, had lost the ability to create large-scale economic growth; indeed, they were now likely actually to retard such growth through anticompetitive practices as they struggled to survive in a more difficult world. One solution, therefore, was vigorous antitrust efforts to restore fluidity to the marketplace. Like Keynes, however, Hansen believed that fluidity alone would not be enough. Government also had a responsibility to sustain and, when necessary, increase purchasing power to keep alive the higher levels of consumption upon which the mature economy would now have to rely. Regulatory and fiscal mechanisms would work together to produce economic growth.

But the partnership of the regulatory and compensatory visions, which for a time had seemed so natural and untroubled, did not last, at least not on equal terms. By 1945 the idea of the administrative state, which had seemed so powerful in the late 1930s, was in decline; and faith in fiscal policy, so tentatively embraced in 1938, had moved to the center of liberal hopes. The reason for that change was not simply that the spending initiatives of the late 1930s seemed to work; even when they did, many liberals continued for a time to consider government spending little more than a temporary stopgap and believed still that more lasting statist solutions were necessary. The change was also a result of the American experience in World War II.

World War I spawned two decades of bitter recriminations among Americans who believed the nation had intervened in the conflict for no useful purpose. But it also helped shape bright dreams among progressives of a more harmonious economic world at home, dreams of a vaguely corporatist economy in which private institutions would learn to cooperate on behalf of the public interest and in which the state would preside benignly over a new era of growth and progress. Those dreams, however untrue to the realities of the wartime experience, fueled a generation of reform efforts and helped shape the early New Deal.[36]

In the 1940s, by contrast, the war itself—the reasons for it, the necessity of it—produced little controversy and few recriminations. But neither did it evoke among liberals anything comparable to the World War I enthusiasm for a reformed and reordered economy. On the contrary, the war helped reduce enthusiasm for a powerful regulatory state and helped legitimize the idea of a primarily compensatory government.

Many factors contributed to this wartime evolution of opinion. The political climate was changing rapidly. The Republicans had rebounded in the 1938 and 1940 elections; conservatives had gained strength in Congress; the public was displaying a growing antipathy toward the more aggressive features of the New Deal and less of an animus against big business. Liberals responded by lowering their sights and modifying their goals.[37] The labor movement, similarly, encountered intense popular hostility during the war, along with strong pressure from the government to abandon its more ambitious political goals. Its accommodation with the state and its alliance with the Democratic party limited its capacity to act as an independent political force and to press for structural economic reforms.[38] Liberals who had once admired the collective character of some European governments looked with horror at the totalitarian states America was now fighting and saw in them a warning about what an excessively powerful state could become. And the emergence of an important American role in the world, which virtually all liberals came to believe must extend indefinitely beyond the end of the war, directed attention and energy away from domestic reform ideas.[39]

The war also forced American government actually to attempt many of the aggressive managerial tasks that reformers had long advocated. The results of those efforts not only failed to increase faith in the ability of the state to administer a rationalized economy but actually diminished it. The War Production Board (WPB), the central institution of the mobilization effort and the World War II equivalent of the War Industries Board of 1918, seemed to liberals to become a tool of its corporate leaders or of the military or both, and to serve the interests of big business at the expense of small entrepreneurs. And it seemed to perform not like the efficient instrument of economic order of which reformers had once dreamed, but like a lumbering, inefficient bureaucracy never quite able to get its signals straight. The WPB managed to avoid any genuine catastrophes, but it was in continual administrative turmoil—crippled from the start by its lack of adequate authority to resist other centers of power (most notably the military) in the battle for control of production decisions.[40] It suffered, too, from the unwillingness of the president to support its decisions unreservedly; Franklin Roosevelt preferred to keep all potential power centers (and thus all possible rivals) in his administration relatively weak.

Even some of the strongest supporters of federal regulatory efforts in the late 1930s found the experience of the war years discouraging. In 1937 Thurman Arnold had called on Americans to develop a "religion of government." By 1943 he was disillusioned and impatient with what he had seen of state control of the economy. "The economic planners are always too complicated for me," he wrote his friend William Allen White. "They were bound to get in power during a period of frustration"; but their time, he implied, had passed.[41] The dreams of an extensive regulatory state were coming to seem unrealistic, perhaps even dangerous. And that realization encouraged a search for other, less intrusive vehicles of economic management.

Declining faith in the managerial capacities of the state coincided with another development that had profound effects on liberal assumptions about the future: the revival of American capitalism. After a decade of Depression, a decade of declining confidence in the economy and despair about the prospects for future growth, the industrial economy restored itself, and what was perhaps more important for the future of national politics, redeemed itself in a single stroke.[42]

In the process it helped erode one of the mainstays of late-Depression liberalism. The wartime economic experience—the booming expansion, the virtual end of unemployment, the creation of new industries, new "frontiers"—served as a rebuke to the "mature-economy" idea and placed the concept of growth at the center of liberal hopes. The capitalist economy, liberals suddenly discovered, was not irretrievably stagnant. Economic expansion could achieve, in fact had achieved, dimensions beyond the wildest dreams of the 1930s. Social and economic advancement could proceed, therefore, without structural changes in capitalism and without continuing, intrusive state management of the economy. It could proceed by virtue of growth.

Assaults on the concept of "economic maturity" began to emerge as early as 1940 and gathered force throughout the war. Alvin Hansen himself partially repudiated the theory in 1941 ("All of us had our sights too low," he admitted).[43] The *New Republic* and the *Nation*, both of which had embraced the idea in 1938 and 1939, openly rejected it in the 1940s—not only rejected it, but celebrated its demise. The country had achieved a "break," the *Nation* insisted, "from the defeatist thinking that held us in economic thraldom through the thirties, when it was assumed that we could not afford full employment or full production in this country."[44]

But to believe that growth was feasible was not necessarily to believe that it was inevitable. "Enough for all is now possible for the first time in history," a 1943 administration study reported. "But the mere existence of plenty of labor, raw materials, capital, and organizing skill is no guarantee that all reasonable wants will be supplied—or that wealth will actually be produced." Except perhaps for the prospect of military defeat (a prospect seldom contemplated by most Americans after the first months of 1942), nothing inspired more fear during the war years than the specter of a peacetime economic collapse and a return to the high levels of unemployment that had been the most troubling and intractable problem of the 1930s. How to prevent that collapse now became the central element on the national political agenda; and for liberals, as for others, that meant a basic change in outlook. Instead of debating how best to distribute limited output and how most efficiently to manage a stagnant economy, reformers began to discuss how to keep the wartime economic boom—and the high levels of income and employment it had produced—alive in the postwar years. "Full employment" was the new rallying cry of liberal economists; all other goals gradually came to seem secondary. And the route to full employment, the war seemed to demonstrate, was not state management of capitalist institutions, but fiscal policies that would promote consumption and thus stimulate economic growth.[45]

The new approach was clearly visible in the deliberations of those committed to the idea of "planning," and above all, perhaps, in the work of the National Resources Planning Board (NRPB). In the first years of the war (before its demise in 1943 at the hands of hostile congressional conservatives), the NRPB produced a series of reports outlining an ambitious program for postwar economic growth and security. It showed in the process how the "planning" ideal was shifting away from the vision of a rationally ordered economy (prominent in the early 1930s), away too from the idea of the activist, regulatory state (a central feature of late 1930s reform), and toward the concept of compensatory action. Planning would enable government to stimulate economic growth through fiscal policies. It would allow the state to make up for the omissions and failings of capitalism through the expansion of welfare programs. It need not involve increased state management of capitalist institutions.[46]

The NRPB had begun its life in 1933 under Harold Ickes in the Interior Department. And during its first half-dozen years of existence (under four different names and several different structures), it had generally reflected a view of planning derived from the city-planning backgrounds of many of its members and from the regional planning experience of the TVA and other, smaller New Deal projects. City planning and regional planning—the coordination of government programs in particular localities to reshape the social, physical, and economic environment—served for a time as microcosmic models for a larger concept of a planned society. The federal government, through a combination of public investment, public welfare, and extensive regulation, could become a major actor in the workings of the national economy, could direct its course, shape its future.[47]

The concept of planning to which the NRPB became principally committed in the first years of the war was subtly yet significantly different. The board continued to outline public works projects and to insist on their importance, but it usually portrayed such projects now less as vehicles for remaking the environment than as opportunities for counter-cyclical government spending. Its mission was to create a "shelf" of potential public undertakings from which the government could draw projects "as insurance against industrial collapse and unemployment"; the intrinsic value of the projects as vehicles for urban or regional planning had become secondary. Welfare programs (and, above all, an expansion of the Social Security system) had, in the meantime, moved to the center of the NRPB prescription for federal social activism—both because such programs now appeared affordable (given the new abundance apparently within the nation's grasp) and because they could themselves serve the cause of growth by increasing and redistributing purchasing power.[48]

The board's 1942 report, *Security, Work, and Relief Policies* (released by the president early in 1943), outlined a program of "social security" of such breadth and ambition that it was widely dubbed the "American Beveridge Report," after the nearly simultaneous study that led to the creation of a new British welfare state. But the NRPB proposals were in fact significantly different from, and in some ways more extensive than, their British counterparts. The Beveridge Report restricted itself to a discussion of social welfare and insurance mechanisms; the NRPB proposed such mechanisms in the context of what it considered a larger goal: the maintenance of full employment.[49] The board's 1943 "National Resources Development Report" called explicitly for government programs to maintain a "dynamic expanding economy on the order of 100 to 125 billions of national income." Only a few years before such a figure would have seemed preposterously high. But now, almost anything seemed possible. "We must plan for full employment," members of the board wrote in a 1942 article explaining their proposals. "We shall plan to balance our national production-consumption budget at a high level with full employment, not at a low level with mass unemployment."[50]

The board did not altogether abandon its concern about state management of economic institutions. Even very late in its existence it continued to include in its reports recommendations for expanded antitrust efforts, for new regulatory mechanisms, and for other extensions of the government's administrative role. One of its 1943 documents, in fact, spoke so explicitly about a drastic expansion of state control of the economy that it evoked rare applause from I. F. Stone, who generally decried the administration's "timidity" but saw in the NRPB proposals "large and historic aims."[51]

But this lingering interest in what Franklin Roosevelt once dismissed as "grandiose schemes" was by then secondary—both to the members of the board themselves and, to an even greater extent, to other liberals interpreting its work—to the larger, simpler task of maintaining economic growth. "We know," the authors of the 1943 "Resources Development Report" wrote, "that the road to the new democracy runs along the highway of a dynamic economy, to the full use of our national resources, to full employment, and increasingly higher standards of living. . . . We stand on the threshold of an economy of abundance. This generation has it within its power not only to produce in plenty but to distribute that plenty." As columnist Ernest K. Lindley noted, "The most striking characteristic of the two [1943 NRPB] reports is their essential conservatism. The postwar is keyed to the restoration of the free enterprise system and its encouragement and stimulation."[52]

Central to this new emphasis on growth was the increasing influence of the ideas of John Maynard Keynes and of the growing number of American economists who were becoming committed to his theories. By the late 1930s Keynes himself was already personally friendly with some of the leading figures of the New Deal. At the same time leading American economists were becoming proponents of Keynesian ideas. Alvin Hansen, Mordecai Ezekiel, and Gardiner Means, for example, all of whom were active on the NRPB and all of whom reached broader audiences through their essays in economic journals and liberal magazines, had by the early years of the war become converted to at least some tenets of Keynes's general theory.[53]

Hansen in particular—one of the principal authors of the 1943 NRPB reports—was in the early 1940s frequently described as "Keynes's American counterpart," "one of the most influential men in Washington," "the leader of a whole new economic school." He served as an illustration not only of the growing impact of Keynes on American economists but of the way in which the American Keynesians were embracing only the most moderate aspects of an economic philosophy that, in Keynes's own hands, at times envisioned far more fundamental change. Hansen's earlier, celebrated concerns about "secular stagnation" were now muted. In their place was a faith in the ability of fiscal policy to ensure continued economic growth. "Clearly fiscal policy is now and will continue to be a powerful factor in the functioning of the modern economy," Hansen wrote in 1942. Such policies should be used "to develop a high-consumption economy so that we can achieve full employment. . . . A higher propensity to consume can in part be achieved by a progressive tax structure combined with social security, social welfare, and community consumption expenditures."[54]

Keynes's economic doctrines (and the larger constellation of ideas derived from them) suggested ways to introduce in peacetime the kinds of stimuli that had created the impressive wartime expansion. They offered, in fact, an escape from one of liberalism's most troubling dilemmas and a mechanism for which reformers had long been groping. They provided a way to manage the economy without directly challenging the prerogatives of capitalists. Growth did not necessarily require constant involvement in the affairs of private institutions, a task that was (as the experience of wartime mobilization helped demonstrate) both endlessly complex and politically difficult; it did not require a drastic expansion of the regulatory functions of the state. "To produce in plenty" required only the indirect manipulation of the economy through the use of fiscal and monetary "levers"; and to "distribute that plenty" required the creation of an efficient welfare system. Such measures were not (as some liberals had once believed) simply temporary stopgaps, keeping things going until some more basic solution could be found. They were themselves the solution.[55]

The renewed wartime faith in economic growth led, in short, to several ideological conclusions of considerable importance to the future of liberalism. It helped relegitimize American capitalism within a circle of men and women who had developed serious doubts about its viability in an advanced economy. It robbed the regulatory reform ideas of the late 1930s of their urgency and gave credence instead to Keynesian ideas of indirect management of the economy. And it fused the idea of the welfare state to the larger vision of sustained economic growth by defining social security mechanisms as ways to distribute income and enhance purchasing power. No other single factor was as central to the redefinition of liberal goals as the simple reality of abundance and the rebirth of faith in capitalism abundance helped to inspire.

By the end of World War II, the concept of New Deal liberalism had assumed a new form; and in its assumptions could be seen the outlines of a transformed political world. Those who were taking the lead in defining a liberal agenda in the aftermath of the war still called themselves New Dealers, but they showed relatively little interest in the corporatist and regulatory ideas that had once played so large a role in shaping the New Deal. They largely ignored the New Deal's abortive experiments in economic planning, its failed efforts to create harmonious associational arrangements, its vigorous if short-lived antimonopoly and regulatory crusades, its open skepticism toward capitalism and its captains, its overt celebration of the state. Instead, they emphasized those New Deal accomplishments that could be reconciled more easily with the vision of an essentially compensatory government. They lauded the New Deal's innovations in social welfare and social insurance; a decade earlier many had considered such initiatives of secondary importance. They credited the New Deal with legitimizing government fiscal policy as a way of dealing with fluctuations in the business cycle and guaranteeing full employment; few liberals in the 1930s had understood, let alone supported, such policies. Above all, perhaps, postwar liberals celebrated the New Deal for having discovered solutions to the problems of capitalism that required no alteration in the structure of capitalism; for having defined a role for the state that did not intrude it too far into the economy. In earlier years many liberals had considered the absence of significant institutional reform one of the New Deal's failures.

This transformation had proceeded slowly, at times almost imperceptibly, so much so that for a time many liberals were unaware that it had even occurred. But for those who cared to look, signs of the change were abundant. It was visible, for example, in the character of the postwar liberal community. The "planners," "regulators," and "antimonopolists" who had dominated liberal circles eight years earlier were now largely in eclipse, without much influence on public discourse. Thurman Arnold, Robert Jackson, and William Douglas were sitting on federal courts. Thomas Corcoran was practicing law. Benjamin Cohen was accepting occasional assignments as a delegate to international conferences. Leon Henderson, one of the last of the true "New Dealers" to hold a major administrative post during the war, had resigned as head of the Office of Price Administration in December 1942 and had become an embittered critic of the government's failures, convinced that without more assertive state planning and regulation the nation faced an economic disaster after the war.[56]

No comparably powerful network could be said to have emerged by 1945 to take their place; indeed many liberals were now so preoccupied with international questions and with the emerging schism within their ranks over the Soviet Union that they paid less attention than they once had to domestic issues. But most of those who did attempt to define a domestic agenda were people fired with enthusiasm for the vision of a full-employment economy, people who considered the New Deal's principal legacy the idea of effective use of fiscal policy and the expansion of social welfare and insurance programs. In place of the "statist" liberals who had helped define public discourse in the 1930s were Keynesians such as Alvin Hansen, one of the architects of the principal liberal initiative of 1945, the Full Employment bill;[57] and Chester Bowles, the last director of the Office of Price Administration, whose 1946 book, *Tomorrow Without Fear*, called not for an expansion or even a continuation of the regulatory experiments with which he had been involved during the war, but for an increased reliance on fiscal policy.[58]

The Democratic platform in 1944 was another sign of the changing political landscape. Four years earlier, the party had filled its platform with calls for attacks on "unbridled concentration of economic power and the exploitation of the consumer and the investor." It had boasted of the New Deal's regulatory innovations, its aggressive antitrust policies, its war on "the extortionate methods of monopoly."[59] The 1944 platform also praised the administration's antimonopoly and regulatory efforts—in a perfunctory sentence near the end. But most of its limited discussion of domestic issues centered on how the New Deal had "found the road to prosperity" through aggressive compensatory measures: fiscal policies and social welfare innovations.[60]

The changing landscape of liberalism was visible as well in some of the first retrospective celebrations of the New Deal, in the way early defenders of its legacy attempted to define its accomplishments. In 1948, Arthur M. Schlesinger, Jr., published an essay entitled "The Broad Accomplishments of the New Deal." The New Deal, he admitted, "made no fundamental attempt to grapple with the problem of the economies of concentration or of the decline in outlets for real investment." But that, he claimed, was not really the point. The New Deal's most significant accomplishments were much simpler and more important: "The New Deal took a broken and despairing land and gave it new confidence in itself. . . . All [Roosevelt's] solutions were incomplete. But then all great problems are insoluble."[61]

The importance of the New Deal lies in large part, of course, in its actual legislative and institutional achievements. But it lies as well in its ideological impact on subsequent generations of liberals and in its effects on two decades of postwar government activism. And in that light, the New Deal appears not just as a bright moment in which reform energies briefly prevailed but as part of a long process of ideological adaptation.

For more than half a century Americans concerned about the impact of industrialization on their society—about the economic instability, the social dislocations, the manifest injustices—had harbored deep and continuing doubts about the institutions of capitalism. Few had wanted to destroy those institutions, but many had wanted to use the powers of government to reshape or at least to tame them. And that desire had been a central element of "progressive" and "liberal" hopes from the late nineteenth century through the late 1930s.

The ideological history of the late New Deal, from the troubled years after 1937 through the conclusion of the war, is the story of a slow repudiation of such commitments and the elevation of other hopes to replace them. By 1945 American liberals, as the result of countless small adaptations to a broad range of experiences, had reached an accommodation with capitalism that served in effect to settle many of the most divisive conflicts of the first decades of the century. They had done so by convincing themselves that the achievements of the New Deal had already eliminated the most dangerous features of the capitalist system; by committing themselves to the belief that economic growth was the surest route to social progress; and by defining a role for the state that would, they believed, permit it to compensate for capitalism's inevitable flaws and omissions without interfering with its internal workings. Thus reconciled to the structure of their economy, liberals of the postwar world could move forward into new crusades—fighting for civil rights, eliminating poverty, saving the environment, protecting communism, reshaping the world—crusades that would produce their own achievements and their own frustrations, and that would one day lead to another, still unfinished, ideological transformation.

4

The New Deal and Southern Politics

In 1949—four years after the death of Franklin Roosevelt, more than a decade after the effective end of the New Deal—V. O. Key, Jr. published an assessment of the state of southern politics that has remained largely unchallenged ever since. He wrote: "When all the exceptions are considered, when all the justifications are made, and when all the invidious comparisons are drawn, those of the South and those who love the South are left with the cold, hard fact that the South as a whole has developed no system or practice of political organization and leadership adequate to cope with its problems."

The problem, he claimed, was not a new one. The political structure of most southern states, Key argued, was in all essential respects the same structure the South had erected for itself at the end of Reconstruction. Politics in most of the South was oligarchic, reactionary, and myopic. It thrived on rigid control of the franchise by conservative political elites, on a fervent commitment to white supremacy, on deep suspicion of "outside interference" in its affairs, and on a one-party system that had faced no real challenge since the 1870s. The southern political system had, in short, prevented the development of effective, class-based interest groups that might have threatened the jarring inequalities in the region's social and economic structure. "The South may not be the nation's number one political problem . . .," Key observed, "but politics is the South's number one problem."[1]

What was striking to Key in 1949, and what remains striking today about southern politics in his time, is how impervious the system appears to have been to a series of extraordinary crises and changes in American life. The South in the 1940s had recently emerged from more than a decade of economic distress that had affected it at least as severely as it had affected any other region. And it had emerged as well from a period of national political reform whose major outlines it had supported, in electoral terms at least, more enthusiastically than had any other area of the nation. And yet neither the Depression nor the New Deal appeared to have wrought any significant changes in the region's internal political organization or in the nature of its political leadership. In other areas of the nation the 1930s had produced powerful new political coalitions capable of challenging and at times toppling old structures of authority. In the South the Depression years had produced little more than what Key described as "weak forays against the established order," forays the established order had generally countered with ease.[2]

The most compelling question about southern politics in the age of the New Deal, then, is why so little seemed to change. Why did the South prove so resistant to the winds of political transformation the New Deal was helping to inspire elsewhere?

Part of the answer, the largest part according to some historians who have examined the South in the 1930s, lies in the nature of the New Deal itself, in its failure or inability to mount any serious challenge to the structure of southern politics. Franklin Roosevelt did, it is true, launch occasional assaults against the conservative political establishment of the South. He did at times attempt to encourage the growth of liberal factions in the region, to promote "forces of change" that might challenge the status quo. But such efforts were infrequent and usually halfhearted. Far more typical of the New Deal were efforts to work closely with existing political elites, attempts that not only failed to challenge the prevailing power structure but often reinforced it.

That Roosevelt chose such a course should not be surprising. The New Deal has in retrospect come to represent a modern, welfare-state liberalism committed to a major expansion of federal power through the creation of great national bureaucracies; it has become a symbol of the shift of authority away from the states and localities and toward Washington. But if that was the New Deal's ultimate effect, it was not its original intent. On the contrary, Franklin Roosevelt and most of those around him were deeply uneasy about the prospect of highly centralized federal authority and bureaucratic expansion; and they sought constantly to limit both, even as they embarked on the new government initiatives they considered necessary in the face of the economic emergency. They were careful, therefore, to place control of most New Deal programs as much in the hands of local officials and institutions as in Washington. Hence the tendency of those programs was often less to challenge than to perpetuate existing structures of local power.

New Deal agricultural programs, for example, almost always scrupulously avoided antagonizing local farm leaders, even when those leaders were—as was often the case in many parts of the South—powerful conservative oligarchs, exercising a rigid and oppressive control over the local economy. The Agricultural Adjustment Administration did have in each state a committee of administrators appointed by Washington. Far more powerful, however, were county-level committees whose members were chosen by local farmers and whose leadership often rested in the hands of established local elites. Chapters of the Farm Bureau Federation, which represented the interests of established commercial farmers and paid scant attention to the needs of the far larger number of marginal, subsistence farmers, played a major role in selecting many county agents.[3]

New Deal relief agencies, similarly, relied heavily on local officials to administer their programs. In northern cities that often meant placing control of work relief programs in the hands of established Democratic bosses, a fact that has caused a growing number of historians in recent years to cast doubt on the so-called "Last Hurrah" thesis—the thesis that the New Deal shattered the power of urban machines.[4] In rural areas of the South, similarly, relief administrators, like AAA county agents, were often established Democratic leaders and were perfectly willing to bend New Deal programs to serve their own conservative interests. Southern relief administrators at times discharged employees from FERA, or later, WPA projects when local landholders needed cheap labor for picking cotton or for other agricultural chores—even though the farm wages were often significantly lower than the relief benefits. Some administrators even complained to Washington that the benefits of their own programs were too high, that they threatened the wage scale of local employers. Such complaints came even though the administration had already agreed to respect the regional wage differentials that kept relief payments in the South lower than those in other regions.[5]

Critics of the New Deal have long maintained that the failure of its programs to challenge the conservative power structure of the South was the result of a failure of will; and it is true that such challenges never seemed to rank very high on the list of New Deal priorities. But even had the administration tried to use its programs to change the political balance in the South, it would have run up against an obstacle far more imposing than insufficient commitment: a lack of bureaucratic capacity. Washington's dependence on local authorities for the administration of its programs was not simply an ideological choice; it was a necessity for a government that lacked any extensive experience of intervention in local economic affairs and that had constructed no institutions to allow it to do so.[6]

At the state level, the Roosevelt administration showed little more interest in challenging the distribution of southern political power than it did at the local level. Rather, as with its treatment of local organizations, the New Deal tended to strengthen, not to challenge, the dominant political factions in state capitals. In part this was a deliberate, perhaps necessary, decision grounded in political self-interest. In many southern states existing statewide political organizations were so firmly entrenched that challenges to them would have been both costly and unlikely to succeed. And those challenges would likely have alienated powerful members of Congress, whose support Roosevelt believed he needed for his legislative initiatives. If he had ever wanted any proof of that, he needed to look no further than his first serious move to confront a hostile, conservative state organization—his attempt in 1936 and 1937 to strengthen the insurgent liberal faction led by James H. Price in Virginia as an alternative to the powerful Byrd machine. That effort resulted only in strained relations with two important United States Senators (Carter Glass and Harry Byrd) and brought no serious reduction in the power of the machine. As soon as the political costs of the challenge became clear to the president, he abandoned Price, restored control of patronage to the Byrd organization, and doomed the insurgents to virtual political extinction. In Virginia, as elsewhere, liberal insurgents found the president an unreliable ally in any battle requiring patience and sustained commitment.[7]

To have expected otherwise from Franklin Roosevelt would have been to misinterpret the president's political instincts in fundamental ways. Roosevelt was a coalition-builder, a compromiser; in purely political terms at least, a conservative. His goal was not to shatter existing political orders and build his own in their place as Huey Long, for example, had tried to do in Louisiana. His inclination, rather, was to conciliate, to broaden his base of support, to win the loyalties of existing leaders. In the South that meant not only remaining solicitous of political elites in the distribution of patronage and the administration of programs. It meant avoiding issues altogether when those issues seemed likely to create regional antagonisms. Hence the New Deal's reluctance to challenge segregation in the South, its willingness to tolerate racial discrimination in the administration of its own relief programs, its acceptance of racial wage differentials, its refusal to endorse antilynching legislation, its notable lack of enthusiasm for supporting union organizing in the South. Franklin Roosevelt was not interested in provoking a political revolution, and except on rare occasions, he balked at doing anything that would inflame regional sensibilities and jeopardize the stability of his political coalition.

Could he have done otherwise? Could the president, had he been so inclined, have used his personal popularity, his patronage, and his funding power to spawn effective "forces of change" in southern politics? Some critics have argued that he could have done so, that in any case there were enough prospects for success that he should have tried.

Among the first to voice this view was James MacGregor Burns, in his 1956 biography of Roosevelt, *The Lion and the Fox*. Burns argued that the president could have made use of "vigorous new elements in the Democratic party that put programs before local patronage, that were chiefly concerned with national policies of reform and recovery," progressive elements that might have lifted the party "out of the ruck of local bickering and orient it toward its national program." Had Roosevelt joined hands with them, he "could have challenged anti-New Deal factions and tried to convert neutralists into backers of the New Deal." But faced with this opportunity, Burns observed, Roosevelt declined to take advantage of it and failed to join hands with progressive forces. He was unwilling "to commit himself to the full implications of party leadership" because "he subordinated the party to his own political needs; he thus failed to exploit its full possibilities as a source of liberal thought and action."[8]

It is true, as Burns claimed, that Roosevelt's efforts to reshape the Democratic party in his own image operated within strict limits. But for the South, at least, there is reason to question Burns's implication that the prospects for the success of such efforts were bright enough to justify the attempt. The pattern of southern politics in the 1930s suggests, on the contrary, that the "forces of change" that Burns and others have touted so enthusiastically were, for the most part, weak and underdeveloped; and that even when strong, they were wedded to visions of change in many ways incompatible with that of the New Deal.[9]

The list of southern progressives who rose to prominence in the 1930s is a familiar and in many respects an impressive one: Governors E. D. Rivers in Georgia, Dave Sholtz in Florida, Olin Johnston and Burnet Maybank in South Carolina; Senators Claude Pepper in Florida and Lister Hill in Alabama; Congressman Lyndon Johnson in Texas, to name only a few. Citing such names, some observers have gone so far as to claim that the South's conservative reputation was really a myth, that the South was actually more progressive than other regions of the country in the 1930s. Others have made the more plausible argument that the list of southern progressives suggests at least the possibility of basic change in the politics of the region.[10]

From another perspective, however, what seems most striking about the roster of southern progressives in the 1930s, aside from its relative brevity, is, first, how fragile the progressives' political bases usually were compared to those of their conservative rivals; and second, how limited was even their commitment to the sorts of liberal reforms that most New Dealers outside the South had come to endorse.

The fragility of the progressives' political base is perhaps best illustrated by what happened to southern New Dealers after their first flush of success. Rivers, for example, managed election to two successive two-year terms as governor of Georgia; but by the end of the second, the public had already grown weary of his relatively modest reform efforts and of what his opponents charged was his reckless spending. Hence Georgians were ready, in 1940, to return the reactionary, anti-Roosevelt Eugene Talmadge to the state house. Claude Pepper managed to hold on to his Senate seat through the 1940s, but finally fell victim to charges that he represented leftist inclinations alien to the South and lost to the conservative George Smathers in 1950. Lyndon Johnson, who posed as an ardent New Dealer in his first campaigns for Congress, discovered in the 1940s that his liberal image was a serious political liability in Texas and henceforth rose to prominence by presenting himself as an archetypal southern conservative. Other progressives who seemed in the 1930s to give promise of regional leadership—

men such as Frank Porter Graham of North Carolina or Hugo Black of Alabama—tended by the end of the decade to find themselves more influential outside the South than within it.

Influential southern liberals were not only few and weak; they were, in comparison with progressives elsewhere, relatively "unliberal." It would be difficult to find a major white politician in the South in the 1930s whose position on the question of race moved very far beyond the region's reactionary norms. But even using more modest standards of judgment, the conservatism of most southern liberals seems striking.[11] One of the shining lights of Depression liberalism in the South was the so-called "Little New Deal" that Dave Sholtz constructed as governor of Florida. And yet what qualified Sholtz for admission to the liberal pantheon was little more than his willingness to permit the federal government to spend money in his state. Harry Hopkins and others complained frequently to the White House that Florida was embracing New Deal relief agencies largely to avoid having to shoulder any responsibility itself for the indigent; that Sholtz consistently failed to contribute the state's expected share to welfare programs. Hopkins refrained from cutting off relief funding to the uncooperative Florida government only because he was reluctant to punish the state's unemployed for the failings of their political leaders.[12]

In South Carolina, two apparently ardent New Dealers—Olin Johnston and Burnet Maybank—won terms as governor during the 1930s and seemed, through much of the decade, not only willing but eager to forge a new relationship with the federal government and the national Democratic party. Like most other southern New Dealers, however, they were willing to consider such a relationship only within rigidly proscribed boundaries. In 1942, when the Roosevelt administration proposed legislation to make it easier for servicemen to vote in federal elections, both Johnston and Maybank (who was by then a United States Senator) responded with outrage at the possible racial implications of the change and demonstrated a parochial belligerence that belied their earlier enthusiasm for the New Deal. Johnston issued a blunt warning to Washington that "we South Carolinians will use the necessary methods to retain white supremacy and to safeguard the homes and happiness of our people," while Maybank promised that the South would retain control of its own institutions "regardless of what decisions the Supreme Court may make and regardless of what laws Congress may pass."[13]

A particularly vivid expression of the suspicion with which southern liberals regarded their counterparts in the rest of the country appeared in a 1939 article by John Temple Graves II. Graves was a syndicated columnist for the *Birmingham Age-Herald;* he was known for his opposition to racial bigotry and the Ku Klux Klan and for his support for most of Franklin Roosevelt's legislative initiatives; he was, by the standards of most of the South, a leading liberal. But he was also a man with a highly defensive vision of his region's progressivism, a vision that reflected the anxieties of many southern New Dealers. The greatest threat to southern liberalism, Graves warned in a 1939 article in the *Nation*, came not from the region's conservatives but from "outside liberals," who attempted to enforce a rigid brand of national reform on a region that had its own special needs. On the surface, at least, it was a reasonable position. But Graves went on to denounce northern liberalism in terms that leave one to wonder whether any meaningful progressive stance could have survived this sort of regional scrutiny.

After expressing his loyalty to Franklin Roosevelt and the New Deal, Graves went on to denounce northern Democrats for their failure, "in their approaches to the South, to separate themselves clearly from a communism which ruling Southerners hate and fear above all else." Organizers of the Southern Conference for Human Welfare, an interracial meeting of liberals in Birmingham in 1938, had, he claimed, done serious damage to the progressive cause in the region by insisting upon defying local segregation laws during their meetings. Liberals throughout the nation who had flocked to the cause of the Scottsboro "boys" had, he argued, "hurt the case for plain justice among a people who might have been persuaded of the innocence of the defendants but who knew that no matter whose the fault, they were individuals of a low order." According to Graves's standards, in short, northern liberals could expect from the South a commitment to progress and reform only if change did not threaten the political status quo, the racial status quo, or even the economic status quo. (He condemned as well agitation to raise industrial wages and strengthen unions in the South.)[14]

It would be unfair, of course, to conclude that the reluctance of southern liberals to endorse open assaults on the status quo always reflected approval of the status quo. Often it did. But there were also many humane and sensitive southern liberals in the 1930s who believed in racial equality, who opposed the political oligarchies, who wanted reform—but who believed that any attempt to promote fundamental change would have catastrophic results, would unleash terrible bigotry and violence. The cure, in short, promised to be worse than the disease. Whatever the reason, whether because of essentially conservative instincts or timidity or some combination of both, most southern liberals came to look on the northern brand of New Deal liberalism with deep suspicion.

At the heart of this suspicion was something more than opposition to specific New Deal programs or proposals. The southern electorate, according to public opinion polls, almost invariably favored Roosevelt's legislative initiatives; a majority even backed the president's ill-fated court-packing plan in 1938. What southern liberals and conservatives alike most feared from the New Deal was intrusion, federal interference in the South's right to manage its own affairs and chart its own future. That fear stemmed, in part, from a very real, if defensive, regional pride, which became evident in 1938 upon the release of the administration's *Report on Economic Conditions of the South.*[15] On the surface, nothing would have seemed more likely to inspire the region's liberals. The report described vividly the South's colonial dependency on northern industry, the tragic conditions of its agricultural economy, the devastating effects of its reactionary politics on the region's economic development.

Virtually all southern leaders endorsed some of the report's specific proposals, especially the proposal to eliminate the discriminatory freight rates that northern industry had used for decades to limit southern competition. But the dominant response to the report, from southern liberals and conservatives alike, was angrily defensive. Southerners denounced it as a slur on the entire region, an official reinforcement of old and unattractive stereotypes. When Franklin Roosevelt read the report and announced that he was now convinced that the South was "the nation's No. 1 economic problem," southern liberals reacted not to the implicit promise of federal action to address the problem, but to the suggestion that the North was holding the South up to judgment and finding it wanting. A chorus of protests—claiming that the region was, in fact, "the nation's No. 1 economic opportunity," that the South was really most striking for the dramatic progress it had made since the devastation wrought on it by the Civil War and Reconstruction, that what it really needed was "to be left alone"—all but drowned out whatever positive impact the report might have had.[16]

But regional pride took second place to regional fears in inspiring southern opposition to outside intervention in its affairs. That was nowhere clearer than in the region's response to Roosevelt's attempt to influence two United States Senate elections in his famous and ill-considered "purge" campaign of 1938. The president was, for once, trying openly to use his popularity in the region to support challenges to two of the South's most reactionary figures: Senator Walter George of Georgia and Senator Ellison D. ("Cotton Ed") Smith of South Carolina. Both were old men who had become deeply alienated from the president and his programs. Both were facing primary challenges from younger politicians who identified themselves openly with the New Deal. George, at least, was, according to early soundings, politically vulnerable.[17]

But when Roosevelt traveled first to Georgia and then to South Carolina and openly appealed to its citizens to unseat the incumbents and send to the Senate men of progressive vision, he evoked reactions so hostile, from across the entire breadth of the political spectrum, that he demolished whatever chance there might once have been of unseating either man. The issue, after the president's visit, became not the records of George and Smith versus the records of their opponents. It became "outside interference," the right of the South to determine its own destiny and choose its own representatives. Walter George, predictably, decried Roosevelt's intervention in the campaign as a "second march through Georgia," a new "carpetbag invasion." Smith, equally predictably, evoked similar images of the Lost Cause with his defiant statement before a statue of the Confederate hero Wade Hampton that "No man dares to come into South Carolina and try to dictate to the sons of those men who held high the hands of Lee and Hampton."[18]

But somewhat less predictable—and certainly more revealing—was that many southern liberals reacted with similar hostility and consternation. Even those who might otherwise have been inclined to support the challenges to George and Smith retreated in the face of Roosevelt's tactics; acquiescence in this "meddling" in state politics, they believed, was both politically and ideologically untenable. One example was the position adopted by the *Atlanta Constitution*, a major organ of moderation and progressivism in the South, and a frequent critic of Walter George's conservative, anti-New Deal stances. After the 1938 primary, the *Constitution* published an editorial assessing the results. It praised Georgia voters for their good sense in reelecting Governor E. D. Rivers over a conservative opponent and defeating Eugene Talmadge's bid for the Senate. But it rejoiced above all in the victory of Senator George. The issue in the race, the paper claimed, "was whether the Democratic voters of a state should decide for themselves who was to speak for them at Washington."[19]

Lurking not far beneath the surface, of course, was a much greater fear, shared by white liberals and conservatives alike: that outside intervention in southern politics, in whatever form, would inevitably lead to an assault on the region's racial institutions. Again, the *Atlanta Constitution* drew the connection as explicitly as the most reactionary southern leader. Roosevelt's attempt to purge Walter George, its editorial writers claimed, was part of the president's effort to win passage of "the vicious, dangerous and cruel anti-lynching bill. A bill that would forever make the sovereign states but chattels of the central government."[20]

If it had not been evident before, the response to Roosevelt's 1938 campaign made clear that the liberal forces in the South were too feeble, too divided, and too limited in their commitment to reform to provide a promising basis for change. But to say that is only to ask, not to answer, the most important questions. Why was southern liberalism so weak? Were the conservative regimes so powerful and popular that they were invulnerable to challenge? Were southern voters so unanimous in their support for the status quo that conflict had disappeared from the region's politics?

Clearly that was not the case. Southern political life in the 1930s was, in most of the region at least, fraught with conflict. In almost every state there were factional divisions that at least vaguely reflected class divisions. Challenges to conservative candidates were constant and not infrequently successful. There was in southern politics a level of conflict and insurgency that seems at first to belie the weak and tentative picture of New Deal challenges to the existing order.

It was, however, an insurgency that had little in common with the New Deal and that often found itself as much opposed to national liberalism as to local conservatism. For the most powerful antiestablishment tradition in the South was not progressivism but populism; and the most successful insurgents in the 1930s, as in the four decades before, were advocates of a vision of reform far different from that of the New Deal.

The most conspicuous and most successful southern insurgent was, of course, Huey Long of Louisiana. Whatever we might think of

Long's methods, he clearly represented the "forces of change" in the politics of his state; his opponents were largely what remained of one of the South's most stubborn and reactionary oligarchies. And yet Long's relationship with the New Deal was troubled from the start; by the end of 1933 he was among Roosevelt's most vociferous and dangerous foes, while the president had allied himself with the conservative opposition in Louisiana.

In part the break between Long and Roosevelt was a result of purely personal and political animosities. Both were powerful, ambitious leaders; neither was willing to contemplate standing in the shadow of the other. But the break also reflected a basic difference in the two visions of reform Long and Roosevelt had come to represent. To Long, the greatest danger to America's future—and the greatest drag on its present prosperity—was concentrated wealth and power, the ability of a few powerful men and institutions to govern the lives of the many. The mission of reformers, therefore, was to oppose centralization of power and restore to individuals and communities control over their own lives. That meant, of course, doing battle against the great financial institutions, against the excessively wealthy, against corporate tyranny. But it also meant resisting the growth of a powerful federal bureaucracy, for an overbearing central government was as capable of oppressing the people as any private power center.

Such concerns put Long squarely at odds with the major thrust of the New Deal. Despite Roosevelt's own reservations about big government, the reforms of the 1930s worked inexorably to create an ever-larger national bureaucracy and to intrude the national government ever deeper into the affairs of individuals and localities, developments against which southern insurgents generally recoiled.[21]

It was not only in Louisiana that they recoiled. Eugene Talmadge in Georgia rose to power, like Long, through strident attacks on the ruling oligarchies, but Talmadge was an equally embittered critic of the "communistic, free-spending" policies of the New Deal. Theodore Bilbo in Mississippi first emerged in state politics as a foe of the Old Guard and won a Senate seat in 1934 as a scourge of the conservative elite; but his subsequent career was characterized by a sour, virulently racist battle against federal incursions into local affairs.[22]

The dominant insurgent force in the Depression South, in short, was not the weak and tentative group of southern liberals who identified with the New Deal. It was a force that drew from the region's own populist traditions, one that could produce both radical and reactionary demands, one that could find expression simultaneously in a Huey Long and a Eugene Talmadge. And it was, above all, a force that looked with almost equal hostility at the conservative aristocrats who dominated Southern politics and the social democratic liberals who were building a powerful and intrusive new federal bureaucracy. Franklin Roosevelt never entirely understood either the strength or the nature of this powerful southern insurgent tradition; but he understood it well enough to know that it was no friend of his New Deal.

What, then, must we conclude about the impact of Franklin Roosevelt and the New Deal on the politics of the South? Clearly the New Deal wrought no internal revolution in southern politics. Few southern states emerged from the Depression with political systems more fluid or progressive than those with which they had entered it. No equivalent appeared in the South of the Roosevelt coalition that was reshaping the Democratic party in the rest of the country. There is, on one level at least, little reason to question the conclusions of such scholars as V. O. Key, Jr., George B. Tindall, James T. Patterson, and others that in political terms the New Deal passed through the South leaving few discernible changes in its wake.[23]

And yet, little more than twenty years after Franklin Roosevelt's election to the presidency, fewer than ten years after his death, a series of profound transformations did begin to occur in southern social, economic, and political life. This Second Reconstruction, arguably the most significant period of change in the entire history of the South, was not the direct work of the New Deal. But it was to a striking degree a result of New Deal policies that, indirectly and often inadvertently, paved the way for the transformation to come.

Some of those policies helped to transform the South's own social and economic structure. New Deal agricultural programs, for example, unintentionally but decisively worked to push southern tenant farmers and sharecroppers off the land. In the short run, the result was enormous hardship for the displaced farmers. In the long run, the result was a radical change in the structure of the South's agricultural economy and a decline in the power of the Black Belts, which had dominated the region's politics since the end of Reconstruction. The exodus of sharecroppers from the land was responsible, too, for a major increase in the African-American population of southern cities; and it was from among these urban blacks that the early civil rights movement drew its greatest strength.[24]

But the New Deal was even more effective in laying the groundwork for the Second Reconstruction through its impact outside the South, and above all through its effect on the national Democratic party. Franklin Roosevelt may not have succeeded in wedding southern Democrats to a modern, statist liberalism, but he was highly successful in imposing a new liberal outlook on the party as a whole. More important, Roosevelt was able to turn the national Democratic party into a powerful new majority coalition capable, as it had never been before, of winning elections and dominating government even without support from the South.

For nearly a century the South's position within the Democratic party had been the region's most effective tool for maintaining its power and autonomy within the larger American society. For the national party to have any hope of victory, it had always needed to rely on the solid, one-party South for support. The Democrats could nominate a presidential candidate uncongenial to its southern members only at the party's peril, as it discovered when it selected Al Smith in 1928. The South, in short, held a crucial balance of power in Democratic politics, and because of that it had almost always been able to prevent any federal initiatives that might have threatened its conservative institutions or its hierarchical social structure.[25]

Franklin Roosevelt's creation of a new and vastly more powerful Democratic coalition shattered the South's grip on the party. No longer could the region hold Democratic presidential candidates hostage to its conservative demands; Roosevelt would have won all four of his national elections even had he received not a single electoral vote from the eleven ex-Confederate states. No longer could the South exercise a veto over the party's choice of national candidates; the traditional two-thirds rule at national Democratic conventions, whereby Southern delegates could block any presidential prospect not to their liking, was abolished in 1936. No longer could the South be certain of dominating the Democratic congressional caucus; it received bitter evidence of that in 1937, when Senate Democrats passed over Pat Harrison of Mississippi, the overwhelming choice of southerners for majority leader, and, responding to presidential pressure, elected the far less conservative Alben Barkley of Kentucky. And no longer could southern Democrats impose their racial views on the party as a whole; the sudden and virtually total shift of northern black voters from the Republican party to the Roosevelt coalition in 1936 meant that the national Democratic leadership could not ignore much longer the legitimate demands of African Americans.[26]

The full implications of such changes were not immediately evident to Franklin Roosevelt. They were not clear to Harry Truman, or even at first to John F. Kennedy. But ultimately the national Democratic party did move, prodded by the courts and by rising black protests, to ally itself firmly with the civil rights movement and to launch a frontal assault on segregation and, through it, the southern political system. It was able to do so in the 1960s at least in part because of the political transformation Franklin Roosevelt had wrought thirty years before. In doing so, it joined a challenge to the nation's oldest and deepest injustice, a challenge Roosevelt himself had not dared to launch. But in doing so, it also proved Roosevelt's political fears to have been in some measure correct. For the price of this historic and honorable stand—as the one-time New Dealer Lyndon Johnson understood better than most of his contemporaries—was, as Roosevelt had warned, the party's loss of its reliable majority in the South and, as a result, a significant weakening of its majority in the nation.[27]

Roosevelt may not have wholly understood what his New Deal had launched in the South. But some of his contemporaries did. Indeed, the most accurate and prescient observers of southern politics in the 1930s were the very men whose bitter opposition to the New Deal made them seem the least enlightened of all political figures: the embittered Old Guard conservatives of the South. For it was they who saw more clearly than anyone else what the political changes of the 1930s would ultimately mean to their region. They were often unhappy, of course, about what the New Deal was doing within the South. But what most alarmed them was what it was doing in the North. They realized that the Democratic party as they had known it was vanishing, and that a new coalition was emerging in which they could never again hope to play a decisive role. They realized that this new coalition, in which African Americans and unions and committed northern liberals played so important a part, would not for long be content to leave the South and its institutions alone. They realized that the South was becoming more isolated from national politics, and thus weaker, more vulnerable to assaults from a hostile outside culture. Resistance to change from within would not be enough in the world the New Deal was shaping.

Political forces were gathering in the North that would ultimately impose changes on the South from without.

"The catering of our National Party to the Negro vote is not only extremely distasteful to me," Josiah Bailey wrote in 1938, "but very alarming to me. Southern people know what this means, and you would have to be in Washington only about three weeks to realize what it is meaning to our party in the Northern states." Carter Glass, a year earlier, expressed similar alarm. "To any discerning person," he wrote, "it is perfectly obvious that the so-called Democratic party at the North is now the negro party, advocating actual social equality for the races; but most of our Southern leaders seem to disregard this socialistic threat to the South in their eagerness to retain Mr. Roosevelt in power."[28]

Such statements clearly exaggerated the Democratic party's commitment to racial reform in the 1930s, but they reflected a remarkably accurate vision of what was to come, a vision that haunted southern conservatives such as Carter Glass with an almost violent intensity. Glass suggested as much in a letter to Lewis Douglas in 1935. "Now is about as good a time as anybody could find to die," he wrote, "when the country is being taken to hell as fast as a lot of miseducated fools can get it there. Nevertheless, it would be interesting to live long enough to see the thing tumble."[29] Glass died in 1946, with the South he knew and loved and defended, a South whose politics rested on white supremacy and on rigid hierarchical rule by conservative political elites, still largely intact. But had he lived a few years longer, he would have seen the thing begin to tumble. And as he had predicted, it would tumble finally in part because of changes that Franklin Roosevelt and his New Deal had set in motion.[30]

5

The Two World Wars and American Liberalism

In the spring of 1917, as the United States prepared finally to enter World War I, Walter Lippmann published an article in the *New Republic* in which he expressed something of the excitement that many Americans felt when they thought about what joining the conflict might do for the nation. "I do not wish to underestimate the forces of reaction in our country," he wrote. But, he added, "We shall know how to deal with them. Forces have been let loose which they can no longer control, and out of this immense horror ideas have arisen to possess men's souls. There are times . . . when new sources of energy are tapped, when the impossible becomes possible, when events outrun our calculations. This may be such a time. . . . We can dare to hope for things we never dared to hope for in the past."[1] Like other progressives, Lippmann hoped for many things from the war: a new international order, or as he put it "a Federation of the World"; moral regeneration at home; and (committed pragmatist that he was) an assault on old orthodoxies and outmoded institutions. But Lippmann had another hope for the war as well, a hope he had first expressed a few years earlier in his precocious second book, *Drift and Mastery*, published when he was only twenty-five: a hope for a new kind of political economy.

The characteristic ailment of modern industrial society, Lippmann believed, both in individual lives and in the public world, was "drift," the tendency to move aimlessly through life buffeted about by great, impersonal forces. "We drift into our work," he had written. "We fall in love, and our lives seem like the intermittent flicker of an obstinate lamp. . . . Men go to war not knowing why, hurl themselves at cannon as if they were bags of flour, seek impossible goals, submit to senseless wrongs, for mankind lives today only in the intervals of a fitful sleep. There is indeed a dreaming quality in life."[2]

But it was not necessary, he argued, for society to drift. The scale of modern life had grown enormously, it was true, and it was now much more difficult for individuals or nations to control their fates. But the scale of human thought had grown enormously too. And so it *was* possible for society to seize control of its destiny, to master the great forces that industrialization had unleashed, if only it had the will to do so. "That is what mastery means," he wrote: "the substitution of conscious intention for unconscious striving. Civilization, it seems to me, is just this constant effort to introduce plan where there has been clash, and purpose into the jungles of disordered growth."[3]

In most respects, the American experience in World War I did very little to reinforce the liberal hopes Lippmann and others had expressed. The dream of a new international order foundered at Versailles and in the bitter political battles at home; the expectations of moral regeneration fell victim to the nativist and antiradical hysteria that gripped the nation both during and after the war; the hopes for a challenge to old orthodoxies collided with a growing popular conservatism, which culminated in the election in 1920 of Warren G. Harding. But there was one respect in which the war did reinforce liberal hopes. It produced a brief experiment in state management of the economy that many progressives, and many others, came to consider a model for the future. Harmony and order, they believed, had, even if briefly, replaced the conflict and disorder of modern industrial life; government, capital, and labor had learned to cooperate with one another on behalf of a great national mission. The war provided an example of what an enlightened state could do (as Lippmann had urged) to replace "clash" with "plan," and "disorder" with "purpose."[4]

The end of the war brought a chorus of tributes, from many sources, to the success of the mobilization effort and to the lessons that could be learned from it. Bernard Baruch, who had served as chairman of the War Industries Board, the chief agency of economic management, argued that "the experience of the War Industries Board points to the desirability of investing some Government agency . . . with constructive as well as inquisitorial powers—an agency whose duty it should be to encourage, under strict Government supervision, such cooperation and coordination in industry as should tend to increase production, eliminate waste, conserve natural resources, improve the quality of products, promote efficiency in operation, and thus reduce costs to the ultimate consumer." The national Chamber of Commerce proclaimed, "War is the stern teacher that is driving home the lessons of cooperative effort." And former Secretary of War Elihu Root predicted, "There will be no withdrawal from these experiments. We shall go on; we shall expand them."[5]

Grosvenor B. Clarkson, who had directed the Council of National Defense during the war and had developed a great admiration for Baruch and his works in the process, incorporated such "lessons" into a massive semi-official history of war mobilization published in 1923:

> If we had a Government business manager with a free hand to run the business side of Government, as free as Baruch had in the War Industries Board, we should have a successful Government of business. . . . It is little wonder that the men who dealt with the industries of a nation, binned and labeled, replenished and drawn on at will for the purposes of war, and its train of consequences, meditated with a sort of intellectual contempt on the huge hit-and-miss confusion of peacetime industry, with its perpetual cycle of surfeit and dearth and its eternal attempt at adjustment after the event. From their meditations arose dreams of an ordered economic world.[6]

The war, in other words, had shown Americans what they could do if they had the will to do it. It had proved that it was indeed possible to create order in the economy, to make it harmonious and efficient, to achieve mastery. And for more than a generation the war remained an inspiration to those progressives who hoped to achieve in peacetime what they liked to think they had achieved in war: "an ordered economic world." The war helped inspire efforts throughout the 1920s to harmonize the business world through the creation of associational arrangements. It supported even larger visions of a "planned economy," in which the government would play a much more intrusive role. It served as a model in 1933 for the creation of the New Deal's National Recovery Administration. And for some, it continued throughout the 1930s, even after the failure and collapse of the NRA, to drive hopes for an economic system in which business, government, and labor would build a working partnership on behalf of the common good.[7]

The outbreak of World War II in 1939 and the American entry into the war two years later seemed at first to encourage some of the same hopes that World War I had inspired twenty years before—including the hopes for a new political economy. "We have learned," the New Deal administrator Clifford Durr wrote in 1943, "that we cannot obtain the production we need for waging the war as an undirected by-product of what we commonly refer to as 'sound business principles.' Neither can we expect such by-product to furnish us after the war with the standard of living which we shall be warranted in expecting. . . . There must be some over-all source of direction more concerned with [these] objectives than with the profits or losses of individual business concerns."[8] Or as Herbert Emmerich, another New Deal official, wrote in 1941, "With a farewell to normalcy and an appreciation of the greater opportunities that the war crisis presents, public administrators today have an opportunity to enhance and permanently to establish the prestige of their calling in the United States."[9] The rhetoric was more muted perhaps, but the hopes seemed much the same: the war would legitimize an expanded state role in economic life and would show the way to new, more cooperative and harmonious economic arrangements; it would help produce "an ordered economic world."

But the end of the Second World War, unlike the end of the first, brought very few public tributes—from liberals or from anyone else—to the achievements of wartime economic mobilization in bringing order and harmony to the economy. There was, to be sure, substantial satisfaction with the way the economy had performed: with the "miracles" of production that had overwhelmed the Germans and the Japanese and with the new prosperity that had finally ended the Great Depression. But little of the credit for those achievements redounded to the government, to the mobilization agencies, or to the concept of a new economic order. Bernard Baruch had emerged from World War I a national hero, a symbol of the nation's hopes for a new political economy; he remained even forty years later a celebrated sage and adviser to presidents. Donald Nelson, Baruch's World War II counterpart, emerged from that war discredited and largely forgotten. Nelson spent his last years serving as a public relations flak for a minor Hollywood trade association and pursuing obscure and unsuccessful business schemes. When he published his tedious memoirs in 1946, many reviewers took the occasion to compare him unfavorably to Baruch.[10]

All this raises an obvious question. Why did these two experiences, in many ways very similar experiences, produce such different political legacies? Why did World War I come to serve as a model to many progressives and liberals of what an enlightened state could do to bring order and harmony to American economic life, while World War II did not?

There were, of course, differences between the two experiments in mobilization, and they account for some of the differences between their legacies. The biggest and most obvious difference was that the United States spent only about two years mobilizing for World War I (and only a little over a year fighting in it), while the World War II mobilization spanned more than five years (and the fighting nearly four). There was much more time during the Second World War for the problems and shortcomings of the mobilization effort to become evident, more time for things to go wrong, more time for grievances to accumulate. There were other differences as well: differences in the way power was delegated among the war agencies, differences in the quality of leadership, and differences in the size and complexity of the economies the war agencies set out to manage.

In most respects, however, the way the federal government mobilized and managed the economy during the two world wars was strikingly similar. Both Woodrow Wilson and Franklin Roosevelt looked beyond the existing federal bureaucracies and created special new agencies to handle the task of war mobilization. (This was not entirely a matter of choice: neither in 1917 nor in 1941—despite the New Deal—did the federal government possess anything approaching sufficient institutional capacity to manage a wartime economy from within the existing bureaucracy.)

In both wars these new agencies staffed themselves almost entirely from the private sector, relying largely on lawyers, businessmen, and financiers (many of them drawn directly from the industries they were then called upon to regulate; many of them still officially in the employ of their prewar firms and paid only a token sum by the government—hence the term, common in both wars, "dollar-a-year men"). At the same time, both in 1917 and in 1942, there were efforts to balance the presence of businessmen in the war agencies with representation from other groups, especially labor: efforts to create tripartite partnerships of business, labor, and government capable of cooperating to increase production and promote the common good.

In both wars the government stumbled through periods of unsuccessful experimentation with various decentralized or divided administrative structures before settling in the end on (to use a phrase popular in 1941, when critics were clamoring for change) "a single responsible agency with a single responsible head." These were the War Industries Board, which Wilson created in 1918, headed by Baruch, and the War Production Board (WPB), which Roosevelt created in 1942, headed by Nelson.

And in both wars the war agencies did on the whole what they were supposed to do. They oversaw impressive feats of production, which tipped the military balance decisively in favor of the United States and its allies; and they avoided major disruptions of civilian life at the same time. If anything, the War Production Board performed rather more impressively than the War Industries Board, if only because World War II was so much larger and (for the United States) so much longer than World War I and hence demanded far greater productive achievements.[11]

The two war mobilization efforts experienced similar failures as well. In neither war did labor ever achieve anything like equal standing in the supposed partnership the government was attempting to create. Labor's wartime gains in World War I were more dramatic, perhaps, than they were in World War II, since unions began the war from a position of less power than they did in 1941; but whatever their modest gains, the unions were unable to retain them once the war ended. In World War II the wartime arrangements were a decidedly mixed blessing for labor, given the great progress unions had been making in the late 1930s; and in the aftermath of the conflict, labor once again lost much of what little it had gained—when Congress passed the Taft-Hartley Act in 1947.

In neither war did business very often subordinate its own interests to a larger public good, as in theory the wartime arrangements required. Complaints about war profiteering were rampant in 1918, and for decades thereafter, just as complaints about corporate greed were rampant in World War II. Some progressives criticized the War Industries Board in 1918 for creating too many millionaires, for discriminating against small business. Twenty-five years later, liberals were criticizing the War Production Board, and the mobilization effort in general, for the same things: for failing to protect small business and for giving too much power to conservative corporate figures more interested in their own profits than in the interests of the nation. I. F. Stone wrote caustically of the WPB in 1942, in a statement typical of liberal complaints: "The arsenal of democracy . . . is still being operated with one eye on the war and the other on the convenience of big business. . . . [T]he men running the program are not willing to fight business interests on behalf of good will and good intentions."[12]

But despite the substantial similarities in both their achievements and failures, even though a strong case could be made that the mobilization experiments of World War II were considerably more successful than those of World War I, the two experiences came to have very different retrospective images. World War I became an inspiration. World War II did not. Indeed, to many liberals, it became a warning of what efforts by the government to coordinate the economy could become: a mechanism by which members of the corporate world could take over (or "capture") the regulatory process and turn it to their own advantage.

What explains that change is less the differences between the ways the United States mobilized for the two wars than the contexts in which those mobilizations occurred, the assumptions and expectations Americans brought to the two experiences. The context changed in many ways between 1918 and 1941. But three changes are particularly useful to an understanding of why many Americans in 1945 thought so differently about the state, and its role in economic life, than they had a generation before.

One of those changes involved the way some Americans viewed the two world wars themselves, the way they explained what the nation was fighting for—and, perhaps more importantly, against. World War I was, in the American imagination, essentially a war against German culture, which in the hysterical anti-German atmosphere of 1917 and 1918 seemed savage, and barbaric, and innately belligerent. As the California Board of Education argued in banning the teaching of the German language in public schools, German culture was steeped in "the ideals of autocracy, brutality, and hatred." Wartime propaganda was filled with personifications of the enemy as the "Prussian cur" and "the German beast." G. Stanley Hall, the eminent American psychologist (and the man who had first brought Freud to America), expressed a widespread assumption when he said, in 1917, "There is something fundamentally wrong with the Teutonic soul."[13] This hostility toward the German people and their society quickly spilled over into a hostility toward German Americans as well.

World War II evoked a different image: less of a barbaric people than of a tyrannical regime; less of a flawed culture than of a flawed political system and a menacing state. Wartime propaganda in World War II did not personify the European enemy, at least, as an evil people (although the same can not be said, of course, about the wartime image of the Japanese). It focused instead on the German and Italian states.[14]

The war, in short, pushed a fear of totalitarianism (and hence a generalized wariness about excessive state power) to the center of American political thought. In particular, it forced a reassessment of the kinds of associational and corporatist arrangements that many had found so attractive in the aftermath of World War I. Those, after all, were the kinds of arrangements Germany and Italy had claimed to be creating. "The rise of totalitarianism," Reinhold Niebuhr noted somberly in 1945, "has prompted the democratic world to view all collectivist answers to our social problems with increased apprehension." Virtually all experiments in state supervision of private institutions, he warned, contained "some peril of compounding economic and political power." Hence "a wise community will walk warily and test the effect of each new adventure before further adventures."[15]

To others, the lesson was even starker. *Any* steps in the direction of state control of economic institutions were (to use the title of Friedrich von Hayek's celebrated antistatist book of 1944) steps along *The Road to Serfdom.* One of those who had by then come to share that fear was Walter Lippmann, whose earlier dreams of an enlightened government creating "mastery" over great social forces had been replaced by a fearful opposition to the growing power of the state. Lippmann spent the war years denouncing the New Deal and corresponding with Hayek, discussing ways to mobilize what he and Hayek called the "real" liberals around the world to rescue liberalism, the liberalism of individual freedom and economic liberty, from its statist traducers.[16]

But Americans in the 1940s did not have to look to Europe for examples of state efforts to solve economic problems. They could look to their own experiences of the preceding two decades. And that, of course, suggests a second important difference between the two world wars. Americans in World War I had very few previous efforts at state management of the economy against which to measure their wartime experiments. Americans in World War II had the New Deal.

We are accustomed to thinking of the New Deal as a phenomenon that created and legitimized much of the modern American state, which in many ways it did. But the New Deal is also important for the options it foreclosed, for the way it tried to take certain paths and failed in the trying, for how it delegitimized certain concepts of the state even as it was legitimizing others. One of those concepts was the vaguely corporatist vision of economic harmony that had emerged from World War I and that culminated in the ill-fated National Recovery Administration of 1933–1935.

The sorry history of the NRA came to an end when the Supreme Court struck down the legislation creating it in 1935. But the memory of the NRA continued to influence the way New Dealers and others thought about what the state could and should do. There were, to be sure, some (including at times Franklin Roosevelt) who continued to defend what came to be known as the "NRA approach." But there were many more who who saw in the NRA experiment a sobering lesson in what *not* to do, who considered it a disastrous mistake never to be repeated again.[17]

Chief among the complaints was that the NRA had, in the name of promoting the common good, become a license for big corporations to collude and hence to threaten the interests of small producers and consumers. The NRA, according to the *New Republic*, "gave employers the opportunity to raise prices and restrict production . . . and so encouraged monopolistic practices that interfered with the very object sought—more abundance." It had, according to the *Nation*, "hindered recovery instead of helping it." It had proved that "whenever business men are allowed to come together to 'cooperate,' the result is almost inevitably an effort to get more profits by some form of price-raising." It was "merely the trust sugar-coated," which had "pinned a policeman's badge" on monopolies.[18]

But the case against the NRA was not just a case against big business; it was also a case against certain kinds of government intervention in the economy, a case against the feasibility of imposing effective public control over the behavior of private institutions, a case against certain notions of planning, regulation, and state management. The NRA had collapsed, Thurman Arnold argued in the late 1930s, for the same reason that all economic "master plans" must collapse—because it could have succeeded only through a "vast extension of state control," an extension that Americans would not (and should not) contemplate. Henry Wallace said of it that "there is something wooden and inhuman about the government interfering in a definite, precise way with the details of our private and business lives. It suggests a time of war with generals and captains telling every individual what he must do each day and hour."[19]

The New Deal, in short, had helped teach liberals not only what the state could do, but what it could not do. And one of the things it could not do, they had come to believe, was reorder the corporate world. Such efforts would lead either to domination by private monopoly or domination by an excessively powerful state. Or it would lead, as many believed the NRA had led, to both. And thus when the United States began, for the second time in a generation, to mobilize the economy for war, liberals brought to that mobilization a much greater sensitivity than had their counterparts two decades earlier to the problems inherent in creating partnerships between the corporate world and the state, and a sensitivity to the problems inherent in giving the state responsibility for managing the affairs of private institutions. Hopes for this second wartime experiment were, as a result, much lower from the beginning; disillusionment set in much more quickly.

But there is a third, and more fundamental, reason for the difference between the way American liberals conceived the role of their state in 1918 and the way they had come to conceive it by 1945. We cannot understand the way liberals defined the state without understanding how they defined the economic problems they were asking the state to resolve. Liberals defined those problems very differently in 1945 from the way their counterparts had in 1918.

At the end of World War I, as for several decades before and for many years after, those who tried to prescribe a more active role for the state tended to think in terms of how the state might change the way private economic institutions behaved: how it might curb monopoly power, promote industrial cooperation, regulate corporate activities. The problem was institutional. The function of the state was to stabilize, or regulate, or even restructure capitalist institutions.

That belief rested not only on uneasiness about the size and power of the new corporate institutions in America. It also reflected an assumption about the way all economies worked, an assumption rooted in classical economic doctrine and in centuries of social experience. The great economic challenge, most American liberals believed in 1917, was to expand society's productive capacities and create enough goods to satisfy everyone's needs. The great economic danger was scarcity. What drove the economy, therefore, was production. The task of economic life (and, to those who believed that the state had a role to play in the economy, the task of public life) was to promote investment and production, to ensure that new factories were built, new crops were harvested, new energy sources were exploited. Economic life also required consumption, of course, but if production could be sustained and enhanced, then consumption would automatically follow.[20]

By the beginning of the 1940s many Americans—and in particular many of those most interested in defining a role for government in the economy—had begun to embrace new assumptions. No longer did the problems of production dominate their thinking about public policy; those problems, they believed, had been largely solved. There was now no real threat of scarcity; the danger now was inadequate consumption. Consumption, not production, was now the principal force in the modern economy. Consumption drove production, not the other way around.[21] This was a significant redefinition of the nation's fundamental economic goals and, by implication, of its political goals. And the question naturally arises why it occurred.

Anyone familiar with recent scholarship in twentieth-century American history is well aware that these new economic assumptions reflect parallel changes in popular culture—changes that have been the subject of an important literature in the last two decades exploring advertising, public education, family behavior, and other social and cultural issues. That literature has made a powerful case for the ways in which the ideas of abundance and consumption were defining the concepts of the "American dream" and the "American way of life" in the first half of the twentieth century. It is reasonable to assume, although hard to demonstrate in decisive ways, that these cultural shifts were penetrating economic and political thought as well.[22]

But it was not just cultural phenomena that were changing political assumptions. It was, among other things, the economy itself, which had come to rely much more heavily on the production and sale of consumer goods than it had in the past. It was the economic boom of the 1920s, which had been driven largely by consumer spending on automobiles, appliances, and housing, and which had suggested that the traditional problems of scarcity and the traditional preoccupation with production might have become obsolete. And most of all, it was the Great Depression, which (whether or not correctly) was widely interpreted not as a problem of inadequate production but as a crisis of underconsumption, and which thus reinforced the idea that the principal mission of economic life should now be to raise purchasing power and stimulate aggregate demand.[23]

The specific implications of these ideas for policy were not, at first, entirely clear through most of the 1930s. Even those who agreed that raising purchasing power and stimulating consumption were the proper aims of policy (which was far from everyone, even within the New Deal) disagreed over the best way to accomplish those goals. To some of these "under-consumptionists" (as they came to be known), the most important goal was organizing consumers as a coherent interest group, able to act in much the same way as organized business and labor interests. To others, the best course was the passage of legislation to protect consumers from misrepresentation and fraud; there were even calls for the creation of a new, cabinet-level Department of the Consumer. There were campaigns to promote "consumer education," modest efforts to create "consumer cooperatives," and generally unsuccessful attempts to organize consumer strikes and boycotts. Indeed, the rhetoric of consumption became at times an almost universal political language used to support antitrust crusades, planning initiatives, regulatory mechanisms, and many other models for policy; it was used by supporters of nearly every position to justify (or at least rationalize) their efforts.[24]

Slowly, however, one set of ideas began to emerge from this welter of approaches, ideas that gradually became central to the liberal concept of the state. Government could stimulate consumption quickly and easily by using its fiscal powers. It could spend money on public works and on jobs programs. It could fund relief and welfare mechanisms. It could accumulate deliberate deficits. Public spending was the best vehicle for attacking deflation and stabilizing the economy. It need no longer be considered a necessary evil, used sparingly to achieve particular ends; it could become a positive good, to be used lavishly to advance the economy as a whole.

These are ideas now associated principally with John Maynard Keynes, who by the end of World War II had developed a substantial following among American economists and in broader liberal circles. But long before Keynes had found any significant audience in America, ideas that are now considered "Keynesian" were receiving independent expression from many sources: from the popular economists William Trufant Foster and Waddill Catchings, who published a series of books in the 1920s and 1930s promoting public spending as the cure for underconsumption;[25] from academic economists such as John M. Clark, Arthur Gayer, and James Harvey Rogers, who promoted the concept of "counter-cyclical" public works spending throughout the 1930s;[26] and from Marriner Eccles, the chairman of the Federal Reserve Board beginning in 1934, who had read Foster and Catchings and admired them, and who was (although he was, as head of the Fed, charged with overseeing monetary policy) principally interested in fiscal matters. Eccles, who never read Keynes, was the leading Keynesian in the New Deal's inner circle in the mid- and late 1930s—a tireless and ultimately effective advocate of using public spending to increase purchasing power.[27]

The spending argument received an important (if indirect) boost in 1937, when the administration made substantial cuts in public funding of relief and public works in order to balance the budget and almost immediately precipitated a severe recession. It received another (more positive) boost in 1938, when (partly in response to Eccles) Roosevelt reversed himself and launched a massive new spending program, justifying it for the first time not in terms of the particular problems the spending might solve but in terms of the way it would contribute to the health of the economy as a whole.[28]

But to most liberals, the clearest confirmation of the value of public spending was World War II itself. Liberals may have derived little comfort from the performance of the War Production Board and the other war agencies. But they could not fail to be impressed with the way in which massive public spending helped end almost overnight a Depression that had proved resistant to institutional reforms for more than a decade. Suddenly the economy, which many Americans had once feared was irretrievably stagnant, was expanding more rapidly and dramatically than almost anyone had believed possible. The lessons for the future seemed obvious: the government's role in supervising the behavior of institutions was less important than its role in sustaining the economy as a whole. Alvin Hansen, the principal Keynesian among the New Dealers in the 1940s, expressed the new faith toward the end of the war. "Clearly fiscal policy is now and will continue to be [the principal] factor in the functioning of the modern economy." Its purpose, he said, was "to develop a high-consumption economy so that we can achieve full employment. . . . A higher propensity to consume can . . . be achieved by a progressive tax structure combined with social security, social welfare, and community consumption expenditures." If World War I's legacy to American political economy was the dream of an "ordered economic world," a more rational distribution and exercise of corporate power, World War II's legacy was the dream of full employment and economic growth.[29]

By 1945, therefore, many American liberals were rallying to a new concept of the state, substantially different from the one their counterparts had embraced at the end of World War I. It was now possible, they believed, to achieve economic growth without intervening in the internal affairs of corporations, which was both endlessly complex and politically difficult. It was now possible for the state to manage the economy without managing the institutions of the economy. The state had already succeeded in curbing the most egregious abuses of corporate behavior through the regulatory initiatives and labor legislation of the 1930s. The task now was to find a way for government to compensate for capitalism's remaining flaws through aggressive fiscal policies and through expanded welfare and social insurance mechanisms. The task was to build not a corporate state nor a regulatory state, but a compensatory state.

Few liberals of the 1940s consciously repudiated the dreams of their forebears of a generation before. They still used much of the same language. They still spoke of planning. They still hoped for economic harmony and order. They still dreamed of what Walter Lippmann, thirty years earlier, had called "mastery." But those words meant different things in 1945 from what they had meant in 1918. They referred, for example, to the principal liberal initiative of 1945: the so-called Full Employment bill, which would commit the federal government to aggressive fiscal policies to sustain purchasing power at high levels at all times. And they referred to the raft of legislative initiatives that Harry Truman promoted throughout his eight years as president: the expansion of Social Security, the creation of national health insurance, the construction of public housing, the protection of the consumer. The older, more institutional dreams—of partnerships between government and business, of planning production and investment (or what we now call "industrial policy"), of extensive state regulation of corporate behavior—had come, in the view of many Americans, to seem politically unrealistic, bureaucratically impossible, and socially dangerous. But most of all, to many liberals at least, they had come to seem irrelevant.

And yet when one looks back from the perspective of a later era at the bright liberal hopes of 1945, it is hard not to sense that the confidence of that time was to some degree misplaced. Liberals in the postwar decades did follow, and to some degree still follow, the path they devised for themselves in the 1940s. But the weak and embattled liberal state that has emerged from their efforts has fallen far short of their hopes—its cumbersome and inadequate welfare mechanisms battling constantly for legitimacy, with dispiriting results; its primitive fiscal mechanisms never coming close to fulfilling the liberal dreams of the

1940s and ultimately, beginning in the 1980s, becoming a grotesque inversion of the Keynesian model; its claim on popular loyalties consistently frail.

Nor is it at all clear that the model of state development liberals rejected in the 1940s—the model of war mobilization, of the War Industries Board and the War Production Board—was as irrelevant to the nation's future as they believed it to be. For in the postwar era there emerged—alongside this frail and struggling liberal state—what became, in a sense, a second government: a national security state, powerful, entrenched, constantly expanding, and largely invulnerable to political attacks; a state that forged intimate partnerships with the corporate world, constantly blurring the distinctions between public and private; and a state that produced some of the very things—strengthened private monopolies and expanded state power to sustain them—that the liberal vision was supposed to prevent.[30]

Sometime in the early 1930s, it is not clear exactly when, Franklin Roosevelt read a book by William T. Foster and Waddill Catchings, the proto-Keynesian popular economists who helped draw public attention to the idea of dealing with economic problems through public spending. The book was called *The Road to Plenty*, and its distinctly Utopian overtones made it reminiscent of William Harvey's free-silver tract of thirty years earlier, *Coin's Financial School*. *The Road to Plenty* outlined what Foster and Catchings considered a safe, painless, and certain route to prosperity and social justice: a redirection of government's efforts away from the profitless (and, in their view, dangerous) effort to manage economic institutions and toward the safer and more promising effort to manage the aggregate economy through taxation and public spending, through attention to consumption instead of to investment. Roosevelt's copy of the book is in the Franklin D. Roosevelt Library in Hyde Park. It contains his marginal commentary, of the sort one sometimes finds scrawled in books in undergraduate libraries. Toward the end, he recorded a general reaction: "Too good to be true—You can't get something for nothing."[31]

Later, of course, Roosevelt seemed to change his mind, if not about Foster and Catchings themselves then about the general constellation of ideas they expressed. But there is room to wonder whether, had Roosevelt lived to see where this new concept of the liberal state would eventually lead, he might have concluded that he had it right the first time.

6

Legacies of World War II

"The great majority of Americans," Archibald MacLeish said in 1943, "understand very well that this war is not a war only, but an end and a beginning—an end to things known and a beginning of things unknown. We have smelled the wind in the streets that changes weather. We know that whatever the world will be when the war ends, the world will be different."[1]

Almost everyone who looked ahead to the postwar era realized, as MacLeish did, that the war had unleashed large forces that would produce a new world and a new American society. But Americans greeted the prospects for change in many different ways. MacLeish—a liberal, a New Dealer, and an administrator in the wartime government—welcomed change and believed it could be harnessed (through the efforts of an enlightened government) to the goal of creating a better and more just society. Others viewed the future with trepidation, many of them hoping to preserve the patterns of power and wealth that had shaped the world they had known before the war. The social and cultural legacy of World War II was the product of broad social forces that no individuals or institutions could ultimately control. But it was also the result of many visions of the postwar world among many groups of Americans—almost all of them certain that the war validated their often sharply different, and even conflicting, expectations.

In the prologue to *Six Armies in Normandy*, his classic portrait of the 1944 Allied invasion of France, the historian John Keegan captured one critical aspect of how the war affected the United States. He wrote of his own wartime experiences as a child in the English countryside when, a few months before D-Day, the Americans arrived. Almost overnight, he recalls, his "backwater" town filled with GIs. "How different they looked from our own jumble-sale champions, beautifully clothed in smooth khaki, as fine in cut and quality as a British officer's—an American private, we confided to each other at school, was paid as much as a British captain, major, colonel." The British army traveled about in "a sad collection of underpowered makeshifts." The Americans rode in "magnificent, gleaming . . . four-wheel-drive juggernauts." For a few months—before they vanished suddenly one night in early June—they dominated the countryside, dazzling girls, overwhelming roads, shops, and pubs, distributing largesse. "Thus," Keegan recalled, "I made my first encounter with the bottomless riches of the American economy."[2]

Even as a child, Keegan had understood the role of abundance in American life and the role of World War II in producing it. The war ended the Depression and made the nation rich again. It created expectations of abundance that would survive for more than a generation. And it removed what had in the 1930s been deep doubts about the ability of the capitalist economy ever again to experience substantial growth. By 1944, as Keegan suggests, American abundance was already capturing the global imagination and firing the hopes of the American people themselves. The vast productive power of the United States supplied both its own armed forces and those of its allies with airplanes, ships, tanks, and ammunition. It fed, clothed, and housed the American people, who experienced only modest privations, and it helped feed, clothe, and house much of the rest of the world as well. Alone among the major nations, the United States faced the future in 1945 with an intact and thriving industrial economy poised to sustain a long period of prosperity and growth. Gross National Product in the war years rose from $91 billion to $166 billion; 15 million new jobs were created, and the most enduring problem of the Depression—massive unemployment—came to an end; industrial production doubled; personal incomes rose (depending on the location) by as much as 200 percent.[3]

Abundance created a striking buoyancy in American life in the early 1940s that the war itself only partially counterbalanced. Suddenly, people had money to spend again and—despite the many shortages of consumer goods—at least some things to spend it on. The theater and movie industries did record business. Resort hotels, casinos, and race tracks were jammed with customers. Advertisers, and at times even the government, exhorted Americans to support the war effort to ensure a future of material comfort and consumer choice for themselves and their children. "Your people are giving their lives in useless sacrifice," the *Saturday Evening Post* wrote in a mock letter to the leaders of wartime Japan. "Ours are fighting for a glorious future of mass employment, mass production and mass distribution and ownership." Even troops at the front seemed at times to justify their efforts with reference to the comforts of home more than to the character of the enemy or the ideals America claimed to be defending. "They are fighting for home," John Hersey once wrote from Guadalcanal (with at least a trace of dismay), because "Home is where the good things are—the generosity, the good pay, the comforts, the democracy, the pie."[4]

One legacy of World War II, therefore, was the return of abundance, and with it the relegitimation of capitalism. Another was a rising popular expectation of economic security and material comfort—of what was already becoming known as "the American dream," a dream that rested on visions of increasing consumption. But abundance also helped strengthen other hopes for change. As Hersey's statement suggests, to some the "American dream" meant more than apple pie alone. Democracy, he said, was part of the mix—not as an alternative to visions of material comfort, but as both a precondition for and a result of them. Defining what democracy meant, mediating among the very different visions the word inspired among Americans, created some of the great struggles of both wartime and the postwar era.

One of the first such conflicts emerged over the political implications of abundance itself, and of the "democratic" initiatives it spawned. Archibald MacLeish and many other liberals eager to see the survival and expansion of the New Deal interpreted the return of economic growth as a mandate to pursue their emerging goal of "full employment" through purposeful government action. A broad coalition of Keynesian economists, union leaders, agricultural activists, consumer groups, and many others rallied in 1944 and 1945 behind what ultimately became the Employment Act of 1946, but which they at first called the "Full Employment" bill—a bill that, had it been passed in its original form, would have committed the government to using Keynesian tools to stimulate economic growth to levels that would ensure very low joblessness.[5] Other liberals rallied around the related proposals that had emerged during the war from the National Resources Planning Board, the New Deal's only real planning agency, which called for, among other things, a major expansion of the welfare programs the New Deal had launched and (in the spirit of full employment) an expansion as well of public works planning to provide the stimuli they believed the postwar economy would often need.[6]

Out of the confluence of abundance and democracy, in other words, had come a vision of an expanded liberal state. Freed from the immediate pressures of the Great Depression, convinced by the wartime growth that the economy was not as irretrievably stagnant as they once had feared, liberals seized on abundance as the basis for an ambitious social and economic agenda that would, if successful, greatly expand the role of the state in ensuring prosperity and protecting the beleaguered.

But to many other Americans, and to the conservative Republicans and Democrats who already by 1943 were coming to dominate the United States Congress, abundance had a very different impact—and the idea of postwar democracy took a very different form. To them the end of the Depression removed whatever justification there had been for the New Deal interventions into the economy and mandated a return to a less regulated market, a less profligate government, and a less expansive welfare state. One by one, in 1943 and 1944, Congress reduced or eliminated New Deal programs that economic growth seemed to have obviated: the Works Progress Administration, the Civilian Conservation Corps, the National Youth Administration, and many others. It abolished the National Resources Planning Board, in retribution for its ambitious and—to conservatives—alarming proposals. It began efforts, which would culminate in 1948, to weaken the Wagner Act. Abundance, they argued, was proof that there was no longer any need for the "socialism" of the New Deal, that it was time to return to what they considered true democracy—a regime of untrammeled economic freedom and minimal government.[7]

Politics was only one of many realms in which the war—the abundance it produced and the hopes for democracy it inspired—provided conflicting lessons and divided legacies. Nowhere was that clearer than in the experiences of African Americans in the 1940s. Prosperity transformed the material circumstances of many black men and women; the war against fascism—and its democratic rationale—transformed their expectations. But the war also reinforced opposition to their hopes.

Two million African Americans left the rural South in the 1940s, more than the total number of migrants in the three decades before (decades that included what is still known as the Great Migration before and during World War I). They moved for many reasons, some of them unrelated to the war. The mechanization of agriculture (and of cotton picking in particular) eliminated the demand for the labor of many black farmers in the South. The sharecropping system, already weakened by the Depression and by New Deal farm subsidies that often made it more profitable for landowners to leave their property fallow than to let it out to tenants, all but disintegrated during the war. Many African Americans also moved because the war created economic opportunities in industrial cities. With millions of men leaving the workforce to join the military, traditional barriers that had kept blacks out of some factories collapsed, at least for a time. The number of blacks employed in manufacturing more than doubled during the war; and there were major increases in the number of African Americans employed as skilled craftsmen or enrolled in unions. There was a substantial movement of black women out of domestic work and into the factory and the shop.

The wartime migration also helped carry the question of race out of the countryside and into the city, out of the South and into the North. The growing concentration of black populations in urban areas made organization and collective action easier and more likely. It made African Americans more important politically. Now that many of them lived in the North, where they could vote more or less at will, they became an increasingly significant force in the Democratic party (to which virtually all African Americans had become committed during the 1930s, in response to the New Deal). Demographic changes, in short, laid the groundwork for the political mobilization of American blacks both during and after the war. There was growing membership and increasing activism in the Urban League, the NAACP, and other existing civil rights organizations. A new and more militant organization emerged: the Congress of Racial Equality—more outspoken, less accommodationist than most older ones. And already during World War II, in Washington, Detroit, and other cities, there were demonstrations against racial discrimination—picketing, sit-ins, occasionally violence—that anticipated the civil rights movement of a decade and more later.[8]

Black Americans who attempted to explain these modest but significant political stirrings did so by pointing to the nature of the war itself. In North Carolina one African American told a visiting journalist: "No clear thinking Negro can afford to ignore our Hitlers here in America. As long as you have men like [Governor Eugene] Talmadge in Georgia [an outspoken white supremacist] we have to think of the home front whether we want to or not." Many black men and women talked openly of the "Double V," which stood for simultaneous victory over the Axis abroad and over racism at home. "If we could not believe in the realization of democratic freedom for ourselves," one black journalist wrote, "certainly no one could ask us to die for the preservation of that ideal for others." To engage in the struggle for freedom in the world while ignoring the struggle for freedom at home was to make a mockery of both.[9]

Some white Americans were beginning to make that connection too. *Fortune* magazine published an article in June 1942 entitled "The Negro's War," which suggested the slow shift in thinking among many whites about the nation's "racial question." The essay catalogued the long list of legitimate grievances African Americans were raising against their country, and it argued, in effect, that the war required America to do something about them. It cited with alarm Japanese propaganda about racial injustice in America, describing a recent race riot in Detroit as "a boon to the Japanese and . . . the German . . . propagandists." And it argued, in terms that clearly resonated with the larger sense of mission that the war had aroused (and that Henry Luce, *Fortune*'s publisher, had endorsed with notable enthusiasm), that

> . . . this is a war in which ideas . . . are sometimes substitutes for armies. The Negro's fate in the U.S. affects the fate of white American soldiers in the Philippines, in the Caribbean, in Africa; bears on the solidity of our alliance with 800 million colored people in China and India; influences the feelings of countless neighbors in South America. In this shrunken world of ours, a fracas in Detroit has an echo in Aden, and what a southern Congressman considers to be a small home-town affair can actually interfere with grand strategy.[10]

This growing awareness of the nation's racial burdens forced many liberals, even if slowly and incompletely, to reconsider one of the staples of New Deal thought: that the principal goal of public life was to confront economic, not racial or cultural, issues. Perhaps, some liberals began now to think, the problems of the modern world were not purely economic. Perhaps class was not the only, or even the best, concept with which to analyze social problems. Perhaps race, ethnicity, religion, and culture—the divisive, "irrational" issues that had so damaged the Democratic party in the 1920s and from which white liberals had taken pains to distance themselves in the 1930s—were, in fact, essential to understanding America after all. "One of the greatest problems of democratic civilization," the great liberal theologian Reinhold Niebuhr wrote in 1944, "is how to integrate the life of its various subordinate ethnic, religious and economic groups in the community in such a way that the richness and harmony of the whole community will be enhanced and not destroyed by them." Niebuhr dismissed the smug liberal confidence of the 1920s that had anticipated what he called a "frictionless harmony of ethnic groups" and the capacity of economic progress alone to achieve "their eventual assimilation in one racial unity." Instead, he called on "democratic society" to use "every strategem of education and every resource of religion" to fight the influence of racial bigotry—a bigotry that would not wither away simply as a result of material prosperity.[11]

Early in 1944 an explosive event helped galvanize this growing but still murky sense of urgency: the publication of Gunnar Myrdal's *An American Dilemma.* Myrdal, an eminent Swedish sociologist whom the Carnegie Foundation had commissioned in the late 1930s to supervise a major examination of America's "race problem," described the "American dilemma" in part as an economic problem—the failure of American society to extend its riches to its black citizens. But it was also a moral dilemma—a problem in the hearts and minds of white Americans, a problem born of the impossible attempt to reconcile a commitment to freedom and democracy with the effort to deny one group of citizens a set of basic rights guaranteed to everyone else. In the shadow of Nazi tyranny, such a contradiction seemed to Myrdal—and to many readers of his book—especially glaring as he made clear in his powerful concluding chapter:

> The three great wars of this country have been fought for the ideals of liberty and equality to which the nation was pledged. . . . Now America is again in a life-and-death struggle for liberty and equality, and the American Negro is again watching for signs of what war and victory will mean in terms of opportunity and rights for him in his native land. To the white American, too, the Negro problem has taken on a sig-

> nificance greater than it has ever had since the Civil War. . . . The world conflict and America's exposed position as the defender of the democratic faith is thus accelerating an ideological process which was well under way.[12]

An American Dilemma became one of those rare books that help define a moment in history, and its reputation grew rapidly over the next several years. That Myrdal was a European and a distinguished scholar; that he couched his findings in the presumably objective language of social science; that a respected, nonpartisan foundation had sponsored the project; that a large number of prominent academics had collaborated with Myrdal on it; that the book itself was nearly 1,500 pages long, with mountains of data and over 500 pages of footnotes, lending it an air of profound scholarly authority: all helped make its findings seem almost unassailable. It was a "study to end all studies," something close to a definitive analysis of the problem.[13]

And yet it would be a mistake to exaggerate the impact of the war on the willingness of Americans to confront the nation's "race problem." For the war did not simply inspire those who believed in racial equality to reconsider the nation's customs and institutions. It also inspired those who did not to defend white supremacy with renewed ardor. Among white Americans, and among white southerners in particular, there were many who considered the war not a challenge to but a confirmation of their commitment to preserving the old racial order. To them democracy meant their right to order their society as they pleased and to sustain the customs and institutions they had always known. This interpretation of democracy was visible, for example, in the Congress, where southern members led by the notorious John Rankin of Mississippi sought to obstruct the GI Bill of Rights until they could feel certain it would not threaten white supremacy. It was evident in the redoubled commitment of many white veterans when they returned home to the South to protect the world they knew. And because much of what they sought to protect was their idealized vision of white women, a vision much romanticized during the war, segregation assumed a specially heightened importance for many of them. In much of the country the World War II generation—the young men who returned from the war fired with determination to make a better world—produced dynamic young leaders impatient with old structures and injustices. In much of the South the new generation of leaders emerging from the war became especially militant defenders of the region's racial institutions.[14]

World War II changed America's racial geography economically, spatially, and ideologically. It ensured that the system of segregation and oppression that had enjoyed a dismal stability for more than half a century would never be entirely stable again. But it ensured, too, that the defenders of that system would confront the new challenges to it with a continued and even strengthened commitment.

In much the same ambiguous, incomplete way the war challenged traditional notions of the role of women in America. Nearly six million women joined the paid workforce during World War II (raising the total number of working women by 60 percent). The new workers were much more likely to be married than earlier female workers had been. They were more likely to have young children. And they were more likely to work in jobs—including some heavy industrial jobs—that had previously been reserved for men (who were now in short supply). Hence the famous image of "Rosie the Riveter." Some women found the experience transforming. In the absence of fathers, brothers, husbands, and boyfriends, many women lived, worked, and traveled alone for the first time in their lives. Some joined unions. Others wore uniforms—as members of the WAACs and WAVEs and other female military organizations.[15]

For many it was an experience of unprecedented freedom; and as a female aircraft worker later recalled, "It really opened up another viewpoint on life." The popular folklore of the time described "Rosie the Riveter" as someone pitching in to win the war but eager to return to home and family. In fact most working women came to the end of the war determined not to return to a purely domestic life. Some lost their jobs when peace arrived and the men came home, but most of those who did looked for work somewhere else. The number of females in the paid workforce never declined to its prewar levels, and it continued to grow throughout the 1950s and beyond.[16]

And yet while the war (and the economic opportunities it opened up) was creating new expectations among many women, it was confirming more traditional expectations among many men. At the front, fighter pilots gave their planes female names and painted bathing beauties on their nosecones. Sailors pasted pin-ups inside their lockers, and infantrymen carried them (along with pictures of wives, mothers, and girlfriends) in their knapsacks. The most popular female icon was Betty Grable, whose picture found its way into the hands of over 5 million fighting men by the end of the war. She was a mildly erotic figure to be sure, but she was not a sex goddess; in her films, she generally played wholesome, innocent young women, the kind any guy would want to marry. And she became a model at the front for the modest, genteel girlfriend or wife many servicemen dreamed of finding on their return. In 1943, when she married the bandleader Harry James and had a child, her popularity actually grew—as if the image of domesticity had enhanced, rather than diminished, her appeal. Thousands of servicemen sent letters to her, suggesting how central her image had become to their own notion of the meaning of the war. "There we were out in those damn dirty trenches," one soldier wrote her, "Machine guns firing. Bombs dropping all around us. We would be exhausted, frightened, confused and sometimes hopeless about our situation. When suddenly someone would pull your picture out of his wallet. Or we'd see a decal of you on a plane and then we'd *know* what we were fighting for."[17] When John Hersey compiled his list of comfortable images that he claimed motivated GIs to fight ("generosity, good pay . . . pie"), he might well have added another vision of the kind of world men were hoping to return to: a world of healthy, heterosexual love, a world in which supportive, nurturing women were waiting to welcome their men back and make a home for them.

For the servicemen who remained in America during the war, and for soldiers and sailors in cities far from home in particular, the company of friendly, "wholesome" women was, the military believed, critical to maintaining morale. USOs recruited thousands of young women to serve as hostesses in their clubs—women who were expected to dress nicely, dance well, and chat happily with lonely men. Other women joined "dance brigades" and traveled by bus to military bases for social evenings with servicemen. They, too, were expected to be pretty, to dress attractively (and conservatively), and to interact comfortably with men they had never met before and would likely never see again. Neither the USO hostesses nor the members of the "dance brigades" were supposed to offer anything more than chaste companionship. The USO actually forbade women to have dates with soldiers after parties in the clubs, and the members of the "dance brigades" were expected to have no contact with servicemen except during the dances. The military sent chaperones to most social events and established clear "rules" for both servicemen and the women who sought to entertain them. Clearly, such regulations were sometimes violated. But while the military took elaborate measures to root out homosexuals and lesbians from their ranks (unceremoniously dismissing many of them with undesirable discharges), it quietly tolerated other relationships. "Healthy" heterosexuality was more important than chastity.[18]

But there was a dark counter-image to this official view of women as wholesome nurturing companions. It was the image of brassy, independent, and hence dangerous women who—in the fluid social atmosphere of the war years—were becoming more numerous, more visible, and more mobile. One result of that anxiety was a new war agency: the Social Protection Division (SPD) of the Office of Community War Services. Its job was, in essence, to protect men from women. Originally, that meant getting rid of the red-light districts that had sprung up around military bases around the country, districts that military leaders feared would expose servicemen to venereal diseases.[19] But before long the SPD was engaged in a more general effort to round up "promiscuous" females (which often meant single women who seemed in any way "loose" or provocative). A battle against venereal disease had quickly escalated to become a larger attack on independent, sexually active women.

For the rest of the war the SPD engaged in something like a witch-hunt, searching out "suspicious" women, or women of "low character" in the vicinity of military bases; enlisting local police and even hotel detectives to spy on suspected women and arrest them if they were found alone anywhere with a serviceman; encouraging citizens to offer anonymous tips. The government was, in effect, waging war on promiscuous women. Servicemen, the SPD implicitly argued, were simply acting out natural urges; they were the victims. The women were the aggressors—"throwing themselves at the soldiers," one official noted, luring presumably helpless men into sin and possibly disease. In enforcing these new directives, the SPD gradually came not to worry very much about whether supposedly "loose" women were, in fact, infected with VD. Any "promiscuous" woman could *become* a carrier, even if she was not yet one. Men needed to be protected from them all. State and local governments were pressured to change their own laws, and in some places there were quite extraordinary measures to restrict the freedom of movement of single, unescorted women, of whom there were, of course, a great many during the war. Some women were summarily arrested and quarantined for weeks, even months, if found to be infected. Some women were detained for many days even without any evidence of infection if there was other evidence that they might be of "loose" morals.[20]

There is an apparent contradiction in American social history in the first decade or so after the war. On one side was the new reality of women moving in unprecedented numbers into the paid workforce. On the other side was the growing power of a more traditional image of women as wives, mothers, and homemakers. But that postwar paradox is simply a continuation of the contrary experiences of women and men during the war itself: for many women, the exhilarating discovery of new freedoms and opportunities; for many men, a fear of independent women and a strengthened expectation of traditional family life.

The conflicting legacies of World War II extended as well to ideology, for the conflict produced at least two very different sets of ideas about the nation, the world, and the future—ideas that reflected conflicting views of history, of human nature, and of the character of "progress." In the struggle to define the meaning of the war could be seen many of the intellectual controversies of the following decades.

One intellectual legacy of the war was a profound anxiety about what it had revealed of humanity's capacity for evil. For some, that led to a new fear of state power—the kind of power that in Germany, Italy, and Japan had produced tyranny, war, and genocide. The fear of the state emerged directly out of the way American liberals (and the American people generally) defined the nature of their enemy in World War II. During the first World War many Americans had believed the enemy was a race, a people: the Germans as beast-like "Huns," and their presumably savage culture. In World War II racial stereotypes continued to play an important role in portrayals of the Japanese; but in defining the enemy in Europe—always the principal enemy in the 1940s to most Americans—the government and most of the media relied less on racial or cultural images than on political ones. The enemy was not the German people; it was their government. The threat of fascism was a threat from the state. And so it was to the state that Americans looked in the 1940s for signs of totalitarian danger at home.[21]

To the Austrian émigré economist Friedrich Hayek, author of the implausible 1944 bestseller *The Road to Serfdom*, the lesson of the war was that any increase in the powers of government (including, he made clear, the New Deal reforms of the 1930s) represented a step toward fascism. "It is necessary now," he wrote in his impassioned introduction, "to state the unpalatable truth that it is Germany whose fate we are in some danger of repeating." But even less conservative figures were suddenly wracked with doubts—Reinhold Niebuhr among them.[22]

Along with this fear of the state emerged another, related fear: a fear of "mass politics" and "mass man"; a fear, in short, of the people. Hitler's Germany, Mussolini's Italy, Stalin's Russia, some intellectuals came to believe, illustrated the dangers inherent in giving the people unmediated control of their political life. The people, the "mass," could too easily be swayed by demagogues and tyrants. They were too susceptible to appeals to their passions, to the dark, intolerant impulses that in a healthy society remained largely repressed and subdued. This fear of the mass lay at the heart of much cultural and intellectual criticism in the first fifteen years after World War II. It found reflection in the writings of Hannah Arendt, Theodor Adorno, Richard Hofstadter, Lionel Trilling, Daniel Bell, Dwight Macdonald, and many others. Like the fear of the state, with which it was closely associated, it reinforced a sense of caution and restraint in liberal thinking; a suspicion of ideology, a commitment to pragmatism, a wariness about moving too quickly to encourage or embrace spontaneous popular movements; indeed, a conviction that one of the purposes of politics was to defend the state against popular movements and their potentially dangerous effects.[23]

There were, in short, powerful voices during and immediately after World War II arguing that the experience of the war had brought a dark cloud of doubt and even despair to human society. A world that could create so terrible a war, a world that could produce Hiroshima, Nagasaki, the Katyn Forest, Auschwitz, a world capable of such profound evil and destruction—such a world, many American liberals argued, must be forever regarded skeptically and suspiciously. Humankind must move cautiously into its uncertain future, wary of unleashing the dark impulses that had produced these horrors.

Some liberal intellectuals went further. Americans, they argued, must resist the temptation to think of themselves, in their hour of triumph, as a chosen people. No people, no nation, could afford to ignore its own capacity for evil. Reinhold Niebuhr spoke for many skeptical liberals when he wrote of the dangers of the "deep layer of Messianic consciousness in the mind of America" and warned of liberal culture's "inability to comprehend the depth of evil to which individuals and communities may sink, particularly when they try to play the role of God in history." Americans, he said, would do well to remember that "no nation is sacred and unique . . . Providence has not set Americans apart from lesser breeds. We too are part of history's seamless web."[24]

But Niebuhr's statements were obviously written to refute a competing assumption. There was another, very different ideological force at work in America during World War II, another form of national self-definition, which affected American thought and behavior at home and in the world, at least as much as the somber assessments of Niebuhr and others. It was the view of America as an anointed nation; America as a special moral force in the world; America as a society with a unique mission born of its righteousness; America as a country insulated from the sins and failures and travails that affect other nations, standing somehow outside of history, protected from it by its own strength and virtue.

World War II did not create those beliefs. They are as old as the nation itself. But the American experience in the conflict, and the radically enhanced international stature and responsibility of the United States in the aftermath of the war, strengthened such ideas and gave them a crusading quality that made them as active and powerful as they had been at any moment in the nation's history.[25]

It was not just the contrast between America's democratic potential and the autocracies of Germany and Japan that shaped this expansive vision of America's moral force in the world. There was also a strengthened sense that the United States—triumphantly prosperous, aglow in victory—had something worth sharing with *all* nations, that it had a commitment to freedom and justice that could serve as a model for the rest of the world. That was the message of, among others, Henry Luce in a celebrated and controversial essay he published in *Life* in 1941 (and later, separately, as a small book) which he entitled "The American Century." In it Luce—the crusading founder and publisher of *Time* and *Life* magazines—sketched a picture of the nation's destiny that probably only slightly exaggerated what would, by the late 1940s, be a widely shared and increasingly powerful view—a vision in which American abundance and American idealism seamlessly merged.

The American Century, Luce wrote, "must be a sharing with all people of our Bill of Rights, our Declaration of Independence, our Constitution, our magnificent industrial products, our technical skills."

America's vision of itself as a world power, he insisted, must include "a passionate devotion to great American ideals . . . a love of freedom, a feeling for the equality of opportunity, a tradition of self-reliance and independence, and also of cooperation." For, he continued, "we are the inheritors of all the great principles of Western civilization—above all Justice, the love of Truth, the ideal of charity. . . . It now becomes our time to be the powerhouse from which the ideals spread throughout the world and do their mysterious work of lifting the life of mankind from the level of the beasts to what the Psalmist called a little lower than the angels."[26]

Luce's occasionally bombastic language was too much for many Americans.[27] Yet even many liberals who disliked him and whose visions of the postwar world were strongly anti-imperialist spoke at times in a similar language, imbued with much the same sense of American mission. Vice President Henry A. Wallace, for example, described America's wartime (and, by implication, postwar) mission to extend democracy, both at home and abroad, in charged, floridly idealistic language in a 1942 speech:

> North, South, East, West, and Middle West—the will of the American people is for complete victory.
>
> No compromise with Satan is possible . . . The people's revolution is on the march, and the devil and all his angels can not prevail against it. They can not prevail, for on the side of the people [America and its allies] is the Lord.
>
> "He [the Lord] giveth power to the faint; to them that have no might He increaseth strength. . . . They that wait upon the Lord shall mount up with wings as eagles; they shall run, and not be weary; they shall walk and not be faint."
>
> Strong in the strength of the Lord, we who fight in the people's cause will never stop until that cause is won.[28]

The belief that America had a powerful destiny in the postwar world, that it had special virtues worth sharing with other peoples, that it could (and should) serve as a model to the democratic strivings of all nations—that belief was penetrating deep into American culture and shaping the concept of the nation's postwar mission. It helped reconcile most Americans to the active, crusading international role victory had thrust upon the nation. It enabled most Americans to rationalize the continued development of methods of mass destruction by harnessing that effort to a perceived moral imperative. It made possible widespread public support for the Cold War. It helped create considerable support for much of the domestic political repression the Cold War later produced, and made it difficult for liberals to find an effective position from which to criticize that repression.

But by increasing popular sensitivity to America's image in the world (and to the impact of its own social problems on that image), it also helped create support for some of the ambitious liberal reform efforts of the postwar era.[29] Theodore White, one of the most eloquent and prolific chroniclers of the experiences of his generation, the World War II generation, suggested something of the ambiguous impact of this sense of world mission when he wrote very near the end of his life:

> For a proper historian of our times, there was only one overtowering beginning—the Year of Victory, 1945.
>
> All things flowed from that victory. . . .
>
> The intoxication of [it] . . . lasted for a generation. First, the sense of power which had convinced a peaceful nation that its armed force . . . could and should forever police and reorder the world. Second, the seductive belief that in any contest between good and evil, good always triumphs. We, our soldiers, had proved that Right makes Might. The imperative legacy of Virtue descended from the war.[30]

The war created other intellectual legacies as well. In the glow of the nation's victory, in the sense of old orders shattered and a new world being born, came an era of exuberant innovation, an era in which, for a time, nothing seemed more appealing than the modern, the new. The allure of the new was visible in the bold works of architectural modernism, whose controversial legacy is so much a part of the postwar American landscape. It was visible in the explosive growth of the innovative and iconoclastic American art world, which made New York in the 1940s and 1950s something of what Paris had been in the nineteenth century. It was visible in the increased stature and boldness of the American scientific community, and in the almost religious faith in technological progress that came to characterize so much of American life and that helped reconcile many people to the continued development of nuclear weapons.[31]

And it was visible in the way it excited, and then frustrated, a generation of American liberals imagining new progress and social justice. In 1943, Archibald MacLeish expressed something of these extravagant hopes by describing what he called the "America of the imagination," the society that the war was encouraging Americans to create:

> We have, and we know we have, the abundant means to bring our boldest dreams to pass—to create for ourselves whatever world we have the courage to desire. We have the metal and the men to take this country down, if we please to take it down, and to build it again as we please to build it. We have the tools and the skill and the intelligence to take our cities apart and put them together, to lead our roads and rivers where we please to lead them, to build our houses where we want our houses, to brighten the air, to clean the wind, to live as men in this Republic, free men, should be living. We have the power and the courage and the resources of good-will and decency and common understanding . . . to create a nation such as men have never seen. . . . We stand at the moment of the building of great lives, for the war's end and our victory in the war will throw that moment and the means before us.[32]

In retrospect, of course, it is easy to see the many flaws in this expansive vision of a brave new postwar world: the dangerous arrogance it at times helped create, the reckless and at times disastrous experiments it helped launch, the intractable problems it helped bring to the surface and then proved unable to solve. But there was also an appealing sense of hope and commitment in that vision—a faith in the possibility of sweeping away old problems and failures, of creating "great lives." Out of such faith came some of the great postwar crusades of American liberals—the battle for racial justice, the effort to combat poverty, the expansion of individual rights. All of those battles had some ambiguous and even unhappy consequences, but all of them reflected a confidence in the character and commitment of American society—and the possibility of creating social justice within it—that few people would express so blithely today.

It is difficult, therefore, to look at today's public world—a world of diminished expectations, dreary resignation, and at times profound cynicism—without finding something appealing about the brief and admittedly deceptive moment when large numbers of Americans, at the close of the most catastrophic war in human history, found it possible to believe that they could create a new and better world.

7

Historians and the Interwar Years

Most Americans who lived through the period from the end of World War I to the end of World War II believed they were experiencing events of special historical importance: an unprecedented capitalist expansion; the greatest economic crisis in the nation's history; a dramatic experiment in political reform; a cataclysmic world conflict; the rise of the United States to unchallenged global preeminence. Contemporaries tried constantly to make sense of their turbulent times, and they produced histories of the era even as it continued. Professional historians were scarcely less eager. Less than a decade after the end of the war, a significant body of scholarship on the interwar years had already begun to emerge.

The initial volume of Frank Freidel's monumental biography of Franklin Roosevelt appeared in 1952, as did Eric Goldman's sweeping (and highly approving) history of twentieth-century liberalism.[1] Three years later Richard Hofstadter published *The Age of Reform*, which (among other things) attempted to situate the New Deal within a broader reform tradition.[2] In 1956 James MacGregor Burns produced *Roosevelt: The Lion and the Fox*, an important biography of Roosevelt as president.[3] And in 1957 the first of three volumes of Arthur M. Schlesinger, Jr.'s *The Age of Roosevelt* appeared, an event that, more than any other, defined the directions in which future scholarship on the era would move.[4] Schlesinger's study was notable for its remarkable breadth (it proposed to chronicle the entire interwar period) and its exceptional literary grace. But it was notable, too, for its powerful interpretive stance, a stance that helped shape both popular and scholarly views of the era for at least a generation and that became the basis of much subsequent historiographical debate.

Central to Schlesinger's interpretation was his belief that American history moves in a discernible cyclical pattern, what he later called "a continuing shift in national involvement, between public purpose and private interest." Periods of energetic public reform occur every twenty to thirty years, run their course, and give way to periods of retrenchment and preoccupation with private goals. During conservative eras, progressive forces slowly regain momentum and in time again prevail. Hence the reform energies of the progressive era gave way to the retrenchment and self-interest of the 1920s, which gave way in turn to the renewal of liberal energies in the 1930s. By the beginning of World War II, the New Deal had largely run its course, and the nation had entered another period of public stasis, which continued until reform energies revived again after 1960.[5]

Schlesinger's cycle theory contained a number of assumptions beyond the obvious one that swings in the political climate occur in predictable patterns. It reflected the belief that political phenomena were the defining events of historical development. Hence the interwar period was, as the title of Schlesinger's series proclaimed, "the age of Roosevelt." Cycle theory also portrayed American history in general (and the interwar years in particular) as a series of sharply discontinuous experiences. The coming of the Great Depression and the advent of the New Deal, for example, marked a sharp break with the 1920s. Similarly, the "New Deal era" was strikingly different from the much more conservative period that followed it. Finally, Schlesinger's interpretation was a highly progressive one. Reform might move in fits and starts, but move it does, pushing the nation inexorably out of an inferior past and toward an improving future. The New Deal, therefore, was part of a long tradition of reform—of popular democratic movements battling successfully against selfish private interests—that stretched back to the early days of the Republic.[6]

The three decades since publication of *The Age of Roosevelt* have been marked by dramatic changes in the nature of American historical scholarship. And while Schlesinger's interpretive premises continue to attract significant attention and respect, they have also encountered vigorous challenges from several alternative historiographical approaches.

One such challenge has come to be known as "the organizational synthesis," an approach to twentieth-century American history that reflects several distinct influences: the ideas of Max Weber, more recent theories of modernization, and most immediately several important works of scholarship that appeared in the 1960s. Alfred D. Chandler, Jr.'s *Strategy and Structure*, the first of his pathbreaking studies of the development of modern business organizations, was a major force in attracting attention to the nature of modern bureaucracies.[7] Robert Wiebe's *The Search for Order*, an influential interpretation of the late nineteenth and early twentieth centuries, emphasized the rise of large-scale national institutions and the demise of localism, shifting attention away from immediate political events and toward large patterns of social and economic change beneath them.[8] Neither Wiebe nor Chandler themselves provided an explicit interpretive framework for the interwar years, but their work helped form the basis for a substantial scholarly redefinition of those years in organizational terms.

The "organizational synthesis" is, in fact, a broad rubric that has been used to embrace widely disparate works. But while its central premises are flexible, they are also distinctive. At its core is the assumption (in the words of Louis Galambos, one of its principal spokesmen):

> . . . that some of the most (if not the single most) important changes which have taken place in modern America have centered about a shift from small-scale, informal, locally or regionally oriented groups to large-scale, national, formal organizations. The new organizations are characterized by a bureaucratic structure of authority. The shift in organization cuts across the traditional boundaries of political, economic, and social history. Businesses, reform groups, professional and labor organizations—all developed along somewhat similar lines.[9]

Organizational historians posed a challenge, therefore, both to Schlesinger's notion of "cycles" and discontinuity and to the general belief among historians in the primacy of political events. Momentary fluctuations in the political and cultural climate (such as the contrast between the "stagnant" politics of the 1920s and the "progressive" nature of the New Deal) have seemed less important to them than the broad adaptations imposed on society by the economic and bureaucratic revolutions.

The organizational synthesis did not, however, necessarily contest the fundamentally "progressive" view of history that Schlesinger shared with most other historians until the 1950s. Organizational historians identified a different engine driving society forward (bureaucratic development, not political reform), but they could still portray history as a continually ameliorative process. The challenge to progressive assumptions came from other directions: from the so-called "consensus" scholars of the 1950s and early 1960s; from historians influenced by the New Left; and from more recent interpretations shaped by (among other things) the sober political realities of the 1970s, 1980s, and 1990s.

Consensus scholarship, which emerged shortly after World War II and flourished in the 1950s and 1960s, has been widely derided by the left as a Cold War effort to celebrate capitalism and delegitimize challenges to it. But the most important consensus historians considered their work highly critical of American values and institutions. At the heart of the American experience, they contended, was what Richard Hofstadter called the "common climate of opinion" that had pervaded most of the nation's history, a climate resting on an almost universal commitment to economic self-aggrandizement through competitive capitalism.[10] Consensus scholars tended to discount the importance (and question the value) of conflict, even as they lamented what they considered the harsh and barren nature of the American political tradition; and they emphasized the limits more than the extent of reform. Hofstadter and others were generally well disposed toward the New Deal, for example, but were more dubious than Schlesinger of its epochal importance.[11]

A less ambiguous assault on progressive assumptions came from historians influenced by the ideas of the New Left, who began in the 1960s to attack the notion, central to Schlesinger's thesis, that liberal reform had been responsible for an increase in democracy and social justice in American life. On the contrary, claimed scholars such as Gabriel Kolko,[12] James Weinstein,[13] and (later) Jeffrey Lustig,[14] the real story of modern America was the decline of genuine democracy and the corresponding increase in the power of private corporate institutions, the growing influence of those institutions over the workings of government, and hence the declining ability of individuals to control the circumstances of their work and their lives. Reform crusades, some leftist scholars contended, did not serve to limit the power of "interests" and increase the power of the people, as Schlesinger and his progressive forebears had argued. They were, rather, the products of a "corporate liberalism" through which powerful capitalist institutions expanded and solidified their influence at the expense of the people.[15]

Still another challenge to progressive assumptions has come from scholars who question not so much the benefits of consolidation and "modernization" as the extent to which they have occurred at all. One of the first explicit efforts to base an interpretive model on the existence of such limits was Barry Karl's *The Uneasy State.* Impressed by the persistence of localistic and "antimodern" forces in late twentieth-century America, Karl suggested that progress toward national unity has not been the hallmark of modern American development. On the contrary, he claimed, twentieth-century society is at least as notable for the degree to which it has *failed* to nationalize, for the extent to which it has *resisted* unity, for the ways in which localism and traditionalism have not only survived but flourished. Such an argument, he conceded, is a challenge to the essentially "nationalist" assumptions that have characterized virtually all previous interpretations of the twentieth century: Schlesinger's progressive view, the interpretations of the "consensus" historians, even the more acerbic arguments of historians of the left. Americans' fervent commitment to the preservation of individual liberties has consistently prevented them from defining themselves clearly as a nation.[16]

Karl's contentions are a reflection (even if perhaps an unintended one) of a larger trend in American historical scholarship as a whole: an emphasis on diversity; a sense that the history of the nation is many different stories, no one of which can be considered the "main" story; a skepticism about finding common definitions of American nationalism or discovering common values among its people. The growing centrality of the concepts of race, ethnicity, gender, and class within historical scholarship—and the highly varied experiences and values that historians have discovered while exploring those categories—has called into question the viability of any effort to define a "central theme" in the nation's past. Even the most fundamental (and presumably unifying) concepts in political language—the ideas of liberty, citizenship, rights, and "Americanism" (as Daniel Rodgers,[17] Roy Rosenzweig,[18] Gary Gerstle,[19] and others demonstrate)—have had very different meanings for different groups and have been the objects of continual contests for definition. Such arguments are part of what some describe as an overdue amplification of historical scholarship and what others describe as its deconstruction. In seeking to explain the experiences of groups and sub-cultures previously consigned to the margins of historical experience, scholars have called into question many of the unifying explanations that once made American history seem whole.

All these broad approaches continue to influence interpretations of the interwar years, even if many individual works do not fit neatly into one or another "school." The result is a scholarly landscape far more varied and conflicted than that of a generation ago.

Historians examining the twentieth century have moved somewhat more slowly than scholars of earlier eras to embrace the movement of modern scholarship away from its concern with politics and toward an increased attention to social and cultural events, but they have moved nonetheless.[20] In particular, scholars have taken an increasing interest in patterns of social and cultural conflict in the 1920s and 1930s.

The first studies of the social and cultural landscape of the interwar years reflected the assumption of those who saw the era as one of sharp discontinuities. The 1920s, according to this view, were not years of conflict so much as a time of stultifying middle-class conformity and bigotry, an interpretation that echoed the opinions of such contemporary social critics as Sinclair Lewis and H. L. Mencken and of Frederick Lewis Allen's influential popular history of the decade, *Only Yesterday*.[21] Mencken, Lewis, Allen, and others portrayed American culture in the 1920s as the product of a narrow-minded, materialistic middle class (what Mencken liked to call the "boobeoisie"); and they tended to link such phenomena as nativism, racism, and fundamentalism with conservative Republican politics and the spread of reactionary bourgeois values. Hence Lewis's character George F. Babbitt could be the epitome of the modern middle-class consumer, celebrating the new business culture, and simultaneously a member of a nativist organization clearly modeled on the Ku Klux Klan. Schlesinger's *The Crisis of the Old Order* accepted the broad outlines of this interpretation.

Even before Schlesinger's study appeared, however, alternative interpretations had emerged. Some consensus scholars, for example, linked the resurgence of the Klan, the Prohibition crusade, and the growth of fundamentalism to such earlier protest movements as greenbackism and populism. All were examples of "symbolic" or "status" politics, which appealed not to the middle class in general but to troubled, usually marginal people who expressed their inchoate anxieties in largely symbolic terms—through a nostalgic call for restoration of a "golden" past or through an embittered attack on symbolic "scapegoats."[22] William Leuchtenburg offered a related but less pejorative explanation in his influential history of the 1920s, *The Perils of Prosperity*. He argued that the intense cultural upheavals of the decade were part of a broad conflict between a new, secular urban culture, committed to cultural pluralism and modernist ideas, and an older, rural America, still wedded to traditional values, largely unconnected to the economic advances of the New Era, and feeling threatened by the changes.[23] These interpretations, unlike earlier views, drew a sharp distinction between members of the "new" middle class and those who gravitated to such movements as fundamentalism and the Klan.

Other scholars have revised such explanations in several ways. Some (following the lead of Lawrence Goodwyn, Steven Hahn, and other historians of populism[24]) have challenged the sharp distinction consensus scholars made between "economic" and "cultural" (or between "rational" and "symbolic") interests. Seemingly rearguard battles to defend "cultural" norms are often, they suggest, democratic efforts to defend rational economic and social interests and to preserve individual and community autonomy. Even some of the unsavory cultural protests of the 1920s, while seldom "democratic" in form, can be seen as an effort to preserve threatened social orders that conferred upon their members not simply "symbolic" rewards but real powers and economic advantages. Kathleen Blee, in examining the women's branch of the Ku Klux Klan, has argued that the women members found in the Klan a source of community that was becoming increasingly difficult to create in ordinary social interaction; and that many women found the women's branch to be a valuable defender of female rights (including suffrage), in addition to being a defender of white supremacy.[25] Leonard Moore's study of the Klan in Indiana suggested, similarly, that many members were driven at least as much by resentments of powerful elites as by racial or ethnic prejudice; that a broad cross-section of middle-class white society rallied to the Klan to defend the values of their community against what they considered menacing outside forces.[26] The Klan, in short, was part of a broader effort by individuals to fight their perceived powerlessness in an increasingly bureaucratized world.

Similarly, many historians have seen Leuchtenburg's "rural-urban" dichotomy as too simple a description of the pattern of conflict. The new bureaucratic order, they argue, was threatening not just to isolated, provincial people, but to everyone whose livelihood or values depended on the survival of local, decentralized institutions. Such people could be either urban or rural; working class or middle class; Protestant or Catholic. The Ku Klux Klan, for example, was not simply an organization of rural Southerners lashing out against changing racial and ethnic norms. As Kenneth Jackson and Leonard Moore have both demonstrated, the Klan had its greatest support in northern and midwestern cities; and it was concerned not just with suppressing blacks, Jews, and immigrants (although racism, anti-Semitism, and nativism were, of course, rife throughout the organization), but also with combating what it considered the moral laxness of modern life. Its members often lashed out at such violations of traditional norms as adultery and divorce.[27] Protestant fundamentalists, George Marsden has argued, were not just the rural "hicks" satirized in popular portrayals of the Scopes trial; they were also intelligent, educated, urban men and women struggling to preserve a traditional faith that was under assault from a newly aggressive secularism (or what David Hollinger, Terry Cooney, and others have called "cosmopolitanism").[28]

By revising the traditional view of conflict in the 1920s, historians have raised new questions about the turbulence of the 1930s. Rather than contrasting the supposedly "cultural" protests of the 1920s with the "economic" dissent of the 1930s, scholars have seen both cultural and economic concerns at work in both periods. One example is the popular dissident movements of the era, such as those associated with Huey Long, Father Charles Coughlin, Dr. Francis Townsend, and others, long dismissed as demagogic aberrations from the generally progressive course of the politics of the era. I myself, and, more recently, Michael Kazin have argued that these phenomena in fact represented an important alternative political vision, often at odds with the ideas of the New Deal. As such, the movements were part of the broad pattern of protest by which "localistic" people were struggling to preserve control of both the economic and the cultural institutions that governed their lives in the face of encroachments from the modern bureaucratic order—a pattern that reflected some of the impulses that scholars of earlier eras have described as republicanism.[29] Leo Ribuffo has suggested that even the far right movements in the 1930s should not be dismissed simply as "extremism," but should be seen as clues to economic and cultural anxieties that affected much of the "mainstream."[30] The turmoil of the 1930s, in short, reflected not just the search for economic advancement but the continuing ambivalence of many Americans about the costs of "modernization."

Not all historians have emphasized conflict in examining the cultural history of the interwar years. To one important group of scholars, what needs explanation in this period is not the extent of conflict but its relative absence. A question that has intrigued Marxist scholars and others on the left for many years is why, given the important inequalities and injustices in modern society, have there been so few class-based challenges to the status quo? Some scholars deny the existence of that anomaly by insisting that there were, in fact, many more such challenges than historians have traditionally been willing to admit. But others have accepted the view that it is the lack of greater conflict that is most in need of explanation. Out of their efforts has emerged a portrait of modern American culture that is in certain ways similar to the critique first advanced by Mencken, Lewis, and other "debunkers" in the 1920s. It emphasizes the rising importance of material consumption, not just to the economy but to the culture.

Warren Susman was among the first to draw attention to the importance of the "consumer culture" in a series of important essays published in the 1960s and 1970s and finally collected in *Culture as History*.[31] Other scholars—among them Christopher Lasch,[32] Jackson Lears,[33] Stuart Ewen,[34] and Roland Marchand[35]—have produced a broad (and highly diverse) literature emphasizing the ways in which material abundance, the increasing availability of consumer goods, the pervasiveness of advertising, and the homogenization of mass culture have worked to define the nation's social and political values. These scholars are highly critical of the "hegemonic" effects of the consumer culture. Ewen, for example, argues that the consumption ethos served the economic needs of industrial capitalists while undermining efforts to address the "human" needs of the larger society. Lasch and Lears portray consumerism as a force that erodes traditional moral or spiritual values in favor of material pleasures and personal fulfillment, and as the source of a "therapeutic" culture (a culture that serves as therapy for the self). But others (Susman among them) have argued, much as Simon Patten and others did early in the century, that consumption has the potential to serve as a force for liberation and human fulfillment.

For scholars interested in the questions that have traditionally dominated discussion of the 1920s and 1930s, the consumer-culture argument helps to explain why so many people seemed to acquiesce in social and economic changes that appeared in many ways contrary to their interests. Although the rise of a new bureaucratic order was eroding the abilities of individuals and small communities to control their lives and livelihoods, consumption and mass culture were opening up new (if, some argue, superficial) vistas that distracted them from their losses.[36]

The political history of the interwar years has undergone substantial revision as well, often as a result of the same impulses that have reshaped interpretations of social and cultural phemonena. In perhaps no area has the traditional view changed more dramatically than in relation to the politics of the 1920s. Until at least the mid-1960s, virtually all scholars accepted the characterization of those years first advanced by Frederick Lewis Allen, then reinforced by several generations of New Deal politicians, and most energetically expressed in Schlesinger's *The Crisis of the Old Order:* that the 1920s were years of political reaction, retreat, and stagnation, a passive interlude between progressivism and the New Deal. By the 1960s, however, historians had begun slowly to revise this essentially negative picture and to see in the politics of those years previously unnoticed progressive impulses. Arthur S. Link, in an influential 1959 article, made a persuasive case that despite the successes of conservative figures such as Harding and Coolidge, important elements of the pre-World War I progressive movement survived into the 1920s and displayed significant strength in Congress and in state and local governments.[37] But the strongest challenge to the old stereotypes has come from scholars contending that the policies of the Republican administrations themselves were far more active and innovative than previously suspected. According to this view, federal public policy in the 1920s represented an important and active effort to bring a measure of rational organization and scientific planning to economic affairs.

"Organizational" historians (Robert Himmelberg,[38] Louis Galambos,[39] and above all Ellis Hawley[40]) have devoted much attention to what they call the "associational" (and what Donald Brand[41] and others call the "corporatist") ideal: the notion that economic order and scientific management could be achieved by creating a cooperative relationship among labor, capital, and the state. Associationalists shared with many progressive reformers a belief in the need for planning and order in the economy. But their real model was the economic mobilization during World War I, when government had worked closely with business to facilitate cooperation and efficiency within the industrial world. The trade association movement of the 1920s, they argue, was an effort to recreate that "ordered economic world" they believed the wartime experiments had produced.[42]

The central figure of the "progressive" 1920s, in this view, was Secretary of Commerce and later President Herbert Hoover, whose historical reputation has been more thoroughly revised in recent years than that of any public figure of his time. Liberal critics of the New Deal era (and after) liked to portray Hoover as a hardened, embittered reactionary, the embodiment of the static old order that the New Deal had triumphantly displaced.[43] Hoover himself, in his later years, did much to support that image. But as Hawley, David Burner,[44] Joan Hoff Wilson,[45] James Stuart Olson,[46] and others have proposed, Hoover in the 1920s (and indeed throughout much of his troubled presidency) was far from reactionary. He was, rather, (to use Wilson's term) a "forgotten progressive," one of the most active and innovative figures in government and the leading advocate of a more forceful federal role in the management of the economy.

Hoover was the champion of the trade association movement in the 1920s and made extensive use of his powers as secretary of commerce and of his influence with other arms of the federal government to promote economic rationalization and limit "destructive competition."[47] As president, Hoover constructed a program of unprecedented federal activism to deal with the Great Depression—price supports for farmers, federal assistance to public works and relief efforts, direct government loans to banks, railroads, and other troubled businesses—and laid the groundwork for many of the achievements of the New Deal. The New Deal, according to this view, was not a sharp and decisive break with a conservative past. It was the culmination of political forces that had been gathering strength for at least a decade before it.

The administration of Franklin D. Roosevelt has long been so central to scholarly views of the interwar years that the slogan "the New Deal" has come to represent not simply a particular set of policies and institutions but, for many historians, the era as a whole. Even those who reject Schlesinger's characterization of the period as the "age of Roosevelt"—even some who doubt the centrality of political history in general—concede that the New Deal was a phenomenon of particular historical importance. As a result, it has generated a larger literature than any other topic in twentieth-century American history. Yet even as studies of the New Deal proliferate, the broad interpretation of the Roosevelt years—as the central event in the progress of the modern United States toward greater unity and democracy—has remained surprisingly impervious to change since Schlesinger and others presented it in the 1950s.

But if there have been few radical revisions in interpretations of the New Deal, there have been significant evolutionary changes. A particularly important moment in that evolution was the appearance in 1963 of William E. Leuchtenburg's influential synthesis, *Franklin D. Roosevelt and the New Deal*, a book that remains the most important single-volume study of the 1930s more than three decades later. Although Leuchtenburg was generally sympathetic to the New Deal, he was more sensitive than earlier scholars to its limits and its failures and assessed its results as no more than a "half-way revolution," which left many problems unresolved and created some new problems of its own. He pointed in particular to the Roosevelt administration's failure to end the Depression before 1940, the absence of significant structural reform in the industrial economy, the limits of the new welfare state, the failure of government relief measures to help those groups most in need of assistance, and the New Deal's modest record on racial issues.[48]

Leuchtenburg's study anticipated many of the arguments that emerged from the left in the late 1960s and was perhaps one reason why revisionist interpretations of the New Deal failed for many years to develop very far beyond a few important essays. Leftist scholars such as Barton Bernstein,[49] Ronald Radosh,[50] and Howard Zinn[51] gave considerably greater emphasis to flaws, limits, and conservative impulses than liberal historians such as Leuchtenburg did; but they failed to make more than vague suggestions of a new theoretical framework for understanding the New Deal. Recently, however, several scholars influenced by the left have produced more sophisticated critiques of the New Deal. Thomas Ferguson argued in several important articles that a rising group of internationalist capitalists shaped and controlled much of the New Deal agenda.[52] Colin Gordon, whose 1994 book *New Deals* was the first full-scale revisionist interpretation of the New Deal in many decades, argued similarly for the direct influence of corporate forces in the construction and management of New Deal programs.[53]

Despite continuing scholarly critiques from the left (and, occasionally, the right), most historians in the last two decades have accepted some variation of Leuchtenburg's stance of muted praise. At the same time, however, they have begun to ask some different questions about the New Deal, questions that are less concerned with establishing whether it was a good or bad thing than with explaining how it took the form it did, what effects it had, and how it helps illuminate larger patterns of political change in the twentieth century.

Historians have paid most attention, perhaps, to the question of constraints, to defining the limits imposed on New Deal reform by the political, social, and economic realities of the 1930s and by the ideological preconceptions of the New Dealers themselves. The first scholars to consider this question focused primarily on political constraints and argued that Franklin Roosevelt, despite his enormous personal popularity, was never able wholly to overcome powerful opposition to his policies both within the government and in the electorate at large. James MacGregor Burns criticized Roosevelt for his failure to make full use of his popularity to challenge his opposition and for his failure genuinely to reshape the party system and provide a secure home for progressives within it.[54] Other scholars, however, have suggested that such a reshaping was never within Roosevelt's power. James Patterson, for example, argued that conservative opposition to the New Deal in Congress was an important factor in the administration's calculations almost from the beginning and became more powerful as time went on.[55] Frank Freidel,[56] Harvard Sitkoff,[57] Nancy Weiss,[58] John B. Kirby,[59] and others have cited the political importance of the South to the New Deal coalition—in Congress and in the electorate—as an explanation for the failure of the administration to take more active measures on behalf of racial equality; while other scholars (myself[60] and Bruce Schulman,[61] for example) have chronicled the failure of New Deal liberalism to take root in the distinctive political environment of the South.

Many scholars have also emphasized ideological constraints: the degree to which Roosevelt and those around him operated in response to the economic and political orthodoxies of their time. Although the New Deal proved more flexible and less ideological than the administrations that preceded it, it too was reined in by powerful conservative assumptions: the belief in a balanced budget, the mistrust of the "dole," the reluctance to intrude the federal government too deeply into the field of microeconomic management, and others. Frank Freidel argued that Roosevelt was an essentially conservative man whose innovations were a result of pragmatic political calculation and instinctive sympathies, not of a genuinely radical temperament.[62] Barry Karl[63] and Otis Graham[64] have pointed to the absence of widespread support within the administration for the advanced forms of planning and organization that some 1930s liberals were proposing. Mark Leff has noted the reluctance of New Dealers to promote a genuinely (as opposed to symbolically) progressive tax system and their reliance instead on a series of highly regressive taxes to finance their programs.[65] Herbert Stein,[66] Robert Lekachman,[67] Margaret Weir,[68] and others have noted the economic conservatism that pervaded New Deal thought at least until 1938, and in particular the unwillingness of the administration to make effective use of federal spending as a tool for fighting the Depression. (They have also pointed out that the economic assumptions that the New Deal resisted—the principles of Keynesian economics—were largely unknown to economists and policymakers alike until the late 1930s.)[69]

Similarly, as James Patterson and others have shown, the clumsy, jerry-built welfare state that emerged from the New Deal (of which the expensive and inefficient Social Security System remains the centerpiece) was in large part a product of the strong ideological opposition, even among many of the most committed liberals, to an overt system of government welfare;[70] and as Jill Quadagno has noted, it reflected too the racist and sexist assumptions of much of the political world through its careful initial exclusion from coverage of those occupations in which African Americans and women were most heavily represented.[71] Institutional constraints—the absence of sufficient bureaucratic capacity or political experience in the running of a national welfare system—also helped shape Social Security, as Theda Skocpol, among others, has suggested.[72] Social Security was also, Linda Gordon has argued, a product of highly gendered assumptions about the proper distribution of benefits. Both men and women involved in the creation of Social Security retained a strong belief in the centrality of the "family wage" and offered the most secure and generous benefits of the system to men. Women were left with the frail Aid to Dependent Children (later Aid to Families with Dependent Children) program, which was based on an assumption of female vulnerability and incapacity.[73]

Nowhere has the argument for the New Deal's ideological conservatism been more forcefully advanced than in the field of labor history. New Deal labor laws and the growth of trade unionism they helped to promote—phenomena liberals have long considered among of the most important progressive triumphs of the 1930s—have received withering reassessments by a host of recent scholars: Karl Klare,[74] Christopher Tomlins,[75] Katherine Stone,[76] Stanley Vittoz,[77] Sanford Jacoby,[78] James Atleson,[79] David Montgomery,[80] David Brody,[81] Ronald Schatz,[82] Bruce Nelson,[83] and others. These scholars disagree on many points, but they are in general agreement that the policy events of the 1930s mark a highly limited victory (if not an actual defeat) for labor; that the great hopes for creating a lasting basis for genuine industrial democracy did not materialize; that the New Deal was never fully committed to achieving it. Other labor historians, however, have seen in the great working-class struggles of the 1930s a striking (if short-lived) effort to redefine democracy and create a central place in it for labor. Gary Gerstle illustrated how immigrant textile workers in Rhode Island found through their organizing efforts a new way to define an Americanism that included them and legitimized their commitment to the union.[84] Lizabeth Cohen's study of steelworkers in Chicago argues that the organizing battles of the 1930s forged a new identity for workers—less ethnically insular, more conscious of class-based grievances—and at least for a time opened up important new democratic possibilities.[85]

Starting in the 1980s, a new body of scholarship began to identify some previously lightly examined constraints on the New Deal—constraints imposed by the nature of American governmental and political institutions. In doing so, it has made a case for considering the structure and character of the state itself as a crucial factor in the actions of government (as opposed to models of state behavior that emphasize the influence of party systems or social forces or constellations of interest groups). Margaret Weir, Anna Shola Orloff, Karen Orren, Kenneth Finegold, and Theda Skocpol (all of them sociologists or political scientists) have been among the many scholars who have shown the importance of political institutions themselves in shaping the results of political battles.[86]

These "state-centered" scholars argue that one reason the New Deal did not do more was because of the absence of sufficient "state capacity"; most of the federal bureaucracy in the 1930s was too small and inexperienced to be able to undertake large tasks. The failure of the National Recovery Administration, according to Finegold and Skocpol, was in large part a result of the lack of government institutions capable of supervising the industrial economy; that absence made it almost inevitable that control of the experiment would fall into the hands of businessmen themselves. The relative success of the Agricultural Adjustment Administration, in contrast, is attributable to the far more highly developed bureaucratic capacity of the Agriculture Department, with its close relationship to powerful farm organizations and its several generations of experience in managing the farm economy.[87]

Even before the emergence of the "state-capacity" argument, a number of historians were examining other aspects of New Deal history that reveal many of the same constraints. As long ago as 1953, Grant McConnell demonstrated the powerlessness of federal agencies to maintain control over agricultural policies in the face of the power of private farm organizations.[88] In 1969 James Patterson revealed the importance of state governments in administering (and hence shaping) programs designed and at least partially funded by the federal government.[89] Bruce Stave,[90] Lyle Dorsett,[91] Charles Trout,[92] and others writing in the 1960s and 1970s challenged what had come to be known as the "Last Hurrah" thesis (after the novel by Edwin O'Connor); they revealed the degree to which the New Deal, far from destroying the power of traditional urban political machines, in fact strengthened many of them by giving them administrative control of new federal programs. That was in part a result of political choice (the kind of choice Burns criticizes Roosevelt for making); but it was also a result of the absence of federal bureaucratic capacity to provide an alternative administrative structure. The "state capacity" literature of recent years, which has slowly found an important audience among historians, suggests some important new directions for these arguments.

Another reflection of this growing interest in bureaucracies is the increasing scholarly attention to the way the consequences of policy initiatives often depart from the intentions behind them. New Deal scholars have only occasionally asked such questions about the programs of the 1930s; but they have made clear nevertheless that some of the New Deal's most important accomplishments were ones that Roosevelt and his associates neither anticipated or desired. In the broadest sense, the unexpected outcomes of New Deal efforts can be seen in the emergence in the 1930s of the so-called "broker state." As Ellis Hawley has shown in *The New Deal and the Problem of Monopoly*, his landmark history of economic policy in the 1930s, by the end of the Depression, important new groups—workers, farmers, and others—were beginning for the first time to exercise meaningful political and economic power. The federal government, in the meantime, had largely rejected the idea of trying to impose any central design on the economy or promoting a transcendent national goal. Its policies worked, rather, to guarantee the rights of particular interest groups and oversee pluralistic competition in the national marketplace. It had become a broker state.[93]

The rise of the broker state is arguably one of the most significant political developments of the New Deal era, and some historians—in talking about the "second New Deal" that emerged in 1935–36—claim that it was the result of a deliberate ideological choice by Roosevelt and those around him.[94] But Hawley makes clear that the broker state was in many respects an unintended result of government policies designed to advance other ends. The NRA, for example, failed in its avowed goal of stabilizing prices and markets and harmonizing industrial relations (which Donald Brand and others have described as part of a broad corporatist impulse powerful within at least the early New Deal[95]). Its most important legacy may have been a partially unintended one: the organization of industrial workers into an important competitive actor in the marketplace (which the NIRA's Section 7a—precursor to the 1935 Wagner Act—did much to promote). Other initiatives designed to promote a planned, harmonious economic world failed in their larger goals but similarly left behind newly organized groups capable for the first time of effectively defending their claims. (Hawley termed this process "counter-organization," the mobilization of weaker groups to allow them to confront stronger ones—an alternative New Dealers gradually came to prefer to the more politically difficult effort to curb the influence of existing centers of power directly.)

Another important shift in the scholarly approach to the New Deal is the tendency to see its achievements less as the result of the political and intellectual impulses of the moment and more as the product of long-term social transformations. This has long been a contention of organizational historians, who see the New Deal as a reflection of the long-term evolution of managerial systems in both private and public life. A related claim is that many New Deal achievements are the result of the emergence in the twentieth century of coherent interest groups, which were steadily gaining influence at the expense of political parties. Richard L. McCormick has chronicled the beginnings of that shift in the late nineteenth and early twentieth centuries;[96] Samuel Hays,[97] Louis Galambos,[98] Anthony Badger,[99] and Bernard Bellush[100] are among the many historians whose work takes account of the impact of that change on the policies of the 1930s. Other historians (among them J. Joseph Huthmacher,[101] Mark Gelfand,[102] William Bremer,[103] Charles Trout,[104] and Bruce Stave[105]) have suggested that urbanization and the growing political power of the city shaped New Deal programs far more than the ideological inclinations of its leaders; the gradual shift in political attention in the 1930s from rural issues toward such matters as public housing, fair labor standards, and public health is evidence of the mobilization of powerful urban forces. Jordan Schwarz proposed that one of the principal legacies of the New Deal was its embrace of an effort, spanning several decades, to use the power of government (what Schwarz calls "state capitalism") to develop previously underdeveloped areas of the country; vast public works projects in the South and the West, he claims, were the fulfillment of a dream stretching back at least to World War I, of using public investment to create a basic infrastructure for those regions.[106]

Still other scholars argue that the New Deal was a reflection of the rising emphasis on consumption in American culture and the American economy alike, and that both the economic and welfare policies of the Roosevelt administration were part of a broad political adaptation to that shift. That transformation found reflection in the policy evolution of the late 1930s and beyond (described in the work of, among others, Herbert Stein,[107] Dean May,[108] Theodore Rosenof,[109] and myself[110]), which introduced Keynesianism to American government.

This emphasis on long-term transformations invites historians to look to earlier eras to find the foundations of many New Deal policies. It also encourages them to look beyond the 1930s for explanations of trends in public policy that have traditionally been attributed to the New Deal. Partly as a result, scholars have begun to show more interest in the domestic impact of World War II.

For many years historians had a simple explanation of the domestic impact of World War II: it ended the Great Depression and launched an era of sustained economic growth; it weakened the liberal coalition and ushered in a period of conservative politics. More recent scholarship has not often challenged those conclusions, but it has begun to amplify and augment them.

Several historians have argued that wartime economic arrangements to promote war production formed the basis of more lasting accommodations between the government and business: a powerful "corporate liberalism" that would survive to dominate public life in the postwar years. John Morton Blum and Richard Polenberg, authors of two valuable overviews of the impact of the war on American society and politics, both chronicle the muting of liberal animus toward the corporate world in the 1940s but stop short of embracing the "corporate liberal" argument"[111] Kim McQuaid and Robert Collins, however, have suggested the outlines of a more explicitly "corporatist" interpretation of the results of wartime mobilization.[112] Political scientist Benjamin Sparrow argues that World War II was crucial to the creation of what came to be known as the New Deal state both in cementing some of the New Deal's social commitments and (in the case of both the welfare state and labor relations) imposing strict limits on those commitments.[113]

In my own work I have argued that the war did not increase federal control of corporate behavior, but contributed instead to a government commitment to indirect management of the economy through Keynesian tools; in the process, liberals in effect repudiated their long battle against "monopoly power" and began instead to construct a "compensatory state." Rather than challenging capitalist institutions, government worked to ensure high levels of growth, "full employment" and a broader distribution of purchasing power among consumers.[114]

Nelson Lichtenstein,[115] Steve Fraser,[116] Howell John Harris[117] and others suggest that far from improving the long-term position of labor, the war undermined the possibility of achieving anything like genuine "industrial democracy." Lichtenstein, in describing the experiences of the CIO during World War II, recounts the failure of efforts by some labor leaders to create power-sharing arrangements by which unions would have won a voice in making basic production decisions. Instead, the unions settled for guarantees of their own institutional survival and higher wages for their members. Harris, similarly, describes ways in which business leaders used the war years to reassert managerial prerogatives they had lost to the unions in the 1930s and to pave the way toward passage of the anti-union Taft-Hartley Act in 1947. Others have portrayed the political alliance between organized labor and the Democratic party (symbolized by the formation of the CIO's Political Action Committee) as a "barren marriage" (Mike Davis's phrase), by which workers sacrificed any hopes for independent political power in exchange for immediate material gains.[118]

The war years also had important, if still imperfectly understood, effects on many other areas of American society. Historians of African-

American life generally agree that the war made an important contribution to the rise of black consciousness and to the mobilization of dissent that would culminate in the civil rights movement. John Blum and Harvard Sitkoff (among many others) emphasize the participation of African Americans in the war (and the rising demands for racial justice that participation inspired) as the most important phenomenon.[119] Arnold Hirsch attributes greater importance to demographic changes. The enormous migration in the 1940s of rural blacks to the cities of both the North and the South greatly increased the size of black urban communities, the principal source of the civil rights movement and black protest. The expanded economic opportunities the war years produced helped enlarge and strengthen the black middle class and made its members less willing to tolerate the barriers that blocked further advances. But the war also helped reinforce the commitment of many southern whites and northern ethnic workers to restore the world they had known before Pearl Harbor. The racial battles of the 1950s and 1960s were in part a result of clashing African-American hopes and white fears, both reinforced by the war.[120]

Scholars working in women's history disagree in some respects about the impact of the war on American women. William Chafe has argued that the war greatly expanded economic opportunities for women,[121] while Leila Rupp has contended that such gains were only temporary.[122] Yet the work of Karen Anderson,[123] Mary Schweitzer,[124] Sara Evans,[125] and others suggests that whatever the immediate impact of the war on women's work, its long-range impact was profound. The war propelled unprecedented numbers of women into the workforce, and many of them stayed there after 1945 (although Alice Kessler-Harris has maintained that this movement of women into paid work would have occurred even without the conflict.[126]) It gave women an experience of independence and self- reliance that many carried with them into the postwar era. And yet among men, as Robert Westbrook and others have suggested, the war worked to strengthen more traditional views of gender roles. Men serving overseas dreamed of returning to a world of traditional gender relationships. Many men (and some women) in the United States during the war looked with alarm at the independence of the many single women entering the workforce and began efforts to limit their autonomy. On issues of gender, as with issues of race, the war created sharply different expectations: a vision of a more independent future among many women; a dream of returning to a traditional male-dominated world among men.[127]

The important social, cultural, and economic transformations that recent scholarship has begun to reveal in the years between 1920 and 1945 have only slowly informed the ways in which historians have explained the public, political life of the era. But it is clear that exploring the connections between great public events and the less visible social phenomena that form their context is emerging as the next important frontier for historians of twentieth-century America.

8

Hofstadter's *The Age of Reform* Reconsidered

Even its detractors (and there are many) might be inclined to agree that Richard Hofstadter's *The Age of Reform* is the most influential book ever published on the history of twentieth-century America. For more than a decade after its appearance in 1955, its interpretations shaped virtually every discussion of modern American reform. For longer than that, its methodological innovations helped recast the writing of history in many fields. Even those historians who have most vigorously and explicitly challenged its interpretations have usually been deeply, if at times unconsciously, in its debt. In this book as in others, Hofstadter's signal achievement, the achievement that has most clearly marked him as one of the century's great American historians, lay less in creating durable interpretations than in raising new questions and establishing new modes of inquiry, in opening hitherto unperceived avenues of exploration. Robert Wiebe spoke for more than his own generation of scholars when he wrote in 1969: "To those of us who encountered *The Age of Reform* in graduate school, [Hofstadter] more than any other writer, framed the problems, explored the techniques, and established the model of literate inquiry that would condition our study of the American past."[1]

The book has most directly influenced the study of populism and progressivism, which Hostadter sought to reinterpret. A remarkable number of the many important studies of both phenomena that have appeared since 1955 were augured, directly or indirectly, by Hofstadter's observations. His discussion of "the struggle over organization," for example, laid much of the groundwork for the important Weberian interpretations of progressivism by Wiebe, Samuel Hays, and others. His examination of the links between political machines and corporate power, and his description of popular resentment of both, foreshadowed some of the significant work of David Thelen on popular reform movements in Wisconsin. His controversial description of the populist mind opened the way for a series of subsequent studies (many of them explicitly critical of Hofstadter, yet nevertheless indebted to him for both interpretive and methodological inspiration) examining populist ideology—an aspect of populism all but ignored in the work of Beard or Hicks and their disciples.

For historians of modern America, *The Age of Reform* has served a role comparable perhaps only to that of C. Vann Woodward's *Origins of the New South* in giving definition to a still undefined field. And yet unlike Woodward's monumental book, which remains the central work in modern southern history and whose interpretation many (if not most) scholars in the field continue to accept, *The Age of Reform* has come to seem something of a relic. It is still widely read and widely cited. It continues to shape arguments and inspire debates. But it is now more often a target than an inspiration, a symbol of abandoned assumptions rather than a guide to further study. It has come, in short, to embody something of a scholarly paradox (to use one of Hofstadter's own favorite words). It is a book whose central interpretations few historians now accept, but one whose influence few historians can escape.

Woodward wrote *Origins of the New South* as part of a lifelong commitment to the field of southern history and after years of immersion in its sources. Hofstadter wrote *The Age of Reform*, by contrast, after a rather short engagement with the subject (neither before nor after did he devote much attention to the populists or progressives) and after a strikingly thin acquaintance with the sources. It was not so much, then, a fascination with the reformers themselves that inspired Hofstadter to examine them, but rather the opportunity they gave him to test certain political, theoretical, and methodological concepts that by the 1950s had come to intrigue him. The self-consciously innovative tone of the study became its greatest strength, but its emphasis on innovation at the expense of evidence was also its most serious weakness.

Critics have most often cited the political concerns of intellectuals of the 1950s, and in particular their immersion in the highly charged atmosphere of the cold war, to explain Hofstadter's interpretations in

The Age of Reform. Shaken by the memory of fascism and the reality of Stalinism, aghast at the success of Joseph McCarthy and other demagogues at home, deeply fearful of the intolerance and bigotry latent in unrestrained mass politics, intellectuals had committed themselves to the defense of what became known as, in Arthur M. Schlesinger, Jr.'s resonant phrase, "the vital center." The task of intellectuals, some believed, was the defense of the pluralistic assumptions of American democracy and the delegitimation of the dangerous ideologies that challenged them from both the left and the right. In the hour of danger, all citizens were soldiers in the cause.[2]

As a member of the close-knit New York intellectual community within which anticommunism and postwar liberalism had seamlessly merged, Hofstadter could not avoid absorbing, and indeed helping to formulate, many of these political concerns. "What started me off as an historian," he once said, "was a sense of engagement with contemporary problems. . . . I still write history out of my engagement with the present." Some of the ideas for *The Age of Reform* emerged from a celebrated 1954 conference at Columbia on the causes of McCarthyism (a conference that resulted in Daniel Bell's 1955 collection, *The New American Right*). And in the introduction to his own book, Hofstadter admitted that he had focused his attention on "that side of Populism and Progressivism—particularly of Populism—which seems very strongly to foreshadow some aspects of the cranky pseudo-conservatism of our time."[3]

But it would be a mistake to attribute too large a role to political commitments in shaping *The Age of Reform,* or to see it—as some critics have—simply as an attempt to read McCarthyism back into the politics of the late nineteenth century. For Hofstadter, these political concerns coexisted with, and were often secondary to, a series of important theoretical and methodological innovations. Even the 1954 Columbia conference, for all its political urgency, influenced many of its participants (and particularly Hofstadter) less by its political agenda than by its illumination of new interdisciplinary approaches to the study of human motivation.

By the early 1950s Hofstadter had been unhappy for some time with the central assumptions of the "progressive historians," most notably Charles Beard, in whose shadow he and his contemporaries continued to work. He considered simplistic and excessively rigid the progressive view that all political alignments derive from the economic interests of contending groups; he questioned its assumption that American history as a whole could be viewed as a persistent conflict between the "people" and the "interests." Historians, he came to believe, must find a place in the scheme of things for ideas. And they must recognize that ideas did not (and here he was challenging, among others, Vernon Parrington) always reflect material concerns.[4]

In searching for new ways to deal with the role of ideas in politics, Hofstadter drew heavily on the social sciences. Like most twentieth-century intellectuals he was deeply affected by Freud (and by contemporary scholars employing Freudian concepts); he made use as well of the work of the German sociologist Karl Mannheim, who had redefined the concept of ideology to permit consideration of noneconomic interests. More immediately, he drew from the work of some of his own colleagues at Columbia: from the literary critic Lionel Trilling, who taught him to appreciate the importance of symbols in the human imagination (Hofstadter told friends that he had read everything Trilling had ever written); from C. Wright Mills, whose *White Collar* (1951) defined the concept of "status" that would prove so crucial to *The Age of Reform* (Mills complained at times that Hofstadter had "stolen" ideas for *The Age of Reform* and other works from him); and perhaps above all from the great sociologist Robert K. Merton, whose ideas about the difference between "latent" and "manifest" functions furnished Hofstadter with a framework for incorporating the "irrational" into historical explanation. *The Age of Reform* became Hofstadter's first systematic effort to put these new approaches into practice.[5]

Hofstadter never claimed to offer a total picture of the reform movements he was examining. *The Age of Reform* was, rather, an effort to address an imbalance in historical understanding. Beard and his disciples had described populism and progressivism almost entirely in terms of clashing economic interests and had celebrated them as expressions of democracy and agents of social progress. Hofstadter did not deny the importance of economic factors, and he conceded that there was much of value in the reform tradition. But—and in this he made clear the central thrust of his argument—he pointed as well to an important strain of illusion and illiberalism in that tradition, which had made it sadly inadequate to the needs of a modern society. "I believe it will be clear," he wrote defensively in his introduction, "that what I am trying to establish is not that the Populist and Progressive movements were foolish and destructive but only that they had, like so many things in life, an ambiguous character." In time, however, as the ideas of the book traveled through the scholarly world, these careful qualifications ceased to be clear at all.[6]

What primarily interested Hofstadter was what he considered a disjunction between the real and perceived interests of the men and women he was describing, a disjunction most clearly visible, he believed, in the ideology of the populists. American farmers, Hofstadter claimed, were by the late nineteenth century as much a part of the world of commerce and entrepreneurship as any other Americans. Yet they denied that reality and embraced instead an "agrarian myth," which encouraged them "to believe that they were not themselves an organic part of the whole order of business enterprise and speculation that flourished in the city . . . but rather the innocent pastoral victims of a conspiracy hatched in the distance." Populist politics, therefore, tended to express less the economic concerns of farmers than the essentially social and psychological anxieties that stemmed from the decline in their "rank in society." Instead of taking purposeful steps to adapt to the modern commercial world, of which they were already—economically—an integral part, they chose to rail defensively against it, taking refuge in a vision of an unrecapturable (and largely imagined) past.[7]

Out of this tension between perception and reality emerged the central assumptions of populist ideology: a dualistic view of social struggle in which the great mass of the people stood pitted against powerful, selfish oligarchies; a "conspiracy theory of history" which attributed to these oligarchies an awesome and diabolical power; and a belief in the primacy of money, control of which had been the key to the ability of elites to subvert democracy, and control of which by the people would be the key to a restoration of democracy. Out of that same tension came the characteristic features of populist resentment: a preoccupation with scapegoats, a belief in ubiquitous plots, and apocalyptic visions of the future. Hence the semi-hysterical flailings at Wall Street, the Bank of England, cities, immigrants, and intellectuals. Hence the tinge of anti-Semitism that ran throughout the movement. ("It is not too much to say," Hofstadter wrote, "that the Greenback-Populist tradition activated most of what we have of modern popular anti-Semitism in the United States," although he was careful to add that such anti-Semitism was "entirely verbal," unaccompanied by any program of repression or violence.)[8]

Hofstadter's picture of the populists found immediate favor among many social scientists; but within the historical profession, the interpretation was from the beginning the target of strenuous (and often vituperative) attacks. One of the first and most thoughtful critiques came in 1959 from Hofstadter's friend C. Vann Woodward, in the influential essay "The Populist Heritage and the Intellectual." Woodward did not single out *The Age of Reform* for criticism. He connected the book with a much larger body of social science literature (among which Hofstadter's book, he claimed, stood out for its balance and sensitivity). Still, his reservations applied to *The Age of Reform* as clearly as they did to other works. The new view of populism was, he argued, fundamentally ahistorical—a deductive interpretation, based on contemporary concerns, that ignored the historical realities of the populist insurgency, especially in the South. The populists, he insisted, were engaged in a real struggle for power based on economic interests; they were not tilting at cultural windmills. Other scholars made similar arguments: Walter T. K. Nugent, in his 1963 study, *The Tolerant Populists,* put Hofstadter's arguments to the test of evidence in Kansas and found little support for the allegations of nativism, anti-Semitism, and xenophobia that were so central to *The Age of Reform;* Michael Rogin (a political scientist), in his *The Intellectuals and McCarthy* (1967), challenged Hofstadter's implication that populism strongly foreshadowed McCarthyism.[9]

Meanwhile, other critics were offering more fundamental (and more explicitly ideological) critiques. Norman Pollack, who for a time made a virtual cottage industry out of attacks on *The Age of Reform,* not only refuted Hofstadter's contention that the populists were motivated by nostalgia, irrational fears, and prejudices. He also challenged the larger view of populists as incipient capitalists working to reform but not fundamentally to alter the economic system. In fact, he argued, the populists were forward-looking radicals who wanted not only a "democratized industrial system" but "a transformation of social values." Their critique "went beyond economic conditions to embrace the question of the individual's plight, his dehumanization, his loss of autonomy in a society which rapidly reduced him to a dependent state."[10]

Pollack was the first of a substantial group of historians whose own experiences with the left in the 1960s led to a new appreciation for the populist past and a new search for an authentic American radicalism within it. Foremost among them was Lawrence Goodwyn, whose *Democratic Promise: The Populist Moment in America,* published in 1976, was the first full-scale study of the movement since John D. Hicks's *The*

Populist Revolt of 1931. A veteran of the civil rights movement and an admirer of the New Left, Goodwyn portrayed populism as a coherent, enlightened, and fundamentally democratic movement (indeed much of his book was devoted to his exploration of the populists' "movement culture"), struggling to produce a cooperative, locally based alternative to the competitive, centralizing tendencies of industrial capitalism. The distinctive expressions of populism were neither fevered resentments nor apocalyptic warnings, but the hopeful, constructive efforts of thousands of communities to build institutions and establish values that would permit an alternative economy (and an alternative value system) to survive. The failure of populism marked the end of America's best (and perhaps last) chance to construct a democratic alternative to modern oligarchic capitalism.[11]

The post-Hofstadter studies of populism were of varying quality. Pollack's, in particular, suffered from a polemicism and an unsystematic use of sources that robbed it of any lasting credibility. Goodwyn's much more important and persuasive study was also at times undermined by the author's unrestrained and uncritical enthusiasm for those he was chronicling. But whatever their limitations, most of these works were far better rooted in the evidence than *The Age of Reform*, and their cumulative effect was, if not to demolish, at least substantially to diminish the persuasiveness of its interpretation.

Critics were not, however, challenging Hofstadter on the basis of evidence alone. They were objecting, at least implicitly, to his apparent animus toward the provincialism he perceived running through the movement, his disdain for what he contemptuously called the "village mind." And they were objecting as well to what they considered his normative view of economic progress, the assumption (which lay at the heart of *The Age of Reform* and, indeed, at the heart of much of the historiography of the 1950s) that industrialization, commercialization, and centralization were at once inevitable and, on the whole, desirable; and that agrarian protest was therefore a futile, flailing effort to stand in the way of progress. (It is significant, perhaps, that the two groups from Hofstadter's own urban world that he chose to equate with the populists were the widely reviled musicians and building trades unions of New York, organizations popularly perceived to be fighting to preserve costly and obsolete work rules regardless of the costs to society.)

Hofstadter's critics viewed populism from a fundamentally different perspective. To them, modernization was a far less happy phenomenon, a process that had exploited and degraded significant segments of the population. Industrialization did not, in their view, evolve naturally from the commercial society of the early nineteenth century; it was a revolution which cut off large groups of Americans from the economic and cultural moorings that had given meaning to their lives. For the rural men and women who became the source of populist strength, this transformation was particularly traumatic—not only psychologically but economically, for what was at stake was not simply the psychic rewards of "rank in society" but the social and economic viability of a distinctive way of life. Steven Hahn's study of the Georgia upcountry in the late nineteenth century, for example, portrays a once independent and virtually self-sufficient white yeomanry being drawn into the jaws of a new commercial system of which they had never been and could never be anything but a subordinate part. For them, Hahn argued, populism would become not only an expression of symbolic, psychic anxieties, but also of real material interests, albeit interests in many ways antithetical to the prevailing order.[12]

The new accounts of populism, as successful as they have been in challenging Hofstadter, have also created problems of their own; and the larger debate over the nature of the agrarian revolt remains to a great degree unresolved. For one thing, none of the major studies has given sufficient attention to the significant regional differences within the movement. Hicks and Hofstadter concentrated primarily on the Midwest, Goodwyn largely on the South, Hahn on two counties in Georgia; most other studies have been similarly provincial in focus. Nor have they dealt adequately with the ambivalence with which farmers appear to have responded to the new market system: the fearful hostility toward the costs of the new market economy combined with the ambitious grasping for its benefits, the simultaneous traditionalism and modernism. (Hofstadter may, in fact, have recognized this ambivalence more clearly than many of his critics, even if he distorted his picture of it by exaggerating the importance of its purely nostalgic elements.) And as James Turner has pointed out, one vital question has received almost no serious attention. Why, in an economy where virtually all farmers were suffering economic difficulties, did some people become populists while others did not? Turner suggests (on the basis of an analysis of populist strength in Texas) that geographical isolation may have been an important factor in determining populist tendencies—both because such isolation placed additional economic strains on struggling farmers, and because it left them bereft of the sorts of social and cultural reinforcements that might have helped reconcile them to the prevailing order. If Turner is correct, therefore, there may still be a place, even if a less central place than *The Age of Reform* suggests, for Hofstadter's emphasis on psychological anxieties, but less as the product of nostalgic mythologizing than as the result of objective conditions.[13]

Progressivism, Hofstadter argued, differed from populism in its location (which was primarily urban), its constituents (who were largely middle-class professionals), and much of its program. But Hofstadter did not share the view of later scholars that progressivism was an impulse fundamentally different from, indeed antithetical to, populism. Instead, he portrayed the two movements as part of the same broad current of reform. The progressives, he argued, shared with the populists a suspicion of modern forms of economic organization, a fear of concentrated power, and perhaps above all an attachment to a vanished and unrecapturable past. And thus, like the populists, they were—despite their many important accomplishments—unable in the end to deal realistically with the problems of their age.

Hofstadter conceded that progressivism "had the adherence of a heterogeneous public whose various segments responded to various needs." But there was, he argued, a core group of progressives "upon whose contributions the movement was politically and intellectually as well as financially dependent, and whose members did much to formulate its ideals."[14] These were men (he gave scant attention to women) of the "mugwump type," mostly from the Northeast. They enjoyed moderate wealth and longtime social standing and considered themselves the natural leaders of society. In the years following the Civil War, such men had looked with contempt on the corrupt and seamy world of politics and had largely withdrawn from it. But by the turn of the century they had become sufficiently alarmed by the rise to power of urban bosses and newly rich industrial titans, and sufficiently distressed at what they considered their own responsibility for having allowed it to happen, that they began to reenter the political arena and to reestablish what they believed was their rightful place as its leaders.[15]

On the surface, at least, progressivism was a phenomenon much better suited than populism to Hofstadter's mode of analysis. The populists had mobilized in the face of genuine economic hardships; the progressives had operated in a climate of general prosperity, in which they themselves (as Hofstadter identified them) were economically comfortable and secure. Thus the "paradox" that Hofstadter had seemed in some measure to invent for the populists appeared real for the progressives: the emergence of a popular reform movement unaccompanied by genuine economic grievances on the part of the reformers.

Hofstadter attempted to solve this paradox by introducing into historical studies the concept of "status," an idea he had extracted from recent works by C. Wright Mills, Seymour Martin Lipset, and other social scientists. This became, in the end, perhaps the most influential and certainly the most controversial of all his many scholarly innovations. The status model was an elaboration and refinement of ideas with which Hofstadter had been wrestling for years: the belief in "multivariate analysis" he had borrowed from Mannheim, the concern with the role of "latent" and "manifest" functions he had derived from Merton, the engagement with the psychological underpinnings of political beliefs he had taken from Freud, Harold Lasswell, and Adorno. And while he had used the model implicitly in his discussion of the populists, he applied it explicitly to the case of the progressive leadership:

> It is my thesis that men of this sort . . . were Progressives not because of economic deprivations but primarily because they were victims of an upheaval in status that took place in the United States during the closing decades of the nineteenth and early years of the twentieth century. Progressivism, in short, was to a very considerable extent led by men who suffered from the events of their time not through a shrinkage in their means but through the changed pattern in the distribution of deference and power.[16]

The progressives, then, were not engaged in "interest" or "class" politics, which Hofstadter elsewhere defined as "the clash of material aims and needs among various groups and blocs," but "status" politics, "the clash of various projective rationalizations arising from status aspirations and other personal motives."[17]

Those "projective rationalizations" did not often take such cranky or irrational forms among the progressives as they had among the populists (although Hofstadter did perceive a strong undercurrent of nativism and moral absolutism running through progressive political thought). The progressives did, however, develop a preoccupation with an imagined past no less central to their ideology than the "agrarian myth" was to the populist mind. In a world coming to be dominated by large, impersonal organizations and bureaucracies, a world in which a few immensely wealthy men seemed to be seizing control of the economy and the society, progressives harked back to an earlier America, one with "a rather broad diffusion of wealth, status, and power, in which the man of moderate means, especially in the many small communities, could command much deference and exert much influence."[18]

It was to restore that world, to destroy the illegitimate concentrations of power that threatened it, that progressives embarked on their various reform crusades. Muckraking journalists attacked powerful urban bosses and the great trusts. Intellectuals and professionals worked to recapture the "moral authority" to which they believed they were entitled and which they feared they had lost. Progressive politicians worked to limit the influence of party organizations and shift power to the people, who could—if properly instructed and led by an enlightened elite—be trusted to resist the destruction of liberty that the rise of organization threatened to produce:

> The American tradition had been one of unusually widespread participation of the citizen in the management of affairs, both political and economic. Now the growth of the large corporation, the labor union, and the big impenetrable political machine was clotting society into large aggregates and presenting to the unorganized citizen the prospect that all these aggregates and interests would be able to act in concert and shut out those men for whom organization was difficult or impossible. . . . The central theme of Progressivism was this revolt against the industrial discipline: the Progressive movement was the complaint of the unorganized against the consequences of organization.[19]

Hofstadter's picture of the progressives was from the beginning more persuasive to historians than his picture of the populists; and so it has remained. But it too soon became the target of important and effective critiques. Much of Hofstadter's interpretation rested on his answer to a single question: who were the progressives? And the most successful challenges to it, therefore, began by challenging his answers to that question. Critics did not often dispute the existence within progressive reform circles of the "displaced elites" Hofstadter described or question their credentials as progressives. They argued, rather, that such people did not constitute the whole, or even the most important segment, of the reform constituency.

David P. Thelen provided one of the boldest challenges by arguing that social tensions (whether the result of class or status conflicts) played almost no role in generating support for progressive reform. Wisconsin Progressives, he argued, emerged from all classes and all social groups more or less equally; and thus the question of who the progressives were was far less important than the question of what they wanted and how they sought to achieve it. Most other studies, however, persisted in the attempt to identify a center of progressive strength and challenged Hofstadter by arguing that it lay in groups other than the "displaced elites" he described. Some located the progressive core in groups "below" Hofstadter's old middle class; Herbert Gutman, J. Joseph Huthmacher, and John D. Buenker, for example, demonstrated how workers, immigrants, and urban machine politicians were central to some of the most important reform crusades of the era.[20] Others looked "above" Hofstadter's constituency: to the same corporate elites and agents of organization against whom Hofstadter had claimed the progressives were reacting. Samuel P. Hays showed how upper-class business leaders dominated several municipal reform movements. Gabriel Kolko described progressive regulatory reforms as an effort by corporate moguls to limit competition and strengthen their own economic hegemony. Robert Wiebe, the most influential of the challengers, viewed progressivism not as the nostalgic flailing of an "old" middle class but as the purposeful efforts of members of a "new middle class," closely tied to the emerging national economy, "to fulfill its destiny through bureaucratic means." Progressivism was, in virtually all such accounts, not an effort to recapture the past, as Hofstadter had described it, but an adaptive, modernizing movement firmly fixed on the future.[21]

Ultimately, however, neither Hofstadter's "traditionalist" model of progressivism nor the "modernizing" view of some of his critics has satisfied scholars attempting to explain the enormous range and variety of early twentieth-century reform. No single class or interest group, most historians tend now to argue (accepting at least some of Thelen's contentions), can lay exclusive claim to the mantle of progressivism, just as no single ideology can account for the sweep of its concerns. Instead of identifying a single, dominant progressive constituency or a clear, common progressive program, scholars now tend to argue for a more pluralistic view that leaves room for many different groups and many different impulses. Some have gone so far as to challenge the existence of a progressive movement at all; others have attempted to divide progressivism into two or three distinct impulses; still others have begun to look beyond the particular issues that dominated progressive rhetoric and to place the phenomenon in the context of a much larger transformation of American political life.[22] As the debate continues, still without any sign of resolution, one thing does seem clear: that Hofstadter's impressively coherent picture of the progressive mind is inadequate as a description of anything but a single segment of the progressive constituency, a segment far less "strategic" in the larger scheme of reform than he claimed.

Like his picture of populism, Hofstadter's analysis of progressivism suffered from its excessive reliance on an explanatory theory—the idea of the dichotomy between "status" and "interest" politics—inadequately tested against the evidence. But it suffered as well from limitations in the theory itself. At the heart of Hofstadter's notion of status was the idea he had borrowed from Merton of "functional" as opposed to "nonfunctional" behavior. When people behaved functionally, they responded directly to their material interests. There were, alas, times when they behaved nonfunctionally, when they responded not to economic but psychic needs, and when their behavior became symbolic and self-defeating. Establishing the dichotomy between "interest politics" and "status politics" meant accepting the progressive historians' assumption that all rational political behavior was rooted in economic concerns, while rejecting their belief that political behavior always *was* rational. The concept of "status," therefore, became a concept oddly similar to the orthodox Marxist idea of "false consciousness," attributing to politics not clearly rooted in class an aberrant, illegitimate quality.

Scholars who shared Hofstadter's dissatisfaction with the economic determinism of the progressive scholars and who absorbed his excitement over the ways in which psychological and sociological tools could deepen historical understanding faced a dilemma. Was it possible to accept the existence of noneconomic factors in history without accepting the rigid and pejorative picture of those factors that the "interests-status" dichotomy suggested? One solution to that dilemma was suggested by Joseph Gusfield, in his 1963 study of the American temperance movement, *Symbolic Crusade.* Gusfield shared Hofstadter's assumption that there was an identifiable difference between class (economic) and status politics; but he rejected the idea that status concerns were in any way less real or less rational than interest ones. David Thelen proposed another solution by contending that there was a realm of political concern independent of either class or status tensions; that, in Wisconsin at least, "issues of corporate irresponsibility and tax evasion" touched virtually everyone, not only in terms of economic self interest but in terms of basic concepts of justice and fairness; such issues thus "transcended the social barriers that had divided individuals and groups" in the past.[23]

What Gusfield and Thelen suggested was perhaps the most fundamental question about the status model: is it possible to distinguish clearly between economic and noneconomic behavior? Are battles over status and power really unrelated to economic interests? There are, of course, times when politics moves in patterns that do not reflect the economic concerns of the actors, even times when people act in direct opposition to their own material interests. But there are also times in which battles over "status" and battles over class are the same battles. Workers fighting for control of the workplace, according to David Montgomery, fought simultaneously for the psychic rewards of greater autonomy and prestige and for the ability to protect their economic interests. Agrarians battling the rise of corporate hegemony, many scholars of populism have argued, struggled not only against cultural obsolescence but also against the economic obsolescence that they perceived—correctly—would accompany it. Even Hofstadter's "displaced elites" were surely aware that their own economic standing was rapidly deteriorating, if not in absolute terms then certainly relative to the great new fortunes they could see springing up around them; and any definition of material interests that does not leave room for the sense of relative deprivation excludes a large portion of the economic concerns of twentieth-century Americans.[24]

In the last years of his life, when Hofstadter attempted on occasion to evaluate the most important achievements of his remarkable scholarly career, he expressed particular pride in having helped to introduce "complexity" to the study of history. It was a real and important contribution; in the wake of Hofstadter's work, few historians attempted to fit all historical causation into a neat pattern of clashing economic interests. But Hofstadter worried that this "keener sense of the structural complexity of our society in the past" might produce as well a paralysis of intellect and a "political immobility," and that both historical study and political thought would descend into a crippling nominalism that would destroy the possibilities for coherent understanding or effective action.[25] Perhaps it had been that fear that led Hofstadter and others to fit their ideas of complexity into the restrictive terms of the "status-interest" model, to replace the simplistic determinism of the progressive historians with a similarly rigid, if less one-dimensional, framework of their own. For Hofstadter had identified a dilemma fundamental to historical studies, one that remains—and will perhaps forever remain—unresolved. Is it possible for scholars to take into account the enormous range of factors that affect human motivation and historical causation and still bring anything like coherence to their picture of the past?

A "total history" of human experience will, clearly, remain forever beyond the grasp of scholars. But thanks in large part to Hofstadter's work—in *The Age of Reform* and elsewhere—it seems unlikely, as he once feared, that "the very idea of complexity will come under fire once again," or that historians will soon argue "that most things in life and in history are not complex but really quite simple." The repudiation by historians of many of the central ideas of Hofstadter's portrait of populism and progressivism is, therefore, to a large degree a measure of his success. For it is the inadequacy of the "status-interest" model's allowance for complexity, not the complexity itself, that has proved its most crippling feature.[26]

Hofstadter's analyses of populism and progressivism, controversial as they were, moved immediately to the center of scholarly debate and framed the discussion of both phenomena for decades. His brief analysis of the New Deal met resistance from the beginning and has had relatively little impact on subsequent interpretations. And yet while the central sections of *The Age of Reform* now seem less persuasive than they once did, the interpretation of the New Deal seems in certain ways more compelling than its earlier critics were willing to admit.

Populism and progressivism had, Hofstadter argued, been part of a long continuum of reform. The New Deal was a sharp break with that continuum, largely unaffected (and hence largely unmarred) by the backward-looking moralism of its predecessors, committed instead to the solution of immediate, debilitating economic problems. No grand strategies or philosophical visions there; Roosevelt and his circle were engaged in a "chaos of experimentation."[27]

Although the New Dealers paid lip service to old progressive verities, in practice they "bypassed, sidestepped" the old progressive issues. The

New Deal made no effort to combat the political machines; instead, Roosevelt attempted to conciliate and forge alliances with them. The New Deal "never developed a clear or consistent line on business consolidation"; the issue of monopoly became secondary to a "restless groping for a means to bring recovery." By the late 1930s the New Deal, without ever expressing (or even recognizing) how sharply it was breaking with the reform past, had revolutionized American liberalism. It had stripped it of its old nostalgic moralism and had added to it "a social-democratic tinge that had never before been present in American reform movements." In the future liberals would be less concerned with "entrepreneurial" reform and would be committed instead to social legislation: "social security, unemployment insurance, wages and hours, and housing." The New Deal, Hofstadter wrote, "represented the triumph of economic emergency and human needs over inherited notions and inhibitions."[28]

There are many problems with this portrait, as critics were quick to point out almost as soon as the book appeared. Hofstadter clearly underestimated the degree to which progressive ideology had influenced New Deal policymakers—in part, perhaps, because his own view of progressive ideology had been so narrow and incomplete.[29] At the same time, however, he had touched on something important when he claimed that liberal ideology emerged from the 1930s fundamentally transformed. That it did so was not, perhaps, because the New Dealers themselves had openly repudiated the grip of the past in favor of pragmatic experimentation; it was because, in the course of more than a decade of political and ideological pulling and tugging, new ideas had slowly and haltingly emerged in response to the failure of old ones to deal with pressing realities. The antimonopoly impulse had ceased to play more than an occasional rhetorical role in reform ideology; the planning ideal had shifted its focus away from the structure of capitalism and toward Keynesian and social welfare goals. The language of liberalism, and the substantive direction of liberalism, had changed.[30] Hofstadter's explanation of how and why was cursory and inadequate; but his identification of that change—and his challenge to the then prevailing view of a long, continuous stream of reform culminating in the New Deal and validating postwar liberal goals[31]—was an important and generally unappreciated accomplishment.

Critics of modern historiography have spent large and perhaps inordinate amounts of time and energy arguing over whether Hofstadter was truly a member of the "consensus school" that came to dominate historical writing in the 1950s. The answer, of course, depends on how that school is defined.[32] Hofstadter certainly shared, and indeed was among the first to state, the "consensus" assumption that economic conflict was not the dominant factor in American history, that beneath the disputes and controversies of the past (and, presumably, the present) lay a "common climate of American opinion," a "general framework" of shared ideas resting on "a belief in the rights of property, the philosophy of economic individualism, the value of competition," and a general acceptance of industrial capitalism.[33] Conflicts that seemed profound on the surface, among them the reform battles of the populists and progressives, had taken place within a relatively narrow ideological framework. Hence most critics of the American political and economic structure could not (or would not) envision a genuinely radical alternative to it; and they vented their frustrations, therefore, not through attacks on bourgeois capitalism but through attachment to "symbols" and "projective rationalizations."

At times in his work (although only passingly in *The Age of Reform*) Hofstadter attempted to qualify his attachment to these consensus assumptions. He pointed to those parts of the American past (the Revolution, the Civil War, moments of racial and religious conflict) that could not be adequately explained in this way; and he conceded that "it is a valid comment on the limits of consensus history to insist that in one form or another conflict finally does remain, and ought to remain, somewhere near the center of our focus of attention."[34] Yet Hofstadter's purpose in most of his own work, and certainly in *The Age of Reform*, was not to place conflict "near the center of our focus of attention." It was precisely the opposite: to refute "the almost obsessive concern with conflict as the central theme of historical writing" that his generation of scholars had inherited from their progressive forebears.[35] Hofstadter was too sensitive and subtle a historian not to recognize the limitations of the approach. But in at least one sense he stands firmly within, indeed very near the center of, the consensus school.

Hofstadter did not, however, always share, and at times strenuously opposed, another distinguishing assumption of many consensus scholars: that this "common climate of opinion," this lack of fundamental conflict, was a good and necessary thing that accounted for America's stability, freedom, and progress. This celebratory use of consensus is most commonly identified with the work of Daniel Boorstin,[36] but a similar (if usually more muted) tone can be found in the work of innumerable scholars of the 1950s and 1960s. Only rarely, however, can it be found in the work of Hofstadter. It may be too much to say, as Arthur Schlesinger, Jr. did in a 1969 essay, that Hofstadter viewed consensus from a "radical perspective . . . and deplored it." But it is certainly true that he viewed it "from the outside," with considerable skepticism, and with occasional alarm.[37] He was not, of course, in any basic sense a critic of American capitalism or American democracy; he was fundamentally unsympathetic to the alternatives. He did, however, recognize that the narrow range of acceptable opinion in American politics, and the centrality within that range of the acquisitive values of competitive capitalism, exacted a significant price—both from the nation's public discourse and from the private lives of its people. The pragmatic opportunism that had played so central a role in shaping American institutions and American values had certain attractions, but it had failed, he believed, to provide a philosophically consistent or morally compelling basis for democratic politics.[38] A society whose greatest political triumph was the New Deal—that stumbling, chaotic exercise in political and economic self-preservation, unconnected to any coherent philosophy or moral vision—was not a society in which a sensitive humanist could take unambiguous pride.

Hofstadter was, in the end, a man caught between two competing, and perhaps incompatible, visions of society. As a scholar committed to the intellectual life and to the tolerant, cosmopolitan values he believed that life represented, he mistrusted the politics of unrestrained popular will and admired the conservative, pluralistic character of American life for providing protections against the far less attractive, far more menacing alternatives. Yet as a twentieth-century man sensitive to the unfulfilled yearnings of many of his world's and his nation's people, he could not help wishing, even if without real hope or definition, for something more. Perhaps that was why, in looking back upon America's past and ahead to its future in one of his last published essays, he could summon up finally only grudging praise and tempered optimism:

> When one considers American history as a whole, it is hard to think of any very long period in which it could be said that the country has been consistently well governed. And yet its political system is, on the whole, a resilient and well-seasoned one, and on the strength of its history one must assume that it can summon enough talent and good

will to cope with its afflictions. To cope with them—but not, I think, to master them in any thoroughly decisive or admirable fashion. The nation seems to slouch onward into its uncertain future like some huge inarticulate beast, too much attainted by wounds and ailments to be robust, but too strong and resourceful to succumb.[39]

9

Robert Penn Warren, T. Harry Williams, and Huey Long

There may be no southern political figure of the first half of the twentieth century whose name is more immediately and widely recognizable outside the South than Huey Long. Memories of him are strongest, and his legacy most obvious, in Louisiana. But more than a century after his birth, more than sixty years after his death, he remains firmly lodged in the larger American imagination as well.

There are many reasons for Long's enduring visibility—his flamboyant personality, his brazen use of political power, his dramatic ascent, his violent death. But among the most important reasons are the two most influential books ever written about him: Robert Penn Warren's novel, *All the King's Men*, first published in 1946, and T. Harry Williams's much celebrated (and much criticized) biography, *Huey Long*, published in 1969. Both books have much to say about Huey Long himself. But they have even more to say about the way Long has been transformed from a political leader of admittedly unusual qualities to a powerful symbol of both the hopes and the fears many Americans entertain when they think about popular democracy. They are, therefore, not just portraits of Long but sources of his literary and historical image.

More than anything else, that image is a product of *All the King's Men*, perhaps the greatest political novel in American literature. Warren always claimed that the connection between Huey Long and the Willie Stark of his novel was indirect; and he also said (along with most critics) that the real center of the novel is not Stark in any case, but Jack Burden, the narrator. But while *All the King's Men* can stand on its own as a novel without connection to Huey Long, the converse is not true, except perhaps in Louisiana. For almost fifty years, the popular image of Long has been in many ways inseparable from Warren's portrayal of Stark.

As a young man in the 1920s and early 1930s, Robert Penn Warren lived off and on in Tennessee—on a farm near Nashville—where he became part of the circle of Fugitive or, later, Agrarian poets who clustered around Vanderbilt University. In 1930 they published their famous manifesto, *I'll Take My Stand*, a defense of what they considered the organic society of the agrarian South. It was, they believed, a humane alternative to the dehumanizing industrial society of the North. Warren's essay in that volume, "The Briar Patch," contained a tortured and ultimately unsuccessful effort to deal with the South's racial dilemma, an effort that later embarrassed him because of its implicit defense of segregation. But it also contained an early, if somewhat cloudy, statement of political concerns that would shape Warren's work for much of the rest of his life.[1] Some years later, looking back on the essay, Warren expressed those concerns explicitly. He wrote of "the sense of the disintegration of the notion of the individual in that society we're living in—it's a common notion, we all know—and the relation of that to democracy. It's the machine of power in this so-called democratic state; the machines disintegrate individuals, so you have no individual sense of responsibility and no awareness that the individual has a past and a place. He's simply the voting machine."[2]

It was with these ideas in mind—his concern about the "disintegration" of the individual, about the loss of the sense of "past" and "place," about the fear of the "machine of power"—that Warren set out in the fall of 1934 to drive from Tennessee to Baton Rouge, to begin an assistant professorship in the English Department at Louisiana State University, widely known at the time as Huey Long's university. As he drove through northern Louisiana, he picked up a hitchhiker—"a country man," he later described him, "the kind you call a red-neck or a wool-hat, aging, aimless, nondescript, beat up by life and hard times and bad luck . . . standing beside the road in an attitude that spoke of infinite patience and considerable fortitude." And it was from this "nameless old hitchhiker" that Warren heard the first of the many stories about Huey Long that would mark his years in Louisiana.[3]

It was a fairly typical story. Long had been standing on a riverbank with the president of a company that owned a toll bridge. Long offered to buy the bridge, so the state could operate it without tolls, and the owner laughed at the offer. But, Warren's hitchhiker told him, "Huey didn' do nothing but lean over and pick him up a chunk of rock and throwed it off a-ways, and asked did that president-feller see whar the rock hit. The feller said yeah, he seen. Wal, Huey said, the next thing you see is gonna be a big new free bridge right whar that rock hit, and you, you son-of-a-bitch, are goen bankrup a-ready and doan even know it."[4]

That story may or may not have been true. There were thousands like it that hovered similarly somewhere between history and myth. But to Warren, the world of myth—what he called the "world of 'Huey'"—was as important as the world of reality, the world of history. Warren saw the real Huey Long only once, from a distance at a luncheon in Baton Rouge to which he had not been invited. He knew almost nothing about him, he later claimed, "except gossip and the local newspaper." He never did "one minute's research" on Long. "What I knew," he said, "was the 'Huey' of the myth." And what he cared about was less Long himself than the effect such a leader had on others.[5]

The Huey of myth, the Huey that his nameless hitchhiker thought he knew, became the basis for a character named Willie Talos in Warren's unpublished play, "Proud Flesh," written in Italy in the late 1930s. ("The thud of boot heels of parading Black Shirts on the cobblestones of Rome seemed to give appropriate sound effects," he later wrote.)[6] A decade later, the play had evolved into the novel *All the King's Men*, and Willie Talos had become Willie Stark. Many readers and most scholars have found unpersuasive Warren's claim that Stark was not modeled on Long.[7] Warren himself has conceded that "if I had never gone to Louisiana and if Huey Long had not existed, the novel would never have been written."[8] Whatever Warren's intentions, *All the King's Men* (the novel and, later, the film based on it) became for many Americans their first, most powerful, and most lasting image of Huey Long.

How did *All the King's Men* affect the way historians and others viewed (and wrote about) Huey Long? Before *All the King's Men*, the prevailing view of Long was that he was an exaggerated version of the traditional southern demagogue—more powerful, more cynical, perhaps more corrupt than others, but not radically outside the much-remarked-upon Southern populist-insurgent tradition. W. J. Cash, for example, wrote of Long in *The Mind of the South* (published in 1941), that "he belonged essentially to the traditional pattern of the Southern demagogue. . . . He was full of the swaggering, hell-for-leather bluster that the South demanded in its heroes and champions; and in addition he had a kind of quizzical, broad, clowning humor, and a capacity for taking on the common touch, that had characteristically been the stock-in-trade not only of the more successful demagogues but even of many of the best of the older leaders." Long was, Cash conceded, "an amazing fellow," who not only exemplified "the traditional pattern" but "carried it forward another great step . . . and greatly modified it in many respects."[9] Unlike most other demagogues of his era, he actually delivered on at least some of his promises. But he was, in the end, part of a familiar breed.

After *All the King's Men*, the emphasis shifted. In the 1950s (and beyond) a strong inclination emerged to view Huey Long as something much greater and much more ominous, as someone largely outside tradition, outside the mainstream, as a kind of primeval force tapping into the darkness in the southern soul, or the American soul, or even—as the novel suggests—the human soul. Long was an incipient fascist. He was a menacing "mass leader," sucking weak, identityless men and women into a "mass movement" in which they surrendered their individuality to a larger cause. He was a symbol of the menacing underside of democracy.[10]

By the time Warren published *All the King's Men* in 1946, he had written at least sixteen drafts of the play ("Proud Flesh") and five more of the novel itself.[11] Over the course of his revisions the political concerns that apparently motivated him to begin the novel broadened to include a set of larger, more existential questions, expressed largely through the character of Jack Burden. But the political message remained, although perhaps never again as clearly stated as in the first fragment of the first draft of the play.

That draft contained a chorus, modeled (somewhat clumsily) on those in Greek tragedies. They represented the "people" of the state Willie Talos (later Willie Stark) had come to control. And in their opening lines, the people contemplate the bond that has been forged between them and their leader:

> Whose hand flings the white road before us?
> What hand over the hills and swampland

Over the damp lands and highlands,
Gully and Bayou? and flings us,
Hard as the lead from the gun-mouth
Hard as the words from his own mouth,
Us nameless—and yet he has named us—
And aimless and yet he has aimed us
And flung us, and flings us, a handful
Of knives hurled, edged errand—O, errand
Blind with the glittering blindness of light![12]

"Nameless" men and women "named" by their leader; "aimless" lives "aimed" by a personality stronger than themselves; empty existences receiving meaning from a hard, strong man, flung forward as "knives hurled, edged errand"; men and women dazzled, "blind with the glittering blindness of light": with these words, Warren suggested what he considered the essence of the phenomenon of Huey Long. In the process, he linked his novel to a burgeoning scholarly literature of the 1940s and 1950s—inspired by the experience of World War II and by the effort to explain European fascism and, later, Soviet communism—warning of the dangers of "mass politics," "mass culture," and "mass man." How much of that literature Warren had read is difficult to determine; some of the most important works appeared after his novel did, in any case. But he certainly echoed its concerns.[13]

This fear of the "mass"—a fear strikingly different from the romanticization of the "people" that had characterized so much of American intellectual life in the 1930s—reflected Warren's belief, and the belief of many other postwar intellectuals, that the twentieth-century world was fundamentally different from those that had preceded it. Individuals, and society as a whole, had rejected their pasts in search of a beckoning, elusive new freedom. They were liberating themselves from the socially imposed repression of Victorian morality. They were becoming free men and women.

But the liberation was not without cost. In rejecting the past—in severing themselves from their traditional moorings in family, community, and church; in spurning the inherited codes of behavior and morality that had once ordered human relations—twentieth-century men and women had assumed a terrible burden. What was to root individual lives once those lives were severed from their pasts? How were men and women to find secure identities in a world in which they had rejected traditional sources of identity? What was to order and stabilize politics once voters and politicians alike were unconstrained by inherited social norms? The search for answers to those questions, Warren believed, was the characteristic intellectual quest of the modern era. It could produce ideas of great profundity and wisdom. But it could also produce simple and dangerous ideologies to which the uprooted individuals of the late twentieth century were particularly vulnerable.

Warren's sense of both the opportunities and the risks of the modern era is the key to his view of Huey Long. Breaking with the past, he recognized, can be a form of liberation—an escape from repression and from the dead hand of tradition. But it can also create an empty, alienated life with no moral center, the kind of life Jack Burden leads through much of *All the King's Men*, a life that leaves Jack unable to believe in anything more than what he calls the "Great Twitch." And liberation can create a man like Willie Stark, who—once released from the moorings of the past—becomes a wholly cynical, amoral person with no moral compass, no guide to what he can and cannot do; an elemental man who seems to operate only on the basis of primal impulses. Perhaps most ominously, in Warren's view, liberation can create a new kind of politics unrestrained by any inhibitions, tapping into the frightening power of the masses.[14]

Warren's dark picture of Willie Stark (and, by implication, of Huey Long) is a reflection of the deep misgivings that he and many other modern intellectuals have felt about a world in which individuals have become free agents. Once detached from traditional moorings, once robbed of old certainties, once stripped of inhibitions, individuals have far fewer defenses against manipulation by demagogues and mass leaders. They can become frenzied and animal-like. They can become a faceless mob capable of almost anything—capable of a purge, a class war, a holocaust. Like Hitler, like Mussolini, like Stalin, Huey Long had forged a political movement out of the fragmented selves of identityless men and women—people whose world had been shattered by the alienating forces of modern industrialism and who, in their weakness, sought strength from a leader who permitted them to lose themselves in him.

Warren's concern about the manipulation of the masses is evident in the image of the crowd, the exhilarating, frightening mass gatherings from which Willie Stark derives his power, an image that is never far from the center of *All the King's Men:* Stark standing, drenched with sweat, his forelock hanging damply down his forehead. "Then he suddenly stretched his arms above his head," Warren describes him at one point, "the coat sleeves drawn tight to expose the shirt sleeves, the hands spread and clutching. . . .

> And the crowd roared.
> He brought both hands slowly down, for silence.
> Then said, "Your will is my strength."
> And after a moment of silence said, "Your need is my justice."[15]

Jack Burden, the narrator, who is himself at times drawn to Stark as an antidote for his own fragility and sense of emptiness, speaks of the effect of the "boss" on the masses who listen to him: "There is nothing like the roar of a crowd when it swells up, all of a sudden at the same time, out of the thing which is in every man in the crowd but is not himself."[16] The people in the crowd are themselves, he suggests, but not themselves. They are individuals, but they are surrendering their individuality, their responsibilities as citizens of a democracy, to a larger force they cannot truly know and can never hope to control. As Warren himself explained it: "The strongman should be seen through the weaknesses of others, or the needs of others, rather than taken as an abstract power represented directly."[17] The idea of the story, he wrote, "was that the dictator, the man of power, is powerful only because he fulfills the blanknesses and needs of people around him. His power is an index to the weaknesses of others . . . the defects of others."[18]

Reflecting on his career in later years, in a series of lectures published in 1975 as *Democracy and Poetry*, Warren spoke again of this concern, which had shaped his thinking about politics throughout his long life: ". . . the tragic ambiguity of the fact that the spirit of the nation we had promised to create has often been the victim of our astonishing objective success, and that, in our success, we have put at pawn the very essence of the nation we had promised to create—that essence being the concept of the free man, the responsible self."[19]

To Robert Penn Warren, and through him to many others, Huey Long came to represent one of the great defects of democracy: the opportunity it provided for unprincipled, ambitious leaders to exploit the weaknesses and the fears of their constituents, to use democratic means for undemocratic ends. In supporting Willie Stark blindly and irrationally, the people were abdicating their responsibilities as members of a democratic society. And in exploiting them as he did, Stark (or

Long) was shirking his own responsibility to communicate with those he presumes to lead. That responsibility, Warren believed, was to learn from as well as to lead them, to respect the ethical norms society has established for those who exercise power within it.[20]

Warren left a large and well-preserved record of his political ideas and of the philosophical concerns that underlay them. T. Harry Williams did not. We do not know very much about why Williams decided to write a biography of Huey Long (other than his claim that he saw it as a vehicle for using the then relatively new technique of oral history). Nor do we know much about what political preconceptions he brought to the project (other than his statement, in the preface, that he believed "that some men, men of power, can influence the course of history"—a statement that no one but the most committed structuralist would likely challenge).[21] And for all the attention and acclaim his biography received, Williams himself never became anything like the object of interest to scholars and intellectuals that Warren was and remains.

Williams was born in 1909. He was of the same generation as Robert Penn Warren, who was born in 1905. But he was a native of Illinois, grew up in the Midwest, and kept a summer home in Wisconsin until he died. He moved to Louisiana to teach at LSU in 1941, after having done his graduate work at the University of Wisconsin; and his view of the South was almost certainly colored by the midwestern progressivism he absorbed in Madison. He never had the same identification with or attachment to the traditional, agrarian society of the South that characterized Warren's early intellectual development. On the contrary, he considered himself a modern man, a man of the twentieth-century North, and throughout his scholarly career he found himself much more drawn than Warren was to "modern" or "pragmatic" men, unencumbered by conservative or aristocratic baggage. He admired Ulysses S. Grant, for example, precisely because he believed Grant was not part of the military establishment (as Lee had been); precisely because he was, as he once wrote, "unhampered by traditional military doctrine." As one critic of Williams has written, "The ornate world of the gentlemen of the Southern past was not a comfortable place for Williams the historian."[22]

Native Louisianans of education and attainment, schooled through much of their lives on stories of the horrors Long visited upon their state, were, for the most part, implacably hostile to the man. But Williams, an outsider with a skeptical view of the southern establishment, was much more inclined to view Long sympathetically and to see in his style of leadership a potential vehicle for shattering the antiquated political norms that still dominated the South in the 1950s, when he began writing his book. It may also be reasonable to suppose that a historian writing in the 1950s and 1960s about a popular leader attacking a reactionary southern oligarchy was influenced in some way by the civil rights movement, an assumption that Williams's rather-too-forgiving picture of Long's record on race relations would seem to support. But this is speculation. In the end, the best clues we have to what Williams intended are within the book itself.

Williams's biography remains the fullest and most exhaustively researched study of Huey Long. No one will ever again have access to the many associates and acquaintances of Long whom Williams interviewed; and since Long left no personal papers of any consequence, it is clear that in that sense at least this is a project that can never be replicated or entirely replaced. But what really distinguishes Williams's *Huey Long* from the numerous other biographies that have appeared both before and since 1969 is its evaluation of Long himself. Williams was a frank, unashamed revisionist who set out to rehabilitate Long's historical reputation. The Huey Long he portrayed was not without flaws, certainly. Williams conceded that he "came to grasp for too much power, to look on power as something to be gained for the sheer pleasure of its use."[23] But Williams's Long was an authentically populist-progressive politician, who shattered an archaic political structure and replaced it with one that, at last, delivered real services to the people who needed them most. Long created an infrastructure in Louisiana that allowed it to emerge from its status as an underdeveloped region and begin to join the modern world. He turned the gaze of white Louisianans away from the "romantic" politics that had enchanted them for generations (the politics of race and white supremacy and the Lost Cause, a politics, Williams argues, that was irrelevant to their real needs). Instead, he introduced a new politics of "economic realism" to Louisiana, one that permitted leaders and voters to discuss issues that were the proper focus of public discourse.[24] Williams was unwilling to call his biography a "pro-Long" book, but few of his readers—and even fewer scholars of Louisiana history—have been so reticent. In its emphasis on Long's achievements and in its tolerance for (and even at times celebration of) Long's unorthodox methods, it is the most sympathetic portrait of Long's career to have been published since Long's own autobiography appeared in 1933.

But while Williams clearly did not view Huey Long with the same sense of danger and menace with which Warren viewed him, his book has much in common with *All the King's Men* nonetheless. That is clear not simply in his statement, in the preface, that he agreed with the thesis of Warren's novel as he (rather incompletely) understood it: "that the politician who wishes to do good may have to do some evil to achieve his goal."[25] The more important similarity is the way in which Williams, like Warren, used the concept of "mass politics" to explain Long's political impact.

Williams was not, if the citations in his biography are any indication, particularly well-versed in the scholarship on "mass politics" and "mass man." He relied primarily on what now seems the somewhat crude work of Eric Hoffer and his 1951 book, *The True Believer* (although he also made use from time to time of the work of Jacques Maritain's *Man and the State*, published the same year).[26] But Williams took from what he read a conception of mass politics in many ways similar to Warren's. "A term that does classify leaders of Huey's type," he wrote, "has been suggested by Eric Hoffer—the mass leader. The mass leader is a man who sets a popular movement in motion. 'He articulates and justifies the resentment dammed up in the souls of the frustrated. He kindles the vision of a breathtaking future.' He does not hesitate to 'harness man's hungers and fears to weld a following and make it zealous unto death in the service of a holy cause.'" Among the qualities a mass leader must have, Williams claims (again citing Hoffer), is "a recognition that the innermost craving of a following is for 'communion' or a sense of collectivity,"[27] an idea very similar to Warren's notion that in a mass society individuals crave, above all, a sense of connection, of belonging, and that they find it at times by subordinating themselves to a person or movement they consider larger than themselves.

Williams differed with Warren, however, on one important point. Mass leaders are capable of great evil, he concedes, as Hitler, Mussolini, and Stalin make clear. But there can also be "good" mass leaders—leaders who "will harness man's hungers and fears to a cause" without trying "to use the frustration of man to build a brave new world." Huey Long, he clearly believed, was a "good mass leader" who used his power within the democratic process to accomplish things of benefit to the people. He was a "prophet leader" (to use Jacques Maritain's words), "whose main mission is 'to *awaken* the people, to awaken them to something better than everyone's daily business, to the sense of a supra-individual task to be performed'."[28]

There are, then, important differences between Warren and Williams on this point. Warren, writing in the 1930s and 1940s, in a time when mass movements seemed menacing and ominous, saw in Long the dark and dangerous aspects of popular politics. Williams, writing in the 1960s, when scholars (and many others) were arguing for the democratic potential of mass movements, saw in Long the progressive and transformative aspects of popular politics. But the similarities are at least as important. Both accepted the model of "mass politics" that the social scientists and philosophers of the postwar era had constructed, and both tried to squeeze Long (in Warren's case a fictional Long, in Williams's a historical one) into that model. Both suggested that Long created a special bond between himself and his followers, that he drew them into a kind of "communion" with a leader and a movement larger than themselves, that he provided them with an identity in a world in which they felt lost and powerless.

All the King's Men is one of the great works of American literature. Williams's *Huey Long* does not have the same classic stature, to be sure, but it is in its own way a great book—a big, powerful, magisterial biography built on what was at the time an extraordinarily innovative kind of research. It is not surprising that these two remarkable books have shaped so much of the popular and scholarly image of Huey Long.

But Warren and Williams were wrong in one of their central claims. Both tried, each in his own way, to push Long into a theoretical model into which he does not fit. Long was not a mass leader in the sense both of them used the concept. There is no evidence that he forged the kind of bond with his followers that both these books suggest, no evidence that the men and women who supported Long—in Louisiana and in the nation—were restless, anomic individuals searching for identity in an alienating world, yearning for "communion" or "collectivity." There may have been some such people among Long's followers, but if so they were probably the exception, not the rule. Long attracted support not by creating a mystical, charismatic bond with lost souls, but by promising—and in Louisiana at least sometimes delivering—solutions to real social and economic grievances. In the absence of evidence to the contrary, it is reasonable to assume that Long's followers had not surrendered their individuality to him or his movement but were, rather, acting rationally as they pursued their economic and political goals; and that they were quite capable of conditioning or even abandoning their support for Long when more attractive alternatives presented themselves (as, outside Lousiana at least, many did once Franklin Roosevelt became president).[29]

None of this, however, suggests that either Long or his supporters were acting wisely or responsibly in any way we would recognize as consistent with the proper character of a democratic society. An effective democracy requires more from its citizens and its leaders than pragmatic calculations of immediate self-interest. It requires reflection—a willingness to examine the world and one's place in it, an openness to knowledge of oneself and one's society, a capacity to evaluate the claims of leaders critically and to balance them against a moral compass of one's own. Here is where Warren, in particular, offers something more important than an accurate portrait of Huey Long and his followers (something he never claimed to do in any case). For Warren used the image of Long (what he calls the "myth of 'Huey'") not just to decry one form of politics but also to suggest the value of another. And in that, he has more to say to those who consider the problems of our own time than Huey Long, however we may judge him, could ever say.

We live in a world in which the gulf separating individuals from the institutions and processes that govern their lives grows ever larger, and in which the entrenched moral and social norms that once shaped, and constrained, the public world have lost much of their power to persuade. One response to such a world is simply to withdraw from it, to retreat into a private universe one can at least pretend to control. Another response is to place faith in leaders who promise simple solutions to complex problems, men like Willie Stark or Huey Long. Both responses, Warren suggests, represent abdications of the responsibilities that come with being part of a democratic community. They represent, in particular, an abdication of the responsibility to seek knowledge. Without knowledge, Warren believes, we have no contact with our past, with our community, and with ourselves. Without knowledge, we become a Jack Burden, moving through the world without really living in it. Or a Willie Stark or a Huey Long: cynical, amoral, with no moral compass, no guide to what one can and cannot do, so lost in the world—so much a creature of empty political ambitions—that there is no longer any difference between a friend and a sycophant, or between a hotel room and a home.

All the King's Men, for all the evil and sadness and emptiness it describes, ends on a note of affirmation—as Jack Burden begins to come to grips with the truth about his own life and begins to find a way to forge a connection with the world. But it is a cautious affirmation, because the world he reenters remains a frightening and dangerous place whatever he may do, just as our own world can never become the safe, secure, homogeneous place we sometimes like to imagine. To live successfully in the world as it is, Warren suggests, we must cultivate knowledge, of ourselves and of it. But we pay a price for that knowledge, and that price is a constant awareness of how much we do not know and cannot know, and a fear of the dark places that lie waiting for us in the world and in ourselves.

That is what makes Warren's fictional portrait of Huey Long—for all its historical flaws—more meaningful to us than T. Harry Williams's rosier portrait: it draws a powerful picture of the cost to individuals and societies of abandoning the quest for understanding, the cost of ceding responsibility to a glib and powerful leader who promises simple answers to all problems. That is what Warren seems to be saying in one of his first passages, in which Jack Burden describes returning home late at night to find a telegram waiting for him and trying to decide whether or not to open it. He fears it contains something terrible, something he doesn't want to know. But he knows, too, that he must know:

> . . . the clammy, sad little foetus which is you way down in the dark which is you too lifts up its sad little face and its eyes are blind, and it shivers inside you for it doesn't want to know what is in that envelope. It wants to lie in the dark and not know, and be warm in its not-knowing. The end of man is knowledge, but there is one thing he can't know. He can't know whether knowledge will save him or kill him. There's the cold in your stomach, but you open the envelope, you have to open the envelope, for the end of man is to know.[30]

10

Icons of the American Establishment

Americans have always been aware, and often suspicious, of the elites among them. But the idea that there is an American "establishment"—a term and a concept both different from and more precise than the somewhat diffuse image of elites that has prevailed through most of our history—is relatively new. As late as 1960 the idea that there was such a thing as an organized "establishment" in the United States had barely occurred to most Americans. The essayist Henry Fairlie had introduced the concept to England in 1955, in a celebrated essay in the London *Spectator* about Britain's ruling elite. But almost no one made a similar case for the existence of an American establishment until Richard Rovere published a half-joking article about it in the *American Scholar* in 1961. By the mid-1960s, however, the idea had found a broad audience; and it has survived ever since as a staple of public discourse and in particular as a description—embraced by both scholars and the larger public—of the small circle of men and women who have framed American foreign policy during at least the first two decades after World War II.[1]

The idea that there was an establishment and that it exercised hidden power was an article of faith in the late 1960s and 1970s to revisionist historians (and to the New Left more generally), who blamed the establishment for locking the United States into a rigidly anticommunist paradigm that culminated in Vietnam; and to the far right, which saw the establishment as an elite conspiracy to destroy freedom. The same idea, turned on its head, has appealed more recently to some "post-revisionists," who credit the establishment with the creation of a stable and intelligent postwar foreign policy that, on the whole, served the nation well from the beginning of the cold war to very near its end. They lament the passing of authority in international relations to a new, more politicized generation of policymakers, who lack the establishment's ability to insulate foreign policy from the vagaries of public opinion.

Most definitions of the establishment rest on two interlocking sets of characteristics: one social and one ideological. Socially, the establishment was characterized by the privilege and self-conscious elitism of its members. Not all were born to wealth and influence, but those who were not usually attained both at a relatively early age. They had the help of connections made at prestigious prep schools (especially Andover and Groton), Ivy League colleges (pre-eminently Yale), and important law schools (above all Harvard). Much of the social cohesion that lay at the heart of the idea of the establishment was, therefore, a result of shared educational experiences and old-school ties. It was a result, too, of Wall Street, where almost everyone identified with the establishment worked for at least some time, either in a law firm or an investment bank; and of New York City, which provided a network of institutions—the Century Association, the Council on Foreign Relations, and others—that helped preserve the sense of community forged first in college clubs and law school seminars.

The ideological affinity that made the establishment an effective force in public policy was in many ways a reflection of these social characteristics. Establishment figures were almost always successful men (and on rare occasions women) who had inherited, or acquired, a sense of entitlement mixed with civic responsibility that in another time or place might be called *noblesse oblige*. Although they were usually Republicans, they were rarely very partisan ones; and, indeed, they looked with some misgivings upon electoral politics and elected politicians. (Relatively few establishment figures ever ran for public office, and even fewer succeeded.) A sound foreign policy, they believed, must be insulated from politics and guided by disinterested people capable of distinguishing the national interest from individual or partisan interests—people schooled in the ethic of public service that permeated the elite educational institutions and the social and familial circles in which most members of the establishment moved. It was therefore the duty of such people to serve the nation when called. Most of all, the establishment's foreign policy rested on the assumption of America's right and obligation to play a leading role in world affairs and on an almost unquestioned faith in the moral and practical wisdom of the nation's values and its capitalist institutions. When Winston Churchill described the Marshall Plan as "the most unsordid act in history," he was, perhaps unintentionally, expressing the essence of the establishment's sense of its goals: that there was a seamless connection between American national interest and the interests of the world.

Establishment figures were determinedly centrist. They deplored the chauvinism of the most militant internationalists as much as they detested isolationism. They also displayed a limited ability to understand social or political systems markedly different from their own. Establishment foreign policy, therefore, was always more successful in dealing with Britain and western Europe (and even, strangely enough, with the entrenched political leaderships of the Soviet Union and later China—who shared the West's own deep faith in existing institutions and in the importance of preserving them) than with the more volatile nations of what is now called the Third World. Establishment figures were skilled at doing business with "gentlemen" (or people who could act like them), but often maladroit in dealing with less polished leaders. They prized stability and identified all but the most modest challenges to the status quo as "radicalism," and hence a danger.

In reality, of course, the establishment was never the coherent entity that its critics (and some of its defenders) claimed. Nor did its members have as much control over American foreign policy as popular myth suggests. Even when establishment figures dominated the policymaking apparatus, they had to contend with presidents, members of Congress, and competing bureaucracies with interests often very different from their own. And yet it is hard to look at the workings of postwar American diplomacy and not be struck by the intimacy, at times bordering on incestuousness, that characterized its leadership for many years. Occasionally the connections were literally ones of blood or kinship (the Bundys, the Dulleses). More often, they were ties of friendship and mentorship. And to a striking extent, the postwar foreign policy elite was bound together by the careers of two men: Henry Stimson and John J. McCloy.

Henry Stimson

For a generation of foreign policy figures, Henry Stimson was both mentor and inspiration. Twice secretary of war, once secretary of state, a longtime Wall Street lawyer, a pillar of the elite social world of New York, he embodied the establishment ideal. He was unwavering in his belief in his own rectitude and firmly wedded to the values and assumptions of his social class. Through most of his long career he associated with few people who were not of his world. At least equally important, Stimson embraced early, and almost never questioned, the vision of the United States as a great world power that had come to enchant so many members of his generation at the turn of the century; and he carried into mid-century the assumptions that had supported that vision—a belief in the moral superiority of the West and of America in particular; a tendency to draw distinctions between what Theodore Roosevelt had liked to call "civilized" countries (mostly the United States and Europe) and "uncivilized" countries (almost everywhere else).[2]

Stimson's towering reputation was in part a product of the offices he held and the milieu he inhabited. But it was also a result of the image of steely integrity he brought to his public life, his impatience with posturing and evasion, his firm belief that most questions had "right" answers and that the task of leadership was to find them and live by them. Few people who knew him, and even fewer who worked with him, could come away from the experience unaffected. Almost no other establishment figures succeeded in creating the aura of power and self-assurance that seemed to come almost naturally to Stimson, but virtually all of them tried to model themselves on him in some way—to ask themselves (as Stimson asked of his own mentor, Theodore Roosevelt's Secretary of War and State Elihu Root) "What would Henry Stimson have done?"

"I was born in New York City on September 21, 1867," Stimson wrote in the preface to his 1948 memoir *On Active Service in Peace and War*. "Less than nine years thereafter my young mother died . . . but the doors of my grandparents' house immediately opened and took us in to the loving care of the large family within." Stimson says almost nothing about what he calls his "hard-working father," but in fact he was all but abandoned by him as well. For all the affection he undoubtedly received in his grandparents' home, for all the cushioning he received from his family's wealth, the loss of his mother and the apparent rejection by his father must have left a deep and painful imprint on him. Perhaps that was one source of Stimson's life-long and, even by the standards of his own time, unusually intense loyalty to almost all the institutions that embraced him in his youth; they gave him a sense of acceptance and security his aloof and disapproving father seldom offered.

Throughout his long life, Stimson remained unwaveringly loyal to

Andover, which he entered at thirteen and which "opened to me a new world of democracy and of companionship with boys from all portions of the United States." His four years at Yale, he recalled, were "most important to my life, both in the character developed and in the friendships formed." Even decades later, he remained active in Yale's exclusive Skull and Bones Society (and was present in the clubhouse one night in the spring of 1947 to initiate a new class of members that included George Bush). Harvard Law School, from which he graduated in 1890, created a "revolution in my power of thinking." Later, as an attorney in New York, he developed similar life-long attachments to his law firm, Winthrop and Stimson, to the Century Association, to the St. Hubert's Club in the Adirondacks (a summer retreat for a closed circle of wealthy, aristocratic New Yorkers). He built a country home on Long Island in 1903 and lived there until he died. He filled his life with invented traditions and unvarying rituals and sought to make all areas of his existence (including, apparently, his long and successful but childless marriage) as stable, correct, and formal as possible.

Stimson developed similarly intense loyalties to several of the aristocratic heroes of his age: to Theodore Roosevelt, whose friend and neighbor he became and whose political causes he championed until they conflicted with his own ambitions; and above all to Elihu Root. Secretary of war, secretary of state, revered statesman, Root was to Stimson's generation what Stimson became to the generation that followed: an exemplar of the ideal of disinterested public service. Shortly after graduating from Harvard Law School, Stimson joined Root's law firm in New York and remained associated with it until he died. His relationship with Root—a man of stern rectitude and unwavering conviction—became one of the most important of his life, both because it immensely aided his advancement and because it provided him with a model for his own public career. Forty years after Root's death, Stimson kept a copy of Root's collected writings within reach of his desk in the War Department.

Although Stimson ultimately became one of the wealthiest and most powerful members of the New York Bar, he never much liked the practice of law (and seemed to suffer most severely from the insomnia and hypochondria that plagued him throughout his life when he was confined within the world of his profession). Unsurprisingly, therefore, he almost always leapt at opportunities to move beyond Wall Street. Theodore Roosevelt appointed him United States attorney for the southern district of New York in 1906. His success there led him into a hopeless race for governor in 1910, where his unfitness for popular politics quickly became clear. "His cultured accent," one journalist later wrote, "his uneasy platform presence, his cold personality, almost every detail of his manner betrayed his birth and breeding, gave his electorate an impression of a young aristocrat who condescends to rule. . . . The opposition press called him 'the human icicle.'" But those same qualities served him well in other settings.

In 1910 Stimson accepted an offer from William Howard Taft to become secretary of war (even though it precipitated a temporary rupture in his friendship with Theodore Roosevelt); and he spent an uneventful but dignified two years presiding over the nation's small and, for the moment, unimportant army. He served briefly as an artillery officer in World War I (at the age of 51), a crucial experience for men of his generation, who had grown up in the shadow of the heroes of the Civil War. "I have seen and felt real war now," Stimson wrote proudly at the time, "and been under more fire (little as it was) than many of the civil war 'patriots' . . . to whom we have so long looked up." He clung tenaciously to his short-lived military title and was known for the rest of his life as "Colonel Stimson."

In late middle age, Stimson had become a widely respected lawyer-statesman with an impressive record of official positions but, as yet, no particularly striking accomplishments. He was a reliable man, of undeniable intelligence and unquestioned integrity, but also, perhaps equally important, of utterly stable and predictable values. Nothing he had confronted in his career to that point, and virtually nothing that would confront him in the far more important career to come, succeeded in shaking the stolid, Victorian morality that produced his memorable denunciation of modern espionage: "Gentlemen do not read each other's mail." Nor did his remarkable experiences ever challenge the extraordinary narrowness of his social world. His circle of friends and associates remained defined by Andover, Yale, Harvard, the Century, St. Hubert's, and the Long Island aristocracy. Divorced people were never welcomed in the Stimson home. Nor, on the whole, were Jews, with such notable exceptions as Stimson's friend and protégé Felix Frankfurter. (He once recommended against donating the proceeds of a bequest to Columbia University by citing, among other things, "the tremendous Jewish influence" there.) An avid hunter and outdoorsman, and an inveterate world traveler, he made many trips to foreign lands and even into the wild and came into contact with many people very different from himself. But much like a serene British colonial official of the nineteenth century, he remained wedded to his secure, unchanging moral and social code no matter what his experiences and associations.

In 1927 Stimson undertook his first major diplomatic assignment when he led an American negotiating team to Nicaragua to mediate a dispute between warring factions in that unstable nation, which had long been, in effect, an American protectorate. His mission was superficially successful, producing a ceasefire in the civil war and free elections supervised by the United States Marines. The lesson of the agreement was a simple one, Stimson observed in his memoirs: "if a man was frank and friendly, and if he treated them as the equals they most certainly were, he could talk turkey with the politicians and other leaders of Latin America as he could with his own American colleagues. And they would not let him down." But the prerequisite for talking turkey was that the "politicians and other leaders" must embrace Stimson's own gentlemanly code. Not all did. The agreement he negotiated conspicuously excluded the rebel general Augusto Sandino, who went on to become the leader of a spirited guerrilla resistance and a revered hero to future generations of Nicaraguan revolutionaries. General Jose Moncada, the rebel leader with whom Stimson did negotiate, was a man whose "manner and bearing" he greatly admired and whom Stimson later pronounced "as good as his word." The rising politician Anastasio Somoza, graced with good manners and fluent English, impressed Stimson "more favorably than almost any other" and struck him as a "very frank, friendly, likeable young liberal." Somoza went on to become one of Latin America's most conspicuously corrupt dictators. Sandino, by contrast, was more common (and more popular) and hence, in Stimson's class-bound view, "a bandit . . . plainly unprincipled and brutal." Future generations of Nicaraguans (and Americans) would pay a high price for Stimson's preference for Somoza—a preference that almost certainly came in part from his serene faith in the good intentions of "gentlemen."

To the government in Washington, however, Stimson's Nicaragua mission was a stunning success and quickly propelled him to larger diplomatic assignments. Early in 1928 he became governor-general of the Philippines, where his subdued and tactful personal style made him immediately popular—particularly since it was such a welcome contrast to the swaggering bravado of his predecessor, General Leonard Wood, who had died suddenly the previous summer. But Stimson was no less an imperialist than Wood, no less certain of the redemptive value of American capitalism, and at least equally committed to the belief that the United States should intervene—both economically and militarily—to help other peoples find the "right path" to their own future, even if it was not the path they themselves wished to take. Stimson spent less than a year in Manila, long enough to soothe the sensitive feelings of local politicians, but not long enough to compile much of a substantive record. When he returned home in March 1929 to become secretary of state in the Hoover administration, however, he was widely praised in the American press for his "brilliant" success.

Much of Stimson's four-year tenure in the State Department was dominated by an unsuccessful effort to find an effective American response to Japanese aggression in Manchuria. A committed internationalist, Stimson was hamstrung and frustrated by the legislated neutrality of United States policy and found himself working to generate international opposition to Japanese aggresssion while he was unable to commit his own country to participate in any boycotts or sanctions that might result from his efforts. He was also alarmed by the growing instability in Europe and the increasing strength of totalitarian movements there. But he never developed as much mistrust and suspicion of the new European leaders as he did of their Japanese counterparts. He was, in fact, rather taken with Mussolini when he and Mrs. Stimson visited Italy in 1931. "He showed his attractive side," Stimson wrote after a Sunday outing in the Duce's new speedboat, "and we both liked him very much." Like most people of his class and generation, he had what a biographer has called "a hierarchical view of the world's nations and peoples," in which Asians ranked consistently below Europeans—and Africans ranked lowest of all. (When Franklin Roosevelt asked him about the prospects of a new Haitian government in 1932, he replied: "I did not think it would stay permanently put and I asked him whether he knew any self-governing Negro community which had stayed put.")

Presiding over American diplomacy in the early years of a great world crisis, Stimson displayed both the strengths and weaknesses of his approach to public life. He recognized the seriousness of the dangers, chafed at the restrictions his country's politics placed on the government's options, and spoke eloquently of the possible costs of inaction. But he showed as well a striking lack of imagination—both in envisioning the likely consequences of the policy failures over which he reluctantly presided and in judging the worth of the leaders with whom he dealt. His leisurely and opulent travels through Europe in 1931 and 1932 were, as one of his biographers uncharitably but not wholly inaccurately describes them, a "rich man's holiday," which Stimson "was somewhat complacently enjoying . . . while the world was falling apart." In Germany he was less impressed with the last of Hitler's foes than with Kurt von Schleicher, who helped pave the way to the Third Reich. In France he was drawn above all to Pierre Laval ("an able, forceful and I think a sincere man"), who was soon to become a notorious Nazi collaborator. Stimson was a skillful negotiator and a superb diplomatic insider when dealing with those he considered his social and moral equals. But only intermittently did he show a real awareness of how obsolete traditional, gentlemanly diplomacy had become as the international system was, in Ramsay MacDonald's words, "crumbling under our feet."

Had Stimson retired from public life in 1933, as he fully expected to do, he would be remembered dimly as a respected but relatively minor notable of the early twentieth century. It was his service as secretary of war during World War II that earned him his place in the pantheon of truly important American statesmen.

Stimson's appointment to the War Department in 1940 was in part a political ploy. Franklin Roosevelt believed adding leading Republicans to his cabinet would undercut his opposition in the presidential election that year (just as William Howard Taft had lured Stimson into his cabinet thirty years earlier to undercut the challenge from Theodore Roosevelt). But Stimson was attractive to Roosevelt for other reasons too. By 1940 Stimson had become an outspoken advocate of a more internationalist foreign policy—including aid to Britain—and would thus be a powerful ally in Roosevelt's battle to move the public, and the Congress, away from isolationism. And the new secretary would give weight and stature to the beleaguered War Department, demoralized by years of bitter infighting between the previous secretary, the feckless isolationist Harry Woodring, and his wildly ambitious undersecretary, Louis Johnson. Stimson cleaned house immediately. He assembled a stable of deputies drawn from his own social and professional milieu—a remarkably able group of younger men (Robert Patterson, John McCloy, Harvey Bundy, Robert Lovett, George Harrison) who would go on to form the nucleus of the postwar foreign policy elite. All were Republicans. Most had graduated from Yale (and Skull and Bones) and Harvard Law School. All but one were veterans of Wall Street. Roosevelt had, in effect, handed control of the War Department over to a tight-knit circle of wealthy Republicans. Throughout the war they consistently frustrated the efforts of liberals and others to democratize the way in which the war economy was governed.

Stimson presided magisterially over the vast bureaucracy. He involved himself directly in broad strategic decisions and a few particularly crucial issues. But he never really ran the army. That was partly because Franklin Roosevelt was himself so directly involved in policy decisions, partly because Stimson's chief of staff, General George C. Marshall, moved outside the chain of command and established direct communications with the president (something Stimson seems not to have opposed). But it was also because Stimson himself chose to leave most daily operations in the hands of trusted subordinates. In fact, Stimson spent relatively little time actually in his office. He returned home by 4:00 P.M. every day to ride or play golf. He spent long weekends on his Long Island estate and took extended vacations every summer. He combined his official travels with long, leisurely visits to exclusive resorts. Stimson's detached management style was no doubt a function of his age. (He was 72 years old when he took office in 1940 and was complaining that "I am pretty near the limit of my strength.") But it was also consistent with the professional and personal style he had honed over many decades. William Bullitt exaggerated in 1942 when he described Stimson (to his face) as a "mere housekeeper of the War Department," but there was enough truth in the stinging remark to irritate the secretary considerably.

Yet Stimson's personal achievements in the War Department were considerable nevertheless. He was one of the few, perhaps the only, official in government who could speak frankly and unfawningly with the evasive Roosevelt. ("Mr. President, I don't like you to dissemble with me," he once reportedly scolded.) In 1940 and 1941, his was one of the most influential voices prodding Roosevelt to move more decisively toward intervention at a time when American policy seemed mired in what Dean Acheson called an "agony of irresolution." Within the War Department he was intolerant of personal rivalries and political ambitions and created an atmosphere of common purpose and stern resolve. His subordinates may have done most of the work, but they did it according to rigorous standards Stimson set and maintained. He was an invaluable asset to the administration in its relations with Congress, a man whose unchallenged integrity helped insulate the administration's military policies from criticism and scrutiny. When Stimson told Senator Harry Truman that a project he was investigating in 1943 was "top secret" (it was, in fact, the Manhattan Project), Truman promptly abandoned the inquiry. "I'll take you at your word," he told the secretary, whose reputation as "a great American patriot and statesman" was assurance enough that nothing was amiss. Stimson's diplomatic skills and his long and close relationships with the ruling circles in Britain were largely responsible for winning Winston Churchill's agreement that the Normandy invasion should be placed under a single (and American) command. His withering attacks on the Morgenthau Plan for the dismantling of Germany's industrial capacity after the war helped consign that radical proposal to prompt oblivion.

Stimson's stern moral code and insular social vision made him a hard man to cross even when his policies were controversial or abhorrent. His support for the unconscionable internment of Japanese-Americans in early 1942 was crucial to the success of the policy. Stimson brushed aside arguments that imprisoning American citizens without due process was both illegal and immoral with a breezy reference to wartime urgencies and the largely un-American idea of *raison d'état.* And perhaps, too, he was receptive to the internment policy because he shared, at least passively, the assumption of the racial inferiority of Asians that had shaped the Pacific policies of his mentors Theodore Roosevelt, Elihu Root, and Leonard Wood. Whatever his reasons, Stimson's reputation for probity helped undercut the position of those within the administration who opposed the decision.

Stimson resolutely and successfully defended the army's control of military contracts against the civilian agencies created to supervise the war mobilization. And he fought effectively against all efforts to increase civilian production, even in the very last days of the war. He blithely undercut the authority of Donald Nelson, the ineffectual director of the civilian War Production Board, who complained that the War Department's goal ("complete authority over the disposition of the nation's resources") would "inevitably produce disorder, and eventually balk their own efforts by undercutting the economy in such a way that it could not meet their demands." Stimson's policies also subverted efforts to assist small businesses and limit corporate profits and helped bring antitrust prosecutions to a virtual halt during the war. He argued that he was simply protecting military production from delay and disruption. But he was doing so on the basis of an unquestioned assumption that production would proceed most efficiently and effectively if left in the hands of the great corporations whose interests he had served for years on Wall Street.

Perhaps the most important, and certainly the most controversial, event of Stimson's career was his crucial role in the development and use of atomic weapons in the last years of the war. Stimson supported and protected the Manhattan Project, ensured that it was generously funded, and pressed its leaders to complete their work speedily. Like most other policymakers aware of the enterprise, Stimson believed (incorrectly, it later turned out) that Germany was nearing completion of an atomic weapon and that the United States must make one first. When Germany surrendered in May 1945, Stimson continued to press the project forward, even though it was clear that the only potential remaining target, Japan, had no nuclear capacity. Roosevelt's death in April had placed the final decision on whether and how to use the new weapon in the hands of Harry Truman, who knew nothing of the bomb's existence until Stimson took him aside in the first moments of his presidency and told him about it. From that moment on, Truman largely deferred to Stimson's judgment. The bomb was simply another weapon, Stimson told him, and should be used to end the war. Truman adopted that position as his own and clung to it for the rest of his life.

Little in Stimson's own record supports the claims of revisionist historians that the United States bombed Japan in an effort to cow the Soviet Union into submitting to its proposals for the postwar world. After the war, in fact, Stimson actively (and unsuccessfully) opposed using America's nuclear potential as a diplomatic tool in its emerging rivalry with the Soviet Union. Instead, he urged Truman to share the new technology with the Soviets unconditionally. "The chief lesson I have learned in a long life," he wrote in an oft-quoted letter to the president, "is that the only way you can make a man trustworthy is to trust him; and the surest way to make him untrustworthy is to distrust him and show your distrust." Nor is there any real evidence to support those who have seen a tinge of racism in the decision to bomb Japan (a decision, some suggest, that would never have been made had Europe been the target). Whatever racist assumptions Stimson may tacitly have embraced, they were nowhere visible in his deliberations on this issue. Indeed, Stimson overrode the wishes of military commanders and ordered that Kyoto, Japan's ancient capital and a major cultural shrine, be stricken from the list of potential targets.

But Stimson's support of the decision to use atomic bombs on Japan, and the apparent absence of any real qualms about the decision, nevertheless reflected the moral coarsening that had by the end of the war affected almost everyone in the American chain of command. Stimson had begun the war deeply concerned about the morality of bombing nonmilitary targets, convinced that there were ethical as well as tactical questions that must be answered when civilians were the likely targets of Allied efforts. As late as early 1945 Stimson was deploring the saturation bombings of Tokyo and Dresden. Little by little, however, the terrible tactics that both sides employed throughout the war seemed to inure him to the civilian costs. And perhaps that is why there was, apparently, no agonizing behind his support for the nuclear destruction of Hiroshima and Nagasaki. In fact he opposed all proposals to give the Japanese advance warning or to drop a "demonstration" bomb on a relatively uninhabited area. The minutes of the crucial meeting record that "the Secretary agreed that the most desirable target would be a vital war plant employing a large number of workers and closely surrounded by workers' houses" and that he recommended "that we should seek to make a profound psychological impression on as many of the inhabitants as possible."

And yet, almost alone among the principal figures in the decision to use the bomb, Stimson sensed the enormity of the step the United States was now taking. He spent much of the remainder of his life in a futile effort to limit the spread of atomic weapons through international control and supervision. "In this last great action of the Second World War we were given final proof that war is death," he wrote in 1947, in an article in *Harper's*. "Now with the release of atomic energy, man's ability to destroy himself is very nearly complete. The bombs dropped on Hiroshima and Nagasaki ended a war. They also made it wholly clear that we must never have another war."

In October 1962, twelve years after Stimson's quiet death at age 83, a group of his protégés gathered in the White House to shape an American response to the Cuban missile crisis. As the meetings began, Robert Lovett told McGeorge Bundy, "Mac, I think the best service we can perform for the President is to try to approach this as Colonel Stimson would." This shopworn anecdote has by now become a staple of the Stimson legend and a widely accepted indication of the extent of Stimson's legacy. But of what does Stimson's legacy actually consist?

Stimson was never a major conceptual architect of American foreign or military policy, and many of the diplomatic efforts with which he was most closely associated—in Nicaragua, the Philippines, and Japan—were ultimately unsuccessful. He was an influential man, of course, but never a genuinely powerful one—never one capable of, or interested in, pursuing an agenda of his own or in any serious way challenging the judgment of his superiors. In the end Stimson's legacy rests less on specific achievements or failures than on the way he conducted himself in public life—and on how his manner of conduct helped shape the ethos of the next generation of the foreign policy elite. Stimson's bequest to them included a stern certitude about the righteousness of American ideals and their suitability for other nations; a conviction that diplomacy must be insulated from popular and legislative whims (and hence from democracy); and a social and cultural elitism—born of his own rarefied station—that survived in diplomatic circles long after it had been repudiated by most of American society.

But Stimson also brought to public life a personal integrity, a resistance to naked self-interest, an absence of hypocrisy, and a commitment to the ideal of public service that compensated for at least some of the shortcomings of his social and political vision. That combination of certitude, elitism, and self-conscious integrity became the defining characteristic of Stimson's successors as leaders of the "establishment"—and of no one more, perhaps, than his protégé John McCloy.

John J. McCloy

If Stimson and Root were the creators of the modern "establishment," John Jay McCloy may have been the most successful postwar exemplar of its culture and its ethos. He was never as famous as his mentor Stimson or as some of his contemporaries in the establishment. Indeed, throughout most of his long career, he was unknown to most Americans. But for more than forty years he was among the most powerful figures in American public and private life. He may have been more actively involved in more areas of national policy, and in more critical decisions, than any figure of his generation. He befriended and advised nine presidents, from Franklin Roosevelt to Ronald Reagan. He knew, and was admired by, almost every Western leader of the postwar era. He was held in such respect, even awe, that he was often called "the most influential private citizen in America" and (by Richard Rovere, in the famous 1961 essay that introduced the idea) "the chairman of the American establishment."[3]

For a time, in the 1940s and early 1950s, McCloy's stature was a result of the important official positions he occupied, which placed him at the center of critical decisions and passionate, enduring controversies. As assistant secretary of war during World War II, he oversaw the American occupations of conquered territories in Europe, Africa, and Asia, and helped draft the plans for the postwar reconstruction of Germany and Japan. He also supervised the wartime internment of Japanese-Americans and helped forestall Allied military action against the Nazi death camps. As president of the World Bank during the critical first years of its existence, he shaped the policies that would guide international development efforts for decades to come. As American high commissioner in occupied West Germany, he presided over the reordering of German political and economic life and helped integrate the nation into the emerging European community.

But for most of his career, until his death in 1989, McCloy operated as a private citizen. Except briefly in 1961, when he served as John Kennedy's disarmament adviser, he held no public office after his return from Germany in 1952. He served as chairman of the board of the nation's second largest bank (Chase Manhattan), its largest private foundation (Ford), its most influential foreign policy organization (the Council on Foreign Relations), and one of its most distinguished colleges (Amherst, his alma mater). He served as a director of more than a dozen major American corporations and countless philanthropic organizations, and as the senior partner of one of Wall Street's largest law firms. He received honorary degrees from more than two dozen universities (Harvard, Princeton, Yale, and Columbia, among others). He was offered, and refused, cabinet appointments in Republican and Democratic administrations alike.

In those years as a private citizen McCloy often exerted more influence, often played a larger role in his country's public life, than he ever did as a government official. Throughout the 1950s he helped articulate many of the guiding assumptions of American foreign policy and helped bring to the fore many of the men who would guide that policy in the years to come. He was a principal presidential adviser on, and envoy to, the NATO alliance; a member of the Warren Commission; a participant in major disarmament negotiations; and a central actor in the resolution of the Cuban missile crisis. At times he exerted even greater influence in the less visible realms of power. As chief counsel to the major American and European oil companies in the 1960s and 1970s, he was a leading figure in the policies and events that led to the creation and radicalization of OPEC and the transformation of the Western economy. Later, he was one of three powerful private citizens who helped persuade the Carter administration to admit the deposed shah of Iran to the United States, a decision that triggered the hostage crisis of 1979 and 1980.

John McCloy personified the establishment tradition openly and unapologetically during the peak of its influence. For more than twenty years after World War II, McCloy's generation of establishment figures—Dean Acheson, Robert Lovett, John Foster Dulles, Douglas Dillon, George Kennan, Charles Bohlen, Averell Harriman, and others—dominated American foreign policy; and they passed their power on to the next generation, to men largely of their own choosing—Dean Rusk, McGeorge Bundy, Robert McNamara, Cyrus Vance—who then threw it away in the jungles of Vietnam. Like Stimson and Root before them, they moved easily in and out of private life, so convinced of their own rectitude—and of the essential unity of interests between government and capital—that they saw virtually no conflict between their roles as public servants and their positions in the world of business and finance.

Henry Kissinger, whose own career owed much to McCloy's patronage, wrote with some amazement in his memoirs of the role McCloy played in American life. "His influence was hard to account for," he admitted, for he "had never served at the Cabinet level." But "presidents and secretaries of state found in John McCloy a reliable pilot through treacherous shoals. . . . He was always available. He was ever wise." Martin Peretz, editor of the *New Republic*, wrote in 1981 with equal certainty, but far less reverence, about the remarkable and, to him, inexplicable stature of this man: "John J. McCloy is mentioned, as if age were virtue, in tones approaching awe." Few who are familiar with McCloy's career would agree with McCloy's own assessment: "I was never that important."

What accounts for this remarkably influential and prestigious career, which spanned more years than that of any modern public figure of comparable importance? Not the advantages of wealth and inherited position, certainly, for McCloy rose from relatively modest circumstances. Not transcendent brilliance or creativity, for McCloy, as he himself readily admitted, was not often a man who initiated policy, not one who shaped the vision of his age. And not the passion or ruthlessness of a towering ambition, for McCloy rarely sought the power that came to him. Several things, it seems, helped elevate McCloy to eminence and, equally important, worked to keep him there. One was his prodigious energy, which Stimson once said enabled him to handle more tasks and balance more responsibilities than any six men would normally undertake. Another was his manner. Gruff, unpretentious, forthright, personable, he avoided publicity and inspired confidence. Still another was his uncanny instinct for implementing policy, for "getting things done," an instinct that enabled him to operate with equal effectiveness in government and in private industry.

But McCloy's stature and longevity are also the result of his unwavering embrace of the ethos of the establishment: his firm confidence in the righteousness and importance of his own and his country's mission. Like many Americans emerging from the crucible of World War II, McCloy saw himself standing at the dawn of a new era, with opportunities and responsibilities that come to few generations in history. And while others grew sour and disillusioned—poisoned by an obsession with communism or, later, shattered by the trauma of Vietnam—McCloy held to that vision, steadily and assuredly, never doubting the vitality of his cause. That supreme assurance, that clear, steady, at times even unconscious commitment, lay at the heart of the many triumphs and the many controversies that marked McCloy's long career.

McCloy never felt entirely comfortable with the establishment label. "Nothing in my background was very established," he insisted. He was born in Philadelphia in 1895—"north of Market Street, on the wrong side of the tracks," he always liked to claim—into a family of modest but by no means desperate means. His father, a self-educated man who worked for an insurance company, died when Jack (as he was always known) was six. But by then he had imbued his young son with his own dreams of accomplishment (he often said that he hoped Jack would become a lawyer) and public service. Jack's mother, a fiercely determined woman who became a beautician ("did heads," as McCloy put it) after her husband's death, worked, saved, and helped her son fulfill his father's dreams. She sent him to private schools and, when he was seventeen, to Amherst. There McCloy studied hard, supported himself by waiting on tables and tutoring, was captain of the varsity tennis team, and engaged in campus politics (arguing, like his fellow Republican Theodore Roosevelt, for American preparedness for war). Immediately after his graduation in 1916, he spent the summer in an army officers' training program in Plattsburg, New York.

The following fall he entered Harvard Law School. But in April 1917, when America declared war on Germany, McCloy left immediately to enlist in the army, where he displayed for the first time the instinct for forming alliances with powerful figures that would characterize the whole of his life. He served as an artillery captain in France, but he managed to become closely acquainted with such future leaders as George Marshall and George Patton. He received an offer of a permanent commission when the war came to an end. But as soon as he could, in the fall of 1919, he quit the army and returned to Harvard.

He was at Harvard what he had been at Amherst: a conscientious, enthusiastic, talented, but less than brilliant student. He did not make the *Law Review*. He was not one of the golden circle of conspicuously bright students Felix Frankfurter gathered under his wing and then dispatched to positions of influence in Washington (although in later years, after McCloy had become a man of eminence, Frankfurter characteristically befriended and cultivated him). Upon his graduation in 1921, he moved to New York and found work, first with the Wall Street firm of Cadwalader, Wickersham & Taft, and then with Cravath, de Gersdorff, Swaine & Wood, where he was to remain for over fifteen years. McCloy rose quickly at Cravath, impressing his colleagues—as he would others throughout his career—with his energy, commitment, and competence. In 1930, at the age of thirty-five, he sailed to France to take over the firm's Paris office. Sailing with him was his new wife, Ellen Zinsser, the sister-in-law of McCloy's Amherst classmate Lew Douglas, who was later to be Franklin Roosevelt's budget director and ambassador to Great Britain.

That same year McCloy became involved with a case that would occupy him for nearly a decade and would change his life. It had its origins in a July night in 1916, when New York City was awakened by the greatest explosion in its—perhaps in any American city's—history.

Thousands of tons of explosives, sitting in the enormous munitions depot on Black Tom Island in New York Harbor awaiting shipment to the Allied powers in Europe, were detonated. The depot was destroyed. Fourteen years later, when McCloy became involved in the case, people on both sides of the Atlantic were still trying to determine the cause. By then, however, what had once been mere rumor—that German saboteurs had caused the explosion—was widely believed by those familiar with the evidence to be true. Among those convinced of German culpability was Cravath's client Bethlehem Steel, one of many companies that had suffered major losses at Black Tom and were seeking redress through the international courts.

The Black Tom case was a landmark in international law. It was also a major international mystery that involved McCloy in a decade-long journey through the world of European politics and espionage, from Dublin to Warsaw, from Vienna to Baltimore, and—in 1936—to meetings in Munich with Rudolf Hess and other Nazi leaders. "It was terrifying," he recalled. "All those goose-stepping soldiers. I could feel war in the air." He spent an afternoon in Adolf Hitler's box at the Olympic Games, and he claimed always to remember his strong reaction to his hosts: "I knew then that they were a bunch of thugs." McCloy was never able to persuade the Germans to settle the case, but by the end of 1936 he had assembled evidence so persuasive that the international courts accepted the American damage claims. And in 1941, only months before the United States would enter another great war with Germany, Bethlehem Steel received a check for $2 million from the German defendants.

For McCloy, however, the most important result of the Black Tom case was that it brought him to the attention of Henry Stimson, who as secretary of state in the early 1930s did battle with (and lost to) McCloy over the propriety of pursuing the litigation further. In 1940, when Franklin Roosevelt made Stimson secretary of war, one of Stimson's first official acts was to appoint McCloy, the young lawyer who had so impressed him several years earlier, as a special consultant to the War Department on German sabotage. ("It never occurred to me to say no," McCloy recalled. "I accepted on the spot.") Within a few months, he had risen to the post of assistant secretary of war. Suddenly, on the eve of America's entry into World War II, a man with no experience in politics or government, a Republican, a conservative corporate lawyer, had become one of the circle of other likeminded conservative Republicans who exercised enormous, and largely unchecked, authority over the life of the nation.

Many believed that McCloy and Stimson's other trusted younger associates "really ran" the War Department. McCloy always insisted that he and his colleagues were only "leg men" for Stimson, George Marshall, and the other "real" leaders of the war effort. But given Stimson's age and seigneurial management style, it is clear that the "leg men" quickly came to exercise a kind of power that in normal times would have been available only to older and more experienced figures.

Years later, Stimson remembered with awe the range of McCloy's wartime activities. "So varied were his interests that they defy summary," he observed in his memoirs. He had sometimes wondered, he claimed, "whether anyone in the administration ever acted without having a word with McCloy." In the months before Pearl Harbor, McCloy was the War Department's representative on Capitol Hill, often sleeping on a cot in the Foreign Relations office so he would always be on call to persuade wavering legislators to support Lend-Lease or the reauthorization of the draft. He created the intelligence office that broke the Japanese codes. He supervised the construction of the new Pentagon building (a project known for a time as "McCloy's folly"). And he made speeches and wrote articles in an effort to alert the still complacent public about the danger from Germany and Japan. Much of the sense of entitlement that McCloy's generation of establishment figures took with them into the postwar era came from their shared sense of having been "right" in the prewar battles over American internationalism, and from the belief they drew from the experience that public opinion could not be trusted to make good policy.

Once America entered the war, McCloy served as Stimson's liaison with the Joint Chiefs of Staff and helped plan most of the major campaigns on the Atlantic and Pacific fronts. He traveled with American troops to North Africa in 1942 and with the advancing armies as they entered Germany in 1944. His hand was visible in wartime legislation regulating labor, conscription, recruitment, promotion, and procurement—always on behalf of "safe," "stable" policies that deferred to the wishes of the military and the demands of manufacturers much more than to the interests of workers and consumers.

He was closely involved as well with some of the most sensitive diplomatic decisions of the war; and in those decisions, as in so many other areas, he displayed what he liked to consider a hardheaded pragmatism that left him largely immune to the moral and emotional concerns of many of those with whom he dealt. He helped persuade Roosevelt to accept Stimson's controversial proposal that the United States form an alliance with Admiral Jean Darlan of Vichy France. The notorious Nazi collaborator was, McCloy insisted, the only man who could bring French forces in North Africa onto the side of the Allies. Later he tried to convince Roosevelt that there was no reasonable alternative to recognizing Charles de Gaulle—whom the president detested and mistrusted—as the leader of the French government-in-exile. And toward the end of the war, he was, along with Stimson, instrumental in defeating Treasury Secretary Henry Morgenthau's radical proposal for the destruction of Germany's industrial capacity and the creation of a "pastoralized" economy. At about the same time, he managed to block Winston Churchill's plan for summary executions of Nazi leaders as they were captured and to generate Allied support for what became the Nuremberg trials.

One area of responsibility, however, was specifically and officially McCloy's own throughout the war: "civil affairs," the handling of civilian populations that came into contact with the American military. For the most part, that meant planning for the occupation and reconstruction of conquered territory. But it also brought him into two of the most controversial decisions of the war—decisions that haunted him for the rest of his life, as they haunt the American conscience still; decisions that displayed in full measure both the power and the myopia that were so central to establishment thinking.

The first involved the approximately 127,000 people of Japanese descent living on the West Coast of the United States, two thirds of them American citizens. In the hysteria following the Japanese attack on Pearl Harbor, they became targets of suspicion and hostility, of wild and utterly groundless charges of conspiracy. And they became as well the objects of a plan—supported by West Coast military commanders, California Attorney General Earl Warren, and others—to "evacuate" all Japanese-Americans from the region. In Washington the proposal generated wide disagreement. Much of the cabinet seemed to favor some sort of relocation; but Attorney General Francis Biddle, the official immediately responsible for the decision, strongly opposed the idea.

The issue found its way to the president, who avoided making a decision and passed the problem on to the War Department.

Stimson apparently decided very quickly to support the relocation proposal, and he sent McCloy as his agent to press the idea on other officials in a series of heated interdepartmental meetings. On February 19, 1942, a formal proposal reached the president's desk calling for the removal of all Japanese-Americans on the Pacific coast to "relocation centers" in the "interior." The president signed it without fanfare, and within days some 116,000 men, women, and children—most of them legal citizens of the United States charged with no crime, only with being of Japanese descent—were rounded up, forced to abandon their property, and delivered to a long, lonely exile in barbed-wire enclosures scattered throughout desolate areas east of the Sierras.

As civil affairs officer of the War Department, McCloy had direct responsibility for both supervising the evacuation and overseeing the internment. He displayed in that role an almost colonial sense of *noblesse oblige*. It was to him that the few friends of this tiny, powerless minority appealed repeatedly during the next four years for a reversal of the policy, or at least a phased return of the interned citizens to their homes. McCloy was utterly unmoved, certain that the decision to relocate them was in the best interests of the nation. Yet he also took pains to ensure that the victims of relocation were treated with at least minimal decency. He attempted (without much success) to get them some compensation for their property. And he sponsored the formation of a special Nisei army unit—the 442nd Combat Team, which fought with conspicuous bravery and enormous losses in Italy and made McCloy an honorary member. (McCloy spoke of the unit with pride for years thereafter, as if it absolved him of any connection with the racism and bigotry that had motivated the internment policy in the first place.)

McCloy did not initiate the relocation plan, and he was not a major figure in the decision to implement it. But neither then nor after did he ever indicate any misgivings about it. "I don't apologize a bit for that," he insisted over forty years later. The relocation was "reasonably undertaken and thoughtfully and humanely conducted." He bitterly opposed the drive in the 1980s to offer compensation to the survivors and descendants of the internees, dismissing it as "extortion." "The war caused disruption in all our lives," he told a congressional committee in 1981. Later he noted defiantly, "There was no compensation for the boys who died at Pearl Harbor." The relocation program, he claimed with stunning imperviousness to decades of recriminations, "was an example of the humanity and the breadth of principle with which the war was conducted." Few Americans today would agree.

A second wartime controversy brought McCloy face-to-face with the horrors of the Holocaust. By 1944, although the full truth about the Nazi death camps in eastern Europe was not yet widely understood among the public, the Allied governments and the leaders of major Jewish organizations were fully aware of at least the broad outlines of what was happening. McCloy received many delegations of Jewish leaders who argued that the rescue of the European Jews should become a major Allied military objective. He responded with rhetorical sympathy, but he offered no help. Bombing the death camps was "impracticable," he claimed (even though, as he likely knew, Allied bombers were already flying missions within a few miles of Auschwitz.) Efforts to stop the Holocaust would divert forces from "decisive operations" elsewhere, he said, and would cause the Allies to lose many planes because of the great distances involved. Bombings would, moreover, kill mainly Jews and "might provoke even more vindictive acts by the Germans." (It is reasonable to wonder what these "more vindictive acts" by Germans against Jews in 1944 could have been.) Proposals to bomb the railroad tracks leading to the camps were equally impractical, he said, because railroad tracks are hard to hit and easy to repair. There was, it seemed, a rational, responsible answer to every proposal—and no sense that the problem he was being asked to confront had any greater moral weight than any other.

"Perhaps an alteration in the tactical situation may make it possible for [the theater commander] to take some effective steps along the lines you propose," he noted in a cool, bureaucratic letter to the head of the World Jewish Congress in September 1944. (No such "alteration" occurred until the war ended.) Perhaps the British would be more helpful, he suggested. (They were not.) In the meantime, he wrote on another occasion, "the positive solution to this problem is the earliest possible victory over Germany." (One of his letters on the subject now rests under glass in the museum at Auschwitz, intended to serve as testimony to the apparent indifference of Allied leaders to the tragedy they were asked to help avert.)

For the rest of his life, McCloy reacted with extraordinary sensitivity to any mention of his role in these always controversial decisions. He often introduced the subject unprompted into conversation, and he offered a vehement defense to counter the harsh charges that even years later were leveled against him. It was Roosevelt and Churchill, not he, who rejected the idea of the bombings; he was only their agent in explaining it. The raids would have accomplished nothing; the costs would have been out of all proportion to any possible benefits.

McCloy was hardly alone among Allied policymakers in responding tepidly to the Holocaust. And it is likely that he was not in a position to have changed the American policy toward it even had he chosen to do so. But what is striking about his connection with this issue is how quickly and easily he was able to fit his position into the simple certitudes on which he based his public life; how little he seemed to be affected by the enormity of the evil he was being asked to confront. He was, of course, horrified by the Holocaust. After the war he was instrumental in winning compensation for its victims from Germany in the form of grants to Israel. But never during the war was he willing to permit the destruction of the Jews to occupy a prominent place on his list of concerns. McCloy and Stimson even argued against a much simpler measure to aid Holocaust victims: a 1944 proposal to increase the number of Jewish refugees admitted to the United States. Any such policy, they claimed, would erode the quota system and weaken the immigration laws.

The reason for this apparent indifference, it seems likely, was not primarily prejudice (although Stimson, at least, displayed throughout his life the genteel anti-Semitism of the Protestant upper class of his generation). It was the unshakable conviction among members of the establishment that their own sense of the national interest transcended what they considered the special claims of particular groups. A nation at war, they argued, had a single, inviolable mission that overshadowed all other goals. In 1944 that mission was victory. Later, during a peace when the sense of national destiny was no less strong, it would be other things.

It would be difficult to exaggerate the effect of World War II on the international outlook of the American people and, perhaps more important, American policymakers. Henry Luce had suggested the new outlook as early as 1941, when he wrote of the coming "American Century." And by the year of victory, 1945, this heady vision had infused an entire generation with a sense of its nation's urgent responsibilities for the future of the world. McCloy, returning home that fall from a tour of the conquered and liberated nations, spoke passionately of a world that "thirsts" for American guidance, a world that looked to the United States "as the one stabilizing influence which can give them the hope of return to decent living." American prestige, he claimed, was "terrifyingly high . . . terrifying when you see how much the rest of the world depends on us for leadership."

These fervent new expectations had implications not only for American policy but for McCloy himself, and for other figures from America's private power centers—the Wall Street lawyers, the corporate leaders—who had moved to the center of government during the war. There could be no abandonment of service as long as the wartime mission remained incomplete. There would be no easy return to private life. "I've always considered that a sort of Periclean age," McCloy later recalled of the postwar years. "There was no intrigue, no fighting for position." The nation remained in the hands of "men of noble, selfless instincts," men whose commitments and personal bonds had been forged by wartime service. When McCloy resigned from the War Department in November 1945, he received a warm letter from Harry Truman expressing the hope that "we can from time to time call upon you." The calls were never to cease, and McCloy was rarely to refuse them.

The first came almost as soon as he returned to New York, as a senior partner in the powerful Wall Street law firm of Milbank, Tweed, Hope, Hadley & (now) McCloy. In 1946 he was named to the new Acheson-Lilienthal committee, charged with drawing up proposals for international control of atomic energy. A few months later he helped negotiate the merger of the armed forces under a single Department of Defense. And little more than a year after his nominal return to private life, he abandoned New York altogether and accepted the intimidating job of president of the World Bank in Washington.

Created by the Bretton Woods monetary conference of 1944 as a lending agency through which affluent countries could assist war-torn or underdeveloped nations, the World Bank (the International Bank for Reconstruction and Development) had yet to float its first bond or make its first loan. Its board of directors—the delegates from the forty-eight member nations—was divided and contentious. Its first president, *Washington Post* publisher Eugene Meyer, had resigned in dismay in

December 1946; and his successor, an acting president, had died just weeks later. When McCloy took office in early 1947, the World Bank, only eight months old, was already in chaos. Its standing within the American financial community, whose confidence it would need if it hoped to sell its bonds, was perilously low.

McCloy's administration of the bank over the next two years was not without its critics. As a condition of accepting the job, he had insisted on much wider powers than his predecessors had had, and soon directors from participating countries were complaining that he treated them with a brusqueness verging on contempt. (McCloy did not deny it. "They were all claimants," he later said. "They were all trying to get money out of the United States.") And liberals complained that McCloy was too cautious, that the bank displayed little of the bold experimentalism its founders had envisioned. But no one questioned McCloy's success in stabilizing the organization and launching it on what he considered a responsible path. In an organization where the most basic questions of authority had never been resolved, he established the prerogatives of the president and his permanent staff and consigned the directors to a decidedly subordinate role. It was vital, he claimed, that power reside with those representing the interests of the bank as a whole, not the interests of their own member countries. McCloy's safe and conservative credit policies won the confidence of Wall Street, which was comforted by his assurance that "This is a bank, not a relief agency." Only months after he took office, the bank's first bond issue of $250 million sold immediately to American investors at above the asking price.

Most important, McCloy launched the real work of the bank: financing reconstruction and development projects. For several critical months, the World Bank was virtually the only source of credit for imperiled European governments. After the creation of the Marshall Plan in 1948, it helped finance major infrastructure projects in underdeveloped nations: roads, bridges, hydroelectric power facilities. In the process, he established a pattern that would characterize the bank's activities for decades to come—a pattern strikingly similar to the one the conservative Texas banker Jesse Jones had created for the Reconstruction Finance Corporation in the first years of the Great Depression. The World Bank, like the RFC, placed a heavy emphasis on making "safe" loans. That ensured it the support and confidence of Wall Street and the Western financial community as a whole, which it badly needed. It also ensured that it would ally itself in one country after another with the most established and usually conservative leaders; that it would forego most efforts to advance democratic reforms in the places it did its work; and that it would promote economic more than social development, convinced that healthy markets would eventually produce healthy societies.

After two years in office, McCloy was comfortable in the job and pleased with the bank's progress. But he did not stay put for long. In the spring of 1949, Harry Truman summoned him to the White House and offered the man who had become known as the government's leading troubleshooter a position that seemed guaranteed to cause him trouble indeed: "the toughest job in the foreign service," the post of American high commissioner in occupied Germany. It was not the first time that a president had tried to lay the problems of Germany in McCloy's lap. In the last days of the war Franklin Roosevelt had offered him the post of high commissioner, and only with difficulty had McCloy managed to persuade the president that a military man, Gen. Lucius Clay, should serve instead. Now, four years later, with the transition from military to civilian rule almost complete, he agreed to succeed Clay. Only a few weeks after his meeting with Truman, he sailed for Germany.

"The German Problem," as it was widely known, was a source of near universal pessimism among American policymakers in 1949. The economy and the social fabric of the defeated nation remained a shambles. Germany was still divided into the four zones of occupation the Allied powers had established, almost inadvertently, in the last days of the war. Only weeks before McCloy's arrival, the year-long communist blockade of West Berlin—which lay entirely within the Soviet zone—had come to an end after a dramatic and effective airlift. But the larger tensions between East and West Germany had made reunification of the nation seem all but impossible. And so the future status of Germany in Europe remained almost as open a question as it had been in 1944, when McCloy had first debated the issue in Washington. American policymakers were torn between their concern over two problems—both vital, both seemingly intractable. They were concerned about Germany itself, concerned that this source of so much violence and horror not be able to disrupt the peace of Europe again. But they were also concerned about the Soviet Union and what they considered its growing threat to western Europe, and they were becoming convinced that West Germany, at least, must somehow be brought into the struggle on the side of the United States and its partners in the new NATO alliance.

Once in Germany, McCloy quickly dropped the title of military governor that Clay had used. He exercised power instead through the indirect authority of the American High Commission, less visibly but no less decisively. He retained final control over virtually all basic policy decisions of Konrad Adenauer's new government. He directed the large American military force that was still in the country. And he was in charge of the $1.5 billion in Marshall Plan aid that the United States had made available for German recovery. In theory, he shared power with the high commissioners of Great Britain and France, but the American High Commission—which was paying most of the bills of the occupation—was clearly the first among equals.

Although the occupying powers were now less concerned with the day-to-day problems of governance than they had been in 1945, they remained responsible for (and divided about) longer-range problems of German reconstruction. Among these problems was the question of what to do about former Nazis. Many of Germany's erstwhile foes insisted on a vigorous campaign of de-Nazification, far more thorough than the Nuremberg trials, to purge German life of all remnants of its fascist past. McCloy rejected the most radical of their proposals (for example, a plan to remove all German children from their parents' homes to prevent Nazi values from being transmitted to the next generation). But he arrived in Germany publicly committed to a vigorous de-Nazification program of his own, and he issued sharp criticisms of "the amazing docility and acquiescence of the greater part of the German population toward Nazi outrages."

Those commitments did not survive for long in the face of growing public pressure in Germany to ease the postwar restrictions and cease "vindictive" purges. As the United States grew increasingly concerned about transforming Germany into a reliable partner in the struggle against the Soviets, McCloy gradually changed his position on the issue—without ever acknowledging, perhaps even to himself, that he was doing so. McCloy was soon arguing that a thorough removal of former Nazis from public life was impossible, that the "little Nazis" who recanted their views should be permitted to work in the new government. And in early 1951, with the same serene certainty with which he had made his earlier pronouncements about the importance of de-Nazification, he took a step that marked the end of any real American involvement with the issue of Nazi influence.

There had been repeated appeals by influential Germans to Lucius Clay, before McCloy's arrival, to review the Nuremberg sentences; Clay had never responded. But McCloy (who had been one of the initiators of the trials) appointed a new panel, headed by an American appellate judge, to study all the decisions of the Nuremberg tribunal. After a hasty (some claimed cursory and even biased) review, in which members accepted briefs from the defense but refused them from the prosecution, the panel sent McCloy a report recommending reductions in prison time for 74 of the 104 convicted former Nazis, and the commutation of most death sentences.

McCloy accepted the majority of their recommendations. He commuted the sentences of twenty-one prisoners who had been sentenced to die at Nuremberg (although, despite substantial public protest in Germany, he allowed seven former Nazis to be executed). And he ordered the unconditional release of Alfried Krupp, heir to the great armaments empire, and the restitution of his family's confiscated property.

Krupp's release was McCloy's most controversial decision during his tenure in Germany. Alfried Krupp had been serving a long sentence for employing slave labor—Jews and other concentration camp inmates—in his family's armaments factories during the war. There was overwhelming evidence that the charges against the company were true, and that the conditions to which the Krupps subjected their prisoners were appalling, even inhuman. But McCloy claimed to have become convinced that Alfried's father had been primarily responsible for the crimes, that the son ("a playboy . . . a weakling," he called him) had been "trotted out as a scapegoat" after the patriarch's death. Other observers, both at the time and since, strongly disagreed, arguing that Alfried not only knew about the Nazi labor policies but was deeply complicit in them; and McCloy never attempted to provide any real evidence to refute these claims. It seems likely, in fact, that the question of Krupp's guilt or innocence played little if any role in McCloy's decision. He claimed to be troubled by what he considered major irregularities in Krupp's trial; but most of all, perhaps, as a product of the world of business and finance, he believed the confiscation of Krupp property—intended as a symbol of the destruction of German militarism—had set a dangerous and illegal precedent that threatened the security of capital everywhere. And so, on January 31, 1951, Alfried Krupp walked out of the gates of Landsberg prison (where he had been living in some comfort and meeting regularly with the directors of his firm), drove to a champagne breakfast at a nearby hotel, and resumed active control of one of the world's largest armaments companies.

McCloy was stung by the fierce criticism that the release of Krupp and others provoked around the world. "All that the French detest in Germany," wrote *Paris-Presse*, "—the Prussian spirit, pan-Germanism, militarism, industrial dumping—is walking abroad again." From the United States came a bitter denunciation from Supreme Court Justice Robert Jackson, the chief prosecutor at Nuremberg, who claimed that to say Krupp was not guilty "would be as true as to say that there had been . . . no [one] slain, no crime, no war." And Eleanor Roosevelt expressed muted concern to McCloy. "Why are we releasing so many Nazis?" she asked him. Krupp had his own answer to that question: "Now that they have Korea on their hands, the Americans are a lot more friendly."

Even decades later, McCloy reacted with particular anger to suggestions that the Korean war had anything to do with his decision to release Krupp. ("It's a damn lie," he said, a "charge from the gutter.") And since he had established the review committee three months before the Korean war began, his denial is at least superficially persuasive, even though Krupp factories did soon become major suppliers of tanks and other supplies to the American war effort in Asia. The Krupp pardon and the other commutations were probably not driven by expediency. They were, more disturbingly, a likely result of real conviction.

Krupp may have been wrong about McCloy's motives in his own case, but he was certainly correct about the impact of the Korean war on American thinking. The invasion of South Korea in June 1950 had transformed the Western—and particularly the American—view of the world. As McCloy wrote a few years later: "Korea brought Europe to its feet. [That it did the same for the United States was a fact too obvious to mention.] The realization that the Soviet was prepared to unleash armed forces to extend its power aroused Europe and particularly Western Germany, whose situation presented a parallel unpleasant to contemplate." In this new context concern about Germany's Nazi past faded quickly, to be replaced by commitment to Germany's anticommunist future. The "German problem" would never seem quite the same again.

Ever since the end of the war, there had been one proposal—often dismissed as visionary—that offered a possible solution to the problem of rebuilding a strong Germany without restoring a German threat to European peace. It was the dream of Jean Monnet, once an important French financier, now a major statesman: the dream of a united, integrated Europe. Monnet proposed a new economic and political entity—modeled, he said, on the United States—so closely bound together by ties of mutual dependence that the "European civil wars" of centuries past would become inconceivable. A resurgent Germany, with an economy linked closely to that of its western neighbors, would not threaten European peace but would contribute to European strength. Monnet's proposals found little support at first among the Allied governments, whose mistrust of France, Germany, and each other remained strong in the early postwar years. But the Korean war, and the added urgency it lent to Europe's fear of the Soviet Union, helped erode doubts. Suddenly the concept of European integration became not a pipedream but a daring, even magical solution to what only recently had seemed intractable problems.

One such problem was the German economy. In the first years after the war, the Allied powers had actually taken steps to dismantle the factories and facilities of the Nazi war machine. And while McCloy put a stop to that on his arrival in 1949, he claimed for a time to remain committed to a vigorous program of "decartelization": breaking up the great financial and industrial combinations that had done so much, many believed, to create the authoritarian climate of German life. But the new German government, to which he entrusted the deconcentration program, showed no inclination to act. And McCloy—never much concerned about economic concentration in America and perhaps not deeply committed to his own stated goals in Germany—was always reluctant to force the issue. Monnet's economic plan (presented by, and named for, French Foreign Minister Robert Schuman) offered a solution to the impasse. It called for a pooling of European coal and steel production into one, unrestricted, continentwide market. Since so many European conflicts had emerged from Franco-German rivalries in these basic industries, removing nationalistic competition from steel and coal production would contribute both to prosperity and peace.

McCloy had played no role in initiating the plan for a European Coal and Steel Community (although, as an old and close friend of Monnet's, he had given it his full support from the start); but he was the principal actor in the arduous negotiations preceding its adoption. A crucial breakthrough was his success in forcing the reluctant Adenauer government to accept French demands for limiting ownership of coal mines by steel companies in the Ruhr Valley, saving the talks from collapse and the American decartelization proposals from oblivion. When the ECSC agreement was successfully concluded (the first step toward what would ultimately become the Common Market and, later, the European Community), both the French and the Germans credited McCloy with rescuing it from defeat.

Even more difficult was the question of German rearmament and its role in European integration. During McCloy's first year in Germany, there was strong sentiment among the Allies and even among some factions in Germany in favor of the neutralization and permanent demilitarization of the nation. Kurt Schumacher, the leader of the Social Democratic Party, regarded this as the only route to a reunified Germany, and McCloy himself had at first insisted that "our fixed policy has been to impose and maintain effective controls against the revival of a German war machine." But after the outbreak of hostilities in Korea, McCloy's inhibitions—and those of the American government—quickly faded. German rearmament now seemed essential not only to the defense of Germany, but also to the larger defense of the West.

Yet McCloy realized, too, that the immediate and unconditional rearmament that the Truman administration was proposing might destabilize German politics and destroy any hopes for future European unity. So he sought instead an approach that would reconcile the need for German forces with the concerns of the French (and the Germans themselves) about the possible consequences of militarization. The central question, he came to believe, was not the size of the new German military, but its relationship to the Western alliance. He worked, therefore, to incorporate Germany into the newly proposed European Defense Community, the military counterpart of Monnet's vision of a European economic community.

As with the ECSC, the major stumbling block was Germany itself. Konrad Adenauer ("a shrewd politician," McCloy later recalled, even if "somewhat naive about the United States and foreign affairs") was pressing for major American concessions. If Germany was to tie itself militarily to the rest of Europe, Adenauer argued, it should expect some real progress on restoring its sovereignty in exchange for even small agreements. Secretary of State Dean Acheson, impatient for movement, was urging McCloy to grant such concessions. But McCloy, although he was willing to restore considerable sovereignty to the German government, believed the Germans should offer more in return. Through long and difficult bargaining, he linked the restoration of German sovereignty to much stronger contractual agreements tying Germany to the Western alliance than Adenauer had originally offered. In May 1952 Germany joined France, Italy, Belgium, and the Netherlands in a treaty establishing a NATO army.

McCloy's role in the EDC negotiations were, he believed, among the great achievement of his life. They "helped create the base for a sense of commonality in Europe," he later claimed. "We sorted out all sorts of obstacles. And Germany ended up our most reliable partner in NATO." The strong and lasting links he helped create between Germany and France became one of the cornerstones of the Western alliance. "We made unthinkable another European civil war," he says. "We ended one of history's longest threats to peace."

McCloy served in Germany with almost unrestricted power. "It was a unique job," he later remembered, with some amazement. "Washington left me alone, and I was like a Roman proconsul." Yet he exercised his power with a public modesty and restraint that won him great poularity among much of the German population. Like an American politician, he traveled constantly, made himself visible and accessible, mingled with the German public. His wife, Ellen—a third-generation German-American, fluent in German and a distant cousin of Konrad Adenauer's second wife (who had died after release from a Nazi concentration camp)—became a popular figure in her own right through her work on behalf of refugees and orphaned children. "I had always felt close to Germany, had always had an affection for it," McCloy recalled. He encouraged the Germans to think of themselves not just as a defeated nation responsible for crimes against humanity but as one with a noble heritage, the nation not only of Hitler but of Goethe, Schiller, and Beethoven. The displays of warmth and gratitude that McCloy received as he prepared to leave the country in the summer of 1952 were a recognition both of his popularity and of his contribution to creating a lasting German-American friendship.

In a sense, McCloy's return from Germany in late 1952 marked the end of his public career. Except briefly in 1961, he was never again to hold a full-time government position. But in a larger sense, 1952 only marked a transition from one kind of public career to another—one in which McCloy was often to wield more influence and touch more areas of national and international life than he had ever done in his official capacities. Few men in the postwar era succeeded better than McCloy at moving into that special realm, perhaps unique to the modern American establishment, where private life and public service seamlessly merge. He became simultaneously a pillar of the corporate world, a key figure in American foreign policy, and a philanthropic leader. These multiple roles, far from conflicting with one another, were mutually reinforcing. They made him a man respected and trusted by his contemporaries as a "disinterested" public servant and revered, even mythologized by the next generation as the carrier of the long tradition of Wall Street in the nation's service.

That McCloy rarely served in official positions after 1952 was not the government's choice but his own. Eisenhower was eager to have him in his cabinet and at one point midway through his administration tried to make him secretary of state. McCloy refused: "Foster Dulles [the incumbent secretary] told me he was going to move over to the White House as an adviser. They wanted me to be a caretaker, a figurehead; and I wouldn't do it." John Kennedy wanted to make him secretary of the treasury; McCloy refused that offer too. He feared his Wall Street connections would prove embarrassing to himself and to the administration (something that seemed not to trouble the Republican investment banker, Douglas Dillon, who accepted the post). And there were repeated rumors of other possibilities: of Supreme Court justiceships, ambassadorships, even (briefly and implausibly in 1956) of a dark-horse nomination for president.

McCloy consistently resisted returning to official life, in part because he had spent so many years of his career—what Wall Street likes to call the "capital-building years"—in low-paying government jobs. And so in 1952 he returned not to Washington but to New York, where in December he became chairman of the board and chief executive officer of the Chase National Bank. For the next eight years McCloy presided over Chase: overseeing its merger in 1955 with the Bank of Manhattan (moving it into retail banking and then making it the second largest financial institution in the nation), lobbying for legislation to permit branch banking in the suburbs, pushing the bank into greatly expanded international activities, and commissioning a towering new building on Wall Street—One Chase Manhattan Plaza, designed in 1961 by Skidmore, Owings & Merrill, one of the defining examples of postwar modernist corporate architecture.

Yet McCloy's Wall Street office was a center not only of financial power but of political and diplomatic influence as well. From it he retained a level of access to the highest reaches of government—not just in Washington, but in European, North African, and Middle Eastern capitals—that few public officials could match. From it he became one of Eisenhower's "inner circle" of unofficial advisers, spending more time with the president than many cabinet officers. From it he became, and for more than twenty years remained, one of the nation's leading authorities on, and defenders of, the Atlantic alliance.

When European leaders visited the United States, they regularly paid a call to McCloy's office, as if to an unofficial foreign ministry. When particularly difficult diplomatic problems arose, McCloy, not the appropriate State Department official, was often dispatched to resolve them. In 1966 and 1967, for example, he was Lyndon Johnson's envoy in the tripartite talks with Britain and France on the touchy issue of sharing the financial burdens of NATO. No one spoke more fervently and ceaselessly than McCloy about the need to protect the Western alliance. There was no stronger critic of the proposed American troop reductions in Europe in the 1960s, no more fervent foe of the new *Ostpolitik*, by which West Germany attempted to improve its ties with the East. And such was McCloy's stature that he could speak bluntly and with impunity of his concerns when most public officials remained discreetly silent. As late as 1981, at a dinner at the German embassy in Washington given by Helmut Schmidt, McCloy rose dramatically to offer an ominous warning about what he saw as a weakening German commitment to the alliance. The imperious Schmidt, who was known to react harshly to criticism from virtually any source, responded with a deferential silence.

McCloy was often called one of the "architects" of postwar American foreign policy. But he was not really a major force in determining the larger strategies of the cold war. In his only extended statement of his international philosophy—a 1953 book entitled *The Challenge to American Foreign Policy* (derived from the Godkin lectures he had recently given at Harvard)—his statement of the basic premises of containment could not have been more orthodox. Yet the book also made clear how little concerned McCloy was with ideology. He devoted most of his attention to questions of implementation: how a bureaucracy should be structured, how decisions should be reached, how negotiations should be conducted. Years later, assessing his own role in American public life, he would call himself an "operator" rather than a policymaker. In his book he made clear how important he believed effective "operators" were to the proper functioning of government.

McCloy's ability to "operate" received an important assist in 1953, when he became chairman of the Council on Foreign Relations. Presiding over the nation's most important private foreign policy organization, he was able not only to organize members of his own generation to influence policy, but also to help determine which members of the next generation would rise to prominence. In 1956, when McCloy chaired a study of American-Soviet relations sponsored by the council, he recruited for its staff a young Harvard scholar little known outside academia at the time. It was one of the first steps in Henry A. Kissinger's ascent into the foreign policy elite.

That McCloy moved so easily into the highest realms of the establishment and stayed there for so long was not just the result of his diplomatic experiences or his corporate eminence; it was also a result of his personality. He was not a remote, intimidating theoretician like George F. Kennan. He was not a moralistic ideologue like John Foster Dulles. He was a warm, personable, unthreatening raconteur, who liked to ramble on amiably about his wartime experiences, his conversations with Stimson, Roosevelt, Churchill, and others, and—as time went on—his connections with even more distant figures from the past. ("I was talking with Bill Taft," he once began a conversation with a Washington reporter in the 1970s.) He could be "time-consuming," Henry Kissinger once recalled, "with his penchant for anecdotes." He seemed at times "more like a genial gnome than a preeminent New York lawyer and perennial counselor of presidents and secretaries of state." But beneath the geniality was a rock-hard certainty about his own basic convictions, and a willingness to support them firmly and vigorously.

These last traits became clear, if they were not so already, in 1953, when he became a target of the rampaging Joe McCarthy. McCloy's career, McCarthy charged, was an "unbelievable, inconceivable, unexplainable record of the deliberate, secret betrayal of the nation to its mortal enemy, the communist conspiracy." More specifically, he said, McCloy had elevated communists to positions of power in the military during World War II and had destroyed incriminating records to cover his tracks. McCloy had, in fact, defended a perfectly reasonable wartime policy of ignoring the political affiliations of officers; he had destroyed no files. And he responded to these accusations with steely outrage, almost regal disdain, and genuine political courage—the kind of courage that only a man who felt wholly apart from politics could muster. He spoke bitterly of the abuses of power of which McCarthy and his minions (Roy Cohn and G. David Schine) were guilty. He defended John Carter Vincent and other maligned State Department officials. He supported J. Robert Oppenheimer when McCarthy and others attacked him. And he fervently defended the accomplishments and integrity of his own generation of policymakers: "We won a war that extended all over the world and touched every shore, and we managed to keep the economy of the world prosperous. That was a great achievement and I'm proud of it. And it was not accomplished by traitors." (At the same time he infuriated many of his liberal friends, who tended to forget how conservative he was at heart, by likening McCarthy's tactics to earlier congressional assaults on the corporate establishment during the New Deal.)

It was inevitable, perhaps, that McCloy would become the target of such abuse from the right (and later from the left); for by the 1950s he had come to represent, as almost no one else could, the powerful network of establishment institutions—the easy mingling of private and public power—that both the right and the left mistrusted and despised. His influence stretched far beyond the already impressive bounds of the Chase Manhattan Bank and the Council on Foreign Relations, beyond his role as adviser to the president, friend and confidant of world leaders. He was chairman of the board of the Ford Foundation, the central agency of establishment philanthropy, and he was a director of countless other charitable and service organizations. He was on the board of Westinghouse, AT&T, Allied Chemical, United Fruit, and other major corporations. He received, almost annually, honorary degrees from the nation's most distinguished universities. In 1953 alone he accepted five: from Princeton, Columbia, Dartmouth, Smith, and New York University. For those convinced that a conspiracy of elites controlled the destiny of ordinary people, McCloy served as the perfect symbol of the interlocking worlds of business, finance, government, and philanthropy.

McCloy reached retirement age, sixty-five, in 1960, and he stepped down as chairman of Chase Manhattan and the Ford Foundation. He did not, however, retreat into obscurity. Almost immediately, he returned to government service as the principal disarmament adviser to John F. Kennedy. To the Kennedy circle, McCloy was a valuable and attractive ally, one of the "tough" pragmatic figures of the World War II generation whom the new, younger leaders hoped to emulate. And McCloy shared their outlook on nuclear weapons: a practical, unemotional belief in the importance of deterrence and a sober recognition of the importance of restraint. His "toughness" on nuclear issues had been apparent as early as 1950, when Harry Truman made his controversial decision to develop the hydrogen bomb. McCloy applauded his resolve. "If there were an oxygen bomb that would be bigger than the H-bomb," he said, "I would build it." Yet McCloy had also been an advocate of moderation from the beginning. In 1945 he was one of a handful in the inner circle of power to question the wisdom of bombing Hiroshima (one of his few disagreements with Henry Stimson). Decades later he continued to "regret that we did it." In the 1950s he served as an adviser to the Eisenhower administration on the disarmament negotiations it began during its final years—the failure of which motivated the Kennedy administration to launch, in addition to its much vaunted missile build-up, new arms control initiatives.

McCloy was in charge of developing the new negotiating position that the United States presented to the Soviets on the immediate issue of concern: a treaty banning the testing of nuclear weapons. He was also the chief negotiator in the protracted talks, in both Washington and Moscow, with his Soviet counterpart, Valerian Zorin, over the specific terms by which formal negotiations might resume. (During one visit to Moscow, he was whisked off—along with his wife, daughter, and niece—for a two-day meeting with Nikita Khrushchev at the premier's Black Sea retreat.) In the meantime McCloy was drafting legislation to create an independent arms control agency within the executive branch, responsible not only for devising negotiating strategy but for conducting the actual talks (thus removing them from the destructive wrangling among existing departments). Kennedy strongly supported the idea through his campaign and first weeks in office. But when McCloy came to the White House with a formal proposal for a new Arms Control and Disarmament Agency (ACDA), he was "shocked" to discover he no longer had the president's full support. "He said he didn't think the votes were there," McCloy recalled, "that he didn't want to risk the prestige of his administration on a bill that wouldn't pass. I was a little shaken that he didn't have the conviction to stick with this issue. . . .

I thought he was taking a very narrow political approach." But Kennedy was adamant. If McCloy wished to pursue the matter, he would have to do so on his own.

McCloy did pursue it. He drew on his own network of friends and colleagues—"all the heroes from World War II"—and paraded them before the appropriate committees in support of the measure: "From Eisenhower and MacArthur down, I had them all!" There was a note of special satisfaction in his description of the bill's smooth passage through Congress, of the overwhelming majorities it received in both houses, of his ability to use the nonpartisan stature of the establishment to achieve something that the president himself had considered too difficult.

In October 1961, only nine months after accepting his post in the administration, McCloy resigned from it. There was speculation that the reason was his dissatisfaction with Kennedy's timidity, or his frustration with the slow pace of his talks with Zorin. (The failure of the two governments to move faster constituted, he said at the time, "the most discouraging exercise in disarmament negotiations since the close of World War II.") But McCloy insisted that he had never planned to stay any longer than he did, that once the ACDA was in place he considered his job complete. Visitors to his cavernous office in the State Department had noted that the room always remained virtually bare, save for an unframed picture of Henry Stimson on the mantel, as if he had been reluctant really to move in. McCloy himself explained, "I couldn't afford to stay any longer. I had to live on my salary; and the money went like hot water on a stove."

Yet Kennedy did not hesitate to call on McCloy again at the most desperate hour of his presidency: the Cuban missile crisis. McCloy was in Germany in October 1962, about to go shooting in the Pyrenees, when he received an urgent call from the president to return home "right away . . . today." And for the next two weeks he was embroiled in the anxious, dangerous confrontation; as a participant in the White House meetings to frame a response to the Soviets, as an unofficial White House presence at the United Nations ("They wanted me to keep an eye on Adlai," he recalled. "They thought he was soft; I didn't think so at all"), and finally as the chief American negotiator, once Khrushchev had conceded the essential point of removing the missiles, on the mechanics of the withdrawal. One crucial meeting occurred at McCloy's rural home near Stamford, Connecticut. The Russian diplomat, Vasily Kuznetsov, suspected that the house was bugged, so the two men sat on a wood-rail fence and finally agreed on procedures and timetables for removal of the missiles. "Everyone thinks it had all been settled by then," McCloy recalled. "But it still wasn't clear that the Soviets were going to remove the missiles. We all knew things could still go wrong. But I held firm, and Kuznetsov knew he had to agree." When they parted, Kuznetsov told McCloy, "We [the Soviets] shall live up to this agreement, but we shall never be in the same position again." It was both a grudging admission of the humiliation his country had suffered and a portent of the intensive arms race of the next twenty years, as the Soviets tried to catch up with the United States and America struggled to retain its lead. (McCloy always cited Kuznetsov's remark as evidence that it was American nuclear superiority that made it possible to resolve the crisis; he dismissed as "nonsense" later claims by some participants that it was U.S. conventional strength that proved decisive.)

McCloy had little contact with Lyndon Johnson during the years of the Kennedy presidency. He remembered the vice president as a quiet, almost shadowy figure who sat in on meetings, listened carefully, and rarely said a word. But Johnson had taken note of McCloy, as he took note of any influential and prestigious man he might one day make use of. And shortly after the assassination of President Kennedy, he asked McCloy to serve on the Warren Commission. "It was a very emotional period," McCloy later said, "and it was so obvious that something like this had to be done." He accepted the appointment immediately. Entering the investigation "thinking there must have been a conspiracy," he left it convinced that Oswald had acted alone. "I never saw a case that I thought was more completely proven," he always claimed. "I just don't have any doubts about it."

As American involvement in Vietnam gradually deepened in the first years of his presidency, Johnson made repeated efforts to drag McCloy, along with virtually every other member of the foreign policy establishment, into the quagmire with him. McCloy resisted better than most. "No one was more adamant than I that we should never get involved on the Asian continent," he recalls. "I always agreed with Ike on that." Americans were incapable of understanding Asia, he had always believed, speaking as the deeply committed Atlanticist he was. (He once described Asia as "a great amorphous mass.") And in the early 1960s he frequently challenged the more hawkish government leaders on the issue of Vietnam: "I argued all the time with them—with that good-looking, tennis playing fellow who always wanted to send troops over there . . . Max Taylor."

So when Johnson called McCloy to the White House in the summer of 1964 and asked him to become American ambassador to South Vietnam, McCloy refused. But not without difficulty. "Talk about twisting your arm!" he recalled. "I will never forget it." It was his first exposure to the "Johnson treatment": the arm around the shoulder, the hand on the lapel, the face so close he could feel the president's breath on his cheek, the unctuous flattery ("I want you to go out there, McCloy, because you're the finest. . . . You're the greatest proconsul the republic has had"), the towering rage ("You're yellow, McCloy. You're afraid of this job"). He nearly succumbed to the onslaught, even felt slightly ashamed that he did not; but he left the White House still a private citizen.

McCloy was too closely tied to the machinery of American foreign policy, however, to remain entirely immune to the ravages of Vietnam. Convinced, in the establishment tradition, that "once we made the commitment we had to honor it," he agreed to serve on the Senior Advisory Group Johnson set up to lend establishment legitimacy to the war. (Dean Acheson was another member.) McCloy was never as zealously hawkish as some others in the group, but he was nevertheless unresponsive to those within the administration who pleaded for a change in policy. George Ball recalled in his memoirs a White House meeting of the "wise old men" in 1967. After he made his "usual plea for extrication to the usual deaf ears," the only response was the "supercilious" claim that the real problem was educating American opinion. As the meeting broke up, Ball turned on McCloy and Acheson and exploded: "I've been watching you across the table. You're like a flock of old buzzards sitting on a fence, sending the young men off to be killed." Ball had been a friend and colleague of McCloy's for twenty years; but the war had now begun to divide even the inner circles of the establishment.

What finally turned McCloy against the war (in a characteristically discreet and gentlemanly way) was what had caused him to support it in the first place: its effect on America's standing elsewhere in the world. By 1968 it was clear that Vietnam was damaging American credibility in Europe. And so McCloy joined other members of the Senior Advisory Group to urge de-escalation. It was only then, many believed—when the president realized he had lost the support not just of the public but of the establishment as well—that the course of American policy slowly began to turn.

McCloy's stature in the corporate world had always been an important source of his power in public life. But his public power also enhanced his influence within the private sector. That was never clearer than in the years following his return to the practice of law—as a senior partner at Milbank, Tweed, Hadley & (once again) McCloy—after his retirement from banking and government.

Milbank was, and is, known in legal circles as the "Rockefeller law firm." It handled the family's personal interests as well as those of Chase Manhattan (whose president, beginning in 1961, was David Rockefeller). And it also handled much of the business of the American oil industry, which the Rockefeller family had done so much to shape and in which it still had substantial interests. No sooner had McCloy returned to Milbank than he became chief counsel in the United States to the so-called Seven Sisters, the major petroleum companies: Exxon, Mobil, BP, Texaco, Shell, Gulf, and Socal. He was also involved in the affairs of more than a dozen smaller companies.

McCloy's involvement with the oil industry resulted in part from the ties to Arab governments he had established through public service. In 1956, in the wake of the Suez crisis, he headed a United Nations mission to negotiate the salvaging and reopening of the canal with Gamal Abdel Nasser. McCloy arranged international financial support for the project and won the confidence of the Egyptian leader. In the next few years he also established comfortable relationships with other, more friendly Middle Eastern leaders: the shah of Iran, the house of Saud, the king of Jordan. Long before the term became fashionable, McCloy had become a leading "Arabist," issuing warnings—which fell, at the time, on deaf ears—that American support of Israel should be tempered by a recognition of the economic importance of the oil-producing countries.

McCloy believed that the continued health of the major oil companies was essential to the stability of the Western economy. "The world was largely rehabilitated," he once said of the postwar decades, "by the cheap oil" that the majors had provided. And he believed that the creation of OPEC in 1960 as a bargaining agent for the oil-producing countries presented dangers that would require a strong, united Western response. Weak and divided at the time of its formation, OPEC could offer no serious threat to the companies' control of prices and production. But McCloy feared the situation might one day change.

In the fall of 1962 he called on Attorney General Robert Kennedy and asked whether the oil companies, if the need arose, would be able to bargain collectively with the producing nations without fear of antitrust prosecution. Kennedy listened to McCloy's arguments and agreed. But lest the agreement be forgotten, McCloy later related, "I made it a point to call on each succeeding attorney general just for the idea of keeping the thing fresh in his mind, because any moment I was afraid we would have to do something."

That moment was slow in coming, but in 1969 it arrived. The government of Libya, now in the hands of the revolutionary regime of Muammar Qaddafi, startled the petroleum world that year by unilaterally demanding substantially higher prices for its crude oil. Ordinarily, a demand by a single government would have had little effect. So powerful were the major companies, so extensive their interests, that they could simply buy elsewhere until the offending government retracted its demands. But Libya, a relative newcomer to the oil-producing world, dealt mainly with aggressive, "independent" companies, some of which had no other supplier. Occidental Petroleum, in particular, was desperately dependent on Libya and could afford no interruption in supply. And when the majors refused to guarantee Occidental the replacement crude it requested, the company had no choice but to accept Qaddafi's new price. The result was precisely what the majors had feared: a chain reaction throughout the oil world, with other independents following Occidental's lead and the producing nations becoming increasingly assertive and profit-hungry. The time had come, the majors believed, to take drastic action to reassert control. "Our best hope of withstanding the pressure being exerted by the members of OPEC," said the president of Shell, "would lie in the companies refusing to be picked off one by one in any country and by declining to deal with the producers except on a total global basis."

In early 1971 the leaders of more than twenty oil companies gathered in McCloy's office at One Chase Manhattan Plaza to devise a strategy for a collective response to OPEC. Outside, in an anteroom, sat representatives of the Justice and State departments, reviewing drafts of the proposed arrangements. In a virtuoso display of private and public power exercised simultaneously, McCloy produced an agreement that won the approval of both the oil companies and the federal government.

The Seven Sisters and the leading independents would present a united front to the producing nations, and they would expect the producers to negotiate in concert as well. Industry strength would be pitted against OPEC strength, and the companies had little doubt that they would prevail. Attorney General Mitchell would grant the industry the antitrust exemption McCloy had first requested in 1962. Secretary of State William Rogers would send his under secretary, John Irwin III, to the Middle East to negotiate on behalf of the companies.

But almost nothing turned out as McCloy and his clients hoped. The industry's united front proved unable to withstand even minimal pressure, and the Justice Department, claiming widespread abuses, finally revoked its antitrust exemption in 1974. OPEC responded to the confrontation with a strength and unity that the oil companies had thought impossible only months earlier. By the end of 1971 OPEC was demanding a new formula for an expanded share of company profits, and even the majors were discovering they had no choice but to accept. Finally came 1973: the Yom Kippur war and the Arab oil embargo, the death blow to company control of Middle Eastern oil. McCloy, sensing the disaster that was to come, repeatedly warned the Nixon administration not to increase military assistance to Israel, not to antagonize the moderate Arab states and threaten access to the oil wells (another reason for the hostility he evoked in later years among some American Jews). The administration at first seemed to agree, and the official American stance—to the distress and anger of Israel and its friends in the United States—was conspicuously aloof during the first days of the war. Eventually, however, Golda Meir received the weapons and supplies for which she had been pleading. And OPEC, having been schooled by masters in the art of cartelization, retaliated with its first embargo of the West, an act that changed the world's economic balance forever.

But the epic failure of his united front policy did nothing to diminish McCloy's influence with either the oil companies or the American government (thus demonstrating another feature of the establishment, the seeming immunity of its members to the consequences of their own failures). On the contrary, now that both the petroleum industry and the Middle East had assumed such vast global importance, McCloy's stature both with the companies and the government seemed, if anything, to increase. When executives of Gulf Oil were accused in 1975 of having made illegal campaign contributions, the company named McCloy to investigate. His stinging report—which not only confirmed the charges, but laid much of the blame on the highest corporate officers—was accepted almost without question by the industry and government alike. (He protected his private-sector credentials by adding a complaint about the "double standard" that led to prosecution of companies that made illegal contributions, but not of the politicians who accepted them.) And when in the fall of 1979 the exiled shah of Iran began seeking permission to enter the United States for medical treatment, McCloy joined with Henry Kissinger and David Rockefeller in pressuring Jimmy Carter to grant it—over the objections of American diplomats in Iran, most members of the State Department, and even some of the White House staff inner circle. Once again, it seemed, the "most influential private citizens in America" had prevailed over the normal channels of official power.

McCloy lived until 1989, well into his nineties, and age gradually took its toll. But until very near the end, he still appeared regularly at his corner office on the forty-sixth floor of One Chase Manhattan Plaza, the building he had commissioned long ago. The walls of his reception room were lined with photographs of the world leaders he had known: Henry Stimson ("my hero statesman"), Franklin Roosevelt (the first president he served), Harry Truman (the president who made him his "proconsul"), George Marshall ("who came closest to wearing the mantle of greatness of any man I ever knew"), Konrad Adenauer (for whose power and longevity in office McCloy was in large part responsible). His own office was relatively plain. From the window, he could look out on New York Harbor, toward Black Tom Island. On one wall hung a painting of the Rhine as viewed from McCloy's house in Germany; the artist was Alice Acheson. Around him in the offices at Milbank, Tweed, and at Chase Manhattan, worked younger men and women, many of them born long after he rose to eminence. To many of them John McCloy was a legend—the subject of a thousand stories, the object of starstruck glances as he stepped in and out of elevators, the embodiment of history, a living symbol of a tradition that was, by the time of his death, rapidly disappearing from American life.

The establishment tradition was not always the "Periclean" force of which McCloy liked to boast. At its worst, it was responsible for some of the most disheartening aspects of postwar American foreign policy: the ideological rigidity, the too easy assumption that corporate interests and public interests are identical, the class-bound assumption that "gentlemen" were more reliable partners than firebrands, the too frequent willingness to use dubious means to achieve righteous ends. And McCloy's career often exemplified the smugness, insularity, and moral myopia of the establishment world. But McCloy also often embodied the tradition at its best. The establishment helped bring a stability and continuity to American policy that some later leaders had reason to envy. It placed decision making in the hands of men who trusted one another, worked comfortably together, and believed that there was such a thing as a true national interest. It insulated international relations from everyday partisanship, and it imposed an ethos on its members that encouraged them to try (even if they never wholly succeeded) to separate their public lives from their political allegiances and even, to a degree, from their personal ambitions.

In the last years of his life, watching the erosion of the tradition that had shaped so much of his career, McCloy worried about the future of the ideal of public service and grew gloomy about the next generation's commitment to sustain that ideal. "These big salaries lawyers are getting make it much harder for them to consider government as part of their careers," he observed. "So many of the younger professionals around here today grew up distrusting government and so they don't think much about serving it. When I was young, the idea of serving in Washington was the most exciting prospect I could imagine."

A story circulated in Washington and New York in the early 1980s about an episode in the 1980 presidential campaign. Rep. John Anderson of Illinois was seeking the Republican nomination for president. In the heat of the early presidential primaries, when it appeared briefly that he might have a chance of wresting the prize from Ronald Reagan, he called John McCloy (as political figures had been doing for forty years) and asked for some advice. He wanted the name of someone in the Stimson-Acheson-McCloy tradition, someone experienced in the corporate establishment and yet wise in international affairs, a Wall Street lawyer who might make a good secretary of state. McCloy hardly paused to think before answering: "You won't find one. Those lawyers don't exist anymore. They're all too busy making money."

11

The Posthumous Lives of John F. Kennedy

The Sunday *New York Times* of November 24, 1963—the day before John Kennedy's funeral—was, of course, filled with stories about the president and his death. Virtually all of those stories, like virtually all other stories in newspapers and magazines, and on television and radio, all over the world that weekend, spoke with anguished reverence about the tragedy the nation had experienced. An extraordinary moment in history had prematurely ended; a bold, inspirational leader was suddenly gone: that was an attitude that anyone reading the paper that day might reasonably conclude was almost universal. When one Kennedy associate was quoted as commenting that "Life goes on, but brightness has fallen from the air. . . . A golden age is over and it will never be again," he was merely expressing sentiments that were already the common coin of public discourse within days of the assassination.[1]

But also in that Sunday paper was a minor, largely unnoticed item with a very different meaning. For sitting at the top of the weekly nonfiction bestseller list of the *New York Times Book Review*, as it had sat for several months before, was a recently published book by the conservative political writer Victor Lasky: *J.F.K.: The Man and the Myth*, a savage (some believed scurrilous) attack designed to persuade the public that the president's alluring image rested on a series of lies and deceptions. It claimed nothing less than that John Kennedy was a fraud, unfit—by character, temperament, and intellect—for the presidency.[2]

In the days after the assassination, many bookstores removed the

Lasky book from their shelves. It fell rapidly from the bestseller lists. And the questions it raised faded into obscurity for a time. But Lasky's dark image of the president, as much as the bright one that prevailed in that day's issue of the *Times*, suggested something important about the way John Kennedy had already entered the American imagination and would continue to live in it after his death, into our own time, and almost certainly beyond. On the one hand, Kennedy was then, and remains still, an embodiment of America's loftiest ideals and boldest hopes: as a gallant warrior whose death marked the end of an age of confidence and optimism and the beginning of an era of conflict and disenchantment; a symbol of the idealism and commitment of his age and an inspiration to countless younger men and women (Bill Clinton among them) to devote their lives to some form of public service. On the other hand, Kennedy was then, and remains now, a symbol of the underside of our political life: as an irresponsible libertine whose election to the presidency marked the triumph of image (and money) over substance. How these two images emerged, and how they have managed to coexist and to exercise such extraordinary power for more than thirty years, reveals the divided character of late twentieth-century cultural and political history.

John Kennedy served in office for fewer than three years. His tangible accomplishments during his foreshortened term were relatively modest. By most of the normal standards by which historians assess presidents, Kennedy seems now to be an undistinguished, even a minor figure. Indeed, a survey of historians in 1981, asking them to rank the presidents, placed Kennedy 13th. Another survey, conducted in 1996 by the *New York Times*, again placed him about in the middle of the pack. The historical John Kennedy, as opposed to the Kennedy of legend, was a cautious, practical, skillful politician, driven by political realism much more than by lofty ideals. Members of his administration boasted that, unlike some of the militant cold warriors of the 1950s, they were pragmatists, not ideologues. Kennedy himself seemed to move through his political life as a slightly bemused observer of his own success, as if reluctant to take himself or anything he did too seriously. It is one of the many ironies of Kennedy's posthumous image that a man who was himself so uncomfortable with passionate commitment would inspire so much of it in others.[3]

As president, as through his pre-presidential career, Kennedy walked gingerly through difficult moments and difficult issues, always searching for a middle ground, always leery of creating unnecessary conflict. He was slow to embrace the civil rights movement, uncertain in his relations with the corporate world, conservative in his embrace of Keynesianism, awkward in his dealings with Congress. Through most of his presidency, his foreign policy was largely reactive, driven by external events rather than by a coherent sense of goals. A plan by the Eisenhower administration drove him into the Bay of Pigs. A decision by Nikita Khrushchev drove him into the Cuban missile crisis. A decade of precedent led him reluctantly into Vietnam.[4]

It is true that Kennedy was hobbled by the slimness of his mandate, by the recalcitrance of Congress, and by a public that was only slowly warming to the idea of liberal activism. It is also true that by the last year of his life, there were indications that Kennedy was changing—becoming more confident, more dynamic, more mature; that in both foreign and domestic policy, he was beginning to suggest a depth of vision and commitment that had been largely lacking previously. But scholars must judge leaders by what they were and what they did, not by what they might have been. And it is not surprising, given the record, that one of the most eminent scholars of the presidency, Richard Neustadt—a great admirer of Kennedy in his lifetime and after, and a man greatly admired by Kennedy in turn—remarked sometime in the 1970s: "He will be just a flicker, forever clouded by the record of his successors. I don't think history will have much space for John Kennedy."

And yet the historical John Kennedy, the Kennedy many scholars try to depict, has proved to be almost irrelevant to the way the people of the United States (and much of the rest of the world) remember him. To them, he remains, and will likely long remain, a great deal more than "just a flicker." As William Leuchtenburg wrote during the wave of observances that marked the twentieth anniversary of Kennedy's death, "In the end the efforts of historians are not likely to have a very considerable effect on Kennedy's reputation, for he has already become part not of history but of myth. . . . Like the fair youth on Keats's Grecian urn, Kennedy will be forever in pursuit, forever unfulfilled, but also 'for ever young,' beyond the power of time and the words of historians."[5] Kennedy's image continues to burn in our historical imagination with an intensity that few other figures of this century can match—and with an intensity that seems to have very little relationship to his actual achievements. These enormously powerful myths are a reflection less of Kennedy himself than of some of the clashing assumptions and values of America's troubled public culture. Powerful sets of cultural and political beliefs shape both versions of the Kennedy myth and make him a larger and more powerful figure in death than he ever was in life.

The heroic myth of John Kennedy, which began to emerge even before the president's death and became enshrined in the public imagination within days of the assassination, was in part the product of efforts by the Kennedy family and its circle to honor him and to make his reputation the basis of their own future political hopes. Grief and emotion combined with ambition and self-interest to create the fuzzy, romantic, almost mystical image of Kennedy that was for many years almost unchallenged. But it was not just relatives and intimates who created the heroic legend. It was a public eager to believe in it, a public that seemed in many ways almost to require it. Even while he lived, as president, he was beginning to become a national obsession: a man who had been elected to the presidency by the narrowest margin in modern history, but who by the middle of 1963 had already become so magnetic a figure that 59 percent of the public surveyed in an opinion poll claimed that they had voted for him (and apparently genuinely believed they had, even though in reality he had received only 49.7 percent of the vote). After his death, his imaginary landslide grew to 65 percent.[6]

Kennedy's death—the horrible, violent death in Dallas that remains one of the great traumas of modern American history, an event that left indelible marks on virtually everyone old enough in 1963 to be aware of it—helped turn this growing obsession into something approaching a religion. Well before the rash of conspiracy theories that have made the Kennedy assassination so continually visible in our culture, it had become an event of mythic proportions. Arthur Schlesinger, Jr., his friend and adviser and one of the nation's pre-eminent historians, wrote of it in his 1965 history/memoir of the Kennedy years, *A Thousand Days*, in phrases so exalted that it is difficult to imagine them being used about anyone today. At the time, however, they expressed ideas so familiar that they were striking only for their eloquence. "One remembered Stephen Spender's poem," he wrote:

> I think continually of those who were truly great . . .
> The names of those who in their lives fought for life,

> Who wore at their hearts the fire's center.
> Born of the sun they traveled a short while towards the sun,
> And left the vivid air signed with their honour.

"It was all gone now—the life-affirming, life-enhancing zest, the brilliance, the wit, the cool commitment, the steady purpose."[7]

The power of the heroic legend, carefully nurtured by Kennedy's family and friends and absorbed by an eager public, grew quickly. Only a year after his death, James Reston, the *New York Times* columnist, wrote: "Deprived of the place he sought in history, he has been given in compensation a place in legend." Two decades later, Kennedy's friend Theodore White, in memoirs White published not long before his death, conveyed something, but only a small part, of the reverence and awe that even then attached to his image:

> I still have difficulty seeing John F. Kennedy clear.
>
> The image of him that comes back to me, as to most who knew him, is so clean and graceful—almost as if I can still see him skip up the steps of his airplane in that half lope, and then turn, flinging out his arm in farewell to the crowd, before disappearing inside. It was a ballet movement. The remembered pleasures of travel with him clutter the outline of history.[8]

The contrasting image of Kennedy, what the revisionists Peter Collier and David Horowitz have called the "counter-myth," was slower to emerge. But beginning in the late 1960s and accelerating rapidly thereafter, it moved out of the shadows of the discredited Victor Lasky and into full public view. Some of the reassessment came from historians and others who saw in Kennedy's policies an intensification of a destructive cold war militancy and the origins of the disastrous war in Vietnam. Some came from disillusioned veterans of the civil rights movement, as they discovered that Kennedy (his forceful public support notwithstanding) had also worked to contain the movement and even, through the FBI, to discredit its leaders. But even more of the reassessment came from those who grew disillusioned with Kennedy the man, who, in an age preoccupied with the personal behavior of public figures, came to doubt his strength and depth of character and to see in him a recklessness and moral emptiness that by the 1970s had come to seem all too characteristic of American political culture. A string of books appeared—by Herbert Parmet, Henry Fairlie, Peter Collier and David Horowitz, Garry Wills, David Halberstam, Richard Walton, Thomas Reeves, and even by such friends and admirers as Harris Wofford and Ben Bradlee—that created a picture of a much shallower and less accomplished figure than most Americans remembered. Some went much further, and offered an image of an exceptionally dangerous and malevolent leader: a man described variously as driven by "an obsessive-compulsive need for power and social recognition," as the "very embodiment of middlebrow culture climbing," as a leader utterly lacking in "depth or seriousness of purpose."[9]

Neither the negative nor the positive image has very much connection with the real John Kennedy (although both versions have now achieved a reality of their own). But both have at least some basis in the same aspects of Kennedy's personality and style—and in three aspects in particular.

First, his youth. Kennedy was the youngest president ever elected to the presidency (succeeding the man who, at the time, was the oldest); he seemed to symbolize—as he perhaps realized better than anyone else—the changing of the guard, the coming of age of a new generation. He was the first person born in the twentieth century and the first member of the World War II generation to become president. (Kennedy's wartime heroism—the celebrated sinking of the ship he captained, PT 109, and his subsequent efforts to save members of his crew, widely publicized by John Hersey in a celebrated *New Yorker* essay—had helped him launch his political career.) In his notable inaugural address, a lofty, almost (but not quite) pretentious piece of oratory with phrases that seemed designed to be carved in stone one day (as, in fact, many of them have been), he said: "Let the word go forth: that the torch has been passed to a new generation of Americans, born in this century, tempered by war, disciplined by a hard and bitter peace." He symbolized in the 1960s a sort of generational imperative: the need for youth to carry forward the battles that the older generation seemed no longer capable of fighting.

And yet Kennedy's youth—his iconoclasm, his orientation toward the new and untried, his impatience with established rules and procedures, the qualities that to many at the time seemed so refreshing and vigorous and even cathartic—later appeared to some critics to have been a source of recklessness, impatience, impetuosity, arrogance. Before he became president, many of his political colleagues considered him simply a rich playboy, whose father had bought him his offices. Nigel Hamilton, author of a generally admiring study of JFK's life up to 1946, concludes after 1,000 pages: "He had the brains, the courage, the shy charisma, good looks, idealism, money. Yet, as always, there was something missing—a certain depth or seriousness of purpose. . . . Once the voters or the women were won, there was a certain vacuousness on Jack's part, a failure to turn conquest into anything very meaningful or profound."[10] That was an assessment of John Kennedy in his youth; some of his friends and acquaintances felt much the same way even fifteen years later, as he entered the presidency: that there was a certain immaturity, shallowness, and even recklessness in him; a callow (and dangerous) disregard for the normal channels and procedures by which the state disciplines and restrains itself; and a gravitation toward a style of governance that Garry Wills has called "guerrilla government," because it set out to circumvent the bureaucracy and even the law.[11]

It is not surprising, perhaps, that a change of attitude has occurred. In the years since the 1960s, the youthful insistence on change and the youthful contempt for the old and the traditional have gradually lost favor. America's traumatic encounters with its own youth in the late 1960s and early 1970s, the social turbulence and intergenerational bitterness they produced, and the memories of those encounters that remain vivid a generation later have tempered enthusiasm for many of Kennedy's qualities. In an era in which many Americans have come to regard bold initiatives with suspicion, in which they look increasingly to the past for guidance and inspiration, Kennedy's sense of a generational imperative has lost much of its allure.

A second quality that helped shape the Kennedy legends was his public presence and his personal charm. He was a man who seemed built for the age of television—gifted, witty, articulate. Even many of those who have become disillusioned with Kennedy over the years are still struck, when they see him on film, by how smooth, polished, and spontaneously eloquent he was, how impressive a presence, how elegant a speaker.

But Kennedy's charm and poise and media skills, which did so much to enhance his image, later came to seem to many people somehow dark and manipulative. Kennedy did not just look good in the media; he *used* the media, carefully, consciously, calculatedly, not only in his campaigns but throughout his presidency. He carefully staged public appearances.

He co-opted journalists and made them into something approaching courtiers (as Ben Bradlee candidly and somewhat ruefully admitted later). He browbeat even friendly reporters when anything appeared in print that he found even mildly irritating. His celebrated press conferences were in many ways exercises in manipulation; they conveyed no more information that those of other presidents, just more charm (and considerable condescension toward women). Malcolm Muggeridge, the acerbic English writer, wrote in the 1970s: "John F. Kennedy, it is now coming to be realized, was a nothing man—an expensively programmed waxwork, a camera-microphone-public relations creation whose career, on examination, turns into a strip cartoon rather than history." I. F. Stone wrote in 1973: "By now he is simply an optical illusion."[12] This is an age in which many Americans look with suspicion on the way politicians use and manipulate the media, in which many have come to fear that the images of public figures have obscured and even replaced their substance. And so it has been tempting to see Kennedy as a media creation, a fraud who, through his charm and eloquence, created an image of himself out of nothing.

A third quality responsible for the Kennedy legends, something deeper than his personal attractiveness, is the image of what many came to call grace. (*That Special Grace* was the title of an admiring book in the 1960s.)[13] Kennedy was not only a man who had grace, in the sense of performing and acting gracefully; he was a man who seemed to *be* graced. ("Charisma," the word so often identified with him, is derived from a Greek word meaning "gift of grace.") Kennedy was handsome and athletic-looking. He was wealthy; his father, Joseph P. Kennedy, was one of the richest men in America and bankrolled his son's campaigns. He had a beautiful wife and appealing children, a large and attractive family. He connected himself with high culture. (Eisenhower had entertained at the White House with middle-brow entertainers such as Guy Lombardo; Kennedy invited the cellist Pablo Casals and the poet Robert Frost and the French writer André Malraux.) He was comfortable with ideas and intellectuals. He sprinkled his public remarks with quotations from poets and philosophers. He had gone to Harvard, written books, won a Pulitzer Prize. He self-consciously surrounded himself in office with "the best and the brightest."

In hindsight, of course, it is clear that Kennedy's image of grace and accomplishment rested in part on a series of carefully crafted illusions and deceptions. Kennedy was not the vigorous, athletic figure he so often appeared to be; he was a remarkably sickly man, who had spent much of his life in the hospital battling various illnesses and who as president suffered from Addison's Disease, a crippling and usually fatal adrenal insufficiency that required him to take cortisone and many other powerful drugs, all carefully concealed from the public. Kennedy was not the contented, loving husband and family man he seemed to be. On the contrary, he led a squalid, covert private life; like his father before him, he was almost obsessed with the ritual of sexual conquest, both before and after his marriage, both before and during his presidency. And Kennedy was not in reality much interested in high culture; he was in fact generally bored by literature and art, uninterested in Robert Frost and Pablo Casals except as props for his public image. He had a stronger attraction to more prosaic cultural figures: Ian Fleming, author of the James Bond novels; Frank Sinatra, who sang at Kennedy's inauguration. And although he was certainly an intelligent and literate man, he was not really much of an intellectual or a writer. There is strong reason to believe (although Kennedy always denied it) that his connection with the writing of *Profiles in Courage*, the book that won him the Pulitzer Prize, was at best casual. His aide Theodore Sorensen and others wrote most of it, and family retainers such as Arthur Krock, enlisted by Kennedy's father, maneuvered it through the jury to secure it the Pulitzer Prize (for which it had not been recommended by the historians on the advisory committee).

Such revelations, seized upon by critics with an almost prurient glee, have turned the image of youth, charisma, accomplishment, and "grace" on its head. They have made it possible to portray Kennedy as a symbol of the fraudulence of public life, of the manipulation of public images, and of the arrogant tendency of public figures to repudiate the values and rules that, in theory, govern more ordinary lives. They have made Kennedy a symbol of the shattered image of the public world that plagues the politics of our own time.

Yet in the end both Kennedy's enormous popularity in the 1960s, and the bitter reassessments of later decades, rested less on these qualities than on another aspect of Kennedy's life—something that transcended his own personality and talents, his own limitations and weaknesses. Kennedy became, both in his life and in his death, an embodiment of a particular moment in American history, a moment that continues, decades later, to shape our view of our world and our politics and to both inspire and confound those who believe in public life. For Kennedy managed, partly by design and partly by historical accident, to represent a growing national desire for activism, for renewed national purpose, for performance. He was the man who, as he liked to put it, would "get the country moving again," at a time when much of the country was ready to move.

The centrality of this idea of action and dynamism is evident in some of Kennedy's own statements, especially during his presidential campaign, when he complained frequently of the stagnation over which Republicans had presided for eight years. He said in his acceptance speech before the 1960 Democratic Convention in Los Angeles: "I have premised my campaign for the presidency on the single assumption that the American people are uneasy at the present drift in our national course . . . and that they have the will and the strength to start the United States moving again." Richard Strout, who wrote the "TRB" column in the *New Republic*, described the candidate shortly after the convention as "a young man offering positive leadership and presidential power to the uttermost." Arthur Schlesinger, Jr. sensed this aspect of the Kennedy years in the contrast he later described between the new administration in 1961 and its predecessor: "The capital city, somnolent in the Eisenhower years, had suddenly come alive. The air had been stale and oppressive; now fresh winds were blowing. There was the excitement which comes from the injection of new men and new ideas, the release of energy which occurs when men of ideas have a chance to put them into practice."[14]

For fifteen years after the end of World War II, a sort of ideological momentum had been slowly building in the United States—fueled by anxieties about the rivalry with the Soviet Union and optimism about the extraordinary performance of the American economy—a momentum behind the active pursuit of a great national goal. Henry Luce, always eager to promote great American missions, recruited a group of eminent scholars and writers to produce a series of essays in 1960, which he collected in a volume entitled *The National Purpose.* (The writers were not entirely in accord about what the national purpose should be, but they never questioned the idea that there was, and should be, one.) The desire for movement and change was, in 1960, still cautious and tentative (as the extraordinarily thin margin by which Kennedy defeated Nixon that year suggests). But the desire was there, and growing. And it continued to do so for several years after Kennedy's death. Kennedy seemed to have seized the moment, to have provided, or at least grasped, the mission, even though it was not at first entirely clear what the mission was.[15]

Kennedy's identification with this moment of unusual public activism helps explain much of his appeal to Americans of the 1960s, and to many Americans today who look back nostalgically on the greater sense of confidence and purpose they remember in those years. It helps explain, too, the bitter disillusionment with the Kennedy myth. On the one hand, Kennedy's image of mission and purpose and idealism serves as an appealing contrast to what often seems the emptiness and aimlessness of today's public world. It reminds many Americans of a time when it was possible to believe that politics could be harnessed to their highest aspirations for themselves and their country, that it could be rooted in a sense of national community, that it could speak to America's moral yearnings. And it suggests, too, that perhaps politics could be that way again.

On the other hand, that same image reminds us of some of the dark or disappointing places to which that sense of mission took the nation: into Vietnam and other dangerous and costly international commitments that the nation later came to regret; into a series of ambitious domestic commitments that later became the source of profound disillusionment. Americans are no longer confident of their nation's capacity to make the world conform to their image of what it should be; and they are no longer confident of government's capacity to solve social problems, to manage the economy, even to manage itself. They have come to doubt the apparently serene assurance of some liberals in the Kennedy years that the answers to the nation's problems were at hand, that all that was lacking was the will to seize them.

Most of all, perhaps, Kennedy reminds Americans of a time when the nation's capacities seemed limitless, when its future seemed unbounded, when it was possible to believe that the United States could solve social problems and accomplish great deeds without great conflict and without great cost. And he is a reminder, too, of how much more difficult it has proved to confront those problems than the promise of the 1960s suggested. Both at home and abroad, the ambitious missions of the 1960s created substantial conflict and brought with them enormous costs. That was a reality that Kennedy and his generation of liberals did very little to prepare themselves, or the nation, to accept. It is a reality that Americans continue to be reluctant to confront. And that, perhaps, is the real reason why, in more recent times, the bright promise of those years has continued to burn so brightly for some and has come to seem fraudulent, even dangerous to others.

Arthur Schlesinger, Jr. wrote in the conclusion of *A Thousand Days* of Kennedy's brief years in office:

> . . . he had accomplished so much. . . . Lifting us beyond our capacities, he gave his country back to its best self, wiping away the world's impression of an old nation of old men, weary, played out, fearful of ideas, change and the future; he taught mankind that the process of rediscovering America was not over. He re-established the republic as the first generation of our leaders saw it—young, brave, civilized, rational, gay, tough, questing, exultant in the excitement and potentiality of history.[16]

Some historians have challenged the heroic Kennedy legend because they see such a glaring contrast between the relatively modest accomplishments of the Kennedy presidency and the extravagant rhetoric in which it has been clothed. But most of the nonscholarly public has little patience with such conventional, empirical assessments. To them, Kennedy is important—for good or for ill—precisely because they sense that in many respects Schlesinger was right. Kennedy did set in motion, even if inadvertently, powerful forces of change. He did evoke a sense of energy and ambition that inspired a generation (and inspires many still). He did come to symbolize, without always meaning to, a new sense of mission in American life, tied to an expansive vision of committed and active government.

To those who yearn for a new age of public activism and commitment, the heroic Kennedy remains a bright and beckoning symbol of the world they have lost. But to many others, disillusioned with idealism and mission and, above all, active government, Kennedy has become a symbol of a heedless, action-oriented impetuosity that led the nation into a series of catastrophes and frustrations from which it has not yet wholly recovered.

Kennedy himself, and to a far greater extent Kennedy's emotional and political legacy, did indeed "accomplish so much," even if not exactly in the ways Schlesinger meant; and that is why he remains an important figure in our national imagination. But not far beneath the clear, cool, graceful image of John Kennedy that still dominates our public memory lies a powerful, nagging doubt: the fear that he may have accomplished too much.

12

The Therapeutic Radicalism of the New Left

For a brief moment in the 1960s, a small group of student radicals managed to do what the American left had largely failed to achieve in almost a century of trying: create a genuine mass movement. The New Left was a short-lived phenomenon, to be sure, which soon collapsed on itself in a paroxysm of frustration, nihilism, and violence. But for a while before the end it penetrated deeply into the heart of American culture, with lasting effects, and profoundly shook (although it failed to transform) the American political system. The New Left is remembered today largely for its failures and excesses. Its history is important, however, not only for how student radicalism ultimately went so wrong, but also for how that radicalism emerged and briefly flourished. It is important above all, perhaps, for what it says about a generation—the largest generation in the nation's history—that produced, and always dominated, the New Left.

The immediate crises of the 1960s explain much of the rise of the New Left. The civil rights movement and the racial turmoil that emerged in its wake had an enormous influence on the reawakening of the left. So did the Vietnam war and the powerful domestic opposition it spawned. But the revolt of the postwar generation was not an American phenomenon alone. It occurred simultaneously through much of the world: in France, Germany, Italy, Mexico, Japan, Korea, and elsewhere. And that suggests that the broad discontents of the "baby boomers" were also a result of a deeper, and more universal, series of changes than the immediate American crises of the time.

The men and women who were coming of age in advanced industrial societies in the late 1960s were part of a distinctive generation. Born in the aftermath of World War II, they were raised in the shadow of the cold war. But they also grew up in the midst of unprecedented prosperity. The dramatic economic growth of the postwar era, and the expectations it produced, had much to do with the explosions in 1968. In the age of abundance and cold war liberalism, according to the dominant messages of both official and popular culture, those who lived in the capitalist world would be blessed with both prosperity and personal freedom. That was what distinguished the West from its communist adversaries: the opportunity of individuals to live their lives as they wished with reasonable comfort and security; the opportunity to pursue not just material success but personal fulfillment. Never before in history had so many people come of age expecting so much of their world, and so much of themselves.

The upheavals among young people in the 1960s—in the United States and throughout the industrial world—reflected, at least in part, the gap between these bright expectations and reality. For as members of the postwar generation moved toward adulthood, they discovered that conservative values and institutions still stood in their way. Colleges and universities remained wedded to patriarchal notions of learning and to rigid codes of conduct. Communities and families still lived by Victorian notions of behavior and decorum. Both the state and society continued to sustain discriminatory structures that oppressed women and minorities and perpetuated old patterns of entrenched privilege. American society, like most other industrial societies, was considerably less rigid and hierarchical in the 1960s than it had been a generation before; but neither was it fluid or tolerant enough to match the expansive expectations of its youth. And so a generation came of age unusually impatient with what to older men and women seemed ordinary restraints and conventions, and unusually outraged by evidence of injustices and inequalities that earlier generations had tolerated or endured. The particular crises of the 1960s in America occurred in the context of this rising determination of many young people across much of the world to seize control of the future.

The distinctive character of the postwar generation helps to explain one of the most striking features of the New Left: that its successes in the 1960s came on the heels of a time of particular discouragement for

American radicalism. Indeed, in the course of the 1950s the Old Left (as it is now known) had come closer to extinction than at any time in this century. It was harried and intimidated by official and popular anticommunist crusades. It was deeply shaken by the 1956 de-Stalinization crisis in the Soviet Union. It grew isolated from its traditional constituency—the working class—by the booming prosperity of the postwar era. As the decade ended, the U.S. Communist party was all but dead; and the independent socialists survived as small, isolated sects waiting for a shift in the climate that might allow their movement to be reborn. When the moment of rebirth finally came in the early 1960s, however, the Old Left was unable to exploit it.

The most promising group within the Old Left in the lean years after 1956 were the Shachtmanites, a small band of Trostskyist socialists led since the 1930s by the talented activist Max Shachtman (once a friend and disciple of Trotsky himself). Shachtman possessed unparalleled political and organizational skills, and after 1958—when he merged his organization with the struggling Socialist party and effectively seized control of its machinery—he and his followers became the dominant force on the socialist left. It was a modest distinction, but one of enormous importance to Shachtman himself—so much so that he steadfastly resisted recruiting new members to the tiny Socialist party from among the now orphaned former communists. "The habits of a lifelong sectarianism reasserted themselves," notes historian Maurice Isserman, "as Shachtman decided it was better to control a narrow group than to risk losing control of a broader movement."[1]

Shachtman came to despair of finding an adequate revolutionary constituency from within the American working class, and by the 1950s he was looking (prophetically) to youth as a potential radical vanguard. But the same preoccupation with Stalinism that constricted Shachtman's ability to resuscitate the Socialist party affected the various student organizations he helped create. (His anti-Stalinism eventually pushed him so far to the right that he supported the war in Vietnam and proclaimed George Meany the principal hope for progressive change.)

The Young Person's Socialist League (YPSL)—which, after a series of arcane organizational maneuverings, emerged at the end of the 1950s as the principal Shachtmanite youth group—had more success than the Socialist party itself in expanding its membership. By 1962 it had over 800 members, far more than any other student organization; among its early leaders was Michael Harrington. But YPSL never managed to free itself from the Old Left's obsession with Stalinism. Its members believed fervently in the Bolshevik tradition as interpreted by Trotsky; they scrutinized potential allies and recruits for signs of insufficient ardor in the campaign against the tradition's Stalinist traducers. The strong internal cohesion and the remarkable organizing skills YPSL had derived from Max Shachtman made it a prime candidate to lead a revived left. But other Shachtman legacies—what Isserman calls its "inward-looking self-preoccupation," its "inflated sense of self-importance," its conviction that "'History' could be relied upon to deliver its 'opportunities'" and that the "real question was the subjective preparation of the revolutionary elite"—all conspired to isolate the organization from the rising tides of student protest in the early 1960s and to consign it, ultimately, to oblivion.[2]

To the radical intellectuals who spent much of the 1950s writing for Irving Howe's *Dissent* and other "little magazines" of the left, the suffocating sectarianism of the Shachtmanites became a model of how not to advance socialism. Howe had grown up politically as a friend and ally of Shachtman, but by the mid-1950s he had charted his own course. Partly, as his memoir makes clear, this was a matter of personal inclination. Howe was simply more comfortable with the literary and academic world than with the intense, hermetic life of the sect. But it was also a political decision. Socialist organizations, Howe came to believe, "did nothing but sit around and talk," mulling endlessly over stale phrases and ancient disputes. Were radicalism to revive, he argued, it "would need to be equipped with something more than the 'correct line.'"[3]

Howe and the "*Dissent* crowd" performed yeomen's service to the left through the 1950s, keeping alive a radical critique of American politics, culture, and foreign policy and opening up discussion of socialist ideas to a larger audience than a disciplined party sect could hope to reach. But if the intellectuals managed to free themselves from the sect, they did not entirely free themselves from sectarianism. They watched aghast in the early 1960s as a new generation of radicals emerged, largely uninterested in the battles their elders had spent so much of their lives fighting. By attempting to impose their own doctrinal purity on the new movement, they created a breach that was never to be repaired. "On many issues they were willing to let the New Left find its own way," Isserman writes. "But there was one issue on which they would not bend: their attitude toward communism. . . . And in a mostly mistaken reading of the temper of the New Left—which was less infatuated with communism than bored by anticommunism—they lost the political opportunity for which they had been waiting a lifetime."

The radical tradition that was perhaps best positioned ideologically to lead a revived left in the early 1960s stood largely outside the incestuous world of the socialists: radical pacifism. American pacifists drew from their own, mostly indigenous traditions—from Quakerism, New England Protestantism and transcendentalism, the memory of the abolitionists, and more recently the example of Gandhi. Unburdened by the baggage of the socialists—free of both the taint of Stalinism and the sectarian preoccupations of the anti-Stalinists—their emphasis on morality and "values" seemed, Isserman notes, "fresh, individualistic, and in tune with both popular cultural assumptions and the anti-ideological predilections of American intellectuals since World War II."[4]

The 1950s were in many ways as lean for the pacifists as they were for the socialists. But pacifists managed nevertheless to keep their tradition alive—through nonviolent action to "bear witness" against nuclear weapons and racism; through the efforts of such talented leaders as A. J. Muste (veteran of many earlier radical battles), David Dellinger, and Bayard Rustin; and through such small but vigorous organizations as the committee for a Sane Nuclear Policy (SANE), the Congress of Racial Equality (CORE), and the Committee for Non-Violent Action. As the civil rights movement and (later) the Vietnam war energized a new generation of student activists in the 1960s, the pacifists were often more influential and more popular among them than other older radicals. Muste, in particular, enjoyed substantial popularity within the new student left; and Dellinger ultimately became a leader of the 1968 Chicago demonstrations (and one of the seven radicals whose trial did so much to publicize the New Left in its waning years).

But pacifism in the end had only marginally greater influence on the New Left than orthodox socialism. Few opponents of the Vietnam war were true pacifists; they opposed a particular war, not all wars. Few white student radicals ever developed a deep commitment to the principles of nonviolent resistance; to most it was simply a tactic, to be abandoned when it ceased to be useful. Many members of Students for a Democratic Society (SDS), after their organization emerged as the principal voice of the New Left, began to see pacifism as an admirable but increasingly irrelevant stance. Eventually, some came to consider it an actual impediment to progress. An SDS Weatherman in 1969, denouncing those who were trying to moderate the movement's increasingly violent course, complained bitterly of "all these old people who came into the Movement at a time when pacifism was important, at a time when there was a total consciousness of defeat, when the only reasons that we were in it were moral reasons, when there was no strategy for victory."[5]

The New Left did not, of course, emerge entirely independently of the Old. The points of connection, in fact, were many. There were the children of radicals and labor organizers ("red diaper babies" and others), who formed much of the early leadership of the movement. There were, in the beginnning at least, important institutional connections. There were innumerable ideological borrowings. For all that, however, the New Left was in the end something genuinely new; and that newness brought both strengths and weaknesses. It brought freedom from the sectarian shibboleths of the Old Left. But it also denied student activists access to the organizational talents, the ideological coherence, and the experience in long-term organizing efforts that the older radicals might have offered.

Both the extent and the limits of the connections between the Old Left and the New are visible in the story of the founding of SDS. It emerged out of the rubble of the Student League for Industrial Democracy (SLID), the obscure student wing of the equally obscure League for Industrial Democracy, an old socialist labor organization. In 1960, SLID renamed itself Students for a Democratic Society (perhaps to eliminate its unfortunate acronym). It retained its organizational and financial ties to the LID, but the relationship soon turned sour.

That was largely because SDS quickly and self-consciously declared its ideological independence both from its parent organization and from the Old Left in general. The independence was clearly visible in, among other places, the Port Huron Statement of 1962, the famous SDS manifesto that has survived as one of the best known documents of the decade. Patched together during a marathon three-day conference at a United Auto Workers conference center in northern Michigan, the Port Huron Statement conspicuously ignored issues of central concern to the older socialists. It included no ringing endorsement of the labor movement. (Indeed, early drafts contained statements that LID leaders considered critical of the working class.) More significant, it contained no strong denunciation of communism. (A symbol of the gulf separating these younger radicals from their anti-Stalinist elders was one delegate's wide-eyed and disappointed response to the early departure from Port Huron of a communist observer: "Do you mean to say there was a *Communist* here? . . . I've never *seen* one.")[6]

Michael Harrington, who briefly attended the conference on behalf of the LID, became (unwittingly, at age 32) a symbol of the Old Left's response to the new generation. Harrington angrily demanded revisions in the Port Huron Statement's discussion of labor and communism; and when informed several days later (falsely) that his suggestions had been ignored, he persuaded the LID to fire the SDS leadership, change the locks on their offices in New York, and repudiate the manifesto altogether. Later, when he saw the document and realized it was less offensive than he had feared, he relented. But hard feelings remained on both sides. The rift never fully healed, and SDS finally severed all its ties to the LID in 1965.

In the meantime, the students who had come together in SDS were engaged in intense intellectual debates of their own as the organization's founders attempted to build a set of theories with which they could live. The movement began, the historian James Miller suggests, as "a kind of freewheeling seminar for young intellectuals," meeting in Ann Arbor coffee houses, basement "offices," and shabby living rooms in graduate student apartments. Members spent more time reading, writing, and talking than they did organizing. Chief among the early leaders were Al Haber, a University of Michigan graduate student and SDS's first president, who described the new organizaton as a vehicle to "formulate radical alternatives to the inadequate society of today"; and Tom Hayden, a talented Michigan undergraduate, recruited by Haber, who became the organization's leading theorist and the principal author of the Port Huron Statement.[7]

Hayden, Haber, and others were responding to many influences. The impersonality of the modern university, the fear of nuclear war, and the memory of McCarthyism were all sources of discontent. The emerging civil rights movement had a profound effect. (Hayden spent much of 1961 in the South, worked with the Student Nonviolent Coordinating Committee [SNCC], and was once badly beaten by local whites in McComb, Mississippi.) But above all, it seems, SDS drew inspiration from the literature of alienation that had emerged with special force in the 1950s among sociologists, psychologists, novelists, filmmakers, Beat poets, and others. Particularly influential was the sociologist C. Wright

Mills—a maverick radical who largely ignored traditional Marxist theory and wrote passionately about the alienation of the middle class in an increasingly bureaucratic, undemocratic world. Mills took a stubborn pride in his isolation from the doctrinal controversies of the socialist left. Once a young socialist grew so frustrated by a conversation in which Mills challenged his every assumption that he shot back, "Just what do you believe in, Mills?" Mills looked up from tinkering with his BMW motorcycle and unhesitatingly replied, "German engines."[8]

SDS theorists were struck in particular by Mills's caustic description of American politics. "By virtue of their increased and centralized power," he once wrote, "political institutions become more objectively important to the course of American history, but because of mass alienation, less and less of subjective interest to the population at large. On the one hand, politics is bureaucratized, and on the other, there is mass indifference."[9] The goal of radicals, the SDS theorists concluded, should be to challenge that indifference and destroy that alienation. It should be to create (in a phrase borrowed from Michigan professor Arnold Kaufman) a "participatory democracy." The key to the future was getting individuals directly involved in the decisions that affected their lives. "The goal of man and society," the Port Huron Statement proclaimed (in the gendered language of its time), "should be human independence: a concern . . . with finding a meaning in life that is personally authentic." The new generation should seek a democracy "governed by two central aims: that the individual share in those social decisions determining the quality and direction of his life; that society be organized to encourage independence in men and provide the media for their common participation."

When compared to most of the Old Left and even when compared to its own later self, SDS in its early years was not a particularly radical organization. It did not repudiate capitalism. It seemed at times to rest its hopes on the Democratic party, believing (as Miller puts it) "that established liberals could be cajoled into changing their errant ways, rather as a tolerant, thoughtful father might be moved to respond to the urgent entreaties of a well-meaning son."[10] The first major SDS political campaign—the Economic Research and Action Project (ERAP), founded in 1963—was in many ways an effort compatible with the mainstream liberalism of its time. SDS volunteers moved into inner-city ghettoes and tried to organize the poor to demand increased attention from established centers of power. When Lyndon Johnson announced the War on Poverty in 1964, some ERAP members, looking at the Community Action program, were briefly ecstatic—convinced that the establishment had embraced their goals.

Even in its later years, when the Vietnam war had pushed some SDS members much further to the left, others continued to hope for a reconciliation with the mainstream. Tom Hayden still retained hopes for liberalism as late as 1968, at the same time that he was participating in the insurrection at Columbia and planning the mayhem in Chicago. Hayden developed a modest personal relationship with Robert Kennedy, whom he came genuinely to admire. On the eve of Kennedy's funeral, he wept in a pew in St. Patrick's Cathedral, then stood in the "honor guard" of friends and family who kept vigil around the coffin through the night. Later, with friends in Ann Arbor, he watched television coverage of Kennedy's burial, wept again, and felt what he remembered as "feelings of loss and despair and grim, grim days ahead."[11]

By 1968 SDS was no longer a small debating society centered in Ann Arbor, no longer a network of modest outposts in inner-city neighborhoods. It was a mass movement, with branches on almost every major campus in America, with perhaps 100,000 members, and with influence far beyond its own ranks.

It is ironic that Vietnam was the agency for this transformation, since many SDS leaders at first took relatively little interest in the war. Plans for the first SDS antiwar march in 1965 sparked bitter internal opposition from Hayden and others, who considered Vietnam a distraction from other, more important undertakings (most notably ERAP); the organization's national leadership only barely passed a resolution to proceed with the demonstration. But when the march succeeded beyond the planners' wildest expectations, attracting at least 15,000 protesters to Washington and wide media attention, the future course of SDS was to some degree set. Over the next three years, opposition to the war gradually became the organization's principal concern and its most effective recruiting device. But as SDS grew larger, it also grew more spontaneous and decentralized. And it developed some glaring weaknesses, which helped ensure that SDS's explosive growth would lead not to triumph but to collapse.[12]

The New Left, unlike the Old, never developed a relationship with, or even a real affinity for, the American working class. And indeed, over time, the idea of class struggle seemed to disappear from all but a few corners of the movement. SDS was born out of efforts by socialists trying to revive an indigenous labor radicalism, and it began, in theory at least, as an auxiliary force in the task of mobilizing and radicalizing workers. (Later in the 1960s, the Progressive Labor party argued that the *only* purpose of the left was to mobilize and radicalize the proletariat; students and other middle-class radicals could play only a secondary role in the process of revolution.) But on the whole, the New Left did not form (or even try very hard to form) any meaningful connection with the working class. More than that, some on the left came to identify the working class not as a potential ally but as one of their most powerful and least redeemable enemies.

Few members of the working class rallied to the support of the left's demands for economic reform. Most unions had purged their leftist members in the 1940s and early 1950s; and while there were some leftists still in the rank and file, they seldom created links with the student left. Relatively few white workers rallied to support the left's demands for racial justice; in fact—despite the conspicuous role of Walter Reuther and some other labor leaders in the civil rights movement—many on the left came to consider working-class whites as the source of reactionary opposition to racial progress. Much of the working class not only did not rally to, but actually opposed, the left's demand for an end to the war in Vietnam; some of the most visible demonstrations of support for the war came from American workers—including an enormous pro-war march in New York in 1967, organized specifically to demonstrate workers' contempt for student dissenters; and a vicious attack by construction workers wearing hardhats on an antiwar march in New York in 1969. A radical journalist in Berkeley wrote, after watching one of these pro-war parades by union members in New York: "A hundred thousand workers marched down Fifth Avenue . . . Seamen, Teamsters, Longshoremen, Auto workers, Carpenters, Bricklayers, and many others. . . . Anyway, the next time some $3.90 an hour AFL-type workers go on strike for a 50 cent raise, I'll remember the day they chanted 'Burn Hanoi, Not Our Flag,' and so help me I'll cross their fucking picket line."

There were fleeting efforts among some white student radicals to forge a relationship with the African-American left (which, having moved decisively in the direction of black nationalism, had no interest in such an alliance) and with the oppressed peoples of the Third World (with whom there were virtually no practical possibilities of any genuine connection). But the New Left's constituency remained overwhelmingly white, middle-class, and young.

The failure to broaden its constituency was, in the end, the New

Left's principal failure. But there were others as well. The new radicals never developed the organizational or institutional skills necessary for building an enduring movement. Nor did they create an ideology sufficiently coherent to sustain the loyalties of its members in the face of the enormous political frustrations they encountered in the late 1960s. Because the movement had no internal discipline, it proved incapable of controlling the new forces it attracted and the passions it gradually unleashed.

In SDS's last stages, some members gave up on the ideals that had once entranced them—participatory democracy and individual regeneration—and seemed driven almost purely by cynicism, hatred, and rage. "I'm a nihilist! I'm proud of it, proud of it!" shouted a delegate to a 1967 SDS meeting in Princeton. "Tactics? It's too late. . . . Let's break what we can. Make as many answer as we can. Tear them apart."[13] This kind of mindless anger and despair produced the final, terrifying remnant of SDS—the Weathermen, who believed in guerrilla warfare, staged the vicious "Days of Rage" in Chicago in 1969 (to "tear pig city apart"), and ultimately perished in the 1970 explosion of their bomb factory in Greenwich Village.

At the same time SDS was attracting the attention of more disciplined outside groups, which recognized the organization's internal weaknesses and saw it as a ripe target for a takeover. In June 1969 members of the Progressive Labor party—a harsh, paramilitary, Marxist-Leninist organization—formally seized control; but they had been infiltrating and poisoning the organization for at least two years before that. Partly because of their influence, the movement began to display a new and troubling characteristic: harsh, dogmatic intolerance. It is unsurprising that at this point Herbert Marcuse began to become an important influence among student radicals, with his critique of liberal tolerance as "serving the cause of oppression" and his belief that society owed no tolerance to ideas that were "radically evil."[14] Among many on the left, definitions of what was "radically evil" quickly became exceptionally broad.

SDS departed in many ways from its original path, and that departure greatly damaged the movement. But there were serious, perhaps fatal weakness at the heart of the New Left from the very beginning. Revolutionary movements are, almost by definition, self-denying phenomena, dependent on the willingness of their members to subordinate individual goals to a larger cause. But from the start the self-denying impulses within SDS were competing with (and as often as not losing to) another impulse: a yearning for personal fulfillment.

The dream of changing oneself by changing the world is a common characteristic of radical commitment. But members of the New Left made these personal goals remarkably central to their political lives—as the Port Huron Statement made clear with its description of "man's unrealized potential for self-cultivation, self-direction, self-understanding" and its call for "a quality of mind . . . which easily unites the fragmented parts of personal history." Indeed, the quest for self-fulfillment was at the core of the New Left's most original and appealing commitment: "participatory democracy" itself.

To the Stalinists, political democracy had been a word without meaning—subordinated always to what they considered the much larger goal of social and economic equality; to the socialists, it was an essential means to greater ends. To the early New Left, democracy was an end in itself, a vehicle through which individuals could feel empowered and enrich their lives. SDS's external efforts may have focused in part on social injustice and concentrations of wealth and power. Internally, however, the organization was an almost entirely shapeless experiment in democratic self-fulfillment. Members fervently resisted anything resembling internal leadership. "Leaders mean organization, organization means hierarchy, and hierarchy is undemocratic," said a delegate to the 1965 annual convention. "It connotes bureaucracy and impersonality." (One result, predictably, was administrative chaos: no one wanted to do mundane office chores, so the chores remained undone. Meetings dragged on interminably and inconclusively in search of an elusive consensus on even the most trivial decisions.)[15]

Volunteers in the ERAP project run by the SDS in the early 1960s were undeterred by the unresponsiveness of urban communities to their organizing efforts; the inner life of the ERAP "communes," the "vitality and intensity of their own group process" was at least equally important. "Discovering authenticity was essential," said Sharon Jeffrey, one of the founders of SDS and an ERAP worker in Cleveland. "This was where my passion was." Another ERAP volunteer, from Hoboken, New Jersey, described his undertaking as a "non-project," without any formal organization, because any "transformation in values . . . had to come through personal relationships."[16]

A similar preoccupation with personal liberation and fulfillment, as opposed to larger visions of social change, was visible on the college campuses that erupted periodically during the heyday of the New Left.

With the notable exception of the broad campus protests of May 1970, in the wake of the American military incursions into Cambodia, most of the major university protests had little to do with the war or the racial crisis. They expressed grievances that emerged more out of the personal experiences and frustrations of the demontrators than out of large public commitments. When students at Columbia University occupied their administration building on April 23, 1968, and marked the real beginning of a sustained period of national campus unrest, Tom Hayden saw in the uprising a process of political engagement that pushed the student left far beyond the relatively tame concerns of the early 1960s. "The issues being considered by seventeen-year-old freshmen at Columbia University," he wrote at the time, "would not have been within the imagination of most 'veteran' student activists five years ago."[17] But the issues he was describing were, on the whole, internal to the university and to the lives of university students. They involved, in large part, what students considered obstacles to personal freedom and fulfillment. At Harvard the following year, there was a similarly polarizing student revolt against the university. In the midst of it protesting architecture students produced a dramatic poster. It expressed the diffuse grievances of many young men and women at Harvard (and, by implication, of students on many other campuses across the country) against their universities, and the society they believed universities represented. Printed across a bold red image of a clenched fist was an impassioned statement of grievances:

> strike because you hate cops / strike because your roommate was clubbed / strike to stop expansion / strike to seize control of your life / strike to become more human . . . / strike because there's no poetry in your lectures / strike because classes are a bore / strike for power / strike to smash the corporation / strike to make yourself free / strike to abolish ROTC / strike because they are trying to squeeze the life out of you.[18]

Of the more than one dozen laments on the Harvard poster, only one (the call for abolishing ROTC) had anything to do with the war; none involved race. At Columbia, too, the grievances centered almost entirely around issues within the university: the plan to build a gymnasium in a nearby park, the behavior of the administration in dealing with demonstrators. At Berkeley in 1969, where perhaps the most profound campus uprising of the decade occurred, the issues centered around the effort of students to create a park on a vacant lot and the efforts of the university to stop them. As at Harvard, the rhetoric of the People's Park crisis emphasized personal more than social frustrations. "You've pushed us to the end of your civilization here, against the sea in Berkeley," one student leader melodramatically proclaimed as the battle for the park was being lost. "Then you pushed us into a square-block area called People's Park. it was the last thing we had to defend, this square block of sanity amid all your madness. . . . We are now homeless in your civilized world. We have become the great American gypsies, with only our mythology for a culture."[19] Students were, in short, demanding not just (often not even primarily) solutions to the immediate issues of the war and race; they were demanding, as well, social and cultural changes that would allow them to find the personal and intellectual release and fulfillment they believed they deserved, changes that would allow them (as the Harvard students declared) to become "more human," to keep the authorities from "squeezing the life out of you," to "make yourself free."

Contemporary observers remarked frequently on this central (and, some believed, crippling) characteristic of the movement. The sociologist Kenneth Keniston wrote in 1968 of "the personal origins of political beliefs," the desire "to start 'to move personally.'"[20] The historian Christopher Lasch noted at about the same time the degree to which "the New Left defined political issues as personal issues."[21] That was, he claimed, both its strength and its weakness. Similar concerns emerged within SDS itself. Richard Flacks, one of the organization's most important early theorists, warned in 1965 (to largely deaf ears) of the movement's excessive emphasis on "personal salvation and gratification," the effort to "reach levels of intimacy and directness with others . . . to be self-expressive, to be free." The result, he feared, would be a breakdown of the radical community.[22]

The subsequent collapse of the New Left appears to justify the fears of Lasch, Flacks, and others. The movement did not entirely disappear—as the political landscape of the 1980s and 1990s suggests. A growing network of grass-roots citizens' movements has emerged, directly and indirectly, out of the continuing political struggles of SDS veterans; Tom Hayden and Al Haber are both deeply involved in such efforts in California today.[23] The women's liberation movement and environmentalism came in significant measure out of the New Left and retain considerable vigor, despite their many problems.[24]

But while particular movements have survived, the larger Movement has not. And that is in part because, by the early 1970s, student radicalism had become almost hopelessly confused with narcissistic cultural impulses that were essentially apolitical. It had fallen victim to the "counter-culture." Disaffection and rebellion that had once led to political commitment were leading instead to the drug culture, the sexual revolution, the cult of eastern religions, rock music, and the world of "hippies" and "dropouts." Woodstock and Altamont were replacing Port Huron and the siege of Chicago as the generation's defining moments. Theodore Roszak might talk exuberantly of the counter-culture's potential for creating social justice and political regeneration. But the real center of attention lay elsewhere.[25] The heart of the counter-culture was the search for what Norman O. Brown called the "Dionysian ego," personal fulfillment through "narcissism and erotic exuberance."[26]

The seductive appeal of the counter-culture undermined the New Left far more effectively than its own political blunders. Even some of SDS's most committed early leaders eventually drifted away from politics in their search for "self-actualization." Sharon Jeffrey, for example, wandered out of the movement in 1967 and in 1973 spent three months at the Esalen Institute at Big Sur—an experience that confirmed her belief that "authenticity was not simply a matter of creating the right kind of social structure." Tom Hayden, after the fiascoes of 1968, moved to Berkeley and settled (briefly) "among the psychedelic daredevils of the counterculture." Drugs, he said, were "a means of deepening self-awareness."[27]

The real story of the New Left's demise, then, is not primarily the mad excesses of the Weathermen nor the harsh authoritarianism of the Progressive Labor party nor the other final, pathetic political efforts of the once expansive movement. It is, primarily, a story of the gradually fading political commitment of thousands of young radicals who, having embraced the left as a vehicle for self-fulfillment, abandoned it for other, more immediately gratifying means to the same end. The New Left ultimately did not so much betray its commitments to "participatory democracy" and "personal authenticity" as succumb to them.

13

Allard Lowenstein and the Ordeal of Liberalism

Allard Lowenstein did not consider himself a symbol. He was an intense, driven political activist and organizer, concerned always with making connections and "making a difference"—with living in his own time and his own world.[1] But he became a symbol despite himself, in part as a result of the frenetic way he lived his life, in part because of his dramatic death in 1980 at the hands of a psychotic former protégé; but most of all, perhaps, because he came to represent—without ever quite meaning to—the effort to preserve the centrist, meritocratic liberalism of the 1950s in the face of the daunting challenges it faced in the 1960s and beyond; to preserve it not by repudiating the new political currents that were coursing through American life, but by absorbing them into liberalism and making them compatible with its assumptions. Lowenstein's own troubled and often unhappy life was in part a product of personal demons he was never able fully to dispel. But it was also a result of the near impossibility of the task he set for himself, and of the many frustrations he encountered before he discovered that.

For most of his life Lowenstein was almost always in the vanguard of liberal activism—embracing causes years, even decades, before they generated broad popular support. He was an early catalyst to student protest against South African *apartheid*, an important figure in the initial struggles of the civil rights movement, one of the first leaders of student protests against the Vietnam war, and perhaps the principal organizer of the movement that, in effect, ousted Lyndon Johnson from the White House in 1968.

Most of all, Lowenstein had an almost mystical ability to inspire and galvanize those who came within his orbit—to transform their sense of themselves and their relationship to the public world. He had a profound effect on the hundreds, even thousands, of younger men and women who experienced his extraordinary presence and who went on to become engaged in political efforts. Many of those he touched are major figures in public life today. (Bill Bradley, Barney Frank, Tom Harkin, and Bob Kerrey are only a few of those whose lives he affected.) He had much of the passion and idealism and energy of the New Left, but he was himself always firmly committed to, even if at times skeptical of, the liberalism of his youth—convinced that within it could be found a way both of creating profound social change and of preserving the essential institutions of American life.

Lowenstein had his greatest impact on the political activism of the 1960s, but he was somewhat older than most of the politically active members of the "sixties generation." (He turned 40 in 1969.) His own character, in fact, was primarily a product of the 1950s, the decade in which he came of age, and almost everything in his life reflected the influence of that very different time. In the eyes of much of the world, he was a man intent on stripping away the masks that had kept white, middle-class Americans from recognizing the injustice in their society. But other masks—constructed by himself and others in an era in which wearing such masks was not yet widely considered "repression"—shaped and even dominated his own personality and allowed him to hide from his complicated, even tortured inner life. It was Lowenstein's need to escape the repressed demons of his own life that made it possible, perhaps even necessary, for him to assist in the liberation of others.

Lowenstein grew up in comfortable middle-class surroundings. His family lived in a substantial home outside New York City and kept an elegant apartment in Manhattan. His father ran a successful New York restaurant business that left Allard financially secure throughout his life and free to pursue political causes that almost never earned him much of an income. He was a brilliant student at the elite Horace Mann School and, from an early age, precociously political; as a seven-year-old boy in 1936, he handed out leaflets for Franklin Roosevelt on Central Park West.

But Lowenstein's childhood, like his adulthood, was also filled with denial and deception—by his parents and by Allard himself. His father,

Gabriel, had come to the United States from Russia in 1906 to avoid being jailed for political activities there. He earned a Ph.D. in biochemistry from Columbia and dreamed of a career in academia; but he was also determined to build a secure, middle-class life for himself and his family in his new world and decided to enter business instead. His regrets about that choice affected, and perhaps poisoned, the rest of his life and encouraged him to transfer his own thwarted ambitions onto his children with a relentless and often suffocating intensity.

So committed was Gabriel to creating a perfect environment for his children that he went to extraordinary lengths to hide from his son one of the most important facts of his own and Allard's life: that Gabriel's first wife, and Allard's mother, had died a year after Allard's birth. Gabriel quickly remarried, and his second wife, Florence, immediately assumed the role of Allard's mother. Not until he was fourteen years old, and then by accident, did Allard learn of his natural mother's existence. Once having learned the secret, he never spoke of it to his father or stepmother. What effect this enormous deception had on father and son is impossible to determine; but it almost certainly reinforced Allard's lifelong pattern of hiding personal truths from others and even from himself.

Keeping secrets, apparently, was part of a larger pathology within the Lowenstein family that may have had terrible effects on all the children. Allard's older brother, Bert, in whom Gabriel at first invested the lion's share of his dreams, fell victim to schizophrenia as a young adult, while Allard watched helplessly and fearfully. Both Gabriel and Florence eventually refocused their oppressive attentions almost exclusively on Allard. Florence wrote him constantly with reports of Gabriel's supposedly deteriorating health, warning him that to disappoint his father might be to kill him. Gabriel redoubled his efforts to force Allard to be the son of his own fevered imaginings. Allard almost always rebelled. His father railed about the importance of neatness, order, and punctuality; Allard became disheveled, disorganized, and notoriously tardy. His father dreamed of sending his son to Harvard or to his own, beloved Columbia; Allard, whose luminous academic record qualified him to go anywhere (and enabled him to graduate from Horace Mann at the age of sixteen), defiantly enrolled at the University of North Carolina at Chapel Hill.

But if Lowenstein struggled with the secrets and deceptions of others, he struggled even more with secrets and deceptions of his own. He made considerable efforts if not actually to hide then at least to de-emphasize his own Jewishness. That was, it seems clear, one of the reasons for his decision to attend Chapel Hill. It was not a place New York Jews ordinarily attended; it would help him learn to live in the non-Jewish world on its own terms. Throughout his life, in fact, he seemed constantly to be in search of assurances that he, a Jew and an immigrant's son, was in fact fully an American; and he defined his American-ness to a large extent by the narrow, constricted standards of the white, Protestant middle class of the 1950s. His most important friends were almost always Protestants (and Lowenstein himself sang and attended services for a time at a Presbyterian church in Chapel Hill). He married a Boston Brahmin, Jennifer Littlefield. He befriended and adopted as role models older men and women who, whatever their other attractions, represented the heart of old-line Protestant culture: Frank Porter Graham, the president of the University of North Carolina; Norman Thomas, the Princeton graduate turned socialist leader; Eleanor Roosevelt.

Lowenstein's greatest deception, of himself and of others, involved his own sexuality. From an early age he recognized that he was sexually attracted to other men. He was ashamed of and horrified by his own longings. "The urge I get when I see certain other boys is getting out-of-control," he wrote in his diary in 1943. "God, God, what will I do?" His fear of exposure was in part, certainly, a product of the culture of his time, in which public acknowledgment of homosexuality brought with it almost certain ostracism and abuse. But it was also, no doubt, a product of what he considered the likely reaction of his parents, whose almost obsessive desire to push themselves and their children into the mainstream of American life—a desire tragically thwarted for Bert—would probably have made it impossible for them to accept so shocking a revelation from their other son. His answer to this dilemma, then and throughout his life, was to try desperately to escape those urges (which, of course, he could never do) and to hide them (which he managed somewhat more successfully).

Lowenstein's sexual ambivalence was one of the fundamental facts of his life. On the one hand, it drew him to scores of attractive young men (most of them tall, blond exemplars of the WASP ideal) and to seek intense friendships with many of them. Lowenstein often took handsome male companions along with him on his travels and sometimes contrived circumstances that required them to stay with him in motel rooms with only one bed. But there was, apparently, little explicit sexuality in his relationships with these friends. Only very late in his life did Lowenstein begin to question the social taboos that made homosexual desire seem impermissible. And so at the same time that he was cultivating male friends and yearning for intimacy with them, he was also careful to prevent any relationship from developing too far, fearful that it would lead him into forbidden territory. Hence his life of ceaseless, restless movement, from place to place and person to person—his almost frenzied effort to find in public activities the fulfillment he could not permit himself in his personal world.

Lowenstein's public life began in earnest when he enrolled at Chapel Hill just after the end of World War II. He quickly befriended the leading figures on campus and became a particular favorite of President Graham—a towering figure in the state and one of its most distinguished and revered progressives. Attaching himself to Graham was, therefore, not only a way for Lowenstein to achieve social distinction and acceptance. It was also a way of entering the world of progressive politics in the state—something he did quickly, intensely, and almost heedlessly.

Interest in challenging racial prejudice was limited in North Carolina in the late 1940s, even among liberals. But Lowenstein, often at considerable personal risk, helped organize campaigns against racism and anti-Semitism on campus and in surrounding communities; and in the process he demonstrated for the first time his remarkable ability to inspire and galvanize others. He seemed to overflow with intellectual energy and to make those around him feel a part of his own excitement. As throughout his life, he conveyed to his friends and admirers a sense that, through him, they could reach into themselves and become more than they were—just as Lowenstein himself appeared to have done. The skinny, gawky, mesmerizing, 16-year-old freshman soon had successful, popular upperclassmen in his thrall. "You see," wrote one such older friend, "in so many ways—and this hasn't happened to me in a long, long time—you are as I should like to be."

Lowenstein's political activism at Chapel Hill revealed the contours of his belief system: a passionate commitment to fighting injustice, and an equally passionate commitment to the ideals of liberal assimilationism. Just as he craved social acceptance for himself, he fought for the acceptance of other, apparently marginal people. But the acceptance he craved, both for himself and for them, was defined by the terms of the middle-class mainstream. Lowenstein was never attracted to class analyses of social problems. He showed little interest in labor politics and even less in Marxist analysis (despite his flirtation with Norman Thomas's democratic socialism). Nor would he have anything to do with racial or ethnic particularism. He was, in fact, adamantly opposed for a time to the establishment of Israel, because he considered Jewishness an inappropriate category for defining nationality. Later, he would equally fervently oppose the demands of black nationalists and others who sought to carve out political identities that challenged American "norms." For all his criticisms of American society, he was deeply patriotic and fervently anticommunist; and like many other liberals of the 1950s, he was at times uncertain whether anticommunism or social justice was his first priority.

In the 1940s, and indeed for many years after, Lowenstein saw nothing incompatible between his commitment to liberal assimilationism and his equally fervent support for racial justice, group rights, and personal liberation. Like many other liberals of his generation, but perhaps more ardently, he assumed that when freed from oppression and discrimination, once-marginalized Americans would freely choose the values of the liberal mainstream; that they would join the middle-class world, accept its values, and play by its rules. He believed that it was possible to generate radical change—an end to racism; a breaking down of social and cultural barriers decades, even centuries in the making; a liberation of individuals from the repressive Victorian values of the past—without producing any genuinely radical results. Neither then, nor later, was he willing to make the leap that so many other activists of the 1960s made—from a repudiation of the evils liberalism had long tolerated to a repudiation of liberalism itself. And so he continued, to the end, in a struggle to redefine liberalism while retaining its core; to demand dramatic changes while defending existing institutions and processes. His faith in the possibility of doing both helped enable many younger idealists to maintain a belief in the "system" as well. But for Lowenstein himself, it produced—in addition to a series of impressive triumphs—years of frustration and disappointment.

While studying at Chapel Hill, Lowenstein began a long involvement with the National Student Association, an organization committed, as Lowenstein himself was, both to promoting liberalism and fighting communism. He dominated the organization for years and became its president in 1950. (He earned a law degree at Yale in the early 1950s, but the NSA occupied almost all his time; his classmates created an award for him at graduation—"the student who graduated from Yale having attended the fewest classes.") Unknown to most NSA members—but almost certainly known to Lowenstein—through most of the 1950s the organization was receiving covert funding and direction from the CIA. It was a measure of Lowenstein's own anticommunism, and of his general faith in the essential beneficence of the American government, that he was apparently untroubled by this deception.

Lowenstein was one of the first young Americans to take an active interest in *apartheid*, and he made a hazardous journey to South Africa in 1959 to gather material for those in America who hoped to organize international action against the white regime. After smuggling documents out of the country at great personal risk, he appeared before the United Nations to testify about conditions in the South African black communities; and in 1962, he published *Brutal Mandate*, his only book, which offered a riveting account of his African travels and a searing critique of the injustices he encountered. "This is a place gnashing her teeth and weeping and bleeding and destroying herself as no other place in the world," he wrote, "a place of ordinary men turned heroes and of ordinary men going mad." He was torn, he said, between his love of this "wounded, crying place" and his dismay at its problems. Someone from Mississippi, he suggested, might understand his conflicted emotions. And it was to the struggle for racial justice at home that he subsequently turned.

Lowenstein spent the year 1961–62 at Stanford University as a minor dean and part-time political science instructor. It was the first of a series of explicitly temporary positions he occupied through much of the next twenty years, and it reflected both his eagerness to allow himself the latitude to continue his political activities and his reluctance to make any deep or lasting commitments to any place (or any person). His presence at Stanford was galvanizing. Almost singlehandedly, he turned the complacent, conservative campus into a center of student protest. He persuaded scores of committed students (among them a young man named Dennis Sweeney) to join him in working for the civil-rights movement that was then making such rapid strides in the South. By 1963, he was traveling frequently to Mississippi and forging a relationship with the Student Nonviolent Coordinating Committee. The following year he organized a group of his Stanford protégés to work in the Freedom Summer Campaign.

But he also began to develop doubts about SNCC. He was concerned that it was not sufficiently anticommunist, worried about the black nationalism that was creeping into its ideology, and perhaps also resentful that the organization was not allowing him to dominate its work as he had long dominated the NSA. By the time of the bitter effort of the Mississippi Freedom Democratic party (MFDP) to be seated at the 1964 Democratic National Convention, Lowenstein had effectively abandoned the crusade; SNCC leaders and many of his own white protégés came to believe (perhaps incorrectly) that he was responsible for the backroom deal that barred most of the MFDP delegates from the convention. Responsible or not, he supported the compromise that so alienated the MFDP that many of its members left the convention, and the party, in despair.

As his relationship with the civil rights movement soured, Lowenstein—like many other young, white activists of his time—moved quickly to the center of another youth crusade: the effort to stop the war in Vietnam. Indeed, beginning in 1965, opposition to the war became the central political reality of his life—the source of both his greatest triumphs and his many frustrations. It also became a test of his belief that the "system" worked. Opposing the war did not require a revolution, he insisted; it need not involve violence or radicalism. Indeed, he was scornful of those on the left who believed bombings and other acts of terrorism were appropriate ways to oppose the war in Vietnam. The institutions that had produced the war, he argued, could also be prodded to end it if enough committed people devoted themselves to the effort. The political system was not a closed world, impervious to popular will, as many on the left had come to believe. It was a repository of organized political belief, and it could be reshaped and redirected by any set of beliefs powerful and well organized enough to make themselves felt. In that he shared the convictions of the great political hero of his life, Robert Kennedy, with whom he developed a warm, if somewhat sycophantic, friendship.

In 1967 he mobilized much of the nascent antiwar movement behind the campaign to drive Lyndon Johnson from the Democratic ticket in 1968. Spurned at first by Kennedy, who was initially unwilling to challenge a sitting president, he helped persuade Eugene McCarthy to challenge the president in the New Hampshire primary. And largely because of Lowenstein's efforts, thousands of students flocked to the state to work for McCarthy's campaign. Their efforts produced McCarthy's stunning moral victory—a virtual tie with a sitting president—and almost certainly contributed to Johnson's decision to withdraw from the race. When Kennedy belatedly entered the race a few days later, Lowenstein remained publicly loyal to McCarthy; privately, however, he built close ties to the Kennedy organization and at times betrayed the interests of his own campaign—rationalizing the betrayal by claiming that Kennedy was the stronger candidate. After Robert Kennedy's death, Lowenstein continued to divide his loyalties. He was among those who tried to persuade Edward Kennedy to challenge Humphrey at the 1968 Democratic convention, even though McCarthy remained the principal antiwar challenger in the race. (Twelve years later, in 1980, he was working for Edward Kennedy's floundering presidential campaign when he himself was murdered.)

Lowenstein was convinced that an antiwar candidate could be elected in 1968, and he attributed Humphrey's defeat to his long support for the bankrupt policies of the Johnson administration in Vietnam. There is little evidence that he was right. Opposition to the war in 1968 was closely tied to another rising passion, very different from Lowenstein's, that in the end did much more to damage liberal hopes than the antiwar movement did to strengthen them. That passion was the cry for "law and order," a cry that expressed a fearful hostility to the instability and seeming radicalism of the left combined with a growing alarm about street crime and urban violence. Some might argue, in fact, that Lowenstein's efforts to topple the Democratic party leadership, far from strengthening liberalism, helped create the disarray that contributed to Nixon's victory that fall.

But 1968 marked, nevertheless, the high point of Lowenstein's public career. Never before, and never again, would he be so central to the nation's political life. As if in confirmation of his momentary importance, he won election himself that fall to a congressional seat from a largely Republican district on Long Island.

Some expected him to be a disruptive firebrand in the House, but that was not Lowenstein's style. Congress was exactly the sort of establishment bastion from which he had always craved acceptance, and he worked hard and successfully to develop friendly relationships with colleagues of all ideological stripes. For a short time at least, he felt finally at home.

But Lowenstein had reached the pinnacle of his career at just the moment when the political currents of the nation were beginning to move decisively away from him. He had always been certain that it was possible to reconcile his passionate commitment to racial and economic justice, to peace, and to a more vigorous democracy with the institutions and norms of mainstream middle-class culture. But increasing numbers of others—on both the right and the left—were rapidly losing faith in the possibility of retaining such a connection. As the nation became increasingly polarized—between advocates of change who had ceased to believe in the "system" and the culture that sustained it, and advocates of "middle-class" values and institutions who grew skeptical of the value of dramatic social change—Lowenstein found himself isolated and marginalized.

In 1970, after the Republican state legislature redrew the boundaries of his district to make it one of the most conservative in the state, he lost his seat in Congress. That was partly because of the gerrymandering; but it was also because his own preoccupation with the war and social reform was coming to be less important to his constituents than the ordinary stuff of local politics: sewers, schools, roads, and other issues in which Lowenstein had no interest at all. For the next six years he tried again and again, with a manic and increasingly self-destructive energy, to return to Congress—running first in an unpromising race in Brooklyn, then, quixotically, in his old district on Long Island, losing so often that his efforts came to seem obsessive, even pathetic. Even more strangely, he spurned an opportunity to run for the House from the upper West Side of Manhattan, the place where he would have had the greatest, and most enduring, political strength, arguing that his real task was to mobilize constituents who were not already disposed to agree with him. His marriage dissolved under the strain of his repeated failures, and Lowenstein himself began to descend into a kind of bitter paranoia—as if unable to comprehend the dramatic change in his political fortunes.

As he drifted halfheartedly from one cause to another and one job to another, he became increasingly absorbed with conspiracy theories, grasping eagerly at every shred of evidence to support stories of CIA plots to murder John and Robert Kennedy, and clinging as well to the belief that a similar conspiracy had destroyed his own political effectiveness. The Watergate revelations, in particular, reinforced his fear of conspiracy; and he plunged into an inquiry into the circumstances of Robert Kennedy's death with the same intensity and commitment he had once brought to his efforts on behalf of the civil rights and antiwar movements. "In our agony," he said, "we have instinctively recoiled from exploring the murky abyss in which may have been interred some of our most cherished assumptions . . . the fantasy that God somehow made all Americans immune to the evils of political murder, [or] that only loose nuts could possibly be involved in these crimes."

In his last years Lowenstein began to ressess his life and his politics in a way that might have allowed him to regain some of his earlier public stature and influence and, perhaps more important, might have permitted him some peace and fulfillment in his private life. Among other things, he developed ties to the rapidly growing gay rights movement (although he never publicly acknowledged his own homosexual leanings).

It seems unlikely, though, that Lowenstein would ever have found the political world of the 1980s and 1990s a comfortable or welcoming place. He spent his public life trying to prove that liberalism could successfully walk a line between the cautious centrism of the 1950s and the searing radicalism of the 1960s and 1970s. He believed in the possibility, and necessity, of fighting for social justice while defending the nation's basic institutions. And he insisted, too, that there was a liberal ideal of freedom and equality to which everyone could and should aspire; that the claim of American democracy to transcend the particularism of racial, ethnic, and social groups was not rhetoric but, potentially, a reality. His biographer William Chafe aptly describes Lowenstein's life as a "struggle to save American liberalism": to save it both from the social injustices it had inadequately addressed in the past and from the cynicism and disillusionment that threatened its future. He believed, in short, in what Martin Luther King had called the "beloved community." And it is hard to imagine him flourishing amid the fragmented cultural politics of the 1980s and 1990s, in which liberalism self-consciously shed the crusading idealism that, to Lowenstein, was its most important and redeeming quality.

In any case, what awaited Lowenstein was not his future but his past: Dennis Sweeney, a protégé of his Stanford year who in the 1970s descended into madness. A victim of adult-onset schizophrenia, Sweeney became convinced that Lowenstein—even now the most important and magnetic figure in his increasingly tortured life—was tormenting him by transmitting voices into his head. He appealed repeatedly to Lowenstein to stop, and Lowenstein—never willing to admit there was anyone he could not help—tried repeatedly to rescue Sweeney from his agony. In March 1980 Sweeney went to Lowenstein's office to ask him once again to stop the imagined torments. Lowenstein—despite repeated warnings from friends that Sweeney was becoming dangerous—agreed to see him and, once again, tried to persuade him to seek psychiatric help. Sweeney pulled out a pistol and shot him seven times, in the leg, the arm, and the abdomen. Lowenstein died a few hours later. Sweeney set the gun down on a table and waited to be arrested.

It would be too much to suggest that this tragic event—a result of a terrible illness and a personal relationship gone sour—had any real connection to the political trials that Lowenstein, and many other liberals, had endured over the previous decade. But it is hard not to be struck by the symbolism of this committed, if frustrated, liberal meeting his end at the hands of a man whose political passions—now run amok—he had once inspired.

In many respects Lowenstein seems today a figure inextricably tied to a vanished moment in our history. He was a product of the naive confidence in the American mission of the 1940s and 1950s, and of the equally naive conviction of the 1960s that passion and idealism could end social injustice without requiring fundamental changes in the nation's values and institutions. But in other respects Lowenstein seems a figure whose beliefs and achievements are as relevant to our own time as they were to his. In a cynical, apolitical age, he taught young men and women to believe that politics mattered, that government mattered, that their lives mattered—that they could play a role in making their world a better place. His dazzling, galvanizing presence helped scores of young people shed apathy and hopelessness and become engaged in the world.

Lowenstein did all this at the cost of repressing his own inner life and failing to find the personal fulfillment he always desperately wanted—a kind of sacrifice our own culture considers almost impermissible. But in an age when the public world is in increasing disrepute, Lowenstein's achievements, and even his sacrifices, provide a healthy rebuke to America's political despair.

14

The Taming of the Political Convention

For nearly a century and a half national party conventions were among the great spectacles of American democracy: sprawling, turbulent passion plays through which the nation played out some of its furies and its hopes.[1] They were forums for political debates, even if they seldom resolved them. They launched political careers and destroyed them. They were the principal events through which local political activists could feel that they were part of a national party. They play those roles no more.

In our own time conventions have become sterile, stage-managed media events—created for television, but so empty and artificial that even television has little interest in them. Conventions have not only been stripped of any power over the selection of candidates. They have also been stripped of almost every other significant function they once performed. They survive, for most viewers, as televised advertisements for presidential campaigns. Their descent into something close to irrelevance is one of the many stories of how our political world has changed.

Critics have long attacked the convention as a relic of corrupt party politics—an anachronism standing in the way of real democracy. But those who organized the first political conventions over a century and a half ago considered their work a great democratic reform. In the first decades of the nineteenth century, presidential candidates were chosen by party caucuses in Congress—closed, clubby groups which their many critics considered corrupt and undemocratic. But in 1824 Andrew Jackson and his followers—who considered themselves outsiders challenging the Eastern elite—revolted against the caucus and effectively destroyed it. And for the next eight years party leaders searched for something with which to replace it. They settled, eventually, on the idea of a national convention—an idea derived, in part, from the revered constitutional conventions of the late eighteenth century that had created the structures of American government. A convention, its defenders argued, would be a great conclave of the people. It would enable ordinary citizens, not just officeholders or political leaders, to shape the party's decisions. Indeed, the creation of the convention was part of a much larger process in the early nineteenth century of extending political democracy in America—a process intended to expand the electorate (at least among white males), assault privilege, and make the political world more responsive to the people and less the tool of elites.

The Anti-Mason party, a short-lived movement designed to counter the supposedly insidious power of the Freemasons, held the first national party meeting in Baltimore in 1831. A year later, the Democrats held their own first convention (also in Baltimore) to nominate Andrew Jackson, the champion of "people's democracy," for a second term. From that point on, the political convention remained the normal vehicle for choosing national candidates and framing party platforms. Every major party has held one in presidential election years ever since.

But it was not long before the convention system began to take on many of the same unpopular characteristics as the caucus system it had replaced. In one state after another, powerful party bosses seized control of their delegations. Before long, relatively few delegates were "ordinary citizens." Most were officials within or allies of local party organizations. On occasion, a convention could spin out of the control of party leaders in the face of popular passions—as the Democratic convention did in 1896, when the young Nebraska congressman William Jennings Bryan electrified the delegates with his famed "Cross of Gold" speech attacking the gold standard and went on to win the nomination (only to lose to William McKinley in November); or again in 1924, when bitter disputes over prohibition and the Ku Klux Klan deadlocked the Democrats for 103 ballots before they selected the esteemed and pallid John W. Davis to face Calvin Coolidge hopelessly that fall. For the most part, however, conventions remained firmly in the hands of the party hierarchy and richly deserved their image as vehicles of "boss rule." It was that image that helped inspire the birth of the primary system early in the twentieth century. Over time the primaries expanded their reach, stripped the power of nominating candidates from party bosses, and delivered it, in theory at least, to the electorate.

By the 1930s conventions were already becoming as much image-making as decision-making events, a change greatly accelerated by the advent of radio. One sign of that change came in 1932. Traditionally, presidential candidates had not addressed the nominating conventions but had waited, usually at home, for a delegation of party leaders to inform them officially of their nomination several weeks later. (This was a reflection of the durable myth that presidents did not actively seek the office but accepted it passively as a gift from the people, that candidates "stood" rather than "ran" for the White House.) But Franklin Roosevelt, aware of how radio had made the convention a potentially powerful vehicle for shaping voter sentiment, shattered that tradition by flying to the Democratic convention in Chicago from his home in New York—thus becoming the first presidential candidate ever to travel by airplane, and the first ever to accept his nomination in person. Roosevelt did so with a speech, broadcast to the nation, in which he promised a "new deal" for the American people.

By the mid-1950s conventions had ceased to play any significant role in choosing candidates; the last convention that needed more than one ballot to select a presidential nominee was in 1952, when the battle between Dwight D. Eisenhower and Robert A. Taft lasted for three ballots before Eisenhower prevailed. But for the next twenty years, it was still at least theoretically possible for the race for the nomination to remain fluid to the end, because significant numbers of delegates remained under the control of party leaders. Many states still had no primaries, and even some that did chose delegates pledged to "favorite sons," to maximize the state's bargaining position in case of a deadlock. In the 1970s even this last vestige of independence disappeared. Spurred by the reforms within the Democratic party devised by the McGovern commission, primaries spread quickly to almost every state. Party bosses and elected officials found themselves almost entirely shut out of the process. And the enormous expense of running a national primary campaign, combined with the pressure by the media to anoint a winner as quickly as possible and the increasing "frontloading" of important primaries in the opening weeks of the season, made it all but impossible for a race to remain seriously contested after the first few elections. By the late 1970s, therefore, conventions had ceased to have any plausible chance of actually choosing a candidate and had begun to assume their modern form as a television spectacle.

It was television that ultimately destroyed whatever serious role remained to conventions in the age of primaries. But it did not do so right away. The networks began covering conventions in 1952 and played the dominant role in them by 1960. And for a time in the 1960s and 1970s television seemed actually to enhance the importance of conventions even as their decision-making role was in decline. It was clear to everyone that something important was at stake in these meetings: access to the airwaves. Every faction within the parties, and many outside them, came to see the conventions as vehicles for airing their enthusiasms, their grievances, their resentments. Party leaders tried to keep abrasive voices and unattractive events out of sight and off the air. But reporters were eager for stories, convention cities drew demonstrators of all kinds, and control of the conventions was divided and still relatively loose. So it was nearly impossible to prevent division and dissent from making its way onto television. In many respects the great days of conventions—at least in terms of their impact on the popular imagination—were the 1960s and early 1970s, not in spite of but precisely because of television.

As late as 1960 the conventions continued to look much as they always had. The parties made few concessions to television, and television (partly because of technological limitations and partly because the networks had not yet begun to think of themselves as active interpreters and shapers of the news) did not intrude very much. But in 1964 the relationship between the media and the conventions began to change—a change first apparent in San Francisco in 1964, where the Republicans met to nominate Barry Goldwater for president. The convention was a major event in the history of the Republican party. It was also a major event in the history of the political conventions itself.

The Goldwater convention had something of the frenzied intensity that the first major-party convention must have had in 1832, when Andrew Jackson's exuberant followers seized control of the Democratic party from the Old Guard and created what they considered a great conclave of the people to replace the elitist congressional caucuses that had nominated candidates in the past. In San Francisco, too, impassioned outsiders were at last taking control of a process from which they had long felt excluded. Finally, after enduring decades of presidential nominees (Dewey, Eisenhower, and Nixon) chosen, as they saw it, by the party's Eastern establishment, the right was choosing one of its own. Phyllis Schlaffly (whose celebrated antifeminism in the 1970s and 1980s was a late chapter in a long career in right-wing politics) joined with other Goldwater enthusiasts to publish an inflammatory pamphlet at the 1964 meeting called "A Choice Not an Echo." It accused the traditional Republican leaders—the "secret kingmakers"—of hijacking the party and betraying the people for over thirty years until the popular triumph in 1964. The pamphlet became one of the founding documents of the New Right.

The zealotry in the hall—the hostility to dissenters and, above all, to the media—was almost palpable. Dwight D. Eisenhower, through most of his career the calmest of men and the dullest of speakers but now, as elder statesman, apparently currying favor with his party's new masters, sent the delegates into a frenzy with his call for rejecting "the divisive efforts of those outside our family, including sensation-seeking columnists and commentators, because, my friends, I assure you that these are people who couldn't care less about the good of our party." The audience exploded, many of them turning and shaking their fists at the television anchormen and the floor reporters they saw around them. Later in the week, some delegates could be seen wearing buttons that read "Stamp Out Huntley-Brinkley." Network correspondents found themselves taunted at times as they walked through the corridors of the convention hall or the lobbies of the large hotels in the city. John Chancellor of NBC was famously arrested on the floor of the Cow Palace, an event he covered himself as it happened—and one that NBC self-referentially repeated so often over the years that it may now be the single best-remembered incident of that week.

It was little wonder, perhaps, that the delegates were reacting so strongly to the media in San Francisco. The right saw the convention as an almost tribal celebration, a coming of age after decades in the wilderness. But it was difficult to look anywhere in the convention hall without being aware of the intrusive and almost imperial presence of the networks: the great glass anchor booths suspended above the floor; the anchormen presiding regally over the proceedings; the knots of cameras and lights that accompanied the roving floor reporters as they moved around the arena; the elaborate, sprawling (and extremely expensive) temporary office spaces surrounding the auditorium with which the networks announced their presence to passersby. Most reporters tried to be fair, but they had a hard time disguising their bewilderment at the strange political culture so suddenly asserting itself around them. And faced with hostility and abuse (such as during the Chancellor arrest), they had a hard time suppressing anger and incredulity.

But television was not the only target of the convention's fury. On the day of Eisenhower's speech, Nelson Rockefeller also addressed the delegates. He had once been the frontrunner for the 1964 Republican nomination, until his ill-timed divorce and remarriage removed him from serious contention. Now he faced an audience that included many people who considered him and his family the leaders of Schlaffly's "secret king-makers"—or worse. (The Rockefeller family had by the 1960s come to occupy a place in the imagination of some members of the far right not unlike that of the Bank of England or the Protocols of the Elders of Zion as a fount of terrible international conspiracies.) On the floor and in the galleries Goldwater loyalists booed, shouted catcalls, and chanted—seemingly interminably—"Go home Rocky!" and "We want Barry." Rockefeller trudged dutifully through his speech, interrupting himself occasionally to say "This is still a free country, ladies and gentlemen," or "Some of you don't like to hear it . . . but it's the truth." Later, he and many of his supporters walked out of the convention altogether—alienated and ostracized by the new Republican leadership.

There was never any real doubt about the outcome of the San Francisco convention—despite a hopeless last-minute mobilization of the party's moderates behind the unlikely candidacy of Bill Scranton, the drab governor of Pennsylvania. But it was a historic moment nevertheless, for it helped give birth to the right-wing resurgence that would eventually dominate the Republican party and, for a time, American politics. Many of the future leaders of the party got their start in the Goldwater campaign and in the rites of admission that the convention represented that year. Some members of Young Americans for Freedom, the conservative youth group that came of age politically in the Goldwater campaign, went on to become prominent figures in the next generation of conservatives, among them Pat Buchanan, Howard Phillips, R. Emmett Tyrell, and Richard Viguerie (who created the great direct-mail operation that helped reinvigorate the right and that started with a list of several thousand Goldwater supporters).

Goldwater himself, of course, was not the real beneficiary of this sea change. His steely, unbending acceptance speech ("Extremism in pursuit of liberty is no vice, and moderation in pursuit of freedom is no virtue") helped doom his candidacy. But already waiting in the wings was another, far more appealing conservative hero, utterly without Goldwater's grim, puritanical fervor. A few months after the convention Ronald Reagan made his national political debut, with a memorable television speech for Goldwater that launched his own sixteen-year march to the White House—much of it guided by the committed young conservatives who had gathered in San Francisco.

After the passions of the Goldwater convention, the Democrats' meeting later that summer in Atlantic City was, on the surface at least, little more than a carefully orchestrated coronation. In the convention hall itself—the high, arched arena best known as the site of the annual Miss America Pageant—huge photographs of Lyndon Johnson and the martyred John Kennedy flanked the podium in a faintly totalitarian display. The Democrats were plainly worried that the delegates, their guests, and (most importantly) the media would grow bored with this orchestrated, suspenseless convention—especially since it was happening in a shabby, crumbling resort still years away from its tawdry splendor as a casino town. They imported popular entertainers (Peter, Paul, and Mary hamfistedly paired with Robert Goulet) for a gala in the convention hall. They tried (and largely failed) to create some excitement over Johnson's choice of a vice president. Lyndon Johnson manufactured some phony suspense over his choice and then broke it with a "surprise" announcement to the delegates that he had selected Hubert Humphrey—a decision widely reported in the press the day before. On the whole, though, there was a grimly dutiful quality to the proceedings. When the Republicans erected a Goldwater billboard on the Boardwalk, the humorless Democratic National Committee Chairman John Bailey released a sanctimonious press release denouncing it. (In the meantime, someone with slightly more wit had attached to the bottom of the poster, which carried Goldwater's campaign slogan "In Your Heart You Know He's Right," a small sign that read, "Yes, Extreme Right.") The ghost of Kennedy, whose convention this was to have been, was everywhere. And the emotional high point of the public proceedings was the appearance of Robert Kennedy on the final night to introduce a filmed tribute to his brother. The applause cascaded over Kennedy in waves. He tried timidly (and perhaps halfheartedly) to stop it, but it continued for nearly half an hour, reportedly embarrassing and infuriating the president. By contrast, Johnson's own acceptance speech later the same evening was utterly forgettable.

But despite the surface torpor, the Atlantic City convention was the scene of a confrontation no less momentous than the coming of age of the Republican right in San Francisco. The Mississippi Freedom Democratic party, a predominantly black organization created out of the tumultuous Freedom Summer voter registration drive that year, was challenging the all-white regular delegation from the state. A slate of MFDP delegates arrived in Atlantic City expecting the convention to seat them in place of the segregationists.

Johnson was reluctant to alienate the white South any more than he already had; and he tried, characteristically, to settle the conflict without antagonizing anyone while obscuring the battle from the public. He failed at both. In the absence of other stories, the media zeroed in on this one. The corridors of the convention hall that week seemed constantly filled with clusters of reporters, cameras, and lights, almost always focused on a party to the MFDP controversy: Martin Luther King, Jr., trying agonizingly to broker a compromise at Johnson's request; Fannie Lou Hamer, Bob Moses, and other MFDP leaders angrily insisting on justice; weary delegates from the all-white regulars talking dismissively of the challengers and trying to present themselves as the reasonable moderates. Johnson seethed watching this televised evidence of a racial schism which, as he knew better than most Democrats, had the capacity to shatter his party.

In the end Humphrey and King pressured the MFDP into accepting a compromise. The convention would seat two at-large delegates from the MFDP. The Mississippi regulars would stay for the moment, but in future conventions delegations from every state would be integrated. These were not trivial concessions. The commitment to ending segregated delegations began the process that weakened the traditional Democratic machines and opened up the party to previously underrepresented groups. Many of the most determinedly liberal figures in the Democratic party—Allard Lowenstein, Joseph Rauh, Roy Wilkins, and Humphrey (whose vice presidential nomination, Johnson made clear, hinged on his success in making the compromise work)—recognized this and struggled to persuade the MFDP to accept the deal. (The Mississippi segregationists recognized this too and walked out of the convention.) But to the MFDP, after their brutal summer of organizing in the face of bigotry, violence, and murder, the only important fact was that the all-white delegation would represent Mississippi at the convention and they would not. Their bitterness was palpable. Many of them left Atlantic City before the convention ended. Some of them gave up on the Democratic party (and mainstream politics) as a result and began moving towards a kind of political separatism. Some months later Robert Moses, one of the organizers of the MFDP, called one night on a white friend with whom he had worked closely in the movement and told him: "This black-white thing doesn't work."

In 1968 the passions and divisions that the 1964 election year had (barely) repressed came bursting to the surface. Not, however, in Miami Beach, where the Republicans met to nominate Richard Nixon. The Nixon organizers—slick, tough advertising men—were in almost complete control, creating a spectacle of order and homogeneity that would, they knew, be a stark contrast to the Democratic meeting a few weeks later. Ronald Reagan had announced his candidacy earlier in the summer, and several hundred bright, shining Reagan supporters from California began showing up in the hotels—one of them, riding in an elevator with a crowd of Nixon supporters, saying, "It may be your turn now, but Ronald Reagan will be president someday." Nelson Rockefeller, too, was engaged in a futile effort to stop the Nixon juggernaut. Inside the convention hall, however, the Reagan and Rockefeller forces were all but invisible. The meeting was a tableau of unity and enthusiasm for the "new Nixon."

Nixon himself made some reference to the furies of 1968 in his acceptance speech (constructed with one eye on George Wallace's independent candidacy that year). He stressed not Barry Goldwater's starchy libertarian orthodoxy, but the new "social" issues that would drive American conservatism for the next twenty-five years: "law and order," immorality, violence, middle-class rage. His biggest applause line was "We're going to have a new attorney general in the United States." But more characteristic of the tone of the convention was his syrupy description of a child "who hears a train go by" and dreams "of faraway places he'd like to go," a description that concluded: "Tonight he stands before you, nominated for President."

In Chicago, everything was different. The three most important actors in the 1964 convention were all missing, all in different ways victims of the passions of their time: Robert Kennedy and Martin Luther

King, Jr. murdered, Lyndon Johnson so fearful of violence (or a hostile reception) he did not dare leave the White House. In their absence the proceedings became a study in acrimony, punctuated by brief explosions of emotion and violence.

The 1968 Democratic convention is best remembered (and appropriately so) for the violent clashes between antiwar demonstrators and the Chicago police in Grant Park. But there was also extraordinary rancor and bitterness inside the convention hall—the cavernous Stockyards Amphitheater—itself. Delegates literally fought each other for access to the microphones stationed around the floor, as credentials and platform battles spun quickly out of control. Party officials grabbed reporters and vented their anger about this or that injustice. Everyone knew that Hubert Humphrey, whom Johnson had chosen as his successor after withdrawing from the race himself in March, would be nominated. Virtually no one was happy about it, and boomlets on behalf of alternatives candidates—Eugene McCarthy, George McGovern, Edward Kennedy—rose defiantly and subsided bitterly during the week. After watching a film honoring Robert Kennedy, delegates began singing the Battle Hymn of the Republic—again and again and again, for more than twenty minutes, turning a teary tribute into an angry demonstration.

The convention organizers tried in vain to keep order. They isolated the antiwar demonstrators in a park miles away (Mayor Daley's idea); the result was the gruesome and politically disastrous battle with the police. They tightened security in the hall by means of a constantly malfunctioning system of electronic credentials that helped produce angry confrontations between some delegates and police. There were efforts to keep controversial issues (the Vietnam war above all) off the floor—a string of party elders, looking like archaic relics in this superheated environment, repeatedly banging the gavel for order—but the delegates refused to be silenced. The Daley administration did its best to prevent the media from covering anything but the official proceedings; the attempted manipulation so angered the journalists that they redoubled their efforts to get the stories.

On the last night of the convention Mayor Daley, after a week of battering by the press, mobilized his machine. Hours before the final session began, buses filled with Chicago wardheelers pulled up to the convention hall and unloaded hundreds of mostly working-class men and women, each carrying a cheap poster-board sign reading "We Love Mayor Daley." They poured into the convention hall and packed the visitors' galleries, leaving space for few of the actual ticket holders, most of whom arrived much later. All through the evening, the Daley partisans waved their posters, cheered loudly for the mayor, tried to drown out speakers they didn't like, and then straggled out of the hall, back onto their buses, and off into the night. It was a last cry of the old, crude, boss-dominated, national politics Daley represented.

Many of those who experienced the Chicago convention remember it with exceptional clarity nearly thirty years later for its air of danger and menace and passion. But it was also an intensely democratic moment, with all the arguing and brawling and agonizing that democracy, in troubled times, produces. And that, for the Democrats, was the problem. Like the 1964 Republican convention in San Francisco, the Chicago meeting had revealed to the world the party's passions and divisions. Nothing, of course, could match the devastating image of bloodied demonstrators being carted away by beefy Chicago policemen, while thousands behind them chanted "The Whole World Is Watching"—a scene played over and over on television throughout the week. But almost as devastating to the party was the scene inside the hall, when Senator Abraham Ribicoff, nominating George McGovern for president, looked down at Mayor Daley, who was sitting just below the podium, and denounced "gestapo tactics in the streets of Chicago." Daley and those around him stood up, red-faced, and shouted obscenities and anti-Semitic slurs at Ribicoff. He gazed back at them tolerantly, shook his head, and said: "How hard it is to accept the truth."

All of this was more democracy than party leaders wanted the voters to see. And so the next twenty years would bring a concerted and in the end largely successful drive to purge the conventions of all conflict and controversy, to turn them into carefully staged promotions for the party's presidential candidates.

The Republicans and the Democrats adopted wildly different strategies in 1972 to ensure tame conventions—with wildly different results. The Republicans, meeting once again in Miami Beach, chose machine-like efficiency. After spending nearly four years battling young antiwar protesters, Nixon apparently decided he wanted some young people of his own (perhaps because in 1972, for the first time, 18-year-olds could vote). The result was a youth movement as Walt Disney might have created it: fresh-scrubbed, neatly dressed young men and women, virtually all them of white, reliably chanting "Four More Years" on cue. This was the first convention to present campaign films as part of the regular proceedings: a long, slickly produced tribute to Nixon shown in the hall (and on the networks, which had not yet caught on to this device and dutifully broadcast all of it during prime time before the president's acceptance speech). Nixon himself appeared in Miami only briefly and gave a solemn, uninspiring address, as if the convention were a tedious distraction from his important duties in Washington. In reality, of course, he had overseen every detail of it with obsessive attention.

The Democrats, who had met a few weeks earlier in the same hall in Miami Beach, had seen one convention threatened and another destroyed by the clamor of the excluded. This time, the party had invited them in. A series of rules changes, the product of the commission that George McGovern had chaired in the aftermath of the Chicago disaster, produced the most diverse group of delegates ever to attend a national convention—more women, more minorities, more young people than ever before. In delegation after delegation, middle-aged men in suits sat uncomfortably alongside feminists, black delegates wearing Afros and dashikis, or blue-jean-clad twenty-year-olds with beards and ponytails. Among the jostling throngs in the convention hall were such luminaries of the counter-culture as Allen Ginsberg, Hunter Thompson, and even at one point some fingerbell-clinking Buddhist monks in saffron robes.

It was not really an angry convention in the way the 1968 brawl in Chicago had been—although there were angry moments, among them the unseating of Richard Daley and the Illinois delegation he led, an act of political suicide gleefully embraced by most present. Most of the time the delegates acted with a kind of jubilant abandon, pursuing one political passion after another. This was the first national convention in which feminism was clearly visible and in which spokesmen for gay rights had any voice. It was the first for all manner of groups and causes long on the margins of political life to say what they wished and do what they pleased. The first, and the last.

On the final night George McGovern had to wait until nearly 3 A.M. to begin his acceptance speech, well after even the West Coast television audience had gone to bed. What prime-time viewers had seen before they feel asleep was the usually perfunctory process of ratifying the vice-presidential candidate (in this case Senator Thomas Eagleton of Missouri) turned into a prolonged demonstration of open politics. The Women's Caucus nominated a candidate (Sissy Farenthold of

Texas) as a symbol of their political awakening; and as the balloting proceeded, individual delegates introduced dozens of names of their own. Mao Zedong, Jerry Rubin, Archie Bunker, Walter Cronkite, Martha Mitchell, César Chávez, and many others received votes before the interminable roll call came to an end. McGovern, trying to make a virtue of necessity, praised the proceedings as evidence of the party's newly democratic character and then gave a very good speech to an ebullient crowd. Many of those standing in the hall that night left exhilarated by the self-consciously democratic (if often sophomoric) character of the convention, a meeting so different from any they had seen before or would see again. But outside the hall, to the dwindling band of bleary-eyed television viewers waiting for McGovern's speech, the convention looked unruly, strident, and irresponsible. For years thereafter, the 1972 convention—even more than the 1968 one—became to many Democrats a model of what should never be allowed to happen again.

How far the party would go to ensure that became clear four years later in New York, where the Democrats met in Madison Square Garden for the first time since 1924. There was no question about the identity of the party's candidate. Jimmy Carter had locked up the Democratic nomination months before. The Democrats had scripted the convention to the minute, carefully excluding anything that might seem controversial and doing their best to avoid anything unexpected.

Perhaps because it was in New York, this convention—more than others—had the feel of a generic celebrity gathering. The V.I.P. galleries were crammed with actors, athletes, actors, models, wealthy businessmen, and others who were there to see and be seen, but who appeared to have no particular interest in the actual proceedings. The jostling for position and attention was reminiscent of the celebrity preening in courtside seats now common at New York Knicks games in the same building. The convention had become an "event," like Wimbledon or the U.S. Open or the Final Four—a magnet for the rich and famous.

The final night was pure Hollywood. A slickly produced film introduced Jimmy Carter as an appealing, softspoken, honest man who disdained pretension and would "never lie to you." It even suggested (falsely) that the famously pious candidate had a sense of humor by including a series of political cartoons that made fun of Carter's well-known smile with faces made up almost entirely of teeth. When the film ended, there was some folksy music as Carter himself entered the hall—walking not from behind the podium, but from in front of it, through the crowds on the floor, accompanied by a gaggle of cameramen. All of this was invisible to 90 percent of those in the convention hall but clearly visible to the television audience. Carter climbed to the podium, unleashed his big smile, and said—as he had countless times in the early months of a campaign that most people had once dismissed as quixotic—"My name is Jimmy Carter, and I'm running for President." The rest of the speech was entirely forgettable.

The Carter convention in 1976 established a pattern that every subsequent convention has imitated: a pattern of careful control, upbeat images, and essential vacuousness. Campaign managers have finally gotten what they have long wanted: conventions that serve their candidates, and only their candidates. But now, most of the time, almost no one watches.

The new age of conventions was clearly visible in 1984—not just in Houston, where the Republicans predictably crowned Ronald Reagan as their nominee without a murmur of dissent, but also in San Francisco, where the once fractious Democrats were staging their own carefully orchestrated event. There were moments of real excitement during that week—Mario Cuomo's stirring keynote address, Jesse Jackson's remarkable speech, the thrill that most women (and many men) felt when Geraldine Ferraro appeared to accept her place as the first woman ever to be on a national ticket; but those moments were rare.

The last national political convention to meet in San Francisco had been twenty years earlier. The 1964 and 1984 events seemed to have nothing in common, not even location. The Democrats were meeting in the sleek new Moscone Center a few blocks from downtown, not in the more distant Cow Palace where the Republicans had nominated Goldwater; and while the Moscone Center was attractive to the media because there was so much room for their facilities, it was actively hostile to the delegates and the audience. The actual meeting hall was, in fact, a large, low-ceilinged, underground exhibition space unsuccessfully converted into an arena.

This was, I believe, the first convention whose proceedings were visible to most of those in the hall only on the giant video screens that now flanked the podium. (Direct visual access to the podium was blocked for many delegates by the large, tall camera platform erected in the center aisle). It was as if the delegates themselves had been reduced at last to part of the television audience. It was also the first convention of the television era that the networks declined to cover "gavel to gavel." They devoted a few prime time hours to it each night (considerably more than they devoted subsequently), but the coverage seemed somehow perfunctory. Nothing of substance was decided, or even debated, in the hall that week. And while that spared Walter Mondale the embarrassment of discord or rancor, it denied him as well any real sense of engagement—either from the delegates or most of the television audience—in the event. At the end of the final night, after an acceptance speech whose most memorable line was Mondale's disastrous pledge to raise taxes, the convention orchestra did not play the Democratic party's traditional closing refrain, "Happy Days Are Here Again," the music that every Democratic candidate since Franklin Roosevelt had heard as he stood on the podium waving to the crowd. Instead, it played "Celebrate," a contemporary soft-rock song that was a favorite of bands at weddings and bar mitzvahs in the mid-1980s.

In 1992 the Democratic convention was again in New York. The glass booths for the networks were gone. Now that "gavel-to-gavel" coverage had ended, most anchors presided over their abbreviated broadcasts from cramped trailers in the bowels of the building. Few reporters were on the convention floor. There was no real news to cover there. People were jammed shoulder to shoulder in the overcrowded Garden, but there was little movement. Everyone was staring at the giant video screens flanking the podium. On the evening of the nomination, as the balloting was coming to its foreordained conclusion, the television screens began to show what looked like a birthday party. It was Bill Clinton, celebrating his nomination with family and friends in Macy's department store across the street. The cameras followed him as he walked with his wife and daughter through the store, outside, into the Garden complex, and finally onto the floor of the convention itself. He climbed up onto a platform just below the massive podium. Someone passed him a hand-held microphone.

Thirty-six years earlier, John Kennedy had paid a surprise visit to the Democratic convention in Los Angeles just after being nominated to thank the delegates. Clinton, whose admiration for Kennedy was well known, referred to that night in 1960 in his brief remarks to the delegates, and then left the hall. It was the only moment of the week that looked unscripted—but of course, it was not really unscripted at all (as the carefully orchestrated television coverage of Clinton's supposedly spontaneous walk to the convention hall made clear). The candidate was trying, it seemed, to find some link to the political world with which he had grown up. But that world no longer existed, and the gesture seemed somehow hollow. Four years later, in Chicago, even that perfunctory gesture toward spontaneity was gone. The Democrats (like the Republicans in San Diego a few weeks earlier) made no effort to disguise their efforts to program the proceedings tightly and precisely to fit the small window of network television time allotted to them.

The transformation of the once turbulent political conventions into shiny, packaged infomercials is now virtually complete—their hollow cores all too visible beneath their slick, media-driven exteriors. They have become an inadvertent symbol of the impoverished state of American politics in our antipolitical age, and it is worth asking what will happen to them now.

They could continue to decline and eventually die. (The Democrats in 1996 flirted briefly with reducing their meeting to three days from the usual four; once that process begins it could be hard to stop.) They could become in fact what they already have become in effect: political advertisements. (The Republicans in 1996 paid Pat Robertson's cable network to run extensive coverage of their convention, coverage the party itself packaged.) They could revive one day, if there are ever enough changes in campaign financing, the primary system, or the conventions' own rules to allow them to perform some real decision-making function again. Or they could continue to stumble along—unloved and widely abused—more or less as they are.

Conventions probably will (and probably should) survive, even if feebly, for several reasons. They offer parties and candidates invaluable free time on television—not nearly as much as they used to get, but the equivalent of millions of dollars of advertising nonetheless. But they serve another function as well. In *The Making of the President 1972*, the fourth in Theodore H. White's series of majestic chronicles of presidential campaigns that began in 1960, White wrote of that year's Republican convention: "Had he wished, Richard Nixon might have accepted the nomination sitting in his office, receiving a delegation of party leaders before television and accepting the honor from their hands, as candidates did of yore." But he went to Miami Beach to the convention, White argued, because "ceremonies are important . . . they are punctuation marks in history as in life."

Individuals have always used ceremonies to mark significant passages in their lives: christenings, bar mitzvahs, graduations, weddings, funerals. Nations need ceremonies to mark the course of their lives too. And conventions are among the few ceremonies Americans have ever had (perhaps the only one they have now) to celebrate the process of politics and to make it seem an activity worthy of attention and concern. They are the only occasions that give our atrophying political parties a sense of identity and purpose. They are, in a time when people across the political spectrum decry the decline of "civic life," among our most conspicuous national civic institutions. Abandoning conventions, even in their present degraded form, would be to surrender a kind of hope for a renewal of public life.

15

The Passions of Oral Roberts

Throughout the more than five decades since World War II, the principal religious activity of millions of Americans has been watching Oral Roberts on television.[1] He has talked to them about the healing power of Jesus from the enormous tents in which he held his great crusades in the 1950s and 1960s; from churches and auditoriums and stadiums around the country and the world; from television studios in New York and Los Angeles; and ultimately from his own broadcast center in Tulsa, Oklahoma, where he has preached from a comfortable living room that looks like the set of a network talk show. Some of Roberts's constituents (whom he calls "partners") have been members of established churches in their own communities. Some have not. But in either case, many have derived from Roberts's television ministry a more vibrant and satisfying religious message than the mainstream Protestant denominations can offer them.

To those unfamiliar with Roberts and his world, the nature of that message has not often been clear, in part because the most striking feature of his broadcasts (and his ministry as a whole) has often appeared to be a relentless and unembarrassed commercialism. In the course of a Sunday morning program, Roberts could spend nearly half of his thirty minutes of airtime promoting a new book or publicizing a ministers' conference to be held on the campus of Oral Roberts University. In the 1980s Roberts's son and heir apparent, Richard, began a daily, hour-long Christian talk show of his own in which promotion was even more conspicuous. The younger Roberts hawked books, pamphlets, tapes, and mementos; and his show was sprinkled with slick commercials urging tourists to visit the new Oral Roberts Healing Outreach Center in Tulsa, which includes a Disneyland-like "Journey Through the Bible" with "state-of-the-art electronics, lasers, sound effects and music, to make the greatest stories of the Bible come alive right before your eyes."

Although Oral Roberts has been more circumspect in appealing for money from his partners than many other television evangelists, contributions flowed into Tulsa at an astonishing rate for decades. During one extraordinary month in 1982, the ministry received gifts totaling $18 million. Even during normal times, Roberts consistently raised more money than any other religious association in the nation. These successes enabled him to build a remarkable empire. Oral Roberts University enrolls over 4,500 students in its fully accredited undergraduate and graduate programs and occupies a complex of lavish new buildings of striking modern design. The City of Faith, an enormous medical complex (whose 60-story tower is the tallest building in Oklahoma), houses a medical school, a dental school, a major hospital, and a research center where Roberts once insisted a "cure for cancer" would soon be found. The new Healing Outreach Center serves as a tourist mecca. A large convention complex enables Roberts to hold enormous conferences and to draw visitors from around the world.

There have been countless disciples and imitators—among them Pat Robertson, once a Roberts protege, who is now a major power in the Republican party and was once a candidate for president. But with the possible exception of Billy Graham, no American religious figure of the last fifty years has had Roberts's reach or impact. Even so, Roberts has received relatively little serious attention outside the circle of the faithful. An examination of his life helps reveal the important religious culture at whose center he has so long stood; and it helps make comprehensible the apparent anomaly of a spiritual movement supposedly grounded in its opposition to mainstream, secular culture but engaging relentlessly (and enormously successfully) in intensely commercial activities.

The Oral Roberts ministry, which began in 1947, is the direct descendant of two great schisms in American Protestantism that emerged in the late nineteenth and early twentieth centuries. One is familiar: the bitter fight over Darwinism that began in the 1870s and that produced a lasting division between modernists and evangelicals.

Protestant modernists (a group that came to include most members of the intelligentsia and the urban upper classes) adapted to Darwinism by discarding from their theology those religious beliefs that contradicted the new teachings of science; for many of them, religious faith became as a result a largely passive experience, consigned to a safe corner of daily life, and—as time went on—easily and frequently abandoned.

Evangelicals, on the other hand, struggled to preserve the tenets and the intensity of traditional faith in the face of the apostasy of the modernists. Evangelicalism (which has generally been most visible through the activities of its most radical adherents, the fundamentalists) was in part a social and cultural protest against an increasingly secular, cosmopolitan world from which many conservative Protestants felt excluded; and as such, it rejected at times not only Darwinism but a wide range of other modern values and assumptions. But the movement was first and foremost a theological crusade, centered around several points of doctrine that modernists had repudiated but that evangelicals continued to cherish: the importance of personal conversion; the infallibility of the Bible, literally interpreted; the factuality of biblical miracles; the importance of the Old Testament and its teachings (modernists tended to prefer the New Testament, with its gentler and more ambiguous messages). Many, although not all, evangelicals accepted as well the doctrine of premillennialism: a belief rooted in biblical prophecies of the second coming of Christ, who would return to earth in the midst of a great apocalypse to redeem those who truly believed in Him and usher in a thousand years of peace and justice. Premillennialism led to a conviction among some evangelicals that the world of man—the world of "kings and nations"—was irrelevant to the lives of true Christians. Their mission was to pray, to evangelize, to believe, and to wait for the end. (Many modernists or progressives rejected all millennial prophecies, but those who accepted them tended to embrace postmillennialism—the belief that the second coming will happen at the end of the millennium of peace and justice; for them postmillennialism became a religious justification for efforts to reform the present world.)

The second schism in American Protestantism is less familiar. On New Year's Day 1901, at Bethel Bible College in Topeka, Kansas, the

Reverend Charles Fox Parham conducted a service during which a female student began "speaking in tongues": praying in an incomprehensible language. To many Christians, the "gift of tongues" (or *glossolalia*) is the sign of a special religious experience: the descent of the Holy Spirit onto a believer, a personal baptism based on direct contact with the Lord. Five years later, at the Azusa Street Mission in Los Angeles, a rash of similar ecstatic conversions sparked a revival that spread rapidly throughout the United States.

The episodes at Bethel and Azusa Street are commonly considered the beginning of the Holiness movement, or modern American pentecostalism—a movement that emerged largely out of fundamentalism but diverged from it on a number of points. Pentecostals rejected the belief of many fundamentalists that the "age of miracles" had passed and that God had ceased to reveal Himself to man. Billy Graham, the most influential fundamentalist of the postwar era, said of man's ability to feel God's presence that faith was like flying a very high kite—you couldn't see it, but now and then you could feel a faint tug on the string. But to the pentecostals the Lord was an immediate presence in the everyday world, communicating directly with the faithful through the Holy Spirit, constantly performing miracles. He could change the life of any Christian at any moment. Speaking in tongues was the first sign of the presence of the Lord in the life of a believer. But certain chosen pentecostals might acquire additional gifts that would enable them to channel the power of the Holy Spirit into the lives of believers: the gift of prophecy, the gift of interpretation of tongues, and above all the gift of healing. Through much of the twentieth century, outsiders have generally become aware of pentecostalism as a result of the activities of the charismatic healers, who claim the ability to channel God's powers into the sick through the "laying on of hands"; and as a result of the ecstatic camp meetings in which rapturous pentecostals toss away their crutches and proclaim miraculous cures.

The pentecostal revival spread rapidly among American Protestants, and particularly rapidly among lower-class men and women seeking a deeper and more spontaneous religious experience than the increasingly staid and middle-class mainstream denominations (both modernist and fundamentalist) had come to offer them. Pentecostalism found its way into many existing churches (and particularly into Methodist congregations in the South and the West); it created denominations of its own (the Assemblies of God, the Church of God, and the Pentecostal Holiness Church); and it spawned a new breed of evangelist, often unattached to any formal church, who created independent ministries of enormous strength. Aimee Semple McPherson, the flamboyant and controversial healing revivalist of the 1920s in California, was among the most prominent of the early pentecostals.

Even more than the fundamentalism from which it had sprung, pentecostalism remained through the first half of the twentieth century an obscure and largely unnoticed subculture, generally ridiculed by the secular mainstream. It was a religion for the poor and the provincial, for men and women isolated from the "great world" and unlikely ever to enter it. But then, in the aftermath of World War II, there was a change. The dramatic postwar capitalist expansion began to lift many of even the most isolated Americans out of poverty and into at least the fringes of the middle class. The pentecostal constituency now could hope not just for spiritual solace, but also for real material gain. And in 1947, perhaps in response to these changes, another great period of pentecostal expansion began, this time in very new directions. Oral Roberts was there to lead it.

Roberts was born in 1918 in rural Oklahoma and grew up in typical pentecostal surroundings. His father was an itinerant preacher of the Pentecostal Holiness Church, and the family moved frequently and lived meagerly. Roberts has described his youth with a combination of horror (at its privations) and pride (in his escape from it). "There were times," he recalled in his 1972 autobiography, *The Call*, "when we were reduced almost to starvation." In 1935 he contracted tuberculosis and seemed unlikely to recover; but in July of that year he attended a camp meeting in Ada, Oklahoma, stood before a pentecostal revivalist, and "felt the healing power of the Lord . . . like electricity going through me." In an instant, he claims (with characteristic overstatement), the tuberculosis left his lungs and he was healed. In fact, his recovery was slow and painful and occupied many more months. But recover he did; and having done so, he dedicated his life to serving the Lord who had, he said, told him to "take the message of my healing power to your generation."

For over a decade, Roberts served, like his father, as a pentecostal minister in small towns and rural communities in the South and West—moving about from North Carolina to Georgia to Oklahoma, supervising modest parishes, and finding himself increasingly restless and frustrated. In 1947, finally, after an extended period of fasting and despair, he once again heard the voice of God as he was praying at his church in Enid, Oklahoma. Then, as on countless other occasions, the Lord chose to convey to Roberts instructions of remarkable triviality: "Stand upon your feet . . . Go and get in your car . . . Drive one block and turn right." (Among the later pieces of arcana God delivered to Roberts were instructions that the three towers of the City of Faith medical center should be 60, 30, and 20 stories tall respectively.) But also on that night in 1947, Roberts claimed, he heard the command that would change his life: "From this hour your ministry of healing will begin."

There is no easy explanation for why Oral Roberts, among so many other pentecostal evangelists, became over the next two decades the giant of healing revivalism. He was always a man of unusual rhetorical power, but so were many others. What perhaps most set him apart was his obsessive determination, his conviction that he was destined for greatness, and his willingness to drive not only himself but those around him—family, friends, associates—with relentless intensity. Whatever the reasons, however, Roberts's crusades throughout the United States and, eventually, the world generated enormous crowds, rapturous enthusiasm, and thousands of testimonials from men and women who insisted that he had healed them.

Almost from the start, it seems clear, Roberts was intent not just on saving souls and curing disease, but on building a large, visible, and permanent empire that would serve as testimony to God's (and his own) achievements. It began in the late 1940s, when he constructed a substantial office building in Tulsa for his Healing Waters evangelistic association. It expanded in 1954, when he began televising his crusades and discovered the enormous financial rewards of soliciting contributions over the air. And it culminated in 1965, when he opened Oral Roberts University—not simply another Bible college, but a degree-granting academic institution that would, he promised, train Christian men and women to move out into the world and serve as missionaries. These would be missionaries not just to the heathen of Africa or Asia or Latin America. They would also carry the gospel to "the board rooms of New York, the offices of Chicago, and the classrooms of Phoenix." They would take pentecostalism out of the hinterland and into the centers of power, and they would break down the barriers that had for so long isolated Roberts and his kind from the world of the American mainstream. Patti Roberts, Oral's former daughter-in-law and a member of the first entering class at ORU in 1965, recalls in her memoirs the excitement of the promise: "He was saying that I could love Jesus and still become all that I could be in His name and take my place in the world community."

A question that arose often in the minds of some of Roberts's fellow pentecostals (although never, he insisted, in his own mind) was whom did this ambitious ministry really change. Did it achieve its ostensible purpose of remaking the secular mainstream, infusing it with Christian faith and rectitude? Or was its real achievement to alter itself so that it would conform to the standards of its new middle-class constituency? In some respects, at least, it is the pentecostals who seem to have adapted to the secular culture and not the other way around.

Evidence for that comes, in part, from the extraordinary degree to which Roberts fused charismatic religion to the consumerist desires of middle-class America. He continued, of course, to talk about God's power to heal the sick and save the unredeemed. But he talked with much greater frequency about other gifts available through the Holy Spirit. For years Roberts's magazine, *Abundant Life*, conveyed this message: Jesus wants those who love him to be not only spiritually and physically whole, but financially whole as well. His controversial doctrine of "seed faith" took the message further, presenting religious conviction as a kind of spiritual mutual fund. Those who made a "seed faith" gift to the Oral Roberts ministry could expect a threefold return on their "investment" from some "unexpected source" within a year; if they did not, Roberts promised, he would return the original contribution.

The promise of immediate material reward was always pervasive throughout the Roberts ministry. To his partners he sent multicolored prayer sheets to be mailed back to him with a list of needs for which he could pray: "The RED area is for your SPIRITUAL healing; the WHITE area is for your PHYSICAL healing; the GREEN area is for your FINANCIAL healing. Check the needs you have and RUSH them back to me." In 1983 he "laid his hands" on a paper napkin for a dinner companion who wanted help in meeting his family's needs. A few weeks later, Roberts received a message of gratitude: "I laid your hands . . . on my daughter for her new computer school that she is starting. I laid them on my billfold for a financial need that I am feeling. . . . Thank you for letting us use this simple table napkin in a simple Act of Faith as a point of contact. OUR MIRACLES ARE ON THE WAY!!" Roberts quickly mailed out thousands of paper napkins to his partners, with the inspiring testimony printed on one side and a tracing of his hands printed on the other.

Roberts himself has never seemed a particularly materialistic man. He has lived comfortably, certainly—in a substantial president's residence at the university in Tulsa; in a vacation home in Palm Springs; and in a $2.4 million house in Beverly Hills (purchased "as an investment" by his ministry). But he has accumulated relatively little personal wealth and has lived much less ostentatiously than some other members of his organization or even than other members of his own family. Nevertheless, he clearly became attuned to the yearning among even the most devout Christians in postwar America for access to the fruits of middle class abundance—a yearning that the "miracle" of economic growth made it possible for them to fulfill in ways that in earlier eras seemed all but impossible. Roberts always attributed his awareness of such desires to a revelation he experienced in 1947, at almost the same time that he received his message from God to begin his healing ministry—a revelation that came from reading a passage in the Book of John: "I wish above all things that thou mayest prosper and be in health, even as thy soul prospereth." The message, he concluded, was that "God is a good God," that it was not necessary to "be poor to be a Christian." As a first test of his faith, he bought a new Buick, which "became a symbol to me of what a man could do if he would believe God."

From that point on, Roberts's message was never one of withdrawal from the world of consumer pleasures, not one of self-denial or Christian asceticism. Least of all was it a message of man's inherent sinfulness and the terrors of damnation. It has been the much more congenial message that God wants those who believe in Him to be prosperous, successful, and happy—a gospel epitomized by such slogans as "Expect a Miracle," "Release Your Faith," or (the phrase with which he opened every television broadcast) "Something Good Is Going to Happen to You." Roberts's wife Evelyn, in her deferential 1976 memoir, makes particularly explicit this religious justification for material ambition. "I think our desires are just as important to God as our needs," she writes. The Lord "is just as concerned about our car payments, dental and medical bills, food bills, and rent as we are. He wants us to prosper."

But Oral Roberts's adaptation to the "great world" went beyond a simple celebration of material success. It embraced a craving for respectability, a desire for movement out of the pentecostal subculture and into the life of mainstream America. Roberts's decision in the 1960s to abandon his much-ridiculed (and by then dwindling) tent campaigns and turn his attention to his university and to television was one of the first indications that he was no longer content with a position of influence among traditional pentecostals alone. And in later years he engaged in relentless efforts to make himself and his ministry palatable to the American mainstream. He produced prime-time television specials with such guest stars as Jerry Lewis, Jimmy Durante, Johnny Mathis, Burl Ives, and Tennessee Ernie Ford. He himself made appearances on Johnny Carson, the Dinah Shore Show, Laugh-In, Hee Haw, and the Jerry Lewis Telethon. At Oral Roberts University, students were encouraged to dress and behave in ways that the middle class would find attractive. Aerobic weight-loss programs were required, and the chronically obese could be expelled. Women were encouraged to wear makeup and fashionable clothes. (Roberts once flew into a rage when conservative pentecostals criticized a student singing group that appeared on his television show for displaying too much "flesh." Who, he asked, would watch a program on which women wore ankle-length dresses?) And in 1968 he left the Pentecostal Holiness Church and became a Methodist; by joining a more "respectable" mainstream denomination, he apparently believed, he would improve his access to the American middle class.

Roberts's own gratitude for signs of acceptance from the larger world verged, at times, on the pathetic. He made that clear, for example, when, on returning from a trip to Hollywood, he told his students: "This sounds crazy . . . but they have my picture up all over the stars in the NBC studio. . . . There's Flip Wilson and I'm right next to the Killer. Then there's Bob Hope. . . . And when I come out there it's just like rolling the red carpet out. . . . The Lord has given us favor with these people." When Ronald Reagan sent a congratulatory telegram to the dedication of the City of Faith in 1981, Roberts was almost speechless: "I just want you to know I'm no longer the little boy from Tulsa, President Ronald Reagan! I didn't know this was coming."

Roberts is a determined, intelligent, and talented man whose accomplishments are, indeed, remarkable. But never, it seems, has he been particularly likable. Throughout his long career, he tyrannized friends and associates, squelching opposition to his plans with the disconcerting habit of claiming to receive his instructions directly from God on even the most trivial of issues. (He almost destroyed his empire in the late 1970s by insisting, over the objections of almost all his associates, that God had ordered him to construct the enormous City of Faith medical complex without delay, no matter what the cost. Once built, it became—as the Tulsa medical community had predicted—an expensive white elephant, unable to fill even a fourth of its hospital beds.) He so inflated claims of his own successes (his production of conversions, healings, and other miracles) that even ORU students at times referred derisively to his magazine, *Abundant Life*, as "Abundant Lies." Indeed, Roberts's obsession with his own empire—with its survival and growth—seemed at times almost monomaniacal. He "will sacrifice anything for his ministry," Patti Roberts insisted.

Roberts is probably not a hypocrite. There is no reason to doubt his claim that he has always believed he was doing the Lord's work. But what is particularly striking about his remarkable career is the degree to which he defined the Lord's work to conform to his own ambitions and to the expectations of middle-class America. A movement that emerged out of the desire to preserve a pure and vital faith from the encroachments of the modern world evolved over time into a movement to make faith compatible with the mundane material desires of the consumer culture. Roberts's God is, as he so often said, a "good God"—a God capable of cleansing sin and healing sickness, to be sure, but a God engaged above all in helping men and women achieve happy, prosperous lives. He is a God who gives evidence of His presence in the world by helping Oral Roberts raise millions of dollars to build gleaming towers of anodized aluminum in Tulsa, Oklahoma; a God who instructs His disciples to fill the airwaves and bookstores with "Eight Steps to Recovery," "Your Key to Financial Health," and countless other counterparts to the secular self-help guides that have been a staple of popular culture since Dale Carnegie; a God whose favor is visible not just through faith or good works but through material success. Patti Roberts, whose personal bitterness toward the Roberts family undoubtedly colored her evaluation of the ministry, nevertheless expressed concerns that many Christians have felt about the direction of modern pentecostalism: "Instead of looking for the marks of the Spirit in a person's life—love, joy, peace, long-suffering, and the others, we have a tendency to consider the cars he drives, the clothes he wears, or the buildings he's built as the measure of God's grace in his life and the quality of his relationship to God."

The increasing strength and visibility of charismatic religion in recent decades has produced bewilderment, contempt, and alarm among secular Americans who not long ago believed active faith to be a vanishing force, consigned to the provincial backwaters of society. To them the Christian right often seems a kind of barbarian horde, storming the gates of the secular world and attempting to supplant it with an alien world of their own. And in some respects, by secular standards at least, that assessment is correct. Many pentecostals and fundamentalists do indeed challenge the deep faith of the modern, secular world in science and rational inquiry. They do indeed question some of the premises of the Enlightenment. They promote an agenda that threatens to undo many of the changes in modern society that most secular Americans consider healthy progress. They struggle to introduce obscurantist religious views (and at times overt bigotry) into schools, public institutions, and popular culture.

But the story of Oral Roberts and his ministry, and the story of many other evangelists who have followed in his wake, suggests another side to modern pentecostalism, many of whose adherents define their challenge in different and much less menacing terms. Theirs is not, on the whole, an effort to destroy or replace the American mainstream, or even to change it except in what they consider relatively limited ways. It is, rather, an effort to have it all: to preserve an active, vital faith while at the same time sharing in the fruits of the modern middle-class world and basking in its approval. The clamor at the gates is not just the sound of a hostile wrath. It is also a simple plea for admission.

16

The Problem of American Conservatism

It will not, I suspect, be very controversial to say that twentieth-century American conservatism has been something of an orphan in historical scholarship. Historians have written books and articles about modern conservatism, of course, some of them quite good. In the last several decades, moreover, both the quantity and the quality of scholarship on the subject has markedly increased. Even so, it would be hard to argue that the American right has received anything like the amount of attention from historians that its role in twentieth-century politics and culture suggests it should.[1] Given the history of the last twenty years, that is coming to seem an ever more curious omission. What follows is an effort to understand why that omission has occurred.

My observations are not the product of any personal scholarly research on conservatism (or of any personal engagement with or sympathy for conservative politics). But for a historian who has been mainly concerned with the history of modern liberalism, this is not so abrupt a departure as it might sound. For me, writing about liberalism has produced considerable skepticism about some of the scholarly assumptions that have governed the study of American political culture in this century. Most historians who have told the story of twentieth-century American political and cultural development have emphasized the triumph of the progressive-liberal state and of the modern, cosmopolitan sensibility that has accompanied and to a large degree supported it. They have argued about the timing of this triumph and about whether it has been a good or bad thing. But until recently, at least, they have seldom doubted that it occurred.

A number of scholars in the last few years, myself among them, have been struck increasingly by other, quite different features of modern America: by the chronic weakness of the progressive state;[2] by the enormous difficulty liberals have had in securing and retaining popular loyalties; and by the persistent strength of forces that, for lack of a better word, we generally call conservative, in a long and still unresolved battle over the nature of American politics and American culture.[3] This is an important and, at least until recently, largely neglected part of the story of twentieth-century America. And so the "problem of American conservatism," as I define it here, is not a problem facing conservatives themselves, and not any of the problems conservatives have created for their opponents. It is a problem of American historical scholarship, the problem of finding a suitable place for the right—for its intellectual traditions and its social and political movements—within our historiographical concerns.

Conservatism has not always been the orphan within American historical scholarship that it is today. The progressive historians who dominated the writing of American history through much of the first half of this century placed conservatives at the center of their interpretive scheme—a scheme that portrayed American history as a long and often intense struggle between popular democratic elements and entrenched antidemocratic interests. But theirs was a constricted view of conservatism, focused almost exclusively on economic elites and their efforts to preserve wealth and privilege. It is not surprising that later generations of scholars have found the progressive framework inadequate.[4]

What succeeded the progressive model, however, was a series of interpretive schemes that did relatively little to enlarge our understanding of conservatism and at times further marginalized the right. That was particularly true of the so-called "consensus" scholarship that briefly dominated American historiography after World War II.[5] The consensus scholars did take note of one of the most serious shortcomings of the progressive view of conservatism. They recognized that the right did not consist only of elites defending wealth and privilege, and that there was a popular, grass-roots right—most immediately visible to them in the alarming rise of McCarthyism in the early 1950s—that needed explanation. But little in their explanations of what such scholars at times called the "radical right," the "new right," or the "pseudo-conservative revolt" suggested that conservatives were people whose ideas or grievances should be taken seriously or that the right deserved attention as a distinct element of the American political tradition. Instead, the consensus approach tended to produce a dismissive view of conservatism, a view suggested by the literary critic Lionel Trilling's famous 1950 statement, in the introduction to *The Liberal Imagination:*

> In the United States at this time liberalism is not only the dominant but even the sole intellectual tradition. For it is the plain fact that nowadays there are no conservative or reactionary ideas in general circulation. This does not mean, of course, that there is no impulse to conservatism or to reaction. Such impulses are certainly very strong, perhaps even stronger than most of us know. But the conservative impulse and the reactionary impulse do not, with some isolated and some ecclesiastical exceptions, express themselves in ideas but only in action or in irritable mental gestures which seem to resemble ideas.[6]

Fourteen years later, in the midst of a presidential campaign that seems in retrospect to have challenged such assumptions, Richard Hofstadter (Trilling's colleague and friend) wrote of Barry Goldwater that he "represents a very special minority point of view which is not even preponderant in his own party." "When, in all our history," he asked, "has anyone with ideas so bizarre, so archaic, so self confounding, so remote from the basic American consensus, ever got so far?"[7] The result of such assumptions was the tendency of consensus scholars to explain much American conservatism as if it were a kind of pathology—a "paranoid style," "symbolic politics," a product of "status anxiety"—an irrational or semi-rational aberration from a firmly established mainstream.[8]

But it was not just "consensus" scholars who had trouble taking conservatism seriously. New Left scholarship, which attacked the consensus with great effectiveness for ignoring or marginalizing the left, had relatively little to say about the right. That was in part because of the way much of the New Left celebrated, even romanticized, "the people." Having repudiated the liberal suspicion of "mass politics" and embraced instead the concept of "participatory democracy," scholars of the left had difficulty conceding that mass movements could be anything but democratic and progressive; they found it difficult to acknowledge that they could emerge from the right.[9] But New Left scholars also neglected conservatism because, no less than the consensus historians they were challenging, they were in large measure preoccupied with the cold war and the liberalism they believed supported it. One of the central assumptions of New Left political history—an assumption that was associated at first with William Appleman Williams and his students but that eventually spread far wider among radical historians—was that the ideology of capitalist hegemony in modern America has not been conventional conservatism but "corporate liberalism," which has shaped American foreign policy and domestic life alike.[10] New Left political scholarship has, therefore, generally been more interested in discrediting liberalism—and, within the academic world, in wresting leadership and initiative from liberal scholars—than in confronting what it has generally considered a less formidable foe: the self-proclaimed right.[11]

Nor has the so-called "organizational synthesis," which has played a large role in recent years in shaping interpretations of twentieth-century America, found much room in its framework for the right. The existence of a conservative tradition is not, perhaps, incompatible with the organizational view that the driving force in the modern world is the emergence of large-scale bureaucratic institutions. But neither does a conservative tradition play a very active role in that view. The organizational approach, therefore, tends to portray conservatism (when it considers it at all) in the same way it considers other forms of dissent: as the futile, and dwindling, resistance of provincial or marginal peoples to the inexorable forces of modernism.[12]

More recently, historians interested in the idea of "republicanism" have done much to revive scholarly interest in resistance to "progress" and the progressive state and to identify a powerful political tradition distinct from liberalism. Most scholars of republicanism, however, identify it as a set of ideas that preceded liberalism and ultimately fell victim to it—at the time of the Revolution, according to some, and in the mid and late nineteenth century according to others. By the twentieth century, most such scholars imply, the nation's ideological landscape was largely devoid of antiprogressive challenges to the liberal center.[13]

But to say that these and other interpretive models have left little room for the right is not to answer the question of why historians have neglected conservatism. It is only to restate it. Why has American conservatism not claimed enough attention from scholars to cause them to revise or overthrow their conceptual models in order to make a place for it? How have scholars managed to content themselves with a set of paradigms in which conservatism plays so small a role? Answering those questions requires considering not just the nature of historiography but the nature of American conservatism itself.

American conservatism is not an easy phenomenon to characterize, even for those who view it sympathetically. Conservatism encompasses a broad range of ideas, impulses, and constituencies, and many conservatives feel no obligation to choose among the conflicting, even incompatible impulses, that fuel their politics. Individual conservatives find it possible, and at times perhaps even necessary, to embrace several clashing ideas at once. Conservatism is not, in short, an "ideology," with a secure and consistent internal structure. It is a cluster of related (and sometimes unrelated) ideas from which those who consider themselves conservatives draw different elements at different times. This ideological juggling makes the American right particularly baffling to those historians who (as most do) stand outside it and try to make sense of it. Still, conservatism is no more inchoate than liberalism, progressivism, socialism, or any other broad political stance that describes a large and diverse group of people.[14] And so its lack of ideological consistency and clarity is not a sufficient answer to the question of why it has received so much less attention than these other clusters of political ideas.

In the twentieth century, at least, American conservatism has also been relatively late in developing as a major intellectual or political force. (In this sense, there is at least some truth to Lionel Trilling's 1950 evaluation of the right.) There have always been conservatives and reactionaries in modern America, but except for defenders of the corporate world and its prerogatives, they have not always been very effective in making themselves heard or felt. George Nash, a sympathetic chronicler, has written that until at least 1945 "no articulate, coordinated, self-consciously conservative intellectual force existed in the United States. There were, at most, scattered voices of protest, profoundly pessimistic about the future of their country."[15] Nor, prior to 1945, did grass-roots American conservatives often constitute an effective political force, as the abysmal performance of such organizational efforts as the Liberty League in the 1930s suggests.[16] Not until the postwar era did large numbers of conservatives manage to articulate a serious and important critique of liberal culture. And only in the 1970s did they begin to make that critique the basis of an effective political movement by creating (among other things) a network of publications, think tanks, and political action committees that have come to rival and often outperform their powerful liberal counterparts.[17] Conservatism as an intellectually serious and politically effective popular movement is, in short, a relatively new phenomenon—born out of the frustrations of political exile in the 1930s and 1940s, the passions of the anticommunist crusades of the late 1940s and early 1950s, and perhaps above all the political and cultural upheavals of the 1960s and 1970s. It has been slow to emerge in a visible and powerful enough form to demand scholarly attention.

But this, too, seems an inadequate explanation for the absence of scholarly attention to the right. If historians have done nothing else in the last twenty years, they have demonstrated their ability to retrieve the experiences of people and groups whose lives and ideas are not immediately visible in mainstream politics and culture. There have, for example, been long periods in the twentieth century when the left has seemed dormant, when its constituencies and goals were not immediately visible. And yet historians have very effectively portrayed the life and ideas of the left during its years in the wilderness. The same case remains to be made for the right.

A better explanation for the inattention of historians may be that much (although by no means all) American conservatism in the twentieth century has rested on a philosophical foundation not readily distinguishable from the liberal tradition to which it is, in theory, opposed. Few historians any longer agree with Louis Hartz's claim that no important political theory has taken root in America that has not been grounded in a commitment to democratic capitalism and Lockean conceptions of freedom. But there was at least some truth in Hartz's claim, and the claim of scholars influenced by him, that "to be an American conservative it is necessary to reassert liberalism."[18] Indeed, the defense of liberty, the preservation of individual freedom, has been as central to much of American conservatism in the twentieth century as it has been to American liberalism. Many conservatives would argue that in the twentieth century it has been much more central to their concerns than to the concerns of liberals.

There is some basis for that claim. Late nineteenth-century (or "classical") liberalism, epitomized in the ideas of the Liberal Republicans of the 1870s and 1880s,[19] rested securely on the individualistic, antistatist assumptions of John Stuart Mill and the Manchester liberals of England. What came to be known as "liberalism" in mid and late twentieth-century America has emerged to a significant extent out of a conscious repudiation of the antistatist elements of that classical tradition. Modern liberalism has been, instead, an effort to build the case for a more active and powerful state (even if one in which ideas of individual rights play an important, often central role). The antistatist liberal tradition of nineteenth-century America has, therefore, increasingly become the property of those who in the twentieth century are generally known as conservatives (or, as some of them prefer, libertarians).

Nothing, in fact, so irritated many conservatives of the 1930s and 1940s as the New Deal's appropriation of the word "liberal." The real liberals, they insisted, were the enemies of New Deal statism, the defenders of individual rights against the "social engineering" and "paternalism" of the left.[20] True liberalism, Herbert Hoover argued in 1938, rested on the "deep realization that economic freedom cannot be sacrificed if political freedom is to be preserved." The New Deal was not liberalism, but a form of "national regimentation" reminiscent of fascism and communism. It was, he argued, "a vast shift from the American concept of human rights which even the government may not infringe to those social philosophies where men are wholly subjective to the state. It is a vast casualty to Liberty if it shall be continued." The true liberalism, which Hoover believed had emerged ascendant from World War I, "is today imperiled and endangered."[21]

Perhaps the single most influential contemporary statement of "conservative" opposition to the New Deal came from a man who always insisted he was a liberal, even as he became a hero to many right-wing intellectuals: Friedrich Hayek. Hayek was a distinguished Austrian economist who emigrated to England in 1931 and later moved to the United States, where he settled at the University of Chicago. With the specter of totalitarian oppression in central Europe in mind, Hayek devoted himself to refurbishing the tattered reputation of the classical, antistatist liberalism of the nineteenth century. He became (along with such others as the economist Milton Friedman and the English philosopher Michael Oakeshott) an important voice on behalf of a form of libertarianism in modern society and a bitter critic of the "collectivism" he saw sweeping through Britain and America in the 1930s.[22]

Out of these concerns emerged Hayek's celebrated 1944 book, *The Road to Serfdom.* It was not a work of scholarship, Hayek readily conceded. It was a "political book," a call to arms—a warning, directed at a general readership, of the dangers confronting the West. (He began writing it in London during the Nazi blitz, so it is perhaps not surprising that it had a superheated, polemical tone.) Somewhat implausibly, it became a major best seller and a *Reader's Digest* condensed book. To many postwar conservatives, Hayek's book served as a philosophical and even programmatic Bible.[23]

The Road to Serfdom was, at its heart, a strenuous polemic against the New Deal on what Hayek insisted were liberal grounds. The New Dealers, he claimed, offered fervent assurances that it was possible to increase the economic power of the state without infringing on personal liberty. But the totalitarian experiences of Germany and the Soviet Union illustrated the impossibility of maintaining that balance. "Economic control," he wrote, "is not merely control of a sector of human life which can be separated from the rest; it is the control of the means of all our ends." And given that connection, the most dangerous form of economic control was statism, for "the separation of economic and political aims is an essential guaranty of individual freedom." And thus, he warned, "It is necessary now to state the unpalatable truth that it is Germany whose fate we are in some danger of repeating." The United States, like Nazi Germany, had embarked on the "road to serfdom."[24]

The centrality to modern conservatism of the essentially liberal concerns that Hayek raised—the fear of the state, the elevation of individual liberty above all other values, the insistence that personal freedom is inseparable from economic freedom—helps explain the dismissive view of conservative intellectual life among many liberal scholars. To them, this libertarian conservatism is simply a rigid and unreflective form of assumptions that liberals themselves share, not a fundamental or intellectually important challenge to the reigning political assumptions of American life.[25]

That much of this individualistic conservatism has had a strong regional base has only added to the tendency of historians to dismiss it. Historians of the South, to be sure, have long acknowledged conservatism as a central element of their region's history. Indeed, in no other field of American scholarship have conservative ideas received such intensive and sophisticated analysis. But relatively few other scholars have until recently shown much interest in, or even recognition of, regionalism as a force in modern American history. According to many influential conceptual models, regionalism is a declining force, overwhelmed by economic centralization and mass culture. The history of modern conservatism—and in particular its close ties to the American West—suggests otherwise.[26]

Conservatism has been an important presence in every area of the United States. But the dramatic rise of the right in the last half century may owe more to the West than to any other region. Of the most successful national conservative leaders of the postwar era—Barry Goldwater, George Wallace, Richard Nixon, and Ronald Reagan—all but Wallace were westerners. George Bush may or not have been a genuine conservative, but it seems clear that he acquired his right-wing credentials (frail as they may have been) from his experience in Texas politics.[27] The most secure voting bloc (and the best source of money) for conservative candidates and conservative causes has been the western states. Conservative intellectual life has found its most prominent homes at universities outside the East: the University of Chicago and, more recently, Stanford and other California universities.[28]

One reason for this is the continuing distinctiveness of the West's social and economic circumstances, and the particular appeal of conservatism's libertarian, antistatist ethos to people dealing with those circumstances. Resentment of presumed domination by the East is one of the oldest themes in western American history. It has helped produce the populist revolt of the late nineteenth century and periodic movements of social and economic protest since. In the past half century, moreover, many westerners have rechanneled the resentments that created populism away from the great private economic institutions that were traditional targets of western anger and toward the federal government, which many westerners believe has assumed the intrusive and oppressive role that banks and railroads once played as the great obstacle to western freedom. That should not perhaps be surprising. The federal government is the greatest landowner in the West. (It owns, for example, 44 percent of the state of Arizona, 90 percent of the state of Alaska). It controls an enormous proportion of the natural resources on which western economic growth largely depends. Many of its environmental regulations impinge on western lifestyles and western enterprises much more directly and severely than on their eastern counterparts. (The revolt against the 55-mile-per-hour speed limit in the 1980s was primarily a phenomenon of western libertarian conservatism, fueled by a sense of the disproportionate burdens the regulation inflicted upon the region.)[29]

The intrusive federal presence has been particularly difficult for many westerners to accept because it has coincided with, and (according to many conservatives) obstructed, the West's rise to economic eminence. In reality, the West's rise to eminence is itself in large part a product of government largesse. Without the great federally funded infrastructure projects of the twentieth century—without the highways, airports, dams, water and irrigation projects, and other facilities the government has provided—the economic development of the Southwest in particular would have been impossible.[30] But few western conservatives have shown much inclination to confront such contradictions. They have focused not on those state initiatives that have benefited them, but on those they believe have served the declining East by curbing westerners' freedom to develop their own region. Kevin Phillips, an energetic chronicler (and, often, defender) of the modern right, makes this point explicitly: that the West (or, to use the term he coined, the "Sun Belt") stands in dramatic contrast to the exhausted regions of the North and East, that it is the engine that can restore America's economic greatness. He wrote in 1982: "I believe that the Sun Belt . . . is the key to making America work again both as a polity and as an economy," that "the frontier Frederick Jackson Turner believed closed is economically and spiritually open once more," that westerners' "churches, their businesses and their patriotism demonstrate the ongoing vitality of old American credos and self-reliant ways of doing things."[31] The belief that unfettered economic freedom has been responsible for western economic growth—that, as Barry Goldwater has written, "individual initiative [has] made the desert bloom"[32]—may be a myth. But if so, it is a durable one, which fuels western conservatism and gives it a powerfully libertarian base.

Libertarian assumptions (reinforced at times by regionalism) have permeated modern American conservatism. But they have not, of course, constituted the whole of it. There are other powerful currents running through conservative thought—currents that have demonstrated growing power in the decades since World War II—that are not libertarian at all, but intensely normative. Relatively few conservatives have been content to base their claims on purely libertarian grounds; and some, at least, have seen in America's "cult of liberty" a dangerous threat to civic virtue and social stability.[33] The forms that these normative concerns have assumed, and the apparent contradiction between them and the libertarianism with which they coexist and in whose language they are often couched, have been especially difficult for historians to explain. This form of conservatism often seems intellectually inconsistent and hence resistant to analysis. Much more important, it has posed a direct challenge to some of modern liberalism's (and the modern left's) most basic assumptions about the nature of modern American society.

The normative assumptions that long informed much European conservatism—the belief that a good society must find its grounding not simply in liberty but in respect for moral traditions, universal values, and inherited social hierarchies—did not find much favor in American thought through most of the nineteenth century and much of the twentieth.[34] To be sure, there were notable exceptions. Such ideas have always had a diffuse appeal to some privileged elites.[35] And they have had a special appeal to elites (and others) in the American South, which has throughout its history bred a number of defenses of hierarchical, organic notions of society—not only as rationalizations for white supremacy and economic oligarchy but also (as the Agrarians made clear in 1930 when they published *I'll Take My Stand*) as expressions of intellectual unhappiness with the progressive norms of the industrial world.[36] Historians, however, have generally explained the South's commitment to organicism and hierarchy as evidence of the region's distinctiveness, not as a sign of broader challenges to America's liberal core.

Until World War II, there was perhaps some justification for such assumptions. In the 1950s, however, a number of conservative intellectuals (many of them neither members of traditional elites nor southerners) launched a strenuous assault on relativistic and libertarian visions of society and built a case for the importance of inherited values and traditional norms that was not rooted in regional concerns.[37] One of the most influential was Russell Kirk, who claimed at times to have been influenced by the Agrarians, and whose 1953 book, *The Conservative Mind*, ultimately became an important force in stimulating the growth of Burkean ideas on the American right (and in encouraging the right to appropriate Tocqueville as a source for its concerns). Kirk included among his six "canons of conservative thought" the "belief that a divine intent rules society as well as conscience" and that "political problems, at bottom, are religious and moral problems"; "affection for the proliferating variety and mystery of traditional life, as distinguished from the narrowing uniformity and equalitarianism and utilitarian aims of most radical systems"; the "conviction that civilized society requires orders and classes"; and the faith that "tradition and sound prejudice provide checks upon man's anarchic impulses." The "true conservative," he wrote,

> may be a resolute and strong-minded clergyman, endeavouring, in his parish, to redeem men and women from their bondage to modern appetites, contending against all the power of the cheap press and the dreary cinema and the blatant radio, reminding them that they are part of a great eternal order, in which it is their lot to serve the ends of love and justice, venerating the mysterious social union of the dead, the living, and those yet to be born.[38]

At about the same time, Leo Strauss and his disciples at the University of Chicago were offering a strenuous defense of Western and classical intellectual traditions as a source of eternal truths and timeless values. Modern social thought, Strauss argued, was not only incapable of improving on its classical forebears; it served actually to erode the moral and intellectual foundations of civilization. Liberal political theory, with its emphasis on individual liberty and subjective morality and its eager rejection of "natural right," leads, Strauss wrote, "to nihilism—nay it is identical with nihilism." For, he argued, "Once we realize that the principles of our actions have no other support than our blind choice, we really do not believe in them any more. We cannot wholeheartedly act upon them any more. We cannot live any more as responsible beings. . . . The more we cultivate reason, the more we cultivate nihilism."[39] The effort to root principles in particular historical circumstances, to deny the existence of "universal norms," to resist "efforts to transcend the actual"—an effort that formed the basis of the modernist project—had, Strauss claimed, produced a society in which no principle or value could withstand attack. The attempt by historicists "to make man absolutely at home in this world ended in man's becoming absolutely homeless."[40]

Neither Kirk nor Strauss enjoyed wide recognition or acclaim in the 1950s, when they were doing their most important work. Kirk remained for many years an isolated, largely unread cult figure (with a very small cult); and Strauss, in part because of his frequent obscurantism and his highly elitist views about the proper audience for philosophical ideas, developed no significant following beyond the fervent circle of admirers he collected (and retains) within academia.[41]

But other intellectual defenders of normative conservatism attracted considerable attention. Catholic conservative intellectuals (among whom William F. Buckley is perhaps the most prominent) have long attacked the relativism and excessive individualism of modern liberalism. At times they have renounced industrialism altogether and have turned instead to an image of a pre-industrial world in which the bonds of community were sustained by timeless values protected by the Church.[42] Some have drawn from the Church's invigorated twentieth-century interest in Thomas Aquinas and his ideas of an organic community, ideas the Catholic left has used at times as well.[43]

Major writers and artists of the first half of the twentieth century (among them T. S. Eliot and Willa Cather) rebelled against the relativism and the acquisitive, materialistic values of modern industrial society—a stance strenuously defended in the 1960s and beyond by, among others, Saul Bellow. "The tendency of unlimited industrialism," Eliot wrote in 1939, "is to create bodies of men and women—of all classes—detached from tradition, alienated from religion, and susceptible to mass suggestion. And a mob will be no less of a mob if it is well fed, well clothed, well housed, and well disciplined."[44] Some Jewish intellectuals have cited the religious and civic traditions of Judaism in an attack on what they consider the excessive emphasis on individual rights and liberties in modern American liberalism; a successful society, they believe, must rest on a set of moral standards shared, and if necessary enforced, by the community.[45]

In the 1970s and 1980s this normative intellectual tradition began to attract a particularly large political and even popular following. The Straussians, for example, were at the center of the intellectual and academic debates of the 1980s and (as the enormous success of Allan Bloom's *The Closing of the American Mind* demonstrated) won considerable sympathy for their argument that tradition can provide society with a much-needed moral and spiritual core.[46] The so-called neoconservatives, most of them former socialists, began in the 1960s to embrace and promote a form of normative conservatism in their effort to discredit the New Left. They did not, on the whole, embrace Strauss or Kirk. But their denunciations of the radicalism and relativism of the 1960s, their calls for a relegitimation of traditional centers of authority, and their cries for a refurbishment of American nationalism and a recognition of the moral claims of American democracy came increasingly to resemble the appeals of other, more longstanding conservatives.[47] (Their appeals have found an echo as well among a group of liberal intellectuals—sometimes described as "neo-liberals"—who on social and cultural issues at least have adopted normative stances in many ways similar to those of some self-proclaimed conservatives.)[48]

If the arguments of these conservative intellectuals were the whole, or even the most important, part of the normative conservatism of recent years, historians would probably have little difficulty explaining and categorizing their ideas. But there is another element of the contemporary right whose demands are considerably more radical, and whose critique of the contemporary world derives not from elitist notions of tradition and morality but from what, for lack of a better term, might be called a deep-seated cultural and religious fundamentalism.[49] This is, in the end, what has constituted the greatest "problem" of American conservatism (for historians and for liberal culture in general): the challenge of understanding and explaining a phenomenon so profoundly at odds with what many Americans have come to believe are the uncontested assumptions of modern Western society.

The dramatic resurgence of fundamentalism as a social and political force took almost all liberals (and almost all historians) by surprise when it became visible in the 1970s. The goal of the fundamentalist right was to challenge the secular, scientific values of modern culture, values most liberals have come to consider norms of modernity. Liberals were, therefore, surprised and even baffled by the suddenly powerful assaults on such symbols of "progress" as the secularization of popular culture, the teaching of evolution, even the principle of the separation of church and state.[50] Fundamentalists on occasion revived ancient quarrels over the banning of books and movies. Some used religious arguments to frame positions on seemingly nonreligious issues, claiming, for example, that the Bible mandated a massive expansion of the American defense budget (an argument that Ronald Reagan, on occasion, appeared to endorse). Others argued that biblical prophecies of the coming millennium should be a factor in the shaping of public policy (a view that James Watt, Secretary of the Interior during part of the Reagan administration, once cited in defense of his opposition to environmental regulations).[51] Many mixed their religious fervor with an essentially secular fundamentalism, which rested on a normative view of "traditional" middle-class constructions of family, community, and morality.

Indeed, the most powerful single strain within fundamentalist conservatism through much of the 1970s and 1980s may have been its assault on the efforts of modern feminists to redefine gender roles. Battles over abortion, birth control, the Equal Rights Amendment, and other gender-based issues (and, more recently, battles over homosexuality) have mobilized the fundamentalist right more successfully and energetically than any other issues.[52] Antifeminist women were especially active in the revival of the fundamentalist right. And they were instrumental in tying it to two important and related claims: that a family structure rooted in traditional notions of gender is the basis of a stable, moral society; and that a moral consensus in society is, in turn, essential to the stability of the family. "The family is the core institution that decisively determines the nature of society itself," one pro-family activist wrote in 1980. It is, she insisted, "the primary source of moral authority for the developing individual. The moral authority anchored in the family is by its very nature dependent on a consensus of core values within society." In that light, the social changes of the 1960s and 1970s appeared a menacing threat to what antifeminists believed were once universally accepted norms. Prior to the 1960s, one activist argued in 1982,

> America was accepted as being a Christian nation. . . . This country was then very much family-oriented. Though divorce, living together outside of marriage, abortion, homosexuality were not uncommon then, they were at least seldom defended in theory. There were moral absolutes that were recognized; and agencies of public expression, including the media and school system, honored those values. Then, unfortunately, over the last twenty years this Judeo-Christian moral consensus has been threatened, challenged, and often times shattered.[53]

This newly powerful challenge to secular culture has been all the more baffling to liberal and leftist scholars because its champions have often couched their essentially normative demands in libertarian language: denouncing a coercive state or an alien "cultural elite" for intruding into the lives of individuals and communities. But the liberal rhetoric should not obscure the larger agenda of many politically active fundamentalists (religious and secular alike), which is not just to protect their own allegiance to "traditional" moral standards, but to impose them on society as a whole.

By the early 1980s it was no longer possible to dismiss conservative fundamentalism in America as a declining rural peculiarity, consigned to oblivion a half-century ago by the Scopes trial and the inexorable forces of modernization. It was necessary to recognize it as a considerable and growing social and political force, which was finding expression at times at the heart of the American state. And while the highly publicized setbacks of some of the most prominent religious fundamentalists of the 1980s considerably weakened their political power, the fundamentalist right remains a potent political force in America (as the continued, indeed growing, strength of the Christian Coalition and other movements of the Christian right suggest), just as it is an important and rapidly growing force in many other areas of the world.[54]

In fact, as George Marsden and other historians of modern evangelicism have revealed, fundamentalism and pentecostalism—the two religious movements that have had the most impact on politics and culture in recent years—were never the dwindling rural phenomena that scholars had assumed they were in the 1950s and 1960s. The traumatic experience of the Scopes trial stilled the public voice of fundamentalism for a time; but throughout the 1930s, and even more aggressively in the 1940s and 1950s, fundamentalist and pentecostal denominations were gaining members faster than any other religious orders.[55] What happened in the 1970s was not so much a sudden explosion in the number of evangelicals in America (although that happened too), but a renewal of cultural and political activism within an already large and well-established religious community.

The resurgence of right-wing fundamentalism in the United States has unsettled many liberal and left-oriented scholars because it has seemed to contradict some of their most basic assumptions about modern society. A rational, economically developed society, progressive intellectuals have tended to believe, does not spurn modernity. It does not reject progress. Liberal scholars have tended, therefore, to explain the phenomenon by stressing economic backwardness and a kind of cultural irrationality, by emphasizing the oddities of the fundamentalist mind and the idiosyncrasies (or pathologies) of provincial cultures. Leftist scholars have stressed class oppression and economic deprivation but have reached essentially the same conclusion: that fundamentalism was a product of social or economic isolation and powerlessness. The fundamentalist right, scholars have been tempted to believe, is a group somehow left behind by the modern world—economically, culturally, psychologically—expressing frustration at their isolation and failure.[56]

And yet the reality of modern American fundamentalism—as recent scholarship has begun to demonstrate—is not always, or even usually, congruent with these assumptions. Who, in fact, are the men and women who have populated the fundamentalist and pentecostal churches; who have protested against "godlessness" and "immorality" in popular culture; who have adopted obscurantist positions on education and publishing; who have joined fundamentalist political crusades to make America a "Christian nation"? Many, perhaps most, of these people have not been poor, provincial folk or helpless victims of economic oppression. They have not been an isolated, rural fringe. They have not been rootless, anomic people searching for personal stability. To an increasing extent in the last fifty years, they have been people who have moved successfully into at least the lower ranks of the middle class, and sometimes much higher; people who have shared in the fruits of the consumer culture; people who have become part of the bureaucratized world of the organizational society. Many of them have been people with stable families and secure roots in their communities; people from urban areas, members of the new service economy; men and women whose new affluence has not weakened their fundamentalist beliefs. If anything, it may have strengthened them.[57]

Recent scholarship on the Ku Klux Klan of the 1920s and 1930s makes clear that much the same can be said about its membership, which consisted heavily of urban, middle-class men and women.[58] Scholarship on right-wing political dissenters in the 1930s suggests that even some of the most extreme and, on the surface, bizarre political leaders of the Depression years attracted supporters who were in all visible respects stable, rational, "normal" people whose deep resentments against the modern world were not rooted in social or economic marginality. That such men and women so often combined a defense of their own moral values with a populist resentment of distant centers of corporate or state power further reinforces this emerging picture of people whose political views are in many ways as fluid, adaptable, pragmatic, and internally inconsistent as any other group and refutes simplistic images of them as obsessive zealots.[59]

The nature of the modern fundamentalist right suggests, in short, that it is possible to be a stable, affluent, middle-class person; to have become part of the modern bureaucratic world and to have embraced the consumer culture; to have achieved and enjoyed worldly success; and to cling nevertheless to a set of cultural and religious beliefs that are at odds with some of the basic assumptions of modernism.[60] And that serves as a challenge to the assumptions of most historians that religious faith and fundamentalist morality should be understood as secondary or dependent characteristics, products of economic or social maladjustment, to be discarded as their adherents move into the modern, cosmopolitan world. The character of the modern fundamentalist right suggests that faith and normative morality may, instead, be primary characteristics, with autonomous power. That they survive and flourish in the midst of a culture many historians (and many others) have assumed is incompatible with them suggests that it is possible to live in the modern world and enjoy its largesse without fully absorbing modernist values. The integrated economy and powerful mass culture of modern America may not have the homogenizing power that many critics have assumed they must have.

Robert Wiebe, an important figure in the growth of the so-called "organizational synthesis," suggested in a small and largely unnoticed book published in 1975 that the nationalizing and consolidating forces he had described so effectively in *The Search for Order* may not be sufficient to explain the nature of modern society. The United States, he argued, is not in fact a truly consolidated nation. It is, in the phrase he uses as the title of his book, a "segmented society." The American people, Wiebe argued, live in a nation of almost unparalleled diversity and complexity. They cope with that diversity less by rallying behind common assumptions and universal values than by "segmenting" their world: creating discrete, isolated social spheres for their private lives separate from the bureaucratized economic system in which they work. America, he argues, is as much a cluster of distinct cultures with divergent worldviews as it is a centralized, consolidated nation. And to the degree that it has maintained stability in modern times, it has done so in large part because its various "segments" have managed to retain a certain autonomy within the larger national culture and have thus managed to avoid the difficult and disorienting task of adapting their lives and their values to the standards of people different from themselves. "What held Americans together," he wrote, "was their ability to live apart. Society depended upon segmentation."[61]

Wiebe's argument, less startling today, in the age of multiculturalism, than it was in the 1970s, suggests at least a partial explanation for America's recent cultural conflicts. For much of the history of the postwar United States has been the story of two intersecting developments. One is the survival of conservative and fundamentalist private values among people who have in other ways adapted themselves to the modern public world. The second is the unprecedentedly vigorous assault on those values by liberal, secular Americans.

To many liberal intellectuals in the 1950s and 1960s, nothing was so alluring as the ideal of what David Hollinger and others have called "cosmopolitanism," an outlook that stressed the virtues of tolerance, relativism, and rationalism and was generally accompanied by strong contempt for what liberals considered the backward "provincial" mind, with its presumed superstitions and prejudices. The cosmopolitan creed argued that "provincialism" (religious provincialism, ethnic provincialism, regional provincialism) accounted for the survival of racism and bigotry; provincialism stood in the way of progress and rationalism. A culturally segmented America was no longer acceptable; only by universalizing the values of cosmopolitanism, by launching an assault on the backwardness and intolerance and antirationalism of the "village mind" could the United States become a truly enlightened society worthy of serving as a model to the world.[62]

The politics of the 1980s and 1990s suggest that this effort—the effort to make the values and assumptions of liberal, secular Americans the values of all Americans—has failed. It has been responsible for some great accomplishments, to be sure: most notably in loosening the grip of racism and sexism on American life. But it has not eliminated, and has in many ways increased, the cultural chasms separating different groups of Americans from each other. Members of the secular center continue to define America as a society committed to modern rationalism, free inquiry, scientific discourse, and above all progress. But members of the fundamentalist right continue, despite (or perhaps because of) the assaults of recent years, to define America as a very different society: as a bastion of traditional (or "family") values and traditional faith in an increasingly godless age; as a citadel of righteousness in a corrupt world; as the earth's only truly Christian nation. It is unthinkable for secular Americans to contemplate any retreat from the rational, progressive course on which they have long assumed the nation is irrevocably embarked. But it is equally unthinkable for fundamentalists to consider abandoning in the name of progress the values and faiths that gives their lives meaning and their communities definition.[63]

It has not been easy or comforting for liberal, secular Americans to assume (as many have done) that the fundamentalist right is an irrational, rootless "lunatic fringe" plagued by cultural and psychological maladjustments. But it may be even more difficult and less comforting for secular intellectuals (and hence for most historians) to accept that fundamentalists can be rational, stable, intelligent people with a world view radically different from their own. For to accept that would be to concede that historians (and many others) may have been wrong in some of their most basic assumptions about America in our time. It is to recognize that the progressive modernism that most scholars have so complacently assumed has become firmly and unassailably established in America—the secularism, the relativism, the celebration of scientific progress—may not in fact be as firmly entrenched as they thought. It is to admit that modernism is not yet truly secure; that even in America, some of the most elementary values and institutions of modern society still have not established full legitimacy within a large—and at times politically powerful—segment of our population.

The "problem" of American conservatism as I have tried to describe it here is, in the end, a problem of the historical imagination. It resembles other problems historians have encountered as they have opened up the world of scholarship and retrieved previously unexamined communities and social experiences. But while historians have displayed impressive powers of imagination in creating empathetic accounts of many once obscure areas of the past, they have seldom done so in considering the character of conservative lives and ideas. That has no doubt been a result in part of a basic lack of sympathy for the right among many scholars. But it is a result, too, of the powerful, if not always fully recognized, progressive assumptions embedded in most of the leading paradigms with which historians approach their work.

Understanding America in the twentieth century requires, ultimately, more than an appreciation of the central role of liberalism (in all its various forms) in our modern history; and more, too, than an understanding of the important role of the left in challenging liberal claims. It requires, as well, a recognition of alternative political traditions on the right. That will not be an easy task. Conservative traditions in America are diverse and inconsistent: both libertarian and normative, both elite and popular, both morally compelling and morally repellent. They fit neatly into no patterns of explanation with which historians are comfortable. But scholars have redefined their categories and paradigms repeatedly in recent decades to help them understand areas of the past they had previously neglected. It may be time for us to do so again.

17

Historians and Their Publics

In the fall of 1994, the Air and Space Museum of the Smithsonian—the most popular single tourist attraction in Washington—installed in its main hall the fuselage of the *Enola Gay*, the airplane that in 1945 dropped on Hiroshima the first atomic bomb used in warfare. The original plans for an exhibit surrounding the installation, strongly influenced by academic historians, included discussions of the still controversial question of whether the United States was justified in using the bomb. The exhibit would have noted—along with the traditional justifications for the decision—the appalling human cost of the attack, the argument that the war against Japan could have been concluded reasonably quickly without it, and the moral qualms that many Americans—both at the time and since—have expressed about the decision. Critics of these plans—led by veterans' groups and joined by, among others, many members of Congress—mobilized rapidly and furiously against the proposed exhibit. They demanded that the Smithsonian express only the official (and, among veterans at least, popular) explanation of 1945: that the bomb saved perhaps a million American lives by removing the necessity of an invasion of the Japanese mainland. In the end, the exhibit presented no interpretation at all. The *Enola Gay* is now simply an object hanging in a large building. The Museum has chosen to provide no guidance at all as to how viewers should evaluate it.

Both the scholars and the veterans who engaged in this controversy believed that their versions of the story were "truer" than those of their adversaries, but the battle over the *Enola Gay* exhibit was not just a battle over historical truth. It was also a struggle for control over the way the past is used to serve present purposes. Such struggles are a constant, if often unnoticed, part of the way societies and individuals try to define themselves; and the *Enola Gay* controversy has been only one of many such arguments in recent years. The debates over the meaning of the Columbus quincentennial in 1992; the ferocious attacks on the National History Standards in 1995; the fight against a Disney historical theme park in Virginia; the continuing battles over Afrocentrism and multiculturalism; and many other controversies have made history a turbulent battleground in contemporary culture. They have revealed as well the ambiguous relationship between academic historians and the various publics they try at times to reach.

Much has been written in recent years about the idea of "memory"—an idea distinct in many ways from the idea of history. "Memory" describes the way individuals and groups choose to remember the past, their own and that of their nations. "History" describes the past as it actually was, and it describes as well the imperfect attempt by scholars to recreate it accurately and, as some historians claim, scientifically. "Memory" is a proper subject for historians of course; it has a "history" of its own. But "memory" is also history's rival, a powerful force that is capable of overwhelming the efforts of scholars to deal honestly and openly with the past. At the Smithsonian, as in many other settings, "memory" confounded the efforts of scholars to present any "history" at all.

In the spring of 1994—the spring of the fiftieth anniversary of the Normandy invasion, a moment when the retrospective image of World War II was much in the public mind—I visited two places in western Europe that made me especially aware of both the power of "memory" and its ability to overwhelm history.

One was the site of Adolf Hitler's home in the mountains near Berchtesgaden, in southern Germany. I had been attending a seminar in Salzburg, a few miles away. And I joined a group of historians (from Poland, Hungary, and the United States) who, out of some perverse curiosity, had arranged an excursion to see the place that, during the Third Reich, was one of the centers of German power. We knew that Hitler's home had been demolished by the new German government in the early 1950s to prevent it from becoming a shrine for unregenerate Nazis. But we were interested in seeing the site, and the ruins, nevertheless.

Finding the place turned out to be very difficult. The area above Berchtesgaden (including the tiny town of Obersalzberg, where Hitler lived) is, as it has always been, a vacation spot popular with skiers, hikers, and others. It is filled with resort hotels and souvenir stands, which service tour buses full of visitors. Nowhere did we see any reference to the Third Reich, to Hitler, or to the "Berghof" in which he had lived. When we asked guides and passersby for directions to Hitler's house, most responded with a baffled gaze or, at best, vague directions to the "Eagle's Nest," a mountaintop structure that Hitler disliked and never lived in but used occasionally for official events. It is now a restaurant. No one seemed to know (or more likely no one was willing to admit knowing) where the house was, or even that it had ever existed. But finally, following directions a colleague in Salzburg had given us, we found the muddy, inconspicuous path (marked with several bright yellow signs reading "Verboten") that led off a paved road into the woods where the house had once stood. As we walked, we passed several groups of German hikers who told us (in what seemed like almost conspiratorial whispers) where to find "das Haus."

All that remains, we discovered, is the brick foundation of the vanished building and the exterior walls of the network of concrete bunkers that ran beneath it. Everything is overgrown. Even the beautiful view that once enchanted Hitler—a view across the valley into his native Austria—is now almost invisible through the trees. The present character of the place—its desolation, its anonymity amidst a modern tourist complex, even the public denial of its existence—gave it an eerier, more haunting quality than the rather undistinguished house itself would have provided had it survived. I stood next to the ruins thinking of the Nazi propaganda pictures I had seen of Hitler incongruously playing with his dogs there or entertaining little children brought in to celebrate his birthday. Remembering the photographs, and thinking of the terrible things they had for a time helped disguise, gave the tranquil landscape a horrible power that the German officials who demolished the building surely did not anticipate.

Later we found an equally inconspicuous entrance to the bunkers themselves, some of which are still more or less intact. After paying a few marks to an impassive attendant, we were able to walk through a series of dank, dimly lit passages, the imagined sounds of jackboots ringing in our ears. Visitors to the complex tended to look away as they passed one another, as if they were doing something vaguely illicit and shameful.

A week later I was in Caen, Normandy, during the commemoration of the fiftieth anniversary of D-Day. Caen is a small commercial city a few miles from the Channel coast. It was once a favorite residence of William the Conqueror. In 1944, during the Allied invasion, it was almost completely (and, as it turned out, unnecessarily) destroyed by American bombers in an effort to drive out the German forces the Allied commanders mistakenly believed were entrenched there. Virtually nothing now remains of the beautiful medieval city that once stood on the site. William the Conqueror's castle, the university (founded in the fifteenth century), the town hall, almost the entire physical fabric that had linked the town to its past is gone. In its place is a pleasant, bustling, largely nondescript postwar city with new homes, new churches, new shops, and a new university campus of stunning banality.

One might expect the destruction of Caen (whose anniversary the West was inadvertently celebrating along with the anniversary of the Normandy invasion) to be remembered there as a kind of holocaust. But in public, at least, the citizens of Caen have chosen to remember it as a heroic moment in the city's history. In one of the few old churches still standing, signs were posted announcing a special mass to commemorate the "bombardment for the liberation of France and the reunification of the peoples of Europe." One of the city's museums had assembled a celebratory exhibit about the rebuilding of the city. It referred to the bombing itself only by way of praise for the courage, vision, and self-sacrifice of the survivors. As the town filled up that week with British and American veterans—some of them, no doubt, members of the bomber crews responsible for Caen's destruction—street lamps, shop windows, and even private homes were festooned with banners reading "Welcome to Our Liberators."

A few miles away are the immaculately manicured and emotionally powerful cemeteries where American, British, and German soldiers who died during the invasion lie buried. But to me, at least, the most memorable experience of the week was walking through the streets of Caen—streets in many ways indistinguishable from those of modern cities in most parts of the world—and seeing the ways in which the city had reconstructed not only itself, but also its memory, to conform to the postwar values its residents have embraced.

What is the actual "history" of these two places? Many of those living in Berchtesgaden in the 1930s and early 1940s, the era of the Third Reich, must have experienced it as a time of eminence, privilege, even glory; some, perhaps, experienced it as a time of horror. No one, certainly, was unaware of its political and military significance. The postwar residents now recognize those years as a time so shameful that they have tried to escape and even to erase them. For the residents of Caen in 1944, the Normandy invasion brought the greatest catastrophe in the city's long history. Today, its people interpret that moment as a source of pride and "liberation." In both cases the true history—to whatever degree there is one—is considerably more ambiguous than the residents of these communities wish to recognize. A carefully reconstructed memory, in service to the needs of the present, has all but replaced the actual history.

This gap between the popular "memory" of the past and the actual "history" of it creates a significant dilemma for scholars. On the one hand, as the *Enola Gay* controversy made clear, it is difficult, and at times impossible, for the academic world to impose its view of history on an unwilling public. The scholarly world does not own the past; societies and individuals are continually creating their own versions of history and using it to suit their personal or political needs. At times the creation of a "useful" history is relatively benign, as in the efforts of Berchtesgaden and Caen to ease the pain of their own pasts. At other times it can be pernicious and dangerous—as in the strenuous efforts of some self-proclaimed historians to deny the existence of the Holocaust or in the spurious efforts of others to describe the slave trade as a Jewish conspiracy. In either case, the process of shaping the past to meet present needs or reflect present prejudices is largely impervious to what historians say or do.

On the other hand, historians do have a distinctive role to play in helping societies understand the past. Although few historians any longer claim that it is possible to create a wholly objective picture of the past, and even fewer would argue that there is a single, settled, "true" answer to any but the most trivial historical questions, we do claim to bring to our examination of history a respect for evidence, an understanding of the contested and ambiguous character of interpretation, and a recognition that while there may be no settled "truth," there are distortions and falsehoods in the presentation of history. The past we create is often very different from the past our various publics want or from the histories governments or popular culture produce. One of the questions scholars need to ask themselves, therefore, is what the value of their work is within a larger world in which popular images of the past float between "history" and "memory."

Yet the historical profession today seems generally uninterested in answering that question. The scholarly world finds itself at odds with official and popular efforts at re-creation. But except when some particular controversy (such as the *Enola Gay* debate or the National History Standards imbroglio) draws public attention—and abuse—to the historical profession, academics are, for the most part, notably absent from the popular battles over the past. Most historians are content to do their work and see it published for an audience of their colleagues and reviewed in professional journals. They hope for little more than that it will become part of the scholarly conversations within their fields. Seldom do they make serious efforts to explain to a skeptical world that their scholarship may have something to contribute to a larger conversation. Within the profession there are new interpretations, new fields of study, and lively new debates. But in much of the broader world the work of academic scholars is barely visible. The great popular battles over the meaning of the past, which sometimes preoccupy public life, go on largely without us.

There are, of course, important exceptions. Scholars in relatively new fields such as women's history, African-American history, ethnic histories, gay and lesbian history, and others have helped many communities create new identities for themselves and pursue social and political efforts. Diplomatic historians have, from time to time, had a direct influence on the shaping of foreign policy. Academic historians of the Civil War, the American Revolution, the American West, and other popular fields have continued to attract wide readerships outside the universities. Scholars have played important roles in the making of documentary films, some of which have had very large audiences.

There is also a growing community of "public" historians, many with backgrounds in and continuing ties to academia. They have transformed the character of museums and historical societies and created vibrant, dynamic new settings in which thousands of people can gain a nontextual understanding of history. And yet, despite all the continuing points of connection between the history profession and the broader world, only a relatively few scholars in the end—and even fewer works of scholarship—manage to cross the boundary between the academy and the public. The disconnection between historians and the larger world is not universal, but it is widespread and, to some of those who experience it, troubling—all the more so because discussions of history are so much a part of contemporary popular (and political) discourse.

The most common explanation of this dilemma (both within the academy and outside it) emphasizes the structure and values of the profession itself. Academia, critics argue, offers few rewards for reaching beyond the scholarly world. Many academics are suspicious of or hostile to public (as opposed to scholarly) discourse, strongly averse to anything that might seem "popularized" or "middlebrow." History departments, scholarly organizations, academic journals, and other institutions that monitor professional activities assign a relatively low value to breadth and accessibility. Younger scholars hoping for tenure often see no reward (and even possible cost) in reaching for a broad audience. The profession as a whole tolerates (even if it does not actively encourage) a great deal of obscure and impenetrable prose. Historians, according to this argument, have abandoned a larger public because they have, in effect, chosen to abandon it.

There is some truth to all these claims. But the difficulties many academics have in reaching the public are at least as much a result of the transformation of historical scholarship over the last thirty years, including the rise of social history, growing attention to the experiences of previously unchronicled groups and individuals, the exploration of private (as opposed to public) worlds, and the rejection of many of the affirmative, nationalistic assumptions that once shaped historical writing. These have been welcome and necessary developments. But this overdue transformation of scholarship has nevertheless helped deepen the gulf between the academy and the public. That is partly because it has produced changes in the style and character of historical writing. The explosion of work in many new fields has fragmented the scholarly world and encouraged increasing specialization. It has also encouraged a growing use of difficult Marxist and post-Marxist, structuralist and post-structuralist, theories. Some academic history is now is so specialized and theoretical that it cannot realistically hope to attract an audience beyond other specialists, and some of it is almost impenetrable to people outside academia (and even to some within).

But the isolation of the academy from the public is not just a result of the often arcane quality of its products. It is also a result of the critical character of much of the new scholarship. No one, of course, should wish to return to a scholarly world in which the experiences of women, minorities, workers, radicals, and others were consistently marginalized and in which the darker and more controversial aspects of American history were only dimly perceived. But the increasingly skeptical stances of scholars—although they have helped attract some new audiences—have alienated other more traditional readers of history, who want the past to serve as a source of inspiration and entertainment. Historians should not seek to tell more affirmative and comforting stories just to satisfy conservative readers. Honest history must often be unsettling, even jarring. But neither can we deny that the academy pays a price for its increasingly intense awareness of the moral ambiguity of the past. Academic scholars once helped confirm many of the comfortable myths with which some (perhaps most) Americans viewed their history. Now that they more often challenge those myths, much of their erstwhile public has responded by turning to other, nonacademic writers whose work is less discomfiting to them.

How, then, do historians find the public ear without abandoning or compromising their convictions? How do academics make the work they consider important seem interesting and significant to others? For one thing, relatively simple changes in style and presentation would help. Better and more accessible writing, less intrusive presentations of theory and methodology, and other modest concessions to the nonacademic reading public would do much to make scholarly work less daunting to those outside the field. There are, certainly, many historians already who are gifted and accessible writers. There are, I suspect, many more who could make their work more appealing to the larger public if they were able to convince themselves that doing so was an important part of their task. And that suggests that one at least equally important task is for scholars to articulate, both to themselves and to others, their own convictions about why it is important to contribute to the public conversation; why there is value in helping others reach an honest understanding of the past—which is, surely, our own central professional goal.

The historical profession has never spent very much time justifying its work either to itself or to the world, possibly because many scholars feel that writing history needs no justification. It is, after all, one of the oldest and most basic of human activities. It expresses a natural, if often unarticulated, yearning for knowledge of the past. In one sense, writing history needs no more justification than does writing poetry or music. It is something human beings do because it brings them pleasure, even joy. But the aesthetic justification of history does little to help scholars when they try to defend the virtues of professional scholarship against the whims of popular memory. If history were important only because it pleased and amused us, why not produce the most pleasing and amusing history possible? Why bother with scholarly rigor and theoretical innovation? History needs another justification as well, one connected to the role it plays in the life of society and in the uses of power.

Such justifications are not easy to create. We cannot justify our work by claiming that we provide "answers" to public questions. Some scholars have tried—at times with impressive results—to make history into a useful tool of decisionmaking and policymaking. But there are severe limits to how far it is possible to move in that direction. History offers many cautions but few "lessons" in any conventional sense of that term. It does not tell us what we should do. It is not a road map for escaping the mistakes of the past.

And yet, whether we like it or not, history has enormous power, even if not the prescriptive power that some try to attribute to it. Supposed historical "lessons" are constant elements of the public conversation, and the more recent the history the more frequently it is used (and often distorted) to serve political ends. In the 1990s, for example, American political discourse is filled with vivid (and often conflicting) uses—by governments, politicians, and many others—of the supposed lessons of Vietnam, the Great Society, the history of social welfare, and the performance of government. Popular assumptions about the lessons of African-American history, labor history, ethnic history, women's history, and the history of sexuality battle one another in the shaping of public policy and public action. Many, if not most, of these "lessons" rest on selective or wholly erroneous pictures of the events from which they are drawn. Similarly glib and mechanical lessons shaped earlier moments in American history: the lessons of Munich, or World War I, or Reconstruction, or the American Revolution. And other nations, of course, have their own list of supposedly instructive moments in their pasts that become the basis of political debate and public policy.

Given how widely and continuously people use history to try to shape public life, it seems reasonable to assume that those who spend their careers trying to understand the past should play some role in that process. Historians have, if not an obligation, then at least an opportunity to help society use the past intelligently and responsibly, to make history a tool for creating reasoned discussions of the issues facing our time and not a vehicle for escaping or short-circuiting such discussions. It would be unrealistic to expect that scholarship will always, or even often, prevail against powerful currents of real or contrived "memory." But it is not unrealistic, I believe, for historians to hope to inject at least some balance into the public conversation, to help people gain a broader understanding of the past with which their culture bombards them so they can form their own judgments about it.

Historians are accustomed to looking beneath the immediate, "epiphenomenal" events of the past for deeper structures of meaning. They are used to dealing with ambiguity, complexity, and uncertainty. They are particularly well equipped to remind us of the chronic shortsightedness of human decisionmaking, the constraints on individual and institutional power, the value of humility in making choices that affect the lives of others. Reminding our personality-obsessed and result-oriented culture that there are forces shaping our world beyond the actions and characters of individuals—and that we will be more successful if we adjust our expectations and our goals to the reality of those forces, and to the difficulty of our fully understanding them—is one of the things we are best equipped to do. And reminding our publics of how often history has become a tool of power, used to advance the political aims of individuals and groups without regard to any standards of evidence or truth, is another role we can hope to play.

At the beginning of *The Book of Laughter and Forgetting*, the 1978 novel by the Czech writer Milan Kundera, there is an account of a famous event in modern Czechoslovakian history. In the winter of 1948, in the aftermath of the coup which brought the Communist party to power, there was a great public assembly in Prague. Hundreds of thousands of Czechs gathered in Wenceslaus Square—the same square where crowds gathered over forty years later to celebrate the collapse of the Communist regime—to salute their new leaders and to usher in the new era. Standing next to the head of the Communist party, Klement Gottwald, was another party leader, Vladimir Clementis. It was cold, some snow was falling, and Clementis solicitously took off his fur cap and put it on Gottwald's head. "The Party propaganda section," Kundera writes, "put out hundreds of thousands of copies of a photograph of that balcony with Gottwald, a fur cap on his head and comrades at his side, speaking to the nation. On that balcony the history of Communist Czechoslovakia was born. Every child knew the photograph from posters, schoolbooks, and museums." In 1952 Clementis was executed for treason. "The propaganda section," Kundera continues, "immediately airbrushed him out of history and, obviously, out of all the photographs as well. Ever since, Gottwald has stood on that balcony alone. Where Clementis one stood, there is only bare palace wall. All that remains of Clementis is the cap on Gottwald's head."

Americans do not live under a regime that controls and alters history in so brutal and heavyhanded a fashion; and now, happily, neither do the people of the Czech Republic and Slovakia. But in every society there are constant efforts—official and unofficial, honest and dishonest—to make use of the past, to control the past, even to erase the past, in the service of present concerns. Much of what is best about the scholarship of the last thirty years has been its effort to retrieve the experiences of the Clementises of history—to reintroduce us to parts of the past that have been figuratively (and at times literally) airbrushed from our consciousness.

The attempt to understand the past, therefore, is not an arcane academic activity. It is part of a society's struggles over policy and belief and present action. It is part of the effort to enable individuals to resist power, to make independent judgments, to evaluate for themselves the claims and counterclaims about the past that form the core of much public discourse. Remembering that, it seems to me, is reason enough for professional scholars to try to restore their much-eroded links to the many publics outside the academy—to insist that popular "memory" be balanced, and at times challenged by, analytical "history."

Battles over the past are never really settled. But neither are they unimportant. If they were, societies would not spend so much time and energy fighting them. Those who have succeeded in presenting the *Enola Gay* as a symbol of American righteousness, or Berchtesgaden as simply a pleasant mountaintop resort, or Caen as a testament to victory and liberation have, for better or worse, exercised power over the way many people relate to both the past and the present. But those who have formed the ability to question these, and other, presentations of the past have themselves acquired a form of power—the capacity to make independent judgments, and to look critically at, even to challenge, the way others attempt to use history. For those without that capacity, the past becomes, at best, a meaningless curiosity and, at worst, a weapon against which they have no defense.

"The struggle of man against power," Milan Kundera writes, "is the struggle of memory against forgetting." If historians choose not to play a role in that struggle, we can be sure that others, not of our choosing, will take our place.

Notes

1. *The Rise of Franklin Roosevelt*

1. The best account of Roosevelt's pre-presidential life is Geoffrey C. Ward, *Before the Trumpet: Young Franklin Roosevelt* (New York: Harper & Row, 1985); and *A First-Class Temperament: The Emergence of Franklin Roosevelt* (New York: Harper & Row, 1989). Ward builds upon the groundbreaking work of Frank Freidel, whose unfinished multivolume biography, *Franklin D. Roosevelt*, 4 vols. (Boston: Little, Brown, 1952–1973), contains three volumes on the years before 1932: *The Apprenticeship*, *The Ordeal*, *The Triumph;* and on Kenneth S. Davis, *FDR: The Beckoning of Destiny, 1882–1928* (New York: G. P. Putnam's Sons, 1972) and *FDR: The New York Years, 1928–1933* (New York: Random House, 1985), the first two volumes of an extended biography of Roosevelt. Nathan Miller, *The Roosevelt Chronicles: The Story of a Great American Family* (Garden City, N.Y.: Doubleday, 1979) is a sketchy account of the long history of the Roosevelt family (both its Hyde Park and Oyster Bay branches) in America. Joseph P. Lash, *Eleanor and Franklin* (New York: W. W. Norton, 1971), and Blanche Wiesen Cook, *Eleanor Roosevelt*, vol 1: *1884–1933* (New York: Viking Press, 1992) are the fullest studies of Eleanor Roosevelt's life and of her relationship with her husband. Hugh Gregory Gallagher, *FDR's Splendid Deception* (New York: Dodd, Mead, 1985), and Richard T. Goldberg, *The Making of Franklin D. Roosevelt: Triumph Over Disability* (Cambridge: Abt Books, 1981) are important, if contrasting, accounts of the impact of polio on Roosevelt; Tony Gould, *A Summer Plague: Polio and Its Survivors* (New Haven: Yale University Press, 1995), is an important social history of the disease with considerable attention to Franklin Roosevelt's significance in the battle against it. David Burner, *The Politics of Provincialism: The Democratic Party in Transition, 1918–1932* (New York: Alfred A. Knopf, 1967), and Allan J. Lichtman, *Prejudice and the Old Politics: The Presidential Election of 1928* (Chapel Hill: University of North Carolina Press, 1979), are valuable studies of the Democratic party in the 1920s. Frank Freidel, *Franklin D. Roosevelt: Launching the New Deal* (Boston: Little, Brown, 1973), and Jordan A. Schwarz, *The Interregnum of Despair: Hoover, the Congress, and the Depression* (Urbana: University of Illinois Press, 1970), are important studies of the transition from Hoover to Roosevelt.

2. *The New Deal Experiments*

1. Richard Hofstadter, *The American Political Tradition and the Men Who Made It* (New York: Alfred A. Knopf, 1948), p. 316; James MacGregor Burns, *Roosevelt: The Lion and the Fox* (New York: Harcourt Brace Jovanovich, 1956), pp. 287–288; Alan Brinkley, *Voices of Protest: Huey Long, Father Coughlin, and the Great Depression* (New York: Alfred A. Knopf, 1982), p. 58.

2. Hofstadter, *The Age of Reform: From Bryan to F.D.R.* (New York: Alfred A. Knopf, 1955), p. 307; Raymond Moley, *After Seven Years: A Political Analysis of the New Deal* (New York: Harper & Row, 1939), pp. 369–370.

3. See Alan Brinkley, *The End of Reform: New Deal Liberalism in Recession and War* (New York: Alfred A. Knopf, 1995), chapters 4–5.

4. Frank Freidel, *Franklin D. Roosevelt: The Triumph* (Boston: Little, Brown, 1956), p. 216.

5. Arthur M. Schlesinger, Jr., *The Coming of the New Deal* (Boston: Houghton Mifflin, 1959), p. 267; Samuel I. Rosenman, ed., *Public Papers and Address of Franklin D. Roosevelt*, 13 vols. (New York: Random House, 1938), III, 420.

6. Anthony J. Badger, *The New Deal: The Depression Years, 1933–1940* (New York: Hill & Wang, 1989), pp. 200–201.

7. Theda Skocpol, *Protecting Soldiers and Mothers: The Political Origins of Social Policy in the United States* (Cambridge, Mass.: Harvard University Press, 1992), and Linda Gordon, *Pitied But Not Entitled: Single Mothers and the History of Welfare* (New York: The Free Press, 1994), are the two most important studies of the gendered quality of the early welfare state. Skocpol's study ends before the New Deal but describes the pre-1930s history of gendered social provision. Gordon's study includes the creation of the Social Security Act itself.

8. Alan Brinkley, "The New Deal: Prelude," *Wilson Quarterly* 6 (1982): 50–61.

9. Jordan Schwarz, *The New Dealers: Power Politics in the Age of FDR* (New York: Alfred A. Knopf, 1993).

10. William E. Leuchtenburg, "The New Deal and the Analogue of War" originally appeared in 1964 and has been republished in Leuchtenburg, *The FDR Years: On Roosevelt and His Legacy* (New York: Columbia University Press, 1995), pp. 35–75.

11. See Robert D. Cuff, *The War Industries Board: Business-Government Relations during World War I* (Baltimore: Johns Hopkins University Press, 1973), and David M. Kennedy, *Over Here: The First World War and American Society* (New York: Oxford University Press, 1980), pp. 126–143, for descriptions of the War Industries Board and its legacy.

12. The best account of the origins, structure, and operations of the NRA is Ellis Hawley, *The New Deal and the Problem of Monopoly: A Study in Economic*

Ambivalence (Princeton: Princeton University Press, 1967), especially pp. 19–146.

13. Rosenman, ed., *Public Papers and Addresses*, II, 252.

14. Kenneth Finegold and Theda Skocpol, "State Capacity and Economic Intervention in the Early New Deal," *Political Science Quarterly* 97 (1982): 255–278; Kenneth Finegold and Theda Skocpol, *State and Party in America's New Deal* (Madison: University of Wisconsin Press, 1995).

15. Rosenman, ed., *Public Papers and Addresses*, V, 568–569.

3. *The Late New Deal and the Idea of the State*

1. Hansen, "Toward Full Employment," speech at the University of Cincinnati, March 15, 1940, Alvin Hansen Papers, 3.10, Harvard University Archives, Cambridge, Mass.

2. See, for example, Morton Keller, *Affairs of State: Public Life in Late Nineteenth-Century America* (Cambridge, Mass.: Harvard University Press, 1977); Stephen Skowronek, *Building an American State: The Expansion of National Administrative Capacities, 1877–1920* (Cambridge: Cambridge University Press, 1982).

3. Richard Hofstadter, *The Age of Reform* (New York: Alfred A. Knopf, 1955), p. 307. William Leuchtenburg challenges the idea of the New Deal's "ideological innocence" in *Franklin D. Roosevelt and the New Deal* (New York: Harper & Row, 1963), p. 34.

4. The best account of the origins of the NRA and its performance is Ellis Hawley, *The New Deal and the Problem of Monopoly* (Princeton: Princeton University Press, 1966), pp. 19–146.

5. Donald Richberg to Marvin McIntyre, March 10, 1938, and FDR to Richberg, January 15, 1941, both in Richberg MSS 2, Manuscripts Division, Library of Congress (hereafter "LC"); James Farley speech in Winston Salem, N.C., February 6, 1940, Joseph Tumulty MSS 60, LC; "What Do They Mean: Monopoly?" *Fortune*, April 1938, p. 126; Robert Jackson, draft of unpublished autobiography, 1944, p. 135, Jackson MSS 188, LC. William Leuchtenburg contends that "the President believed deeply in the NRA approach and never gave up trying to restore it" (*Franklin D. Roosevelt and the New Deal*, p. 146).

6. George Soule, "Toward a Planned Society," *New Republic*, November 8, 1939, p. 31; "A New NRA," *Nation*, March 25, 1939, p. 337; Thurman Arnold, *The Folklore of Capitalism* (New Haven: Yale University Press, 1937), pp. 221, 268; Arnold, "Feathers and Prices," *Common Sense*, July 1939, p. 6; David Cushman Coyle, "The Twilight of National Planning," *Harper's*, October 1935, pp. 557–559. See also Hawley, *The New Deal and the Problem of Monopoly*, pp. 143–146.

7. The existence of an informal network of liberals in the late 1930s was

the subject of frequent comment in the popular press. See, for example, Joseph Alsop and Robert Kintner, "We Shall Make America Over: The New Dealers Move In," *Saturday Evening Post*, November 12, 1938, pp. 8–9; Beverly Smith, "Corcoran and Cohen, *American Magazine*, August 1937, p. 22; Alva Johnston, "White House Tommy," *Saturday Evening Post*, July 31, 1937, pp. 5–7; "A New NRA," p. 337. Surviving correspondence among members of the group helps confirm such reports. See, for example, Archibald MacLeish to Thomas Corcoran, May 2, 1942, MacLeish MSS 5, LC; MacLeish to Felix Frankfurter, January 26, 1940, MacLeish MSS 8, LC; William Douglas to Thurman Arnold, February 8, 1938, and Arnold to Douglas, February 11, 1938, both in Douglas MSS 14, LC; Hugo Black to Harold Ickes, August 15, 1935, Black MSS 34, LC; Benjamin Cohen to Hugo Black, February 2, 1938, Black MSS 23, LC.

8. The idea of a "capital strike" was most prominently associated at the time with Assistant Attorney General Robert Jackson, known in 1937 as a favorite of the president. Jackson used the phrase and explained the concept in a controversial speech before the American Political Science Association on December 29, 1937 (Jackson MSS 30, LC). So eager was the administration to believe this explanation that late in 1937 the president ordered the FBI to launch an investigation into the possibility of a criminal conspiracy. His evidence for the charge was extraordinarily frail: an unsubstantiated letter from a hotel waiter in Chicago who reported overhearing a conversation among railroad executives. They were, the waiter reported, conspiring to lay off workers as part of an "unemployment boycott" that would force Roosevelt "and his gang" to "come to terms." The FBI found no evidence to support the charge. (Vasilia N. Getz to Roosevelt, November 19, 1937, Roosevelt to Homer Cummings, November 26, 1937, and J. Edgar Hoover to Roosevelt, December 11, 1937, all in Corcoran MSS 203, LC.) See also "The Administration Strikes Back," *New Republic*, January 5, 1938, p. 240; Arthur D. Gayer, "What Is Ahead?" *New Republic*, February 2, 1938, p. 391; George Soule, "What Has Happened—And Whose Fault Is It?" *New Republic*, February 2, 1938, p. 381; Irving Brant to Thomas Corcoran, January 5, 1938, Brant MSS 5, LC.

9. FDR to Robert Jackson, August 19, 1937, and Isador Lubin to Marvin McIntyre, August 25, 1937, both in President's Secretary's File (hereafter, "PSF") 77, Franklin D. Roosevelt Library, Hyde Park, New York (hereafter, "FDRL"). Wayne C. Taylor to FDR, March 26, 1938; draft of "Monopoly Message," n.d., 1938; Huston Thompson to McIntyre, April 25, 1938: all in Official File (hereafter, "OF") 277, FDRL. Samuel Rosenman, ed., *The Public Papers and Addresses of Franklin D. Roosevelt*, 13 vols. (New York: Random House, 1938–1950), VIII, 305–320; Alsop and Kintner, "We Shall Make America Over," p. 86; Public Resolution No. 113, 75th Congress, "To create a temporary national economic committee," OF 3322, FDRL; "Trustbuster's Goal," *Business Week*, February 22, 1941, p. 35; Homer Cummings to FDR, April 21,

1938 (and accompanying memorandum from Arnold), OF 277, FDRL; Gene M. Gressley, "Thurman Arnold, Antitrust, and the New Deal," *Business History Review* 38 (1964): 217; Walter Millis, "Cross Purposes in the New Deal," *Virginia Quarterly Review* 14 (1938): 359–361.

10. "Trust Buster Benched," *Time*, February 22, 1943, pp. 32–34; Corwin Edwards, "Thurman Arnold and the Antitrust Laws," *Political Science Quarterly* 58 (1943): 353–355; J. David Stern to Robert S. Allen, December 9, 1939, Thurman Arnold MSS, University of Wyoming; Leuchtenburg, *Franklin D. Roosevelt and the New Deal*, pp. 259–260.

11. "Do Monopolies Retard or Advance Business Recovery?" *Town Meeting*, January 30, 1939, 11–12, 16; "How Far Should Government Control Business?" *Consensus* 23 (March 1939): 17; Arnold R. Sweezy, "Mr. Arnold and the Trusts," *New Republic* June 8, 1942, pp. 803–804.

12. Arnold, *The Folklore of Capitalism*, p. 211.

13. Arnold, "Feathers and Prices," pp. 5–6; Arnold, "Confidence Must Replace Fear," *Vital Speeches*, July 1, 1942, p. 561. See also Arnold, *The Bottlenecks of Business* (New York: Harcourt Brace Jovanovich, 1940), p. 124; Arnold, "The Abuse of Patents," *Atlantic Monthly*, July 1942, p. 16.

14. Even Brandeis, the patron saint of antimonopoly, viewed the antitrust laws more as regulatory mechanisms than as vehicles for overt "trust-busting." But Brandeis and his allies always believed that regulation could itself prevent economic concentration; that restriction of unfair trade practices would forestall the creation of large combinations. He wrote in 1933: "I am so firmly convinced that the large unit is not as efficient—I mean the very large unit—as the smaller unit, that I believe that if it were possible today to make the corporations act in accordance with what doubtless all of us would agree should be the rules of trade no huge corporation would be created, or if created, would be successful." Arnold embraced no such assumptions. For an important discussion of Brandeis's regulatory philosophy, see Thomas K. McCraw, *Prophets of Regulation* (Cambridge, Mass.: Harvard University Press, 1984), pp. 94–109, 135–142; and McCraw, "Rethinking the Trust Question," in McCraw, ed., *Regulation in Perspective: Historical Essays* (Boston: Harvard Business School, 1981), pp. 1–55.

15. Hearings before a subcommittee of the Committee on the Judiciary, United States Senate, 75th Cong., 3d sess., March 11, 1938, in Wendell Berge MSS 15, LC; Henry Hyde to William Borah, July 6, 1938, Walter Williams to Borah, February 23, 1939, both in Borah MSS 772, LC. Borah's hostility toward Arnold was undoubtedly in part a result of the condescending description of Borah's own career in *The Folklore of Capitalism:* "Men like Senator Borah founded political careers on the continuance of such [antitrust] crusades, which were entirely futile but enormously picturesque, and which paid big dividends in terms of personal prestige" (p. 217).

16. Max Lerner to Thurman Arnold, December 4, 1938, Arnold MSS. See, especially, Adolf A. Berle, Jr., "Memorandum of Suggestions," July 12, 1938, and Berle to Steve Early, July 15, 1938, both in OF 3322, FDRL. Berle's lengthy memorandum, written at the request of Jerome Frank and Thurman Arnold, was intended to provide a "foundation for one branch of the investigation," and its suggestions were apparently of significant influence. Much of the report focused on what Berle called "unwarranted assumptions" the TNEC should avoid—most notably the assumption that there was any inherent connection between the size of an enterprise and its efficiency, competitiveness, or humaneness.

17. "Final Statement of Senator Joseph C. O'Mahoney, Chairman of the TNEC, at the Closing Public Session," March 11, 1941, reprint in Raymond Clapper MSS 182, LC; O'Mahoney to FDR, April 2, 1941, OF 3322, FDRL; Raymond Moley, "Monopoly Mystery," *Saturday Evening Post*, March 30, 1940, pp. 9–11, and "Business in the Woodshed," ibid., May 6, 1940, pp. 62, 68; Emmet F. Connely, "Let Business Roll Its Own: The TNEC, Stuart Chase, and the New Financing," *Harper's*, May 1940, pp. 644–651; Lawrence Dennis, "The Essential Factual Details about the TNEC," privately circulated business newsletter, October 17, 1938, OF 3322, FDRL; "Twilight of TNEC," *Time*, April 14, 1941, pp. 86–87; "TNEC: Magnificent Failure," *Business Week*, March 22, 1941, pp. 22–27; Robert Brady, "Reports and Conclusions of the TNEC," *Economic Journal* 53 (1943): 415; Richard N. Chapman, "Contours of Public Policy, 1939–1945," (Ph.D. diss., Yale University, 1976), pp. 152–153.

18. William Douglas to Karl Llewelyn, December 20, 1938, Douglas MSS 18, LC; Arnold, *The Folklore of Capitalism*, p. 389.

19. James M. Landis, *The Administrative Process* (New Haven: Yale University Press, 1938), pp. 24–25. McCraw, *Prophets of Regulation*, pp. 212–216, analyzes Landis's argument.

20. Arnold, *Bottlenecks of Business*, pp. 122–126.

21. Herbert Stein, *The Fiscal Revolution in America* (Chicago: University of Chicago Press, 1969), pp. 114–118; Dean L. May, *From New Deal to New Economics: The American Liberal Response to the Recession of 1937* (New York: Garland Books, 1981), p. 95.

22. Stein, *Fiscal Revolution*, pp. 91–100; May, *From New Deal to New Economics*, pp. 17–37.

23. Stein, *Fiscal Revolution*, p. 93. The quoted phrases are from Morgenthau's description of Eccles's advice to the president.

24. May, *From New Deal to New Economics*, p. 89.

25. Bruce Bliven, "Confidential: To the President," *New Republic*, April 20, 1938, p. 328.

26. May, *From New Deal to New Economics*, pp. 123–125, 132–133.

27. Stein, *Fiscal Revolution*, pp. 109–115.

28. Theda Skocpol and Margaret Weir, "State Structures and the Possibilities for Keynesian Responses to the Great Depression in Sweden, Britain, and the United States," in Peter B. Evans, Dietrich Rueschemeyer, and Skocpol, eds., *Bringing the State Back In* (New York: Cambridge University Press, 1985), pp. 132–136.

29. Franklin D. Roosevelt, *The Public Papers and Addresses of Franklin D. Roosevelt* (New York: Macmillan, 1941), 7 (1938 volume): 240–241, 243.

30. Hansen, "Toward Full Employment," March 15, 1940, Hansen MSS, 3.10. "Perhaps I am getting too Keynesian," Hansen joked to Sir Dennis H. Robertson. Hansen to Robertson, September 29, 1939, ibid. See also Hansen, "Economic Progress and Declining Population Growth," *American Economic Review* 29 (1939): 1–15, a published version of Hansen's presidential address of the previous year before the American Economic Association.

31. Leon Henderson, for example, served simultaneously as one of the leading advocates of increased spending and one of the architects of such regulatory efforts as the TNEC. When Roosevelt traveled back to Washington after the meeting in Warm Springs at which he agreed to increase his budget requests, Robert Jackson and Benjamin Cohen joined him on the train. In the course of the trip, they persuaded him to launch a vigorous antitrust campaign as a natural complement to the spending efforts. (See Robert H. Jackson, draft of unpublished autobiography, 1944, p. 131, Jackson MSS 188, LC).

32. For a thoughtful analysis of the "mature economy" idea, see Theodore Rosenof, *Patterns of Political Economy in America: The Failure to Develop a Democratic Left Synthesis, 1933–1950* (New York: Garland Publishing, 1983), pp. 39–46.

33. Schwellenbach speech in Seattle, July 15, 1938, Schwellenbach MSS 3, LC.

34. The prediction came from a 1938 report—*The Problems of a Changing Population*—published by the National Resources Committee (which later became the National Resource Planning Board). In fact, the population exceeded 175 million before the 1960 census (Philip W. Warken, *A History of the National Resource Planning Board, 1933–1943* [New York: Garland Books, 1979], pp. 85–86).

35. Stuart Chase, "Freedom from Want," *Harper's*, October 1942, p. 468.

36. The best description of the World War I economic mobilization and of the gap between the reality of its performance and its later image is Robert D. Cuff's *The War Industries Board: Business-Government Relations during World War I* (Baltimore: Johns Hopkins University Press), pp. 7, 147–155, 220, 268–269, and passim. See also Robert D. Cuff, "American Mobilization for War 1917–1945: Political Culture vs. Bureaucratic Administration," in N.F. Dreisziger, ed., *Mobilization for Total War: The Canadian, American, and British Experience, 1914–1918, 1937–1945* (Waterloo, Ont.: Wilfred Laurier University

Press, 1981), p. 80; David M. Kennedy, *Over Here: The First World War and American Society* (New York: Oxford University Press, 1980), pp. 113–43. William E. Leuchtenburg, "The New Deal and the Analogue of War," in John Braeman et al., eds., *Change and Continuity in Twentieth-Century America* (Columbus: Ohio State University Press, 1964), pp. 81–143, suggests the degree to which the legacy of World War I served as an inspiration to New Deal efforts.

37. On public attitudes toward big business in the 1930s, see Louis Galambos, *The Public Image of Big Business in America, 1880–1940* (Baltimore: Johns Hopkins University Press, 1975), pp. 222–252. "In the Great Depression," Galambos argues, "middle-class Americans mounted only a brief and rather feeble attack on big business. . . . [N]ew bureaucratic norms muffled hostility toward corporate enterprise, and on the eve of the Second World War they helped to ease Americans into an acceptance of big business" (pp. 246–247).

38. See Nelson Lichtenstein, *Labor's War at Home: The CIO in World War II* (New York: Cambridge University Press, 1982), pp. 9–25; Bruce Catton, *The War Lords of Washington* (New York: Harcourt, Brace, 1948), pp. 92–96; Mike Davis, "The Barren Marriage of American Labor and the Democratic Party," *New Left Review* 124 (1980): 43–50.

39. Barry D. Karl, *The Uneasy State: The United States from 1915 to 1945* (Chicago: University of Chicago Press, 1983), makes a case for the central importance of anti-statism in twentieth century America; see esp. pp. 1–7, 155–181, 205–239. See also Theodore Rosenof, "Freedom, Planning, and Totalitarianism: The Reception of F.A. Hayek's *Road to Serfdom*," *Canadian Review of American Studies* 5 (Fall 1974): 149–165, which assesses the impact of von Hayek's antistatist tract of 1940 on American liberal thought; and Robert D. Cuff, "Commentary," in James Titus, ed., *The Home Front and War in the Twentieth Century* (United States Air Force Academy, 1984), pp. 114–116.

40. Ibid., pp. 310–11; John Morton Blum, *V Was for Victory: Politics and American Culture During World War II* (New York: Harcourt Brace Jovanovich, 1976), pp. 124–131; Nelson, *Arsenal of Democracy*, pp. 269–289; Jim F. Heath, "American War Mobilization and the Use of Small Manufacturers, 1939–1943," *Business History Review* 46 (1972): 317–319. Roosevelt wrote James F. Byrnes late in 1942: "This Small Business problem has baffled me, as you know, for nearly two years. We have not met it—and I am not sure that it can be met." He raised the "wild idea" of appointing Joseph Kennedy to head the Smaller War Plants Corporation, an agency he had created within the WPB to protect the interests of small business. Kennedy refused the offer, explaining (according to Byrnes) that he doubted "that anyone could accomplish anything of value to small business," and that certainly no accomplishments were possible given the limited authority of the SWPC (FDR to Byrnes, December 18, 1942, and Byrnes to FDR, January 14, 1943, OF 4735-F, FDRL).

41. Arnold to White, September 9, 1943, White MSS C413, LC.

42. Between 1939 and 1944, the American GNP (measured in constant dollars) grew by more than 50 percent. Although the bulk of the growth was a result of military production, the consumer economy expanded by 12 percent during the same years. Unemployment, the most persistent and troubling economic problem of the 1930s, all but vanished (Alan S. Milward, *War, Economy and Society: 1939–1945* [Berkeley: University of California Press, 1977], pp. 63–65; Blum, *V Was for Victory*, pp. 90–93).

43. Alvin Hansen, "Planning Full Employment," *Nation*, October 21, 1941, p. 492.

44. "Is There a New Frontier?" *New Republic*, November 27, 1944, pp. 708–710; "A New Bill of Rights," *Nation*, March 20, 1943, p. 402; Stein, *The Fiscal Revolution in America*, pp. 175–177.

45. National Resources Planning Board (hereafter, "NRPB"), "National Resources Development Report for 1943," p. 4, PSF 185, FDRL; Milward, *War, Economy, and Society*, p. 330. Wartime public opinion polls suggested that the majority of the public was coming to believe that postwar economic growth offered the best route to meeting the nation's social needs and that interest in government job programs was waning (see Office of Public Opinion Research, "Presenting Post-War Planning to the Public," OF 4351, FDRL; Harlow S. Person to Morris L. Cooke, October 3, 1944, President's Personal File, 940, FDRL).

46. Chapman, "Contours of Public Policy," pp. 30–31, 342–345, 358; Office of Facts and Figures, "War Aims and Postwar Policies," March 17, 1942, MacLeish MSS 5, LC; Milward, *War, Economy, and Society*, p. 330.

47. Philip J. Funigiello, *The Challenge to Urban Liberalism: Federal-City Relations during World War II* (Knoxville: University of Tennessee Press, 1978), pp. 11, 180–185, 197; Graham, *Toward a Planned Society*, pp. 52–58; Chapman, "Contours of Public Policy," pp. 342–343.

48. Frederic Delano et al. to FDR, August 24, 1943, OF 1092, FDRL; NRPB, "Post-War Plan and Program," February 1943, Senatorial File 43, HSTL.

49. NRPB, *Security, Work, and Relief Policies* (Washington, D.C.: Government Printing Office, 1942). Beveridge claimed that full employment was a "basic assumption" of his own plan, and it is clear that he believed his social welfare and insurance proposals—proposals considerably more extensive than those of the NRPB—would contribute to that end. But the Beveridge Report contained no direct mechanisms for ensuring full employment, and indeed Beveridge himself warned against the accumulation of public debt in pursuit of social goals. The NRPB proposed, in addition to aggressive use of federal spending, making the government the employer of last resort; and its members had few inhibitions about deficit spending as a means to that end (see, e.g., Eveline M. Burns, "Comparison of the NRPB Report with the Beveridge Re-

port," December 26, 1942, PIN.8, 167, Public Records Office [hereafter, "PRO"], London). T. J. Woofter, Jr., to Roger Evans, April 20, 1943, and Alvin Hansen to Beveridge, July 3, 1943, both in William Beveridge MSS, XI-31, British Library of Political and Economic Science, London School of Economics.

50. NRPB, "National Resources Development Report"; NRPB, "The NRPB in Wartime," *Frontiers of Democracy* 8 (February 1942): 143. See also memorandum to Stephen Early (telephone summaries), February 4, 1943, OF 1092 (5), FDRL; L.B. Parker to Rep. Harry Sheppard, March 11, 1943, OF 4351 (2), FDRL; Bruce Bliven, Max Lerner, and George Soule, "Charter for America," *New Republic*, April 19, 1943, p. 528; J. Raymond Walsh, "Action for Postwar Planning," *Antioch Review* 3 (1943): 153–161.

51. I. F. Stone, "Planning and Politics," *Nation*, March 20, 1943, p. 405. See also "Postwar Portent," *Newsweek*, March 22, 1943, pp. 31–34, and L. G. Rockwell, "The National Resource Planning Board in the United States," *Public Affairs* 6 (1942): 9–13.

52. NRPB, "National Resources Development Report," p. 4; Ernest K. Lindley, "How the Postwar Reports Came to Be," *Newsweek*, March 22, 1943, p. 27. Bliven, "Charter for America," pp. 539–542, is a good example of how some liberals gave more emphasis to the NRPB's proposals for structural reform than did the NRPB itself. See also Chapman, "Contours of Public Policy," p. 363; Harold Smith to FDR, April 27, 1942, OF 788, FDRL.

53. William O. Douglas to Keynes, July 29, 1937, Douglas MSS 8, LC; Felix Frankfurter to Alfred Harcourt, February 2, 1939, MacLeish MSS 8, LC; Archibald MacLeish to Keynes, July 8, 1941 and October 10, 1944, both in MacLeish MSS 12, LC; Chapman, "Contours of Public Policy," pp. 11–13. See Robert Lekachman, *The Age of Keynes* (New York: Random House, 1966), pp. 124–143, for a discussion of the rise of an indigenous American "Keynesian school" of economists after 1937.

54. Richard Strout, "Hansen of Harvard," *New Republic* December 29, 1941, pp. 888–889; Alvin Hansen and Guy Greer, "The Federal Debt and the Future," *Harper's*, April 1942, p. 500; Hansen, "Wanted: Ten Million Jobs," *Atlantic*, September 1943, pp. 68–69.

55. Skidelsky, "Keynes and the Reconstruction of Liberalism," *Encounter*, pp. 29–32; Stein, *Fiscal Revolution*, pp. 169–196; Donald T. Critchlow, "The Political Control of the Economy: Deficit Spending as a Political Belief, 1932–1952," *Public Historian* 3 (1981): 5–22; Herbert Feis, "Keynes in Retrospect," *Foreign Affairs* 29 (1951): 576–577; Alfred H. Bornemann, "The Keynesian Paradigm and Economic Policy," *American Journal of Economics and Sociology* 35 (1976): 126–128.

56. One revealing glimpse of Henderson's bitterness after 1942 is in a report by Richard Miles of the British embassy in Washington of a dinner party in late

1943 at which Henderson was a guest and during which he spoke harshly (and apparently constantly) about the abysmal state of liberal government (Redvers Opie to Gladwyn Jebb, November 30, 1943, FO371–35368, PRO).

57. Alvin Hansen, "Suggested Revision of the Full Employment Bill," Hansen MSS, 3.10.

58. Chester Bowles, *Tomorrow Without Fear* (New York: Simon & Schuster, 1946).

59. "Democratic Platform of 1940," reprinted in Democratic National Committee, *Democratic Campaign Handbook* (1940), pp. 84–90.

60. "The 1944 Democratic Platform," *Democratic Digest*, August 1944, pp. 13, 27.

61. Arthur M. Schlesinger, Jr., "The Broad Accomplishments of the New Deal," in Seymour Harris, ed., *Saving American Capitalism* (New York: Alfred A. Knopf, 1948), pp. 78, 80.

4. *The New Deal and Southern Politics*

1. V. O. Key, Jr., *Southern Politics in State and Nation* (New York: Alfred A. Knopf, 1949), pp. 3–4.

2. Ibid., p. 645.

3. Henry C. Dethloff, "Missouri Farmers and the New Deal," *Agricultural History* 39 (July 1965): 142–144; J. Wayne Flynt, *Dixie's Forgotten People: The South's Poor Whites* (Bloomington: Indiana University Press, 1979), pp. 78–79.

4. See, e. g., Lyle W. Dorsett, *Franklin D. Roosevelt and the City Bosses* (Port Washington, N.Y.: Kennikat Press, 1977), and Bruce M. Stave, *The New Deal and the Last Hurrah: Pittsburgh Machine Politics* (Pittsburgh: University of Pittsburgh Press, 1970).

5. Paul E. Mertz, *New Deal Policy and Southern Rural Poverty* (Baton Rouge: Louisiana State University Press, 1978), pp. 40–49, 53–54, 61, 83.

6. Theda Skocpol, "Political Response to Capitalist Crisis," *Politics and Society* 10 No. 2 (1980): 155–201; Skocpol and Kenneth Finegold, "State Capacity and Economic Intervention in the New Deal," *Political Science Quarterly* 97 (Summer 1982): 255–278; James T. Patterson, *The New Deal and the States: Federalism in Transition* (Princeton: Princeton University Press, 1969), pp. 201–207.

7. A. Cash Koeniger, "The New Deal and the States: Roosevelt versus the Byrd Organization in Virginia," *Journal of American History* 68 (March 1982): 876–896. According to Koeniger, "The demise of the Price faction was not the fault of its Virginia leaders, whose efforts has been marked by dedication and teamwork throughout. Nor did it result from Virginia's disillusionment with the New Deal. . . . Rather, Roosevelt himself sacrificed the Price faction, denying it the patronage that its leaders frantically insisted they must have to 'save

face' in Virginia" after a 1938 electoral setback." Ibid., p. 895. See also Robert F. Hunter, "Virginia and the New Deal," in John Braeman et al., eds., *The New Deal;* vol. II: *The State and Local Levels* (Columbus: Ohio State University Press, 1975), pp. 103–133; and Hunter, "The AAA Between Neighbors: Virginia, North Carolina, and the New Deal Farm Program," *Journal of Southern History* 44 (November 1978): 537–570.

8. James MacGregor Burns, *Roosevelt: The Lion and the Fox* (New York: Harcourt, Brace & World, 1956), pp. 379–380.

9. Bruce J. Schulman offers a contrasting view of the New Deal's impact on the South in *From Cotton Belt to Sunbelt: Federal Policy, Economic Development, and the Transformation of the South, 1938–1980* (New York: Oxford University Press, 1991). According to Schulman, the New Deal—hesitant to challenge the existing patterns of southern authority in its early years—"went south" in 1938, when it released its celebrated *Report on Economic Conditions of the South*, contributed greatly to the economic development of the region, and created an important progressive constituency there for its emerging brand of Keynesian/welfare-state liberalism, which was later shattered during the Cold War.

10. See, e. g., William G. Carleton, "The Conservative South—A Political Myth," *Virginia Quarterly Review* 22 (Spring 1946): 179–192; Carleton, "The Southern Politician—1900 and 1950," *Journal of Politics* 13 (May 1951): 215–231; Norman Phillips, "The Question of Southern Conservatism," *South Atlantic Quarterly* 54 (January 1955): 1–10; Lee Coller, "The Solid South Cracks," *New Republic* 94 (March 23, 1938): 185–186. Historians who maintain that the New Deal helped sow "seeds of change," but who stop short of the larger claims of Carleton and Phillips, include Frank Freidel, *The New Deal and the South* (Baton Rouge: Louisiana State University Press, 1965), pp. 99–101; George B. Tindall, *The Emergence of the New South, 1913–1945* (Baton Rouge: Louisiana State University Press, 1967), pp. 631–639; and Dewey Grantham, Jr., *The Democratic South* (Athens: University of Georgia Press, 1963), pp. 67–70. Marian D. Irish, "The Southern One-Party System and National Politics," *Journal of Politics* 4 (February 1942): 80–94, offers a contemporary assessment.

11. Douglas Carl Abrams, *Conservative Constraints: North Carolina and the New Deal* (Jackson: University of Mississippi Press, 1992), pp. 215–262.

12. James W. Dunn, "The New Deal and Florida Politics" (Ph.D. diss., Florida State University, 1971), pp. 169–171, 201; Merlin G. Cox, "David Sholtz: New Deal Governor of Florida," *Florida Historical Quarterly* 43 (October 1964): 142–152.

13. Tindall, *Emergence of the New South*, pp. 726–727.

14. John Temple Graves II, "This is America: III. The South Still Loves Roosevelt." *Nation* 149 (July 1, 1939): 12; *Newsweek*, October 4, 1937, pp. 34–36.

15. National Emergency Council, *Report on Economic Conditions of the South* (Washington, D.C.: Goverment Printing Office, 1938).

16. Schulman, *From Cotton Belt to Sunbelt*, pp. 50–53; Tindall, *Emergence of the New South*, pp. 598–600; Tindall, "The 'Colonial Economy' and the Growth Psychology: The South in the 1930s," *South Atlantic Quarterly* 64 (Autumn 1965): 473–474; Mertz, *New Deal and Southern Rural Poverty*, pp. 247–248; Steve Davis, "The South as 'the Nation's No. 1 Economic Problem: The NEC Report of 1938," *Georgia Historical Quarterly* 62 (Summer 1978): 119–131.

17. Patterson, *Congressional Conservatism*, pp. 250–297; James C. Cobb, "Not Gone, But Forgotten: Eugene Talmadge and the 1938 Purge Campaign," *Georgia Historical Quarterly* 59 (Summer 1975): 197–209. Cobb claims that had Roosevelt not intervened in the race, George might well have been defeated—not by Lawrence Camp, the New Deal candidate whom the President endorsed, but by Eugene Talmadge.

18. "My Party & Myself," *Time*, August 22, 1938, pp. 19–20; "50¢ Fight," ibid., (August 29, 1938); Roy E. Fossett, "The Impact of the New Deal on Georgia Politics, 1933–1941" (Ph.D. diss., University of Florida, 1960), pp. 295–306; Tindall, *Emergence of the New South*, p. 629.

19. *Atlanta Constitution*, September 16, 1938. See ibid., September 1, 1938; *Charlotte Observer*, September 1, 1938; "It's a Bust," *Time*, September 26, 1938, p. 13; Patterson, *Congressional Conservatism*, pp. 283–287; J. B. Shannon, "Presidential Politics in the South, 1938, I," *Journal of Politics* 1 (May 1939): 146–170; and Shannon, "Presidential Politics . . . II," ibid., pp. 278–298.

20. *Atlanta Constitution*, September 11, 1938.

21. T. Harry Williams, *Huey Long* (New York: Alfred A. Knopf, 1969), pp. 619–706; Alan Brinkley, *Voices of Protest: Huey Long, Father Coughlin, and the Great Depression* (New York: Alfred A. Knopf, 1982), pp. 36–81, 143–168, 276–283.

22. Ibid., pp. 216–222; A. Wigfall Green, *The Man Bilbo* (Baton Rouge: Louisiana State University Press, 1963), pp. 9–97; William Anderson, *The Wild Man from Sugar Creek* (Baton Rouge: Louisiana State University Press, 1975).

23. Key, *Southern Politics*, p. 645; Tindall, *Emergence of the New South*, p. 649; Patterson, "The Failure of Party Realignment in the South," *Journal of Politics* 27 (August 1965): 617.

24. David Conrad, *The Forgotten Farmer: The Story of the Sharecroppers in the New Deal* (Urbana: University of Illinois Press, 1965), pp. 64–82, 205–209, and passim; Donald H. Grubbs, *Cry from the Cotton: The Southern Tenant Farmers' Union and the New Deal* (Chapel Hill: University of North Carolina Press, 1971), pp. 3–61; Jonathan M. Wiener, "Class Structure and Economic Development in the American South, 1865–1955," *American Historical Review* 84 (October 1979): 970–992.

25. See David Potter, *The South and the Concurrent Majority* (Baton Rouge: Louisiana State University Press, 1972).

26. Ibid., pp. 67–73; John M. Allswang, *The New Deal and American Politics*

(New York: John Wiley & Sons, 1978), pp. 53–56, 101–103; Harvard Sitkoff, *A New Deal for Blacks. The Emergence of Civil Rights as a National Issue* (New York: Oxford University Press, 1978), pp. 84–138; Nancy J. Weiss, *Farewell to the Party of Lincoln: Black Politics in the Age of FDR* (Princeton: Princeton University Press, 1983), passim.

27. Other discussions of the relationship between changes in national Democratic politics and the politics of the South in the 1930s include Monroe Lee Billington, *The Political South in the Twentieth Century* (New York: Charles Scribner's Sons, 1975), pp. 67–68; Grantham, *The Democratic South*, pp. 70–75; Potter, *The South and the Concurrent Majority*, pp. 61–89.

28. Patterson, "Failure of Party Realignment in the South," p. 603; Freidel, *FDR and the South*, pp. 91–92.

29. Patterson, *Congressional Conservatism and the New Deal*, p. 20.

30. The essay that formed the basis of this chapter was published well before the appearance of several recent studies of the New Deal and the South. They include, in addition to Schulman, Roger Biles, *The South and the New Deal* (Lexington: University Press of Kentucky, 1994), a broad synthesis that largely supports the argument presented here; Jeannie M. Whayne, *A New Plantation South: Land, Labor, and Federal Favor in Twentieth-Century Arkansas* (Charlottesville: University Press of Virginia, 1996), a local study of a county in Arkansas that emphasizes the essential conservatism of New Deal programs at the local level; George T. Blaskey, *Hard Times and New Deal in Kentucky, 1929–1939* (Lexington: University Press of Kentucky, 1986), which traces the changes the New Deal brought to Kentucky; James Hodges, *New Deal Labor Policy and the Southern Cotton Textile Industry, 1933–1941* (Knoxville: University of Tennessee Press, 1986), which examines the weakness of New Deal labor policies in the South; and Douglas L. Smith, *The New Deal in the Urban South* (Baton Rouge: Louisiana State University Press, 1988).

5. *The Two World Wars and American Liberalism*

1. Walter Lippmann, "The World Conflict In its Relation to American Democracy," *The Annals* 72 (July 1917): 7–8.

2. Walter Lippmann, *Drift and Mastery: An Attempt to Diagnose the Current Unrest* (New York: Mitchell Kennerley, 1914), pp. 147–148.

3. Ibid., p. 148.

4. David Kennedy, *Over Here: The First World War and American Society* (New York: Oxford University Press, 1980), chapters 1, 2, 6; Alan Dawley, *Struggles for Justice: Social Responsibility and the Liberal State* (Cambridge, Mass.: Harvard University Press, 1991), pp. 254–294.

5. Bernard M. Baruch, *American Industry in the War* (New York: Prentice-Hall, 1941), pp. 105–106; Paul A. C. Koistinen, "The 'Industrial-Military

Complex' in Historical Perspective: World War I," *Business History Review* 41 (1967): 393.

6. Grosvenor B. Clarkson, *Industrial America in the World War: The Strategy Behind the Lines, 1917–1918* (Boston: Houghton Mifflin, 1923), pp. 312, 475–488.

7. Ellis W. Hawley, "Herbert Hoover and Economic Stabilization, 1921–22," in Hawley, ed., *Herbert Hoover as Secretary of Commerce* (Iowa City: University of Iowa Press, 1981), pp. 43–77; Robert F. Himmelberg, *The Origins of the National Recovery Administration: Business, Government, and the Trade Association Issue, 1921–1933* (New York: Fordham University Press, 1976), pp. 43–74; Louis Galambos, *Competition and Cooperation: The Emergence of a National Trade Association* (Baltimore: Johns Hopkins University Press, 1966), pp. 89–138; Rexford G. Tugwell, *The Industrial Discipline and the Governmental Arts* (New York: Columbia University Press, 1933), pp. 4–6, 189–219; Tugwell, *The Democratic Roosevelt* (Garden City: Doubleday, 1957), pp. 229–230, 284–286, 308–311; Adolf A. Berle, Jr. and Gardiner C. Means, *The Modern Corporation and Private Property* (New York: Macmillan, 1932), pp. v., 124–125, 352, 356, and passim; Charles R. Van Hise, *Concentration and Control: A Solution of the Trust Problem in the United States* (New York: Macmillan, 1912), esp. pp. 8–20, 277–278. For a discussion of the roots of New Deal corporatism in the decades preceding the Depression, see (in addition to the works cited above) Donald Brand, *Corporatism and the Rule of Law: A Study of the National Recovery Administration* (Ithaca: Cornell University Press, 1988), part I.

8. Clifford Durr, "The Postwar Relationship Between Government and Business," *American Economic Review* 33 (1943): 47. See also George Soule, "The War in Washington," *New Republic*, September 27, 1939, pp. 205–206; "New Deal Plans Industry Council," *Business Week*, March 20, 1943, p. 15.

9. Robert D. Cuff, "American Mobilization for War 1917–1945: Political Culture vs Bureaucratic Administration," in N. F. Dreisziger, ed., *Mobilization for Total War: The Canadian, American, and British Experience, 1914–1918, 1937–1945* (Waterloo, Ont.: Wilfred Laurier University Press, 1981), p. 80.

10. *New York Times*, September 21, 1948; *New York World Telegram and Sun*, March 10, 1950; W. M. Jeffers to Eberstadt, March 20, 1950, Eberstadt Papers, Box 116, Princeton University Library; Eliot Janeway, "Where Was Mr. Nelson?" *Saturday Review*, September 7, 1946, p. 11; Eberstadt letter to multiple correspondents, August 23, 1946, Eberstadt Papers, Box 116.

11. The best account of economic mobilization during World War I is Robert D. Cuff, *The War Industries Board: Business-Government Relations during World War I* (Baltimore: Johns Hopkins University Press, 1973). For World War II, see Richard Polenberg, *War and Society: The United States, 1941–1945* (Philadelphia: J. B. Lippincott, 1972), chapters 1, 6; and Alan Brinkley, *The End of Reform: New Deal Liberalism in Recession and War* (New York: Alfred A. Knopf, 1995), chapter 8.

12. I. F. Stone, "Donald Nelson Has Chosen," *Nation*, March 21, 1942, p. 332. See also Stone, "Nelson and Guthrie," ibid., June 27, 1942, p. 731; Michael Straight, "Dollar-a-Year Sabotage," *New Republic*, March 30, 1942, p. 418; "Don Nelson's Men," *Business Week*, July 4, 1942, pp. 50–52; "The Pain and the Necessity," *Time*, June 29, 1942, p. 18; *Kiplinger Washington Letter*, August 15, 1942, Nelson Papers, Box 2, Huntington Library, San Marino, Calif.; Bruce Bliven to Max Lerner, August 24, 1942, Lerner Papers, Box 1, Yale University Library.

13. Kennedy, *Over Here*, pp. 55–56, 62–69; John Higham, *Strangers in the Land* (New Brunswick: Rutgers University Press, 1963), pp. 201–202; Paul L. Murphy, *World War I and the Origin of Civil Liberties in the United States* (New York: W. W. Norton, 1979), chapters 4–5.

14. See Allan M. Winkler, *The Politics of Propaganda: The Office of War Information, 1942–1945* (New Haven: Yale University Press, 1978), pp. 38–72; John Morton Blum, *V Was for Victory* (New York: Harcourt Brace Jovanovich, 1976), pp. 45–52; Clayton R. Koppes and Gregory D. Black, *Hollywood Goes to War: How Politics, Profits and Propaganda Shaped World War II Movies* (Berkeley: University of California Press, 1987), pp. 82–112, 278–316.

15. Reinhold Niebuhr, *The Children of Light and the Children of Darkness* (New York: Charles Scribner's Sons, 1945), p. 117. See also Niebuhr, "The Collectivist Bogy," *Nation*, October 21, 1944, pp. 478–480.

16. Friedrich A. Hayek, *The Road to Serfdom* (Chicago: University of Chicago Press, 1944); Hayek to Walter Lippmann, April 6, 1937, Walter Lippmann Papers, Series III, Box 77, Yale University Library. See also Theodore Rosenof, *Patterns of Political Economy: The Failure to Develop a Democratic Left Synthesis in America, 1933–1950* (New York: Garland, 1983), pp. 228–232; Rosenof, "Freedom, Planning, and Totalitarianism: The Reception of F. A. Hayek's *Road to Serfdom*." *Canadian Review of American Studies* 5 (Fall 1974): 150–160.

17. James T. Flynn, "Other People's Money," *New Republic*, January 26, 1938, p. 337; Walter Millis, "Cross Purposes in the New Deal," *Virginia Quarterly Review* 14 (Summer 1938): 357–367. The best account of the NRA is Ellis W. Hawley, *The New Deal and the Problem of Monopoly* (Princeton: Princeton University Press, 1966), chapters 1–7. See also Donald R. Brand, *Corporatism and the Rule of Law* (Ithaca: Cornell University Press, 1988).

18. "National Minima for Labor," *New Republic*, December 1, 1937, p. 88; "Again—The Trust Problem," *New Republic*, January 19, 1938, p. 295; "A New NRA," *Nation*, March 25, 1939, p. 337; "Liberals Never Learn," *Nation*, March 18, 1939, p. 309; George Soule, "This Recovery: What Brought It? Will It Last?" *Harper's*, March 1937, p. 342; Robert Jackson, speech entitled "Business Confidence and Government Policy," December 26, 1937, Raymond Clapper Papers, Box 200, Manuscripts Division, LC.

19. Thurman Arnold, *The Folklore of Capitalism* (New Haven: Yale Univer-

sity Press, 1937), pp. 221, 268; Arnold, "Feathers and Prices," *Common Sense*, July, 1939, p. 6; William E. Leuchtenburg, "The New Deal and the Analogue of War," in John Braeman et al., eds., *Change and Continuity in Twentieth-Century America* (Columbus: Ohio State University Press, 1964), p. 135.

20. Alan Brinkley, "Origins of the 'Fiscal Revolution,'" *Storia NordAmericana* 6 (1989): 37–39.

21. Ibid., pp. 37–42.

22. On the role of the advertising industry in encouraging and legitimizing consumption, see Roland Marchand, *Advertising the American Dream, 1920–1940* (Berkeley: University of California Press, 1985) 25–43, 120–163, and passim; Stuart Ewen, *Captains of Consciousness: Advertising and the Social Roots of the Consumer Culture* (New York: McGraw-Hill, 1976), pp. 81–109 and passim: T. J. Jackson Lears, "From Salvation to Self-Realization: Advertising and the Therapeutic Roots of the Consumer Culture, 1880–1930," in Lears and Richard Wightman Fox, eds., *The Culture of Consumption: Critical Essays in American History, 1880–1890* (New York: Pantheon, 1983), pp. 1–38.

23. Michael Bernstein, *The Great Depression: Delayed Recovery and Economic Change in America, 1929–1939* (New York: Cambridge University Press, 1987), pp. 21–40; Stanley Lebergott, *Pursuing Happiness: American Consumers in the Twentieth Century* (Princeton: Princeton University Press, 1993), pp. 69–72, 148.

24. On the rise of consumer activism, see Horace M. Kallen, *The Decline and Rise of the Consumer* (New York: D. Appleton-Century, 1936), pp. 153–200; Helen Sorenson, *The Consumer Movement: What It Is and What It Means* (New York: Harper & Brothers, 1941), pp. 3–30 and passim. The growing importance of consumer activism was not lost on the Roosevelt administration. Tugwell, among others, courted consumer groups and told one of them in 1934 that "the organization of consumers' leagues in the United States has been a recognition of the inherent power of organized consumer action. Historically your organizations have endeavored to use this latent power . . . in support of numerous attempts by various groups to raise living standards for working people." Tugwell speech draft, May 1, 1934, Thomas Blaisdell Papers, Box 40, National Resources Planning Board Archives, Record Group 187, National Archives.

25. William Trufant Foster and Waddill Catchings, *Money* (Boston: Houghton Mifflin, 1923), pp. 351–356 and passim; Foster and Catchings, *Profits* (Boston: Houghton Mifflin, 1925), pp. v–vi, 223–246, 398–418; Foster and Catchings, *Business Without a Buyer* (Boston: Houghton Mifflin, 1927), pp. v–vii; Foster and Catchings, *The Road to Plenty* (Boston: Houghton Mifflin, 1928), pp. 3–10, and passim.

26. Arthur D. Gayer, *Public Works in Prosperity and Depression* (New York: National Bureau of Economic Research, 1935), pp. 366–401; John M. Clark,

Economics of Planning Public Works (Washington: The National Planning Board, 1935), pp. 155–159. Alan Sweezy, "The Keynesians and Government Policy, 1933–1939," *American Economic Review* 62 (May 1972), 118–119; James Harvey Rogers to Marvin McIntyre, October 28, 1937, James Roosevelt to Rogers, November 8, 1937, Rogers to Robert S. Shriver, December 9, 1937, all in Rogers Papers, Box 21, Yale University Library; Byrd L. Jones, "James Harvey Rogers: An Intellectual Biography" (Ph.D. diss., Yale University, 1966), pp. 146, 175, 210–211, 297, 506–507.

27. Brinkley, "Origins of the 'Fiscal Revolution,'" pp. 48–56.

28. Herbert Stein, *The Fiscal Revolution in America* (Chicago: University of Chicago Press, 1969), chapters 6–7; Dean L. May, *From New Deal to New Economics: The American Liberal Response to the Recession of 1937* (New York: Garland, 1981).

29. Alvin Hansen, "Planning Full Employment," *Nation*, October 21, 1941, p. 492; Hansen to Marriner Eccles, August 18, 1944, enclosing a copy of "Post-war Employment Program," August 17, 1944, Eccles Papers, Box 7, Folder 12, University of Utah Library; "Is There a New Frontier?" *New Republic*, November 27, 1944, pp. 708–710; "A New Bill of Rights," *Nation*, March 20, 1943, p. 402; Stein, *Fiscal Revolution*, pp. 175–77.

30. The literature describing the origins and character of what has come to be known as the military-industrial complex is vast. C. Wright Mills was among the first scholars to describe its characteristics in *The Power Elite* (New York: Oxford University Press, 1956), pp. 171–224. William Appleman Williams, similarly, cited the "military-industrial complex" as part of "an imperial complex" that dominated American foreign policy and political economy; see *Americans in a Changing World: A History of the United States in the Twentieth Century* (New York: Harper & Row, 1978), p. 375. Daniel Yergin describes the complex as a central element of the "national-security state" in *Shattered Peace: The Origins of The Cold War and the National Security State* (Boston: Houghton Mifflin, 1977). See also Paul A. C. Koistinen, *The Military-Industrial Complex: A Historical Perspective* (New York: Praeger, 1980), and "Mobilizing the World War II Economy"; Bruce G. Brunton, "The Origins and Early Development of the American Military-Industrial Complex" (Ph.D. diss., University of Utah, 1989) and "An Historical Perspective on the Future of the Military-Industrial Complex," *Social Science Journal* 28 (1991): 45–62; Charles A. Cannon, "The Military-Industrial Complex in American Politics, 1953–1970" (Ph.D. diss., Stanford, 1975); Gregory Hooks, *Forging the Military-Industrial Complex: World War II's Battle of the Potomac* (Urbana: University of Illinois Press, 1991); Steve Fraser, *Labor Will Rule: Sidney Hillman and the Rise of American Labor* (New York: The Free Press, 1991), pp. 481–483; Gerald D. Nash, "The West and the Military-Industrial Complex," *Montana* 40 (1990): 72–75; Ben Baack and Edward Ray, "The Political Economy of the Origins of the Military-Industrial

Complex in the United States," *Journal of Economic History* 45 (1985): 369–375; Roger W. Lotchin, "The Political Culture of the Metropolitan-Military Complex," *Social Science History* 16 (1992): 275–299; Huntington, *The Soldier and the State*, chapters 12–13; Gautam Sen, "The Economics of US Defense: The Military Industrial Complex and Neo-Marxist Economic Theories Reconsidered," *Millennium: Journal of International Studies* 15 (1986): 179–195.

31. Foster and Catchings, *The Road to Plenty*, pp. 3–10, and passim; Schlesinger, *Crisis of the Old Order*, pp. 134–136.

6. *Legacies of World War II*

1. Archibald MacLeish, "The Unimagined America," *Atlantic*, June 1943, pp. 59–63.

2. John Keegan, *Six Armies in Normandy* (New York: The Viking Press, 1982), pp. 11–14.

3. Although the bulk of the growth was a result of military production, the consumer economy expanded by 12 percent during the same years. Alan S. Milward, *War, Economy and Society: 1939–1945* (Berkeley: University of California Press, 1977), pp. 63–65; John Morton Blum, *V Was for Victory* (New York: Harcourt, Brace Jovanovich, 1976), pp. 90–93.

4. Blum, *V Was for Victory*, p. 67.

5. "For Full Employment," *Nation*, December 23, 1944, p. 761; James G. Patton and James Loeb, Jr., "The Challenge to Progressives," *New Republic*, February 5, 1945, pp. 187–206; Alvin H. Hansen, "Suggested Revision of Full Employment Bill," July 28, 1945, Hansen MSS 3.10; Stephen K. Bailey, *Congress Makes a Law: The Story Behind the Employment Act of 1946* (New York: Columbia University Press, 1950), pp. 92–96.

6. National Resources Planning Board, *Security, Work, and Relief Policies* (Washington, D.C.: U.S. Government Printing Office, 1942), pp. 1–3, 325–328, 546–549.

7. Robert N. Chapman, *Contours of Public Policy, 1939–1945* (New York: Garland, 1981), pp. 33–35–45–53, 56–57; "Defeatist Liberals," *New Republic*, March 6, 1944, p. 302.

8. Arnold R. Hirsch, *Making the Second Ghetto: Race and Housing in Chicago, 1940–1960* (New York; Cambridge University Press, 1983), pp. 1–39; Nicholas Lemann, *The Promised Land: The Great Black Migration and How It Changed America* (New York: Alfred A. Knopf, 1991), pp. 1–10; Jacqueline Jones, *Labor of Love, Labor of Sorrow: Black Women, Work and the Family, from Slavery to the Present* (New York: Basic Books, 1985), pp. 232–256; Blum, *V Was for Victory*, pp. 182–207; "The Negro's War," *Fortune*, June 1942, pp. 77–80, 157–164

9. Charles W. Eagles, "Two 'Double V's': Jonathan Daniels, FDR, and

Race Relations during World War II," *North Carolina Historical Review* 59 (1982), 252–270.

10. "The Negro's War," pp. 77–80, 157–164.

11. Reinhold Niebuhr, *The Children of Light and the Children of Darkness: A Vindication of Democracy and a Critique of Its Traditional Defence* (New York: Charles Scribner's Sons, 1944), pp. 140–144; Niebuhr, "Christian Faith and the Race Problem," *Christianity and Society* (Spring 1945): 21–24.

12. Gunnar Myrdal, *An American Dilemma: The Negro Problem and Modern Democracy*, 2 vols. (New York: Harper & Row, 1944), I, lxix–lxxii; II, 997, 1009.

13. On the making of and responses to Myrdal's book, see Walter A. Jackson, *Gunnar Myrdal and America's Conscience: Social Engineering and Racial Liberalism, 1938–1987* (Chapel Hill: University of North Carolina Press, 1990), esp. chapters 5–7; David W. Southern, *Gunnar Myrdal and Black-White Relations: The Use and Abuse of 'An American Dilemma,' 1944–1969* (Baton Rouge: Louisiana State University Press, 1987); Sissela Bok, unpublished "Introductory Remarks" at a conference on "An American Dilemma Revisited: Race Relations in a Changing World," April 20, 1994, Morehouse College.

14. John T. Kneebone, *Southern Liberal Journalists and the Issue of Race, 1920–1944* (Chapel Hill: University of North Carolina Press, 1985), chapter 10; John Egerton, *Speak Now Against the Day: The Generation Before the Civil Rights Movement in the South* (Chapel Hill: University of North Carolina Press, 1994), parts II and III; Numan V. Bartley, *The New South, 1945–1980)* (Baton Rouge: Louisiana State University Press, 1995), chapters 1-3.

15. See Maureen Honey, *Creating Rosie the Riveter: Class, Gender, and Propaganda during World War II* (Amherst: University of Massachusetts Press, 1984), pp. 19–27, 47–59.

16. Sherna Berger Gluck, *Rosie the Riveter Revisited: Women, the War, and Social Change* (Boston: Twayne, 1987) is an important oral history of women war workers. Susan M. Hartman, *The Home Front and Beyond: American Women in the 1940s* (Boston: Twayne, 1982) is a general history. Alice Kessler-Harris minimizes the impact of the war in moving women into the workplace, although she concedes that the conflict had some important effects on the attitude of many women toward their relationship to the economy. *Out to Work: A History of Wage-Earning Women in America* (New York: Oxford University Press, 1982), pp. 273–299.

17. Robert Westbrook, "Fighting for the American Family: Private Interests and Political Obligations in World War II," in Richard Wightman Fox and Jackson Lears, *The Power of Culture* (Chicago: University of Chicago Press, 1993), pp. 195–221.

18. D'Ann Campbell, *Women at War with America: Private Lives in a Patriotic Era* (Cambridge, Mass.: Harvard University Press, 1984), pp. 68–71, 208.

19. Bascom Johnson, "The Vice Problem and Defense," *Survey Midmonthly*, May 1941, pp. 141–143; Kathryn Close, "In May Act Areas," ibid., March

1943, pp. 67–70; Samuel Tennenbaum, "Venereal Disease and War," *American Mercury*, November 1944, pp. 578–582; Eliot Ness, "Venereal Disease Control in Defense," *Annals of the American Academy* 220 (1942): 89–93.

20. "The Public's Health," *Survey Midmonthly*, May 1943, pp. 152–153; Close, "In May Act Areas," pp. 69–70; *New York Times*, August 10, 1942; Campbell, *Women at War with America*, p. 208; Karen Anderson, *Wartime Women: Sex Roles, Family Relations, and the Status of Women during World War II* (Westport, Conn.: Greenwood Press, 1981), pp. 104–111; Beth Bailey and David Farber, "Hotel Street: Prostitution and the Politics of War," *Radical History Review* 52 (1992): 54–77.

21. Winkler, *Politics of Propaganda*, pp. 38–72; Blum, *V Was for Victory*, pp. 45–52.

22. Niebuhr, *The Children of Light and the Children of Darkness*, p. 117; Friedrich A. Hayek, *The Road to Serfdom* (Chicago: University of Chicago Press, 1944); Theodore Rosenof, "Freedom, Planning, and Totalitarianism: The Reception of F.A. Hayek's *Road to Serfdom*," *Canadian Review of American Studies* 5 (1974): 149–165; Rosenof, *Patterns of Political Economy*, pp. 228–232.

23. The preoccupation with mass politics, "mass man," and "mass culture" was a pervasive theme in the intellectual life of the 1940s and 1950s and remains a pervasive theme in the historical scholarship on that era. See, for example, Christopher Brookeman, *American Culture and Society since the 1930s* (New York: Schocken Books, 1984); Richard H. Pells, *The Liberal Mind in a Conservative Age: American Intellectuals in the 1940s and 1950s* (New York: Harper & Row, 1985); Stephen J. Whitfield, *The Culture of the Cold War* (Baltimore: Johns Hopkins University Press, 1991); William S. Graebner, *The Age of Doubt: American Thought and Culture in the 1940s* (Boston: Twayne, 1991).

24. Reinhold Niebuhr, *The Irony of American History* (New York: Charles Scribner's Sons, 1952) pp. 69, 173; Arthur M. Schlesinger, Jr., *The Cycles of American History* (Boston: Houghton Mifflin, 1986), pp. 19–20.

25. Arthur Schlesinger's 1977 essay "The Theory of America: Experiment or Destiny?" evaluates the tension between the doubting and messianic visions of America. It is republished in ibid., pp. 3–22.

26. Henry R. Luce, *The American Century* (New York: Farrar and Rinehart, 1941), pp. 32–34, 38–39. The essay appeared originally in *Life*, February 17, 1941; it is reprinted in John K. Jessup, *The Ideas of Henry Luce* (New York: Atheneum, 1969), pp. 105–120.

27. See James L. Baughman, *Henry R. Luce and the Rise of the American News Media* (Boston: Twayne, 1987), esp. chapters 8–9.

28. Henry A. Wallace, *Democracy Reborn*, Russell Lord, ed. (New York: Reynal & Hitchcock, 1944), pp. 195–196; Edward L. and Frederick H. Schapsmeier, *Prophet in Politics: Henry A. Wallace and the War Years, 1940–1965* (Ames: Iowa State University Press, 1970), p. 32.

29. Alan Brinkley, "Dilemmas of Modern Liberalism," in John F. Sears, ed.,

Franklin D. Roosevelt and the Future of Liberalism (Westport, Conn.: Meckler, 1991), pp. 17–24.

30. Theodore H. White, *America in Search of Itself* (New York: Harper & Row, 1982), pp. 3–4.

31. Godfrey Hodgson, *America in Our Time* (Garden City, N.Y.: Doubleday, 1976), pp. 6–8.

32. MacLeish, "The Unimagined America," pp. 59–63.

7. *Historians and the Interwar Years*

1. *Franklin D. Roosevelt: The Apprenticeship* (Boston: Little, Brown, 1952). Subsequent volumes were *The Ordeal* (Boston: Little, Brown, 1954), *The Triumph* (Boston: Little, Brown, 1956), and *Launching the New Deal* (Boston: Little, Brown, 1973). Freidel also published a one-volume biography: *Franklin D. Roosevelt: A Rendezvous with Destiny* (Boston: Little, Brown, 1990).

2. Richard Hofstadter, *The Age of Reform: From Bryan to FDR* (New York: Alfred A. Knopf, 1955).

3. James MacGregor Burns, *Roosevelt: The Lion and the Fox* (New York: Harcourt Brace, 1956). The second and concluding volume of Burns's biography is *Roosevelt: The Soldier of Freedom* (New York: Harcourt Brace Jovanovich, 1970).

4. Arthur M. Schlesinger, Jr., *The Age of Roosevelt:* vol. 1, *The Crisis of the Old Order;* vol. 2, *The Coming of the New Deal;* vol. 3, *The Politics of Upheaval* (Boston: Houghton Mifflin, 1957, 1959, 1960).

5. Schlesinger derived the "cycle theory" in part from the work of his father, the historian Arthur M. Schlesinger, Sr. and from the political scientist V. O. Key. Schlesinger, Jr.'s *The Cycles of American History* (Boston: Houghton Mifflin, 1986) contains his most recent explanation of the theory.

6. An important recent study of the "progressive" approach to American history (and of other approaches discussed below) is Peter Novick, *That Noble Dream: The "Objectivity Question" and the American Historical Profession* (Chicago: University of Chicago Press, 1988).

7. Alfred D. Chandler, Jr., *Strategy and Structure: Chapters in the History of the American Industrial Enterprise* (Cambridge, Mass.: MIT Press, 1962). Among other important works by Chandler that have contributed to the development of organizational history is *The Visible Hand: The Managerial Revolution in American Business* (Cambridge, Mass.: Harvard University Press, 1977).

8. Robert H. Wiebe, *The Search for Order, 1877–1920* (New York: Hill & Wang, 1967).

9. Louis Galambos, "The Emerging Organizational Synthesis in Modern American History," *Business History Review* 44 (1970): 279–290.

10. Richard Hofstadter, *The American Political Tradition and the Men Who*

Made It (New York: Alfred A. Knopf, 1948), p. vii. For a contemporary comment on the rise of "consensus" history, see John Higham, "The Cult of the 'American Consensus': Homogenizing Our History," *Commentary* 27 (1959): 94–95.

11. Hofstadter, *The Age of Reform*, Chapter 8.

12. Gabriel Kolko, *Main Currents in Modern American History* (New York: Harper & Row, 1976), and *The Triumph of Conservatism: A Reinterpretation of American History, 1900–1916* (New York: Free Press of Glencoe, 1963).

13. James Weinstein, *The Corporate Ideal in the Liberal State, 1900–1918* (Boston: Beacon Press, 1968).

14. R. Jeffrey Lustig, *Corporate Liberalism: The Origins of Modern American Political Theory, 1890–1920* (Berkeley: University of California Press, 1982).

15. As Galambos has noted, the "corporate liberal" synthesis is in most respects compatible with the "organizational synthesis," although it contains a normative element the organizational historians do not generally embrace.

16. Barry D. Karl, *The Uneasy State: The United States from 1915 to 1945* (Chicago: University of Chicago Press, 1983).

17. Daniel T. Rodgers, *Contested Truths: Key Words in American Politics Since Independence* (New York: Basic Books, 1987).

18. Roy Rosenzweig, *Eight Hours for What We Will: Workers and Leisure in an Industrial City, 1870–1920* (New York: Cambridge University Press, 1983).

19. Gary Gerstle, *Working-Class Americanism: The Politics of Labor in a Textile City, 1914–1960* (New York, Cambridge University Press, 1989).

20. Scholarship shaped by the premises of the "new" history has been particularly plentiful for the interwar years in the areas of labor and gender history. Because other essays in the collection for which I originally wrote this essay dealt specifically and exclusively with those fields, they have received less attention here than their importance would normally suggest they should.

21. Frederick Lewis Allen, *Only Yesterday: An Informal History of the 1920's* (New York: Harper & Row, 1931).

22. Joseph R. Gusfield, *Symbolic Crusade: Status Politics and the American Temperance Movement* (Urbana: University of Illinois Press, 1963).

23. William E. Leuchtenburg, *The Perils of Prosperity, 1914–1932* (Chicago: University of Chicago Press, 1958).

24. Lawrence Goodwyn, *Democratic Promise: The Populism Movement in America* (New York: Oxford University Press, 1976); Steven Hahn, *The Roots of Southern Populism: Yeoman Farmers and the Transformation of the Georgia Upcountry, 1850–1890* (New York: Oxford University Press, 1983).

25. Kathleen M. Blee, *Women of the Klan: Racism and Gender in the 1920s* (Berkeley: University of California Press, 1991).

26. Leonard J. Moore, *Citizen Klansmen: The Ku Klux Klan in Indiana, 1921–1928* (Chapel Hill: University of North Carolina Press, 1991).

27. Moore, *Citizen Klansmen;* Kenneth T. Jackson, *The Ku Klux Klan in the City, 1915–1930* (New York: Oxford University Press, 1967).

28. George M. Marsden, *Fundamentalism and American Culture: The Shaping of Twentieth-Century Evangelicalism, 1870–1925* (New York: Oxford University Press, 1980); Terry A. Cooney, "Cosmopolitan Values and the Identification of Reaction: *Partisan Review* in the 1930s," *Journal of American History* 68 (1981): 580–598; David A. Hollinger, "Ethnic Diversity, Cosmopolitanism and the Emergence of the American Liberal Intelligentsia," *American Quarterly* 27 (1975): 133–151.

29. Alan Brinkley, *Voices of Protest: Huey Long, Father Coughlin, and the Great Depression* (New York: Alfred A. Knopf, 1982); Michael Kazin, *The Populist Persuasion: An American History* (New York: Basic Books, 1994).

30. Leo P. Ribuffo, *The Old Christian Right: The Protestant Far Right from the Great Depression to the Cold War* (Philadelphia: Temple University Press, 1983).

31. Warren I. Susman, *Culture as History: The Transformation of American Society in the Twentieth Century* (New York: Pantheon, 1984).

32. See, among many others, Christopher Lasch, *The Culture of Narcissism: American Life in an Age of Diminishing Expectations* (New York: Norton, 1978); and Lasch, *The True and Only Heaven: Progress and Its Critics* (New York: Norton, 1991).

33. Jackson Lears, *Fables of Abundance: A Cultural History of Advertising in America* (New York: Basic Books, 1994).

34. Stuart Ewen, *Captains of Consciousness: Advertising and the Social Roots of the Consumer Culture* (New York: McGraw-Hill, 1976).

35. Roland Marchand, *Advertising the American Dream: Making Way for Modernity, 1920–1940* (Berkeley: University of California Press, 1985).

36. The sociologists Robert and Helen Merrell Lynd had made similar observations in the 1920s about life in the city of Muncie, Indiana, in their famous study, *Middletown* (New York: Harcourt, Brace & World, 1929).

37. Arthur S. Link, "What Happened to the Progressive Movement in the 1920's?" *American Historical Review* 64 (1959): 833–851.

38. Robert F. Himmelberg, *The Origins of the National Recovery Administration: Business, Government, and the Trade Association Issue, 1921–1933* (New York: Fordham University Press, 1976).

39. Louis Galambos, *Competition and Cooperation: The Emergence of a National Trade Association* (Baltimore: Johns Hopkins University Press, 1966).

40. Ellis W. Hawley, *The Great War and the Search for a Modern Order: A History of the American People and Their Institutions, 1917–1933* (New York: St. Martin's Press, 1979); Hawley, ed., *Herbert Hoover as Secretary of Commerce: Studies in New Era Thought and Practice* (West Branch, Iowa: Herbert Hoover Presidential Library Association, 1974).

41. Donald R. Brand, *Corporatism and the Rule of Law: A Study of the National Recovery Administration* (Ithaca: Cornell University Press, 1988).

42. Hawley's *The Great War and the Search for a Modern Order* is a particularly useful summary of this argument for the period from World War I to the New Deal.

43. See Schlesinger, "Vicissitudes of Presidential Reputations," *The Cycles of American History*, pp. 374–387, for a restatement (tempered by the findings of recent scholarship) of the liberal case for Hoover as a conservative starkly different from Roosevelt.

44. David Burner, *Herbert Hoover: A Public Life* (New York: Alfred A. Knopf, 1979).

45. Joan Hoff Wilson, *Herbert Hoover: Forgotten Progressive* (Boston: Little, Brown, 1975).

46. James Stuart Olson, *Herbert Hoover and the Reconstruction Finance Corporation, 1931–1933* (Ames: Iowa State University Press, 1977).

47. See Galambos, *Competition and Cooperation*.

48. William E. Leuchtenburg, *Franklin D. Roosevelt and the New Deal, 1932–1940* (New York: Harper & Row, 1963).

49. Barton J. Bernstein, "The New Deal: The Conservative Achievements of Liberal Reform," in Bernstein, ed. *Towards a New Past: Dissenting Essays in American History* (New York: Alfred A. Knopf, 1968), pp. 263–288.

50. Ronald Radosh, "The Myth of the New Deal," in Radosh and Murray Rothbard, eds. *A New History of the Leviathan* (New York: Dutton, 1972), pp. 146–187.

51. See the introduction to Howard Zinn, ed., *New Deal Thought* (Indianapolis: Bobbs-Merrill, 1966).

52. Thomas Ferguson, "From Normalcy to New Deal: Industrial Structure, Party Competition, and American Public Policy in the Great Depression," *International Organization* 38 (1984): 41–94. A revised version of this essay is "Industrial Conflict and the Coming of the New Deal: The Triumph of Multinational Liberalism in America,," in Steve Fraser and Gary Gerstle, eds., *The Rise and Fall of the New Deal Order* (Princeton: Princeton University Press, 1989), pp. 3–31.

53. Colin Gordon, *New Deals: Business, Labor, and Politics in America, 1920–1935* (New York: Cambridge University Press, 1994).

54. James MacGregor Burns, *Roosevelt: The Lion and the Fox* (New York: Harcourt Brace, 1956).

55. James T. Patterson, *Congressional Conservatism and the New Deal: The Growth of the Conservative Coalition in Congress, 1933–1939* (Lexington: University of Kentucky Press, 1967).

56. Frank Freidel, *F.D.R. and the South* (Baton Rouge: Louisiana State University Press, 1965).

57. Harvard Sitkoff, ed., *Fifty Years Later: The New Deal Evaluated* (New York: Alfred A. Knopf, 1985); Sitkoff, *A New Deal for Blacks. The Emergence of Civil Rights as a National Issue: The Depression Decade* (New York: Oxford University Press, 1978).

58. Nancy J. Weiss, *Farewell to the Party of Lincoln: Black Politics in the Age of FDR* (Princeton: Princeton University Press, 1983).

59. John B. Kirby, *Black Americans in the Roosevelt Era: Liberalism and Race* (Knoxville: University of Tennessee Press, 1980).

60. Alan Brinkley, "The New Deal and Southern Politics." in James C. Cobb and Michael V. Namarato, eds., *The New Deal and the South* (Oxford, Miss.: University of Mississippi Press, 1984), pp. 97–116.

61. Bruce Schulman, *From Cotton Belt to Sunbelt: Federal Policy, Economic Development, and the Transformation of the South, 1938–1980* (New York: Oxford University Press, 1991).

62. Freidel suggests this view throughout his work on Roosevelt, especially in *FDR: Launching the New Deal.*

63. Barry D. Karl, *Executive Reorganization and Reform in the New Deal: The Genesis of Administrative Management, 1900–1939* (Chicago: University of Chicago Press, 1963).

64. Otis L. Graham, Jr., "Franklin Roosevelt and the Intended New Deal," in Michael R. Beschloss and Thomas C. Cronin, *Essays in Honor of James MacGregor Burns* (Englewood Cliffs, N.J.: Prentice Hall, 1989), pp. 75–95.

65. Mark Leff, *The Limits of Symbolic Reform: The New Deal and Taxation, 1933–1939* (New York: Cambridge University Press, 1984).

66. Herbert Stein, *The Fiscal Revolution in America* (Chicago: University of Chicago Press, 1969).

67. Robert Lekachman, *The Age of Keynes* (New York: Random House, 1966).

68. Margaret Weir, "The Federal Government and Unemployment: The Frustration of Policy Innovation from the New Deal to the Great Society," in Weir, Ann Shola Orloff, and Theda Skocpol, eds., *The Politics of Social Policy in the United States* (Princeton: Princeton University Press, 1988), pp. 149–190.

69. Thomas Ferguson and Colin Gordon have gone considerably further and portrayed New Deal economic policy as the product, at least in part, of the influence of powerful corporate interests with close ties to the administration. Gordon notes that these interests became sympathetic to some moderate New Deal reforms, but he argues that they were a powerful inhibition against more extensive measures.

70. James T. Patterson, *America's Struggle Against Poverty, 1900–1980* (Cambridge, Mass.: Harvard University Press, 1981).

71. Jill S. Quadagno, *The Transformation of Old Age Security: Class and Politics in the American Welfare State* (Chicago: University of Chicago Press, 1988).

72. Theda Skocpol, "The Limits of the New Deal System and the Roots of Contemporary Welfare Dilemmas," in Weir, Orloff, and Skocpol, eds., *The Politics of Social Policy*, pp. 293–312. Skocpol makes a broader argument about the institutional constraints that have inhibited the growth of the American welfare state in *Protecting Soldiers and Mothers; The Political Origins of Social Policy in the United States* (Cambridge, Mass.: Harvard University Press, 1992), although the study does not examine the New Deal itself.

73. Linda Gordon, *Pitied But Not Entitled: Single Mothers and the History of Welfare* (New York: The Free Press, 1994).

74. Karl E. Klare,"Judicial Deradicalization of the Wagner Act and the Origins of Modern Legal Consciousness, 1937–1941," *Minnesota Law Review* 65 (1978): 265–339.

75. Christopher Tomlins, *The State and the Unions: Labor Relations, Law, and the Organized Labor Movement in America, 1880–1960* (Cambridge: Cambridge University Press, 1985).

76. Katherine Van Wenzel Stone, "The Post-War Paradigm in American Labor Law," *Yale Law Journal* 4 (1981): 1509–1580.

77. Stanley Vittoz, *New Deal Labor Policy and the American Industrial Economy* (Chapel Hill: University of North Carolina Press, 1987).

78. Sanford Jacoby, *Employing Bureaucracy: Managers, Unions, and the Transformation of Work in American Industry, 1900–1945* (New York: Columbia University Press, 1985).

79. James Atleson, *Values and Assumptions in American Labor Law* (Amherst: University of Massachusetts, 1983).

80. David Montgomery, *Workers' Control in America: Studies in the History of Work, Technology, and Labor Struggles* (Cambridge: Cambridge University Press, 1979).

81. David Brody, *Workers in Industrial America: Essays on the Twentieth Century Struggle* (New York: Oxford University Press, 1980).

82. Ronald W. Schatz, *The Electrical Workers: A History of Labor at General Electric and Westinghouse, 1923–60* (Urbana: University of Illinois Press, 1983).

83. Bruce Nelson, *Workers on the Waterfront: Seamen, Longshoremen, and Unionism in the 1930s* (Urbana: University of Illinois Press, 1988).

84. Gary Gerstle, *Working-Class Americanism: The Politics of Labor in a Textile City, 1914–1960* (New York: Cambridge University Press, 1989).

85. Lizabeth Cohen, *Making a New Deal: Industrial Workers in Chicago, 1919–1939* (New York: Cambridge University Press, 1990).

86. Two collections of essays represent much of this new literature: Peter B. Evans, Dietrich Rueschemeyer, and Theda Skocpol, eds., *Bringing the State Back In* (New York: Cambridge University Press, 1985); and Weir, Orloff, and Skocpol, eds., *The Politics of Social Policy*.

87. Kenneth Finegold and Theda Skocpol, *State and Party in America's New Deal* (Madison: University of Wisconsin Press, 1995).

88. Grant McConnell, *The Decline of Agrarian Democracy* (Berkeley: University of California Press, 1953).

89. James T. Patterson, *The New Deal and the States: Federalism in Transition* (Princeton: Princeton University Press, 1969).

90. Bruce M. Stave, *The New Deal and the Last Hurrah: Pittsburgh Machine Politics* (Pittsburgh: University of Pittsburgh Press, 1970).

91. Lyle W. Dorsett, *Franklin D. Roosevelt and the City Bosses* (Port Washington, N.Y.: Kennikat, 1977).

92. Charles H. Trout, *Boston: The Great Depression and the New Deal* (New York: Oxford University Press, 1977).

93. Ellis W. Hawley, *The New Deal and the Problem of Monopoly: A Study in Economic Ambivalence* (Princeton: Princeton University Press, 1966).

94. Graham, "Franklin Roosevelt and the Intended New Deal"; Karl, *The Uneasy State.*

95. Brand, *Corporatism and the Rule of Law.*

96. Richard L. McCormick, *From Realignment to Reform: Political Change in New York State, 1893–1910* (Ithaca: Cornell University Press, 1981).

97. Samuel P. Hays, "Politics and Society: Beyond the Political Party," in Paul Kleppner, ed. *The Evolution of American Electoral Systems* (Westport, Conn.: Greenwood, 1981), pp. 243–267.

98. Louis Galambos, *The Rise of the Corporate Commonwealth: United States Business and Public Policy in the Twentieth Century* (New York: Basic Books, 1988); and Galambos, "Technology, Political Economy, and Professionalization: Central Themes of the Organizational Synthesis," *Business History Review* 57 (1983): 471–493.

99. Anthony J. Badger, *The New Deal: The Depression Years, 1933–1940* (New York: Hill & Wang, 1988).

100. Bernard W. Bellush, *The Failure of the NRA* (New York: Norton, 1975).

101. J. Joseph Huthmacher, *Senator Robert F. Wagner and the Rise of Urban Liberalism* (Cambridge, Mass.: Harvard University Press, 1968).

102. Mark I. Gelfand, *A Nation of Cities: The Federal Government and Urban America, 1933–1965* (New York: Oxford University Press, 1975).

103. William W. Bremer, *Depression Winters: New York Social Workers and the New Deal* (Philadelphia: Temple University Press, 1984).

104. Trout, *Boston: The Great Depression and the New Deal.*

105. Stave, *The New Deal and the Last Hurrah.*

106. Jordan Schwarz, *The New Dealers: Power Politics in the Age of Roosevelt* (New York: Alfred A. Knopf, 1993).

107. Stein, *The Fiscal Revolution.*

108. Dean L. May, *From New Deal to New Economics: The American Liberal Response to the Recession of 1937* (New York: Garland, 1981).

109. Theodore Rosenof, *Patterns of Political Economy in America: The Failure to Develop a Democratic Left Synthesis, 1933–1950* (New York, Garland, 1983).

110. Alan Brinkley, *The End of Reform: New Deal Liberalism in Recession and War* (New York: Alfred A. Knopf, 1995).

111. John Morton Blum, *V Was for Victory: Politics and American Culture During World War II* (New York: Harcourt Brace Jovanovich, 1976); Richard Polenberg, *War and Society: The United States, 1941–1945* (Philadelphia: Lippincott, 1972).

112. Kim McQuaid, *Big Business and Presidential Power: From FDR to Reagan* (New York: William Morrow, 1982); Robert M. Collins, *The Business Response to Keynes, 1929–1964* (New York: Columbia University Press, 1981).

113. Bartholomew H. Sparrow, *From the Outside In: World War II and the American State* (Princeton: Princeton University Press, 1996).

114. Brinkley, *The End of Reform.* See also in this volume Chapter 3, "The Late New Deal and the Idea of the State," and Chapter 5, "The Two World Wars and American Liberalism."

115. Nelson Lichtenstein, *Labor's War at Home: The CIO and World War II* (New York: Cambridge University Press, 1982) and *The Most Dangerous Man in Detroit: Walter Reuther and the Fate of American Labor* (New York: Basic Books, 1995).

116. Steve Fraser, *Labor Will Rule: Sidney Hillman and the Rise of American Labor* (New York: The Free Press, 1991).

117. Howell John Harris, *The Right to Manage: Industrial Relations Policies of American Business in the 1940s* (Madison: University of Wisconsin Press, 1982).

118. Mike Davis, "The Barren Marriage of American Labor and the Democratic Party," *New Left Review* 124 (1980): 43–84.

119. Blum, *V Was for Victory;* Sitkoff, *A New Deal for Blacks.*

120. Arnold R. Hirsch, *Making the Second Ghetto: Race and Housing in Chicago, 1940–1960* (New York: Cambridge University Press, 1983).

121. William H. Chafe, *The American Woman* (New York: Oxford University Press, 1972).

122. Leila J. Rupp, *Mobilizing Women for War: German and American Propaganda, 1939–1945* (Princeton: Princeton University Press, 1978).

123. Karen Anderson, *Wartime Women: Sex Roles, Family Relations, and the Status of Women During World War II* (Westport, Conn.: Greenwood, 1981).

124. Mary Schweitzer, "World War II and Female Labor Participation Rates," *Journal of Economic History* 40 (March 1980): pp. 89–95.

125. Sara M. Evans, *Born for Liberty: A History of Women in America* (New York: The Free Press, 1989).

126. Alice Kessler-Harris, *Out to Work: A History of Wage-Earning Women in the United States* (New York: Oxford University Press, 1992).

127. Robert Westbrook, "Fighting for the American Family: Private Inter-

ests and Political Obligations in World War II," in Richard Wightman Fox and Jackson Lears, *The Power of Culture* (Chicago: University of Chicago Press, 1993), pp. 195–221.

8. *Hofstadter's* The Age of Reform *Reconsidered*

1. Robert Wiebe, "Views But No Vista," *The Progressive* 33 (1969): 47.

2. Arthur M. Schlesinger, Jr., *The Vital Center* (Boston: Houghton Mifflin, 1949). For a thoughtful assessment of Hofstadter's political and intellectual assumptions and of the role they played in shaping his scholarship, see Daniel Joseph Singal, "Beyond Consensus: Richard Hofstadter and American Historiography," *American Historical Review* 89 (1984): 976–981. Singal describes Hofstadter as a historical modernist whose outlook reflected a set of values he and others have described as "cosmopolitanism"—an essentially urban cast of mind and one that attributed particular importance to such worldly values as tolerance of diversity and skepticism of inherited faiths. Hofstadter himself spoke frequently of his reverence for the skeptical, relativistic world of scholarship and—sometimes by implication, sometimes explicitly—of his mistrust of provincialism. For other discussions of the emergence of this "cosmopolitan ideal," see Terry A. Cooney, "Cosmopolitan Values and the Identification of Reaction: Partisan Review in the 1930s," *Journal of American History* 68 (1981): 580–598; and David A. Hollinger, "Ethnic Diversity, Cosmopolitanism and the Emergence of the American Liberal Intelligentsia," *American Quarterly* 27 (1975): 133–151. Richard Pells attempts to place Hofstadter (and *The Age of Reform* in particular) in the context of the intellectual history of the 1950s in *The Liberal Mind in a Conservative Age* (1985), pp. 150–155 and ch. 3 *passim.*

3. Richard Hofstadter, *The Age of Reform: From Bryan to FDR* (New York: Alfred A. Knopf, 1955), p. 20; David Hawke, "Interview: Richard Hofstadter," *History* 3 (1960): 136; Daniel Bell, ed., *The New American Right* (1955).

4. See, e.g., Charles A. and Mary Beard, *The Rise of American Civilization* (1927); and Vernon L. Parrington, *Main Currents of American Thought*, 3 vols. (1927–1930).

5. Karl Mannheim, *Ideology and Utopia: An Introduction to the Sociology of Knowledge*, trans. Louis Wirth and Edward Shils (1957), esp. pp. 58–70; Lionel Trilling, "Reality in America," *The Liberal Imagination* (1950), pp. 3–21; C. Wright Mills, *White Collar* (1951), pp. 239–258 and passim; and Robert K. Merton, *Social Theory and Social Structure*, enlarged ed. (1968), pp. 73–118. Hofstadter acknowledged his debts to these and other social scientists in his essay "History and the Social Sciences," in Fritz Stern, ed., *The Varieties of History: From Voltaire to the Present* (1956), pp. 359–370 and in the introduction to *The Age of Reform*, p. 13. Fuller discussions of the importance of Hofstadter's interdisciplinary interests can be found in Singal, "Beyond Consensus,"

pp. 986–988; Daniel Walker Howe and Peter Elliott Finn, "Richard Hofstadter: The Ironies of an American Historian," *Pacific Historical Review* 43 (1974): 7–11; Richard Gillam, "Richard Hofstadter, C. Wright Mills, and 'the Critical Ideal,'" *The American Scholar* 57 (1977–78): 72–73, 79–81; and Stanley Elkins and Eric McKitrick, "Richard Hofstadter: A Progress," in *The Hofstadter Aegis* (New York: Alfred A. Knopf, 1974), pp. 309–310, 317–322.

6. Hofstadter, *Age of Reform*, p. 18.

7. Ibid., p. 35.

8. Ibid., pp. 61–62, 80.

9. C. Vann Woodward, "The Populist Heritage and the Intellectual," *The Burden of Southern History* (1968), pp. 141–66 (originally published in *The American Scholar* in 1959). Walter T. K. Nugent, *The Tolerant Populists* (1963); Michael Rogin, *The Intellectuals and McCarthy* (1967). Rogin's argument involved, as well, a much broader critique of the pluralistic assumptions that dominated American intellectual life and a charge that the work of Hofstadter and others represented an antidemocratic elitism.

10. Norman Pollack, *The Populist Response to Industrial America* (1962). See also the following essays by Pollack: "Hofstadter on Populism: A Critique of 'The Age of Reform,'" *Journal of Southern History* 26 (1960): 478–500; "The Myth of Populist Anti-Semitism," *American Historical Review* 68 (1962): 76–80; and "Fear of Man: Populism, Authoritarianism, and the Historian," *Agricultural History* 39 (1965): 59–67, from which the quoted passages are drawn (p. 59). Rejoinders include Oscar Handlin, "Reconsidering the Populists," *Agricultural History* 39 (1965): 68–74, and Irwin Unger, "Critique of Norman Pollack's 'Fear of Man,'" ibid., 75–80. On the especially sensitive question of populist anti-Semitism, see, in addition to the Pollack and Handlin essays above, Handlin, "American Views of the Jew at the Opening of the Twentieth Century," *Publication of the American Jewish Historical Society* 40 (1951): 323–344; and John Higham, "Anti-Semitism in the Gilded Age: A Reinterpretation," *Mississippi Valley Historical Review* 43 (1957): 559–579.

11. Lawrence Goodwyn, *Democratic Promise: The Populist Moment in America* (1976); John D. Hicks, *The Populist Revolt* (1931). Bruce Palmer, in *Man Over Money: The Southern Populist Critique of American Capitalism* (1980), offers an even starker statement of some of Goodwyn's assumptions, emphasizing the populist critique of the acquisitive individualism of American society.

12. Steven Hahn, *The Roots of Southern Populism: Yeoman Farmers and the Transformation of the Georgia Upcountry, 1850–1890* (1983), esp. pp. 1–10, 137–169, 269–289.

13. James Turner, "Understanding the Populists," *Journal of American History* 67 (1980): 354–373. Martin Ridge, "Populism Redux: John D. Hicks and *The Populist Revolt*," *Reviews in American History* 13 (1983): 142–154, offers an overview of populist historiography.

14. Hofstadter, *Age of Reform*, p. 135.

15. Hofstadter's portrait of the progressives drew from (although it did not always fully agree with) earlier studies by George Mowry and Alfred D. Chandler, both of whom had emphasized the relatively affluent, middle-class origins of reformers, hence raising a challenge to the then prevailing stereotype of progressives as tribunes of the common man. See George Mowry, *The California Progressives* (1951) and Alfred D. Chandler, "The Origins of Progressive Leadership," in Elting Morison, ed., *The Letters of Theodore Roosevelt*, vol. 8 (1954), pp. 1462–65.

16. Hofstadter, *Age of Reform*, p. 135.

17. Hofstadter, "The Pseudo-Conservative Revolt," in Daniel Bell, ed., *The Radical Right* (1964), p. 84. This is a revised edition of *The New American Right* (1955). Hofstadter's essay appears as well in his *The Paranoid Style in American Politics and Other Essays* (1965), where the quoted passage can be found on p. 53. See also Paula Fass, "Richard Hofstadter," *Dictionary of Literary Biography* 17 (1983): 219–222.

18. Hofstadter, *Age of Reform*, p. 135.

19. Ibid., pp. 215–216.

20. David P. Thelen, "Social Tensions and the Origins of Progressivism," *Journal of American History* 56 (1969): 323–341; Thelen, *The New Citizenship: Origins of Progressivism in Wisconsin, 1885–1900* (1972), passim; J. Joseph Huthmacher, "Urban Liberalism and the Age of Reform," *Mississippi Valley Historical Review* 59 (1962): 231–241, and *Senator Robert F. Wagner and the Rise of Urban Liberalism* (1968), chs. 2–3; Herbert G. Gutman, "Protestantism and the American Labor Movement: The Christian Spirit in the Gilded Age," in *Work, Culture, and Society in Industrializing America* (1976), pp. 79–117; John D. Buenker, "The Urban Political Machine and the Seventeenth Amendment," *Journal of American History* 56 (1969): 305–322. See also Richard Abrams, *Conservatism in a Progressive Era: Massachusetts Politics, 1900–1912* (1964), pp. 132–133, which identifies the working-class Irish as the truly reform-minded "insurgent" groups in Massachusetts.

21. Samuel P. Hays, "The Politics of Reform in Municipal Government in the Progressive Era," *Pacific Northwest Quarterly* 55 (1964): 159–169; Gabriel Kolko, *The Triumph of Conservatism* (1963); Robert Wiebe, *The Search for Order, 1877–1920* (1967), p. 166 and passim. In an earlier study, *Businessmen and Reform: A Study of the Progressive Movement* (1962), Wiebe argued, like Kolko, that business leaders had been at the forefront of progressive reform efforts, although he was more careful than Kolko to distinguish among different segments of the business community.

22. See, e.g., Peter G. Filene, "An Obituary for the Progressive Movement," *American Quarterly* 22 (1970): 20–34; and John D. Buenker, "The Progressive Era: A Search for a Synthesis," *Mid-America* 51 (1969): 175–193, both of whom

attack the notion of a progressive "movement." The work of Richard L. McCormick on the rise of a politics of interest groups to replace the older politics of party is particularly important. See, especially, *From Realignment to Reform: Political Change in New York State, 1893–1910* (1981). A particularly valuable discussion of the many-sided debate over the nature of progressivism may be found in Daniel Rodgers, "In Search of Progressivism," *Reviews in American History* 10 (1982): 113–132.

23. Joseph R. Gusfield, *Symbolic Crusade: Status Politics and the American Temperance Movement* (1963), esp. pp. 1–24, 166–188; Thelen, *The New Citizenship*, pp. 2–3, 309–310; Thelen, "Social Tensions," pp. 323–330. See also Elkins and McKitrick, "Richard Hofstadter," pp. 338–342.

24. David Montgomery, *Workers' Control in America: Studies in the History of Work, Technology, and Labor Struggles* (1979); Hahn, *The Roots of Southern Populism;* Goodwyn, *Democratic Promise.* An early effort to express this objection, although one weakened by its stridency, is William Appleman Williams, "The Age of Re-Forming History," *The Nation,* June 30, 1956, pp. 552–554.

25. Hofstadter, *The Progressive Historians: Turner, Beard, Parrington* (1968), p. 466.

26. Ibid. For a discussion of this and other dilemmas facing modern historians, see Bernard Bailyn, "The Challenge of Modern Historiography," *American Historical Review* 87 (1982): 1–24.

27. Hofstadter, *Age of Reform*, p. 307.

28. Ibid., pp. 307–316.

29. See, esp., Ellis Hawley, *The New Deal and the Problem of Monopoly: A Study in Economic Ambivalence* (Princeton: Princeton University Press, 1966). Otis Graham, *Encore for Reform: The Old Progressives and the New Deal* (1967), provides a different perspective on the role of progressive ideology in the 1930s.

30. See Alan Brinkley, *The End of Reform: New Deal Liberalism in Recession and War* (New York: Alfred A. Knopf, 1995).

31. See Eric Goldman, *Rendezvous with Destiny: A History of Modern American Reform* (New York: Alfred A. Knopf, 1952).

32. The most thoughtful contemporary efforts to define consensus historiography came from John Higham, who first gave the school its name in his famous article "The Cult of the 'American Consensus': Homogenizing Our History," *Commentary*, February 1959, pp. 93–100. He has since revised and moderated this initial assessment in *History: Professional Scholarship in America* (1965), pp. 212–232.

33. Hofstadter first expressed what became the basic assumptions of "consensus history" in his brief preface to *The American Political Tradition* (1948), pp. v–xi.

34. Hofstadter, *The Progressive Historians*, p. 458.

35. Hofstadter, "History and Sociology in the United States," in Hofstadter and Seymour Martin Lipset, eds., *Sociology and History: Methods* (1968), p. 18.

36. See, e.g., Boorstin, *The Genius of American Politics* (1953) and *The Americans*, 3 vols. (1958–1973).

37. Arthur M. Schlesinger, Jr., "Richard Hofstadter," in Marcus Cunliffe and Robin W. Winks, eds., *Pastmasters: Some Essays on American Historians* (1969), p. 289. Hofstadter offered a series of ambiguous assessments of his own of the consensus school, and of his place within it; see, e.g., "Communication," *Journal of the History of Ideas* 15 (1954): 328, and *The Progressive Historians* (1968), pp. 437–66.

38. In this, he shared many of the reservations expressed by Louis Hartz in *The Liberal Tradition in America: An Interpretation of American Political Thought Since the Revolution* (New York: Harcourt, Brace & World, 1955).

39. Hofstadter, "Reflections on Violence in the United States," in Hofstadter and Michael Wallace, eds., *American Violence: A Documentary History* (1970), p. 43.

9. Robert Penn Warren, T. Harry Williams, and Huey Long

1. Robert Penn Warren, "The Briar Patch," in Twelve Southerners, *I'll Take My Stand: The South and the Agrarian Tradition* (New York: Harper, 1930), pp. 246–264.

2. Rob Roy Purdy, ed., *Fugitives' Reunion: Conversations at Vanderbilt, May 3–5, 1956* (Nashville: Vanderbilt University Press, 1959), p. 209.

3. Robert Penn Warren, "*All the King's Men:* The Matrix of Experience," *Yale Review* 53 (December 1963): 161–162.

4. Ibid., pp. 162–173.

5. Ibid., p. 166; Warren memoir, Columbia Oral History Project, p. 123. Daniel Singal suggests that Warren's claim to have done no research is, to some degree, disingenuous. See Singal, *The War Within: From Victorian to Modernist Thought in the South, 1919–1945* (Chapel Hill: University of North Carolina Press, 1982), p. 361.

6. Unpublished preface to an unidentified draft of the Talos/Stark project, Robert Penn Warren Papers, Box 103, Folder 1904, Beinecke Library, Yale University.

7. See, for example, Ladell Payne, "Willie Stark and Huey Long: Atmosphere, Myth or Suggestion," *American Quarterly* 20 (Fall 1968): 580–595.

8. Warren, "*All the King's Men:* The Matrix of Experience," p. 161.

9. W. J. Cash, *The Mind of the South* (New York: Alfred A. Knopf, 1941), pp. 290–291.

10. See, for example, Victor Ferkiss, "The Political and Economic Philosophy of American Fascism" (Ph.D. dissertation: University of Chicago, 1954),

pp. 131–138; Seymour Lipsett and Earl Raab, *The Politics of Unreason* (New York: Harper & Row, 1970); Hodding Carter, "Huey Long: American Dictator," in Isabel Leighton, ed., *The Aspirin Age: 1919–1941* (New York: Simon & Schuster, 1949).

11. The many drafts are in the Warren Papers. The only published version of the play—from a very late draft—appeared well after publication of the novel, under the title *All the King's Men: a Play* (New York: Random House, 1960). The character Willie Talos had become Willie Stark, and the focus of the play now resembled that of the novel; Jack Burden had become the central character.

12. This fragment, which appears in other versions in full drafts of the play (sometimes spoken by a "patrolman," who becomes the character Sugar-Boy in *All the King's Men*), can be found in a folder of draft material with a note from Warren stating: "This was the first fragment written for 'Proud Flesh,' which later became *All the King's Men*." Warren Papers, Box 97, Folder 1812.

13. See, for example, Harold Lasswell, "The Psychology of Hitlerism," *Political Science Quarterly* 4 (1933): 378–382; Daniel Bell, ed., *The New American Right* (New York: Doubleday, 1954).

14. Daniel Singal provides an excellent analysis of Warren's relationship to the transition from Victorianism to modernism in *The War Within*, pp. 339–371.

15. Robert Penn Warren, *All the King's Men* (New York: Harcourt Brace, 1946), p. 262.

16. Ibid., p. 146.

17. Floyd C. Watkins and John T. Hiers, eds., *Robert Penn Warren Talking: Interviews, 1950–1978* (New York: Random House, 1980), p. 179.

18. Ibid., p. 176.

19. Robert Penn Warren, *Democracy and Poetry* (Cambridge: Harvard University Press, 1975), p. 31.

20. Jonathan Baumbach, "The Metaphysics of Demagoguery: *All the King's Men* by Robert Penn Warren," in Baumbach, *The Landscape of Nightmare* (New York: New York University Press, 1965), pp. 16–34.

21. T. Harry Williams, *Huey Long* (New York: Alfred A. Knopf, 1969), pp. vii–x.

22. Michael Kreyling, "One History, Many Hands?" *Mississippi Quarterly* 37 (Winter 1983–1984): 100–101. See also Peggy Ann Brock, "An Exclusive Interview with T. Harry Williams," *Writer's Digest*, September 1970, pp. 26–27, 40–41; Louis D. Rubin, Jr., "Versions of the Kingfish," *Sewanee Review* 101 (Fall 1993): 622–636.

23. T. Harry Williams, "Introduction," *Every Man a King: The Autobiography of Huey P. Long* (Chicago: Quandrangle Books, 1964).

24. See T. Harry Williams, "Huey Long and the Politics of Realism," in

Harold M. Hollingsworth, ed., *Essays on Recent Southern Politics* (Austin: University of Texas Press, 1970), pp. 95–115.

25. Williams, *Huey Long*, p. x.

26. Williams, "The Gentleman from Louisiana: Demagogue or Democrat," *Journal of Southern History* 26 (February 1960): 19–21. See Eric Hoffer, *The True Believer: Thoughts on the Nature of Mass Movements* (New York: Harper & Row, 1951); Jacques Maritain, *Man and the State* (Chicago: University of Chicago Press, 1951).

27. Williams, *Huey Long*, pp. 414–415.

28. Ibid., p. 415; Williams, "The Gentleman from Louisiana," p. 21.

29. This assessment of Long's impact relies on research of my own, presented in *Voices of Protest: Huey Long, Father Coughlin, and the Great Depression* (New York: Alfred A. Knopf, 1982); and "Huey Long, the Share-Our-Wealth Movement, and the Limits of Depression Dissidence," *Louisiana History* 22 (1981): 117–134, which is more explicit on this point.

30. Warren, *All the King's Men*, p. 9.

10. Icons of the American Establishment

1. There have been many studies of the American establishment since Richard Rovere introduced the idea into public discourse in 1962, among them Rovere's own *The American Establishment and Other Reports, Opinions, and Speculations* (New York: Harcourt, Brace & World, 1962); E. Digby Baltzell, *The Protestant Establishment: Aristocracy & Caste in America* (New York: Random House, 1964); Leonard Silk and Mark Silk, *The American Establishment* (New York: Basic Books, 1980). Godfrey Hodgson, *America in Our Time* (New York: Doubleday, 1976) contains a provocative discussion of the establishment in chapter 6. So do Walter Isaacson and Evan Thomas in *The Wise Men: Six Friends and the World They Made* (New York: Simon & Schuster, 1986). David Halberstam, *The Best and the Brightest* (New York: Random House, 1971) is perhaps the best known (if far from the most strident) attack on the establishment from the left. Phyllis Schlafly, *A Choice Not an Echo*, 3rd ed. (Milwaukee: Pere Marquette Press, 1964) is an example of the attack from the right.

2. There are two thorough biographies of Henry Stimson: Elting E. Morison, *Turmoil and Tradition: A Study of the Life and Times of Henry L. Stimson* (New York: Atheneum, 1964), a scrupulously researched and admiring portrait; and Godfrey Hodgson, *The Colonel: The Life and Wars of Henry Stimson, 1867–1950* (New York: Alfred A. Knopf, 1990). Richard N. Current, *Secretary Stimson: A Study in Statecraft* (New Brunswick: Rutgers University Press, 1954) is a briefer and much more skeptical profile. Henry L. Stimson and McGeorge Bundy, *On Active Service in Peace and War* (New York: Harper & Brothers, 1948) is a hybrid: part memoir, mostly a third-person account of Stimson's

career based on Stimson's own memories, by Bundy. Larry G. Gerber makes a forceful if at times somewhat exaggerated case for the importance of Stimson's capitalist convictions in *The Limits of Liberalism* (New York: New York University Press, 1983). The fullest account of Stimson's involvement with the Manchurian crisis is Armin Rappaport, *Henry L. Stimson and Japan, 1931–33* (Chicago: University of Chicago Press, 1963). Dean Acheson, *Present at the Creation* (New York: Norton, 1969); Harry S. Truman, *Memoirs*, vol. 1, *Year of Decisions* (Garden City, N.Y.: Doubleday, 1955); and Donald M. Nelson, *Arsenal of Democracy* (New York: Harcourt Brace Jovanovich, 1946) are among the many memoirs of Stimson's contemporaries with extensive reflections on the man. Gar Alperovitz, *Atomic Diplomacy* (New York: Simon & Schuster, 1965) and *The Decision to Use the Atomic Bomb and the Architecture of an American Myth* (New York: Alfred A. Knopf, 1995) are the two most important revisionist arguments about the Hiroshima and Nagasaki decisions, highly critical of Stimson. Otis Cary, "The Sparing of Kyoto: Mr. Stimson's 'Pet City,'" *Japan Quarterly* 22 (1975): 229–245 attempts to explain Stimson's decision not to bomb that ancient capital.

3. Three important studies of John J. McCloy have appeared since I wrote the 1983 article from which the profile here is derived: Isaacson and Thomas, *The Wise Men*, which profiles McCloy along with five other establishment figures of his generation; Thomas Alan Schwartz, *America's Germany: John J. McCloy and the Federal Republic of Germany* (Cambridge, Mass.: Harvard University Press, 1991), an excellent study of McCloy's work as American High Commissioner in occupied Germany; and Kai Bird, *The Chairman: John J. McCloy. The Making of the American Establishment* (New York: Simon & Schuster, 1992), the only full-scale biography yet to appear, and one based on enormous research. McCloy himself never wrote a memoir.

My own study of McCloy, republished here with minor revisions, was based on extensive research in published primary and secondary materials. It relied primarily on scattered newspaper and news magazine accounts of McCloy's activities as well as on secondary studies of the many issues and controversies with which he had been involved. I relied, too, on several lengthy interviews with McCloy himself, who very generously agreed to speak frankly if sometimes testily with me about almost all the aspects of his past about which I have written (and who complained vigorously about portions of the article when it appeared).

11. The Posthumous Lives of John F. Kennedy

1. *New York Times*, November 24, 1963; William E. Leuchtenburg, "John F. Kennedy Twenty Years Later," *American Heritage*, December 1983, p. 51.

2. *New York Times Book Review*, November 24, 1963, p. 8; Victor Lasky, *JFK:*

The Man and the Myth (New Rochelle, N.Y.: Arlington House, 1963). Lasky's *JFK* was the third best-selling nonfiction title of the year according to *Publisher's Weekly;* Alice Payne Hackett and James Henry Burke, *80 Years of Best Sellers: 1895–1975* (New York, London: R. R. Bowker Company, 1977), pp. 189–191.

3. *Time*, November 14, 1983, p. 67; Arthur M. Schlesinger, "The Ultimate Approval Rating," *New York Times Magazine*, December 15, 1996, pp. 46–47; Norman Mailer, "Enter Prince Jack," *Esquire*, June 1983, pp. 204–208.

4. A skeptical view of Kennedy's foreign policy is Richard J. Walton, *Cold War and Counterrevolution* (New York: Viking, 1972); Carl Brauer, *John F. Kennedy and the Second Reconstruction* (New York: Columbia University Press, 1977) is the fullest account of Kennedy's slow movement toward support of the civil rights movement.

5. Leuchtenburg, "John F. Kennedy," p. 59.

6. Christopher Lasch, "The Life of Kennedy's Death," *Harper's*, October 1983, pp. 32–36; Godfrey Hodgson, *America in Our Time* (New York: Doubleday, 1976), p. 5.

7. Arthur M. Schlesinger, Jr., *A Thousand Days: John F. Kennedy in the White House* (Boston: Houghton Mifflin, 1965), p. 1029–1030.

8. Leuchtenburg, "John F. Kennedy," p. 58; Theodore H. White, *In Search of History: A Personal Adventure* (New York: Harper & Row, 1978), p. 457.

9. Among the many books that have supported a more skeptical view of Kennedy are Peter Collier and David Horowitz, *The Kennedys: An American Drama* (New York: Summit Books, 1984), a family history; Herbert Parmet, *Jack: The Struggles of John F. Kennedy* (New York: Dial, 1980), and *JFK: The Presidency of John F. Kennedy* (New York: Dial, 1983), a carefully researched biography that strips away many layers of myth; Garry Wills, *The Kennedy Imprisonment: A Meditation on Power* (Boston: Atlantic—Little, Brown, 1983), a brilliantly polemical attack on the Kennedy legend; Henry Fairlie, *The Kennedy Promise: The Politics of Expectation* (Garden City, N.Y.: Doubleday, 1973), a relatively early expression of disillusionment; Lewis J. Paper, *The Promise and the Performance: The Leadership of John F. Kennedy* (New York: Crown, 1975), which emphasizes Kennedy's inability to break through the constraints on his exercise of power; Thomas C. Reeves, *A Question of Character: A Life of John F. Kennedy* (New York: The Free Press, 1991), a bitterly critical discussion of the president's character and morality; Richard Reeves, *President Kennedy: Profile of Power* (New York: Simon & Schuster, 1993), a scrupulously researched and largely nonjudgmental narrative that nevertheless supports the picture many revisions have offered of a man without any strong commitments and not fully engaged with his responsibilities as president; and most recently, Seymour Hersh, *The Dark Side of Camelot* (Boston: Little, Brown, 1997), a relentlessly (and recklessly) scathing portrait of Kennedy, much of which rests on vague or misleading evidence and speculative argument. David Halberstam, *The Best and the Brightest* (New York: Random House, 1972) and Walton, *Cold War and*

Counterrevolution are sharply critical of the Kennedy administration's approach to foreign policy. Among friends and associates of President Kennedy who have, even if unintentionally, contributed to the reassessment of his character and legacy are Harris Wofford, *Of Kennedys and Kings: Making Sense of the Sixties* (New York: Farrar, Straus, Giroux, 1980), and Benjamin C. Bradlee, *Conversations with Kennedy* (New York: W. W. Norton, 1976).

10. Nigel Hamilton, *JFK: Life and Death of an American President, Volume One: Reckless Youth* (New York: Random House, 1992), p. 780.

11. Wills, *The Kennedy Imprisonment*, pp. 163–174.

12. Leuchtenburg, "John F. Kennedy," p. 53.

13. Benjamin C. Bradlee, *That Special Grace* (Philadelphia: Lippincott, 1964).

14. *New York Times*, July 16, 1960; Schlesinger, *A Thousand Days*, pp. 206, 210–215.

15. John K. Jessup, et al., *The National Purpose* (New York: Holt, Rinehart, and Winston, 1960). The essays had all appeared originally in *Life* magazine.

16. Schlesinger, *A Thousand Days*, p. 1031.

12. *The Therapeutic Radicalism of the New Left*

1. Maurice Isserman, *If I Had a Hammer: The Death of the Old Left and the Birth of the New Left* (New York: Basic Books, 1987), p. 68.

2. Ibid., pp 174–175.

3. Irving Howe, *A Margin of Hope: An Intellectual Autobiography* (New York: Harcourt, Brace, Jovanovich, 1982), pp. 122–127; Isserman, *If I Had a Hammer*, pp. 73–74.

4. Ibid., p. 118.

5. Ibid., p. 153.

6. James Miller, *"Democracy Is in the Streets": From Port Huron to the Siege of Chicago* (New York: Simon & Schuster, 1987), p. 117.

7. Ibid., p. 194.

8. Ibid., p. 81.

9. C. Wright Mills, *White Collar* (New York: Oxford University Press, 1951), p. 350.

10. Miller, *"Democracy Is in the Streets,"* p. 182.

11. Ibid., p. 294.

12. A somewhat broader, although less satisfactory, picture of the movement at high tide is Kirkpatrick Sale, *SDS* (New York: Random House, 1973).

13. Dotson Rader, "Princeton Weekend with the SDS," *The New Republic*, December 9, 1967, p. 15.

14. Herbert Marcuse, "Repressive Tolerance," in Robert Paull Wolff et al., *A Critique of Pure Tolerance* (Boston: Beacon Press, 1965), pp. 81–84.

15. Miller, *"Democracy Is in the Streets,"* p. 240.

16. Ibid., pp. 205–205, 240.
17. Ibid., pp. 290–292.
18. *Atlantic Monthly*, November 1986, p. 24.
19. Godfrey Hodgson, *America In Our Time* (Garden City, N.Y.: Doubleday, 1976), pp. 300–305.
20. Kenneth Kenniston, *Young Radicals* (Harcourt, Brace & World, 1968), pp. 26–27.
21. Christopher Lasch, *The Agony of the American Left* (New York: Alfred A. Knopf, 1968), p. 180.
22. Miller, *"Democracy Is in the Streets,"* p. 238.
23. Sara M. Evans and Harry C. Boyte, *Free Spaces: The Sources of Democratic Change in America* (New York: Harper & Row, 1986).
24. Sara Evans, *Personal Politics: The Roots of Women's Liberation in the Civil Rights Movement and the New Left* (New York: Alfred A. Knopf, 1979).
25. Roszak wrote admiringly of SDS and other New Left groups. His admiration rested, however, less on their political or economic agenda than on their "extraordinary personalism," the "irreducible element of human tenderness in their politicking." *The Making of a Counter Culture* (New York: Doubleday, 1969), pp. 56–57.
26. Norman O. Brown, *Life Against Death: The Psychoanalytical Meaning of History* (Wesleyan, Conn.: Wesleyan University Press, 1959), pp. 175, 307. See also Allen J. Matusow, *The Unraveling of America* (New York: Harper & Row, 1984), pp. 277–280.
27. Miller, *"Democracy Is in the Streets,"* pp. 307, 319.

13. *Allard Lowenstein and the Ordeal of Liberalism*

1. Lowenstein's only book was *Brutal Mandate: A Journey to South West Africa* (New York: Macmillan, 1962). The best and fullest account of his life and career, based on extensive research in his papers at the University of North Carolina at Chapel Hill and on many interviews, is William H. Chafe, *Never Stop Running: Allard Lowenstein and the Struggle to Save American Liberalism* (New York: Basic Books, 1993). David Harris,"Bloody End of a 60's Dream," *New York Times Magazine*, August 17, 1980, pp. 34–36 ff., and Harris, *Dreams Die Hard* (New York: St. Martin's/Marek, 1982) are accounts of his life (and death) by a former colleague. Teresa Carpenter, "From Heroism to Madness: The Odyssey of the Man Who Shot Al Lowenstein," *Village Voice*, May 12, 1980, pp. 1, 24–27 is a valuable contemporary discussion of Lowenstein's life.

14. *The Taming of the Political Convention*

1. This essay is based in considerable part on my own memories of the ten political conventions I attended from 1964 to 1992. I have, of course, vicari-

ously attended many others—along with a large if dwindling number of Americans—through television coverage. I have checked my own memories against the published proceedings of the conventions, against contemporary accounts in major newspapers and newsmagazines, and against some of the fine published histories of presidential campaigns of the last several decades. Among the most notable are the five volumes in Theodore H. White's *The Making of the President* series (New York: Atheneum, 1961, 1965, 1969, 1973; Harper & Row, 1981); Lewis Chester, Godfrey Hodgson, Bruce Page, *An American Melodrama* (New York: Viking, 1969); and David Farber, *Chicago '68* (Chicago: University of Chicago, 1988).

15. *The Passions of Oral Roberts*

1. Oral Roberts is the author of many books, including several versions of his autobiography: *The Call* (Garden City, N.Y.: Doubleday, 1972) and *Expect a Miracle* (Nashville: T. Nelson, 1995). In *How I Learned Jesus Was Not Poor* (Altamone Springs, Fla.: Creation House, 1989), he gives the fullest description of his recognition of the link between faith and material success. *Your Road to Recovery* (Nashville: Oliver-Nelson, 1986) describes some of the tenets of his message of material and spiritual salvation. His wife, Evelyn Roberts, describes their marriage cloyingly in *His Darling Wife, Evelyn* (New York: Dial Press, 1976). Patti Roberts Thompson, his former daughter-in-law, describes her disillusionment in *Ashes to Gold* (Waco, Texas: Word Books, 1982).

David Edwin Harrell, Jr., *Oral Roberts: An American Life* (Bloomington: Indiana University Press, 1985) is the only scholarly biography of Roberts and recounts his life into the 1980s. Harrell is also the author of *All Things Are Possible: The Healing and Charismatic Revivals in Modern America* (Bloomington: Indiana University Press, 1975), which examines, among other things, modern pentecostalism; and editor of *Varieties of Southern Evangelism* (Macon, Ga.: Mercer University Press, 1981).

16. *The Problem of American Conservatism*

1. In a recently published study of scholarship about the right since the mid-1950s, William B. Hixson claims to "have covered all the relevant scholarly material published by sociologists, psychologists, political scientists, and historians." Social scientists, he notes, have produced an enormous quantity of scholarship, but "historians as a group play a minor role in this study." Hixson, *Search for the American Right Wing: An Analysis of the Social Science Record, 1955–1987* (Princeton: Princeton University Press, 1992), pp. xvii–xix.

2. Skepticism about the progressive assumptions of much twentieth-century political history can be found in Barry D. Karl, *The Uneasy State* (Chicago: University of Chicago Press, 1983). Some more specialized studies that raise

challenges to the assumption that the United States has been moving steadily toward greater political unity include Ellis Hawley, *The New Deal and the Problem of Monopoly* (Princeton: Princeton University Press, 1967), which chronicles the many frustrations New Dealers encountered in attempting to impose various forms of order on the industrial economy; Stephen Skowronek, *Building a New American State: The Expansion of National Administrative Capacities, 1877–1920* (New York: Cambridge University Press, 1982), which describes the halting, piecemeal process by which Americans "patched" together a modern state; James Patterson, *Congressional Conservatism and the New Deal* (Lexington: University of Kentucky Press, 1967) and *The New Deal and the States: Federalism in Transition* (Princeton: Princeton University Press, 1969), which describe the obstacles to centralization the New Deal encountered and never entirely overcame; Alan Brinkley, "The New Deal and the Idea of the State," in Steve Fraser and Gary Gerstle, eds., *The Rise and Fall of the New Deal Order* (Princeton: Princeton University Press, 1989), pp. 85–121, and *The End of Reform: New Deal Liberalism in Recession and War* (New York: Alfred A. Knopf, 1995), which describe the way in which liberals modified or abandoned many of their most ambitious plans for consolidating and rationalizing the economy in response to substantial political, ideological, and economic obstacles.

3. Writers from both the right and the left have chronicled the survival of an antiprogressive, antistatist tradition in twentieth-century America. Robert Nisbet, *The Quest for Community* (New York: Oxford University Press, 1953) offers a conservative intellectual critique of the rise of the modern state and an account of the continuing struggle against its influence by individuals and nongovernmental institutions and associations. Christopher Lasch, writing from the left, has identified a tradition in American culture of important antiprogressive intellectuals (a tradition of which he is an outstanding contemporary example) in *The True and Only Heaven: Progress and Its Critics* (New York: Norton, 1991) and other works. The short-lived *democracy: A Journal of Political Renewal and Radical Change* (edited by Sheldon Wolin and with which Lasch was connected for a time) provided a running critique of progressive centralization and expressed the belief (and hope) that it was not, in fact, securely or inevitably entrenched as the governing dynamic of American life.

4. Perhaps the most influential version of the "progressive" version of American history is Charles A. Beard and Mary R. Beard, *The Rise of American Civilization*, 2 vols. (New York: Macmillan, 1927). Among the discussions (and critiques) of progressive scholarship and the assumptions behind it are Richard Hofstadter, *The Progressive Historians: Turner, Beard, Parrington* (New York: Alfred A. Knopf, 1968) and Peter Novick, *That Noble Dream: The "Objectivity" Question and the American Historical Profession* (New York: Cambridge University Press, 1988), esp. pp. 92–108, 206–278.

5. Richard Hofstadter, *The American Political Tradition and the Men Who*

Made It (New York: Alfred A. Knopf, 1948) was one of the first expressions of what later came to be known as "consensus" assumptions. Louis Hartz, *The Liberal Tradition in America: An Interpretation of American Political Thought Since the Revolution* (New York: Harcourt, Brace & World, 1955) is perhaps the purest expression of those ideas, including a brusque dismissal of the influence of the right: "The ironic flaw in American liberalism lies in the fact that we have never had a real conservative tradition" (p. 57). John Higham, "The Cult of the 'American Consensus': Homogenizing Our History," *Commentary* 27 (1959): 94–95 is the critical assessment that gave the "consensus school" its name. Novick, *That Noble Dream*, pp. 320–360, examines and criticizes consensus scholarship.

6. Lionel Trilling, *The Liberal Imagination* (New York: Viking Press, 1950), p. ix. Trilling was, however, more willing than many of his liberal contemporaries to concede that conservatism retained considerable strength in American culture, even as he dismissed it as a serious intellectual movement.

7. Richard Hofstadter, "A Long View: Goldwater in History," *New York Review of Books*, October 8, 1964, pp. 17–20. Peter Viereck, one of the contributors to *The New American Right* in 1955, had by 1963—when a second edition of the book was published—partially disavowed his own earlier, dismissive view of conservatism, and by implication Hofstadter's as well. He had failed, he acknowledged, to recognize "something far more serious intellectually [than McCarthyism]— the non-McCarthyite, non-thought-controlling movement known as 'the new conservatism.'" Viereck, "The Philosophical 'New Conservatism,'" in Daniel Bell, ed., *The Radical Right* (Garden City, N.Y.: Doubleday, 1963), p. 185.

8. The most celebrated expressions of the "consensus" approach to nonelite conservative dissent were the essays collected in Daniel Bell, ed., *The New American Right* (New York: Criterion Books, 1955). Richard Hofstadter was the leading historical voice in this reassessment, especially in *The Paranoid Style in American Politics and Other Essays* (New York: Alfred A. Knopf, 1965), which included his influential essay "The Pseudo-Conservative Revolt," first published in *The New American Right*. Clinton Rossiter, *Conservatism in America: The Thankless Persuasion* (New York: Random House, 1955) is a partial exception to this trend. Rossiter never doubted the primacy of the liberal tradition in America, but he treated conservatism as a serious (if marginal) alternative intellectual stance. According to two recent, sympathetic historians of the right, Rossiter "announced to the academic world that right of center was intellectually respectable." Charles W. Dunn and J. David Woodard, *American Conservatism from Burke to Bush: An Introduction* (New York: Madison Books, 1991), p. 4.

9. The ferocity with which the New Left attacked consensus scholarship for linking populism with such apparently antidemocratic movements as McCarthyism reflected, at least in part, this reluctance to accept that mass popular

politics could embrace the right. Scholarly work that attempted to rehabilitate the populists (and mass movements in general) includes Norman Pollack, *The Populist Response to Industrial America* (New York: Norton, 1962); Lawrence Goodwyn, *Democratic Promise: The Populist Moment in America* (New York: Oxford University Press, 1976); Bruce Palmer, *"Man Over Money": The Southern Populist Critique of American Capitalism* (Chapel Hill: University of North Carolina Press, 1980). C. Vann Woodward, "The Populist Heritage and the Intellectual," *The American Scholar* 28 (1959): 55–72, republished in Woodward, *The Burden of Southern History* (Baton Rouge: Louisiana State University Press, 1968), 141–166, was one of the first important challenges to the Hofstadter view of populism. Michael Paul Rogin, *The Intellectuals and McCarthy: The Radical Specter* (Cambridge, Mass.: MIT Press, 1967) argued, further, that support for McCarthy did not arise from "populist" impulses but from among traditionally right-wing, conservative groups.

10. Williams suggested the outlines of the "corporate liberal" approach to twentieth-century history in his classic *The Tragedy of American Diplomacy* (Cleveland: World, 1959), but he gave fuller expression to the idea in *Americans in a Changing World: A History of the United States in the Twentieth Century* (New York: Harper & Row, 1978). See also, among many other works, R. Jeffrey Lustig, *Corporate Liberalism: The Origins of Modern American Political Theory* (Berkeley: University of California Press, 1982) and Martin Sklar, *The Corporate Reconstruction of American Capitalism, 1890–1916: The Market, the Law, and Politics* (New York: Cambridge University Press, 1988).

11. Robert Nisbet, recalling his own experiences as a conservative in the academic world of the 1960s, noted that "the Left never hassled me as they did the Kennedy liberals and also Old Socialists. . . . In later years, other conservatives . . . told me their experience had been the same as mine; they were largely left alone, at least in comparison with those who weakly or despairingly kept trying to remind the Rudds and Savios of the nation that they were friends of the Revolution by other means." *The Making of Modern Society* (New York: New York University Press, 1986), p. 17.

12. One of the earliest and clearest statements of the assumptions of the "organizational synthesis" is Louis Galambos, "The Emerging Organizational Synthesis in Modern American History," *Business History Review* 44 (1970); a later evaluation is Galambos, "Technology, Political Economy, and Professionalization: Central Themes of the Organizational Synthesis," *Business History Review* 57 (1983): 472–493. A recent reconsideration is Brian Balogh, "Reorganizing the Organizational Synthesis," *Studies in American Political Development* 5 (1991): 119–172. A more skeptical view of the organizational synthesis can be found in Alan Brinkley, "Writing the History of Contemporary America: Dilemmas and Challenges," *Daedalus* 113 (1984): 121–142.

13. Daniel Rodgers, "Republicanism: The Career of a Concept," *Journal of*

American History 79 (June 1992), 11–38 is a thoughtful, if skeptical, account of the influence of republicanism on modern scholarship. Gary Gerstle, *Working-Class Americanism: The Politics of Labor in a Textile City, 1914–1960* (New York: Cambridge University Press, 1989), esp. pp. 183–195, 331–336, argues that republican traditions remained hardy well into the twentieth century.

14. Daniel Rodgers has written provocatively about the diversity of meanings of conventional political labels in "In Search of Progressivism," *Reviews in American History* 10 (December 1982): 113–132, and in *Contested Truths: Key Words in American Politics Since Independence* (New York: Basic Books, 1987).

15. George H. Nash, *The Conservative Intellectual Movement in America: Since 1945* (New York: Basic Books, 1976), p. xiii.

16. George Wolfskill, *The Revolt of the Conservatives: A History of the American Liberty League, 1934–1940* (Boston: Houghton Mifflin, 1962); Robert F. Burk, *The Corporate State and the Broker State: The Du Ponts and American National Politics, 1925–1940* (Cambridge, Mass.: Harvard University Press, 1990), esp. pp. 143–253.

17. Sidney Blumenthal, *The Rise of the Counter-Establishment* (New York: Times Books, 1986).

18. Hartz, *The Liberal Tradition in America*, pp. 145–177; Peter Viereck said much the same thing in 1963 when he wrote that "our conservatism, in the absence of medieval feudal relics, must grudgingly admit it has little real tradition to conserve except that of liberalism" ("The Philosophical 'New Conservatism,'" p. 199). See also Stuart Gerry Brown, "Democracy, the New Conservatism, and the Liberal Tradition in America," *Ethics* 66 (October 1955): 8.

19. John G. Sproat, *The Best Men: Liberal Reformers in the Gilded Age* (New York: Oxford University Press,, 1968), pp. 3–10, 143–168.

20. Michael W. Miles, *The Odyssey of the American Right* (New York: Oxford University Press, 1980), pp. 18–20.

21. Herbert Hoover, *Addresses Upon the American Road, 1933–1938* (New York: Charles Scribner's Sons, 1938), p. 138; Hoover, *The Challenge to Liberty* (New York: Charles Scribner's Sons, 1934), pp. 103, 190.

22. C. Hartley Grattan, "Hayek's Hayride," *Harper's*, July 1945, pp. 48–49; Hayek to Walter Lippmann, April 6, 1937, Lippmann Papers, Sterling Library, Yale University, III, 77.

23. Friedrich A. Hayek, *The Road to Serfdom* (Chicago: University of Chicago Press, 1944). For a discussion of the impact of the book, see Theodore Rosenof, "Freedom, Planning, and Totalitarianism: The Reception of F.A. Hayek's *Road to Serfdom*," *Canadian Review of American Studies* 5 (1974): 149–165. Nash, *Conservative Intellectual Movement in America*, pp. 34–37 discusses the impact of Hayek's book on American conservatives.

24. Hayek, *Road to Serfdom*, pp. ix, 2, 92, 145–146.

25. Examples of the liberal response to Hayek's book include Alvin Hansen,

"The New Crusade Against Planning," *New Republic*, January 1, 1945, pp. 9–12, and Seymour E. Harris, "Breaking a Lance with Mr. Hayek," *New York Times Book Review*, December 9, 1945, pp. 3, 14, 16.

26. The emergence in the last decade or so of an energetic group of younger scholars engaged in a "new western history" has served as an important challenge to the tendency of many twentieth-century American historians to neglect regionalism as an important force in modern society. Two collections of essays that lay out some of the premises of the "new western history" are William Cronon, George Miles, and Jay Gitlin. eds., *Under an Open Sky: Rethinking America's Western Past* (New York: Norton, 1992), and Patricia Nelson Limerick, Clyde A. Milner II, and Charles E. Rankin, eds., *Trails: Toward a New Western History* (Lawrence: University Press of Kansas, 1992). So far, however, few of the new western historians have devoted much attention to the right.

27. Garry Wills, "The Hostage," *New York Review of Books*, August 13, 1992, pp. 21–28.

28. Richard White, *"It's Your Misfortune and None of My Own": A New History of the American West* (Norman: University of Oklahoma Press, 1991), pp. 601–611, summarizes the history of the rise of the western right.

29. Michael McGerr, "Is There a Twentieth-Century West?" Cronon, Miles, Gitlin, eds., *Under an Open Sky*, pp. 248–250; Gerald D. Nash, "Bureaucracy and Reform in the West: Notes on the Influence of a Neglected Interest Group," *Western Historical Quarterly* 2 (July 1971): 295–305.

30. See, for example, Jordan Schwarz, *The New Dealers: Power Politics in the Age of Roosevelt* (New York: Alfred A. Knopf, 1993); Leonard Arrington, *The Changing Economic Structure of the Mountain West, 1850–1950* (Logan: Utah State University Press, 1963; Monograph Series X, 3); James L. Clayton, "The Impact of the Cold War on the Economy of California and Utah, 1946–1965," *Pacific Historical Review* 36 (November 1967): 449–473.

31. Kevin Phillips, *Post-Conservative America* (New York: Random House, 1982), pp. 237–238; Phillips introduced the idea of the "sunbelt" in *The Emerging Republican Majority* (New Rochelle, N.Y.: Arlington Books, 1969).

32. Barry Goldwater with Jack Casserly, *Goldwater* (New York: Doubleday, 1988), p. 35.

33. See, for example, Robert Nisbet, "Conservatives and Libertarians: Uneasy Cousins," *Modern Age* 24 (1980), 4–5; Nash, *Conservative Intellectual Movement*, pp. 76–81.

34. George Nash notes, for example, that "Burke was not highly esteemed in American academic circles in the 1930s." Ibid., p. 69. Robert Nisbet observed similarly that Burke and Tocqueville were almost entirely absent from twentieth-century intellectual life, even among conservatives, until the 1940s. *Making of Modern Society*, p. 8.

35. T. J. Jackson Lears, *No Place of Grace: Antimodernism and the Transforma-*

tion of American Culture, 1880–1920 (New York: Pantheon: 1981), offers a provocative and largely sympathetic view of a form of normative cultural conservatism among elites in the late nineteenth and early twentieth centuries. See esp. chaps. 4, 5, and 7.

36. Twelve Southerners, *I'll Take My Stand: The South and the Agrarian Tradition* (New York: Harper, 1930).

37. Paul Gottfried and Thomas Fleming, *The Conservative Movement* (Boston: Twayne, 1988), give special attention to the normative qualities of modern conservatism. "Conservatives, as much as Leftists," they write, "are united by a distinctive approach to reality—particularly nature. For the Left, the concept 'nature' suggests infinite plasticity; for the Right, by contrast, it is something fixed, and even normative" (pp. ix–x).

38. Russell Kirk, *The Conservative Mind* (London: Faber and Faber, 1954), pp. 17–18, 140–165, 436; originally published by University of Chicago Press, 1953. On the positive reaction to Kirk among conservative intellectuals, see Nash, *Conservative Intellectual Movement*, p. 74. Kirk's book followed, and built upon, other less widely noted texts of the postwar period that offered similar defenses of a more normative conservatism. See, for example, Nisbet, *The Quest for Community;* Richard M. Weaver, *Ideas Have Consequences* (Chicago: University of Chicago Press, 1948); Peter Viereck, *Conservatism Revisited: The Revolt Against Revolt, 1815–1949* (London: John Lehman, 1950).

39. Leo Strauss, *Natural Right and History* (Chicago: University of Chicago Press, 1953), pp. 4–5.

40. Ibid., pp. 16–18.

41. Alan Udoff, ed., *Leo Strauss's Thought: Toward a Critical Engagement* (Boulder: Lynne Rienner, 1991) contains recent appreciative critiques of Strauss's work. Shadia Drury, *The Political Ideas of Leo Strauss* (Houndsmill, England: Macmillan, 1988), and Stephen Holmes, "Truths for Philosophers Alone?" *Times Literary Supplement*, December 1–7, 1989, pp. 1319–1324 are less sympathetic.

42. William F. Buckley, Jr., *God and Man at Yale: The Superstitions of 'Academic Freedom'"* (Chicago: Henry Regnery, 1951) was perhaps the most visible example of this Catholic social conservatism in the early postwar period. See also Ross Hoffman, *The Organic State: An Historical View of Contemporary Politics* (New York: Sheed and Ward, 1939). Patrick Allitt, *Catholic Intellectuals and Conservative Politics in America, 1950–1985* (Ithaca: Cornell University Press, 1993) is an important recent study.

43. George Q. Flynn, *American Catholics and the Roosevelt Presidency* (Lexington: University of Kentucky Press, 1968), pp. 22–35. The revived interest in Aquinas was sparked, or at least signaled, by the 1891 publication of Leo XII's encyclical *Rerum Novarum* or *On the Condition of the Working Class* and reinforced by Pius XI's 1931 encyclical *Quadragesimo Anno* or *Forty Years After: On*

Reconstructing the Social Order; see Leo XIII and Pius XI, *Two Basic Social Encyclicals* (New York: Benzinger Brothers, 1943).

44. See, for example, Eliot's 1939 lectures at Corpus Christi College, Cambridge, published as *The Idea of a Christian Society* (London: Faber and Faber, 1939). Quotation is from p. 21. Saul Bellow's attraction to a normative conservatism is evident in his admiring, if somewhat guarded, introduction to Allan Bloom, *The Closing of the American Mind* (New York: Simon & Schuster, 1987), pp. 11–18.

45. Daniel Bell, for example, told an interviewer in 1978 of "a fear of mass action, a fear of passions let loose. A lot of this goes back to a particularly Jewish fear. In traditional Jewish life, going back particularly to the Assyrian and Babylonian episodes . . . there's a fear of what happens when man is let loose. When man doesn't have *halacha,* the law, he becomes *chaia,* an animal." Nathan Liebowitz, *Daniel Bell and the Agony of Modern Liberalism* (Westport, Conn.: Greenwood, 1985), p. 70.

46. Richard Rorty and Harvey C. Mansfield, Jr. debate the implications of Bloom's book in "Straussianism, Democracy, and Allan Bloom," *New Republic,* April 4, 1988, pp. 28–37.

47. Irving Kristol, *On the Democratic Idea in America* (New York: Harper & Row, 1972), p. 330–333; Kevin Phillips, *Post-Conservative America* (New York: Random House, 1982), pp. 5–49. Robert Nisbet, *Twilight of Authority* (New York: Oxford University Press, 1975), especially in chapter 5, suggests the confluence of neo-conservative thought with an older tradition of normative conservatism. Critical discussion of the neo-conservative movement includes Peter Steinfels, *The Neo-Conservatives: The Men Who Are Changing America's Politics* (New York: Simon & Schuster, 1979); Nathan Glazer, Peter Steinfels, James Q. Wilson, Norman Birnbaum, "'Neoconservatism: Pro and Con," *Partisan Review* 47 (1980): 497–521; Amitai Etzioni, "The Neoconservatives," *Partisan Review* 44 (1977): 431–437; Seymour Martin Lipset, "Neoconservatism: Myth and Reality," *Society* 25 (July/August 1988): 29–37.

48. See, for example, Michael J. Sandel, *Liberalism and the Limits of Justice* (New York: Cambridge University Press, 1982), and Michael Walzer, *Spheres of Justice* (New York: Basic Books, 1983). These new critiques of liberalism, many of them ostensibly from the left, are often difficult to distinguish from neo-conservative and even older conservative critiques. Some have much in common with the work of the English political theorist Michael Oakeshott, a major spokesman for an older conservative tradition. Jeremy Waldron, for example, notes a similarity between Oakeshott's description of a modern, liberal rationalist ("Like a man whose only language is Esperanto, he has no means of knowing that the world did not begin in the twentieth century") and Sandel's ("a person wholly without character, without moral depth, for to have character is to know that I move in a history I neither summon nor command"). Waldron,

"Politics Without Purpose?" *Times Literary Supplement*, July 6–12, 1990, pp. 715–716.

49. I use the term "fundamentalism" not simply to describe people with fundamentalist religious beliefs (some of whom are involved in the so-called Christian right, but many of whom are not politically active) but a larger group, often described as the "new right" or the "populist right," who share a commitment to purging American culture and politics of what they consider its relativistic, antitraditional character.

50. "The conflict," writes Christian conservative Carl Horn, "is between those who believe that law and public policy derive from religious belief and those who reject such an assumption." Gottfried and Fleming, *The Conservative Movement*, p. 85.

51. Paul Boyer, *When Time Shall Be No More: Prophecy Belief in Modern American Culture* (Cambridge, Mass.: Harvard University Press, 1992), pp. 140–151, 304–324.

52. Jane Sherron De Hart has contrasted the normative quality of the antifeminist position to the more relativistic stance of feminists. "Gender," she writes (characterizing the right-wing position) "was sacred. It was a given: a biologically, physically, spiritually defined thing; an unambiguous, clear, definite division of humanity into two. Feminists, however, insisted that gender, like race, was a social construction; the meaning attached to sexual difference was actually made by humans, not God or Nature, and therefore could be changed." De Hart, "Gender on the Right: Meanings Behind the Existential Scream," *Gender & History* 3 (Autumn 1991): 256. See also Kristin Luker, *Abortion and the Politics of Motherhood* (Berkeley: University of California Press, 1984), pp. 158–175. Zillah R. Eisenstein, "The Sexual Politics of the New Right," *Feminist Theory* 7 (Spring 1982).

53. Rebecca E. Klatch, *Women of the New Right* (Philadelphia: Temple University Press, 1987), pp. 23–25. The statements, quoted in Klatch, are by Onalee McGraw and Virginia Bessey.

54. Martin Marty and R. Scott Appleby have edited a series of volumes, known collectively as The Fundamentalist Project, at the University of Chicago Divinity School in an effort to identify both the international character of fundamentalism and the wide-ranging utility of the concept. Three volumes were in print as of mid-1993, all published by University of Chicago Press: *Fundamentalisms Observed* (1991); *Fundamentalisms and Society: Reclaiming the Religious Sciences, the Family, and Education* (1993); and *Fundamentalisms and the State: Remaking Polities, Economies, and Militance*. See also Malise Ruthven, "The Fundamentalist Project," *Times Literary Supplement*, April 30, 1993, p. 14.

55. George Marsden, *Fundamentalism and American Culture* (New York: Oxford University Press, 1980), pp. 176–198.

56. A classic example is Seymour Martin Lipset and Earl Rabb, *The Politics of*

Unreason: Right-Wing Extremism in America (New York: Harper & Row, 1970), written before the resurgence of the right in the 1980s and largely concerned with right-wing movements of the 1930s, 1940s, and 1950s. Daniel Bell's *The New American Right* was republished in 1963 under the title *The Radical Right* (Garden City, N.Y.: Doubleday, 1963), with new essays by Bell and others reinforcing the implication of the earlier volume that the normative right was the product of social and psychological dislocation. Among other examples of such analyses, see Dean M. Kelley, *Why Conservative Churches Are Growing: A Study in Sociology of Religion* (New York: Harper & Row, 1972). For an extensive discussion of this literature, see Hixson, *Search for the American Right Wing*, pp. 9–26, 61–112.

57. Recent work on religious fundamentalism and pentecostalism that supports such a conclusion includes Marsden, *Fundamentalism and American Culture;* Gillian Peele, *Revival and Reaction: The Right in Contemporary America* (New York: Oxford University Press, 1984); David Edwin Harrell, Jr., *Oral Roberts: An American Life* (Bloomington: Indiana University Press, 1985); Harrell, *All Things Are Possible: The Healing and Charismatic Revivals in Modern America* (Bloomington: Indiana University Press, 1975). David H. Bennett, *The Party of Fear: From Nativist Movements to the New Right in American History* (Chapel Hill: University of North Carolina Press, 1988) chronicles the history of the many Nativist movements (some of them with fundamentalist roots) that have surfaced repeatedly throughout American history.

58. Two important new books that explore the social roots of the Klan and dispute earlier "paranoid-style" characterizations are Leonard J. Moore, *Citizen Klansmen: The Ku Klux Klan in Indiana, 1921–1928* (Chapel Hill: University of North Carolina Press, 1991), and Kathleen M. Blee, *Women of the Klan: Racism and Gender in the 1920s* (Berkeley: University of California Press, 1991). Kenneth Jackson, *The Ku Klux Klan in the City, 1915–1930* (New York: Oxford University Press, 1967) was an early challenge to the portrait of the Klan as a rural, provincial peculiarity.

59. Alan Brinkley, *Voices of Protest: Huey Long, Father Coughlin, and the Great Depression* (New York: Alfred A. Knopf, 1982) considers two protest movements of the 1930s that have often been considered right-wing and even fascist and suggests that they were rooted in rational economic grievances and a broad populist sensibility. Leo P. Ribuffo, *The Old Christian Right: The Protestant Far Right from the Great Depression to the Cold War* (Philadelphia: Temple University Press, 1983) considers several of the most extreme right-wing leaders of the interwar years and suggests that even their unattractive views were not radically at odds with those of mainstream Americans.

60. Among important recent work that suggests the stability and rationality of the nonelite right is Jerome L. Himmelstein, *To the Right: The Transformation of American Conservatism* (Berkeley: University of California Press, 1990);

Klatch, *Women of the New Right;* Jonathan Rieder, *Canarsie: The Jews and Italians of Brooklyn against Liberalism* (Cambridge, Mass.: Harvard University Press, 1985); Ronald P. Formisano, *Boston Against Busing: Race, Class, and Ethnicity in the 1960s and 1970s* (Chapel Hill: University of North Carolina Press, 1991). See also Alan Wolfe, "Sociology, Liberalism, and the Radical Right," *New Left Review* 128 (July–August 1981): 3–27, for a discussion of the way sociologists have viewed the right, and Michael Kazin, "The Grass-Roots Right: New Histories of U.S. Conservatism in the Twentieth Century," *American Historical Review* 97 (February 1992): 136–155 for a perceptive overview of recent historical and sociological scholarship. Recent nonscholarly books that have tried to treat the populist right as a political force with rational grievances include Thomas Byrne Edsall and Mary E. Edsall, *Chain Reaction: The Impact of Race, Rights, and Taxes on American Politics* (New York: Norton, 1991) and E. J. Dionne, Jr., *Why Americans Hate Politics* (New York: Simon & Schuster, 1991).

61. Robert Wiebe, *The Segmented Society: An Introduction to the Meaning of America* (New York: Oxford University Press, 1975), p. 46.

62. See, for example, David A. Hollinger, "Ethnic Diversity, Cosmopolitanism and the Emergence of the American Liberal Intelligentsia," *American Quarterly* 27 (1975): 133–151; Terry A. Cooney, "Cosmopolitan Values and the Identification of Reaction: *Partisan Review* in the 1930s," *Journal of American History* 68 (1981): 580–598; Daniel Joseph Singal, "Beyond Consensus: Richard Hofstadter and American Historiography," *American Historical Review* 89 (1984): 976–1004.

63. For an exploration of the centrality of religion to much of American life, and a critique of intellectuals, scholars, and others for attacking or ignoring it, see Stephen L. Carter, *The Culture of Disbelief: How American Law and Politics Trivialize Religious Devotion* (New York: Basic Books, 1993).

Sources

1. The Rise of Franklin Roosevelt
   Portions adapted from "Franklin D. Roosevelt," an entry in *American National Biography*, forthcoming from Oxford University Press, and from "The New Deal: Prelude," *Wilson Quarterly* 6 (1982): 50–61.
2. The New Deal Experiments
   Portions adapted from lectures given at Oxford University under the auspices of the Astor Trust, in February 1997.
3. The Late New Deal and the Idea of the State
   Appeared in a slightly different form as "The New Deal and the Idea of the State" in Steve Fraser and Gary Gerstle, eds., *The Rise and Fall of the New Deal Order* (Princeton: Princeton University Press, 1989), pp. 85–121.
4. The New Deal and Southern Politics
   An earlier version appeared in James C. Cobb and Michael V. Namarato, eds., *The New Deal and the South* (Jackson: University Press of Mississippi, 1984), pp. 97–117.
5. The Two World Wars and American Liberalism
   A briefer version appeared in John P. Diggins, ed., *The Liberal Persuasion: Arthur Schlesinger, Jr. and the Challenge of the American Past* (Princeton: Princeton University Press, 1997), pp. 127–141.
6. Legacies of World War II
   Portions appeared as "World War II and American Liberalism" in Lewis A. Erenberg and Susan E. Hirsch, eds., *The War and American Culture: Society and Consciousness during World War II* (Chicago: University of Chicago Press, 1995), pp. 313–330. © 1995 by the University of Chicago Press. All rights reserved. Portions also appeared in "For America, It Truly Was a Great War," *New York Times Magazine*, May 7, 1995, pp. 54–57. © 1995 by The New York Times Company. Reprinted by permission.
7. Historians and the Interwar Years
   An earlier version appeared as "Prosperity, Depression, and War: Patterns of Historical Explanation, 1920–1945," in Eric Foner, ed., *The New American History*, rev. ed. (Philadelphia: Temple University Press, 1997), pp. 133–158.

8. Hofstadter's *The Age of Reform* Reconsidered
   First published as "Richard Hofstadter's *The Age of Reform:* A Reconsideration," in *Reviews in American History* 13 (September 1985): 462–480 (published by the John Hopkins University Press).
9. Robert Penn Warren, T. Harry Williams, and Huey Long
   An earlier version appeared as "Robert Penn Warren, T. Harry Williams, and Huey Long: Mass Politics in the Literary and Historical Imaginations," in Glen Jeansonne, ed., *Huey at 100: Centennial Essays on Huey P. Long* (Ruston, La.: McGinty Press, 1994), pp. 17–32.
10. Icons of the American Establishment
    Portions appeared under the title "The Good Old Days" in the *New York Review of Books,* January 17, 1991, pp. 24–31; and "Minister Without Portfolio," *Harper's,* February 1983, pp. 31–46. Copyright © 1983 by *Harper's Magazine.* All rights reserved. Reproduced from the February issue by special permission.
11. The Posthumous Lives of John F. Kennedy
    An earlier version was delivered as a lecture for the conference "The Legacy of John F. Kennedy," The Stanton Sharp Symposium at Southern Methodist University, Dallas, November 8–9, 1993.
12. The Therapeutic Radicalism of the New Left
    An earlier version appeared under the title "Dreams of the Sixties" in the *New York Review of Books,* October 22, 1987, pp. 10–16.
13. Allard Lowenstein and the Ordeal of Liberalism
    An earlier version appeared under the title "The Rise and Fall of an Idealist" in the *New York Review of Books,* November 3, 1994, pp. 44–46.
14. The Taming of the Political Convention
    Portions appeared under the title "Unceremony" in the *New Yorker,* August 12, 1996.
15. The Passions of Oral Roberts
    An earlier version appeared under the title "The Oral Majority" in *New Republic,* September 29, 1986, pp. 28–33.
16. The Problem of American Conservatism
    Appeared in the *American Historical Review* 99 (April 1994): 409–429.
17. Historians and Their Publics
    Portions appeared in the *Journal of American History* 81 (December 1994): 1027–1030.

Index